Cher Oncle, Cher Papa

The Letters of Francois and Berenice Chouteau

By
Dorothy Brandt Marra

Translated by
Marie-Laure Dionne Pal

Edited by
David Boutros

Foreword by William E. Foley, Ph.D.

Western Historical Manuscript Collection-Kansas City
a joint collection of the University of Missouri
and the State Historical Society of Missouri

Copyright © 2001 by the
Western Historical Manuscript Collection-Kansas City
University of Missouri
5100 Rockhill Road
Kansas City, Missouri 64110-2499
http://www.umkc.edu/WHMCKC/

All rights reserved. No part of this book may be reproduced, in any form or by any means, without permission in writing from the publisher.

ISBN 0-9710496-0-2

Library of Congress Control Number: 2001096389

Printed and bound in the United States.

∞ This paper meets the requirements of the American National Standard for Permanence of Paper for Printed Library Materials, Z39.48, 1984.

Cover Illustration and Design: Sylvia D. Mooney
Printer and Binder: Cushing-Malloy, Inc.
Typeface: Palatino, *Monotype Corsiva*

Cher Oncle, Cher Papa

is dedicated,

with great respect, to the staunch and courageous

peoples – both Native Americans and immigrant Europeans –

who braved the wilderness to establish the first homes and commerce

in the valley of the Missouri and Kansas Rivers,

clearing the way for Kansas City.

Contents

Key to Abbreviations vi
Illustrations and Maps vii
Foreword x
Acknowledgments xii
Chapter 1   Of Frontier, Furs, and Family 1
Chapter 2   "Filled with Respect and Affection": The Early Letters 23
Chapter 3   Gains and Losses: A Balance Sheet 47
Chapter 4   New Faces on the Frontier 77
Chapter 5   At Home on the Chouteau Farm 109
Chapter 6   "We Have a Lot of Disappointment This Year...." 125
Chapter 7   End of the Pioneer Era 151
Chapter 8   Berenice's Later Life 183
Appendixes
    1 – *Confluence of People and Place: The Chouteau Posts on the Missouri and Kansas Rivers* by David Boutros. 191
    2 – Pierre (Cadet) Chouteau Jr. to Gabriel (Seres) Chouteau, July 19, 1822. (Subject: Where Gabriel (Seres) Chouteau will operate a post.) 205
    3 – Pierre Menard to Francois Chouteau, 1829-1836. 207
    4 – Pierre Menard Chouteau to Pierre Menard, June 24, 1835. (Subject: Pierre Menard Chouteau greets his grandfather, Pierre Menard.) 214
    5 – Edmond Francois (Gesseau) Chouteau to Pierre Menard, Jan. 15, 1836. (Subject: Gesseau's apology to his Grandfather Menard after being expelled from school.) 215
    6 – Facsimile of Francois Chouteau and Berenice Chouteau letters. 216
Pieces of the Puzzle: A Glossary of People, Places, and Things 219
Bibliography 269
Index 281
Contributors' Biographies 304

Key to Abbreviations

ASJCF – Archives de la Compagnie de Jesus, province du Canada frantais
BIA – Bureau of Indian Affairs
IHS – Illinois Historical Survey, University of Illinois Library, Urbana-Champaign, Illinois
ISHL – Illinois State Historical Library, Springfield, Illinois
KHC – *Kansas Historical Collection*
KHQ – *Kansas Historical Quarterly*
KSHS – Kansas State Historical Society, Topeka, Kansas
MHR – *Missouri Historical Review*
MHS – Missouri Historical Society, St. Louis, Missouri
NARA – National Archives and Records Administration
NSA – *Native Sons Archives*, Western Historical Manuscript Collection-Kansas City
OIA – Office of Indian Affairs
PMC – *Pierre Menard Collection,* Illinois State Historical Library, Springfield, Illinois
SIA – Superintendent of Indian Affairs
WSUL – Manuscripts, Archives, and Special Collections, Washington State University Libraries
WHMC-C – Western Historical Manuscript Collection-Columbia
WHMC-KC – Western Historical Manuscript Collection-Kansas City

Illustrations and Maps

James Anderson (1884-1967). Historian, Native Sons of Kansas City. WHMC-KC. xii
Louise Barry (1910-1974). Librarian/historian, Kansas State Historical Society. KSHS. xii
"*Aspect general des prairies occidentales de l'amerique – dites vulgairement La Grand-prairie*"
[General appearance of America's western prairies – commonly called the Great
Prairie]. *Père Nicolas Point, S.J., Collection*, Archives de la Compagnie de Jesus,
province du Canada frantais (ASJCF). 1
Pierre Menard's home, *Illustrated Historical Atlas Map of Randolph County, Illinois*, 1875. 5
Pierre Chouteau Residence, S.W. corner Main and Washington, St. Louis, Missouri.
Ink on paper by Clarence Hoblitzelle, 1897. Acc. #1897.22.15. Missouri Historical
Society Art Collection, Missouri Historical Society (MHS). 7
"Keel-boat moving up the Mississippi. From a picture belonging to Mr. Pierre Chouteau."
Western Historical Manuscript Collection-Kansas City (WHMC-KC). 14
American Fur Company Warehouse, 1835. North side of Walnut Street between Main
and Levee Streets, St. Louis, Missouri. Ink on paper by Clarence Hoblitzelle, 1897.
[neg PB 0109]. MHS. 20
Second map of the State of Missouri. Drawn and published by F. Lucas Jr., Baltimore,
1823. WHMC-KC. 21
Portion of map drawn by Isaac McCoy, ca. 1830, showing the mouth of the Kansas
River. *Isaac McCoy Papers*, Kansas State Historical Society (KSHS). 22
"*Barge du Fort Louis*" [Barge of (from) Fort Lewis]. *Père Nicolas Point, S.J., Collection*,
ASJCF. 23
Portion of map drawn by Isaac McCoy, 1830, showing the locations of the various
tribal lands in the vicinity of the mouth of the Kansas River. *Isaac McCoy Papers*,
KSHS. 45
Portion of map drawn by Isaac McCoy, 1839, showing the locations of the Shawnee
and Delaware villages and the Shawnee Agency. *Isaac McCoy Papers*, KSHS. 46
"*Presse des ballots*" [Press of the packages (packs of furs)].
Père Nicolas Point, S.J., Collection, ASJCF. 47
"*Free hunter*." Drawn by Nicolas Point, S.J. *Pierre Jean De Smet (1801-1873) Papers*,
Manuscripts, Archives, and Special Collections, Washington State University
Libraries (WSUL). 77

Map drawn by John Calvin McCoy of the Kansa Agency (1827-1834). KSHS. 106

[Map of] *Missouri*. Published by A. Finley, Philadelphia, 1831. WHMC-KC. 107

"*Vue de la premiere hutte des Kants avant d'arrivier a la riviere du meme nom. Village des Kants*" [View of the first hut of the Kansas before the arrival at the river of the same name. Village of the Kansas]. Drawn by Nicolas Point. *Pierre Jean De Smet (1801-1873) Papers*, WSUL. 108

Section of Nicolas Point's "*Plan de Westport (Missouri)*". *Père Nicolas Point, S.J., Collection*, ASJCF. 109

"*Depart de Westport.*" Drawn by Nicolas Point, S.J., *Pierre Jean De Smet (1801-1873) Papers*, WSUL. 125

Francois Chouteau's land holdings in sections 33 and 28, Township 50 N, Range 33 W. WHMC-KC. 150

"*Maison Emportee*" [House carried away]. *Père Nicolas Point, S.J., Collection*, ASJCF. 151

"*Plan de Westport (Missouri)*". *Père Nicolas Point, S.J., Collection*, ASJCF. 182

Portion of "*Kansas City, 1855*," drawn by F. Buckeridge. MHS. 183

The 1827 Jackson County survey of T50N R33W and a portion of the 1819 Clay County survey including Section 18 of T50N R32W are overlaid on a current U.S. Geological Survey map to show the location of the Missouri River relative to today's channel. WHMC-KC. 197

A portion of the 1827 Jackson County survey and the 1819 Clay County survey overlaid on a current U.S. Geological Survey map. WHMC-KC. 198

A portion of Angus Langham's survey map (1826) of the Kansas River from its mouth to about fifteen miles out. KSHS. 200

A portion of the 1827 Jackson County survey of T50N R33W overlaid on a current U.S. Geological Survey map. WHMC-KC. 201

A portion of Plat XIV of the 1878 survey of the Missouri River. WHMC-KC. 203

A sample of Francois Chouteau's scribe. Illinois State Historical Library (ISHL). 216

The handwriting of Berenice Chouteau. ISHL 218

American Fur Company Warehouse, 1835. North side of Walnut Street between Main and Levee Streets, St. Louis, Missouri. Ink on paper by Clarence Hoblitzelle, 1897. [neg PB 0109]. MHS. 220

"The Barrens" – St. Mary's of the Barrens, in Perryville, Missouri. De Andreis Rosati Memorial Archives, DePaul University Archives, Chicago. 221

Lt. Auguste Pierre Chouteau (1786-1838). Photograph, 1899 of watercolor copy of oil on ivory miniature. [Neg Por C-29]. MHS. 225

Benjamin Chouteau (1828-1876). WHMC-KC. 225

Cyprien Chouteau (1802-1879). WHMC-KC. 227

Frederick Chouteau (1809-1891). KSHS. 229

Marie Therese Chouteau (1733-1814). WHMC-KC. 230

Mary Brigitte Chouteau (1835-1864). WHMC-KC. 231

Pierre Chouteau, Jr. [Cadet] (1789-1865). Oil on canvas. Acc. # 1922.24.1. MHS. 231

Pierre Chouteau Sr. (1758-1849). WHMC-KC. 232

Pierre Menard Chouteau (1822-1885). WHMC-KC. 232

"*Westport.*" [St. Francis Regis Church]. Drawn by Nicolas Point, S.J. ASJCF. 233

Marston Greene Clark (1769-1846). WHMC-KC. 233

William Clark (1770-1838). WHMC-KC 234
Maj. John Dougherty (1791-1860). Copy photograph by J. Edward Roesch,
    ca. 1900 of daguerreotype. IM 001-001525. [Neg Por D-6]. MHS. 237
Major Andrew Drips (1789-1860). Copy photograph of daguerreotype.
    IM 001-001571. [Neg GPN Por D-16]. MHS. 238
Reconstructed Fort Osage. WHMC-KC. 239
William Gilliss, (1788?-1869). WHMC-KC. 240
Major Richard Graham (1780-1857). Oil on canvas by Chester Harding.
    Acc. # 1913.36.1. Photograph by Allied Photocolor, 1984. MHS. 241
John Grey (179?-1843?) drawn by Nicolas Point, S.J. WSUL. 241
Mary Ann Charles Grey (?) drawn by Nicolas Point, S.J. WSUL. 241
Thomas Johnson (1802-1865). WHMC-KC. 243
Shawnee Methodist Mission and School located near present
    Turner (1830). WHMC-KC. 244
"First White settlement in Kansas, established 1827, by Col. Daniel Morgan Boone,
    'Farmer' for the Kansas Indians. Site, seven miles northwest of
    Lawrence." KSHS. 244
Portion of map *Missouri* showing the towns of southeast Missouri and
    western Illinois. Published by A. Finley, Philadelphia, 1831. WHMC-KC. 246
Keelboat on the Missouri River. WHMC-KC. 247
Captain George Hancock Kennerly (1790-1867). Photograph, ca. 1910 of painting
    loaned by Mrs. Abbie H. Haines. IM 001-002802. [Neg GPN Por K-9]. MHS. 247
Colonel Henry Leavenworth (1785-1834). KSHS. 248
Isaac McCoy (1784-1846). KSHS. 250
John Calvin McCoy (1811-1889). KSHS. 251
Pierre Menard Sr. (1766-1844). Photograph of a lithograph, n.d. (ICHi-32527)
    Chicago Historical Society (CHS). 252
Felix Valley Home (1814), Ste. Genevieve, Missouri. WHMC-KC. 253
Samuel Owens (d. 1847). WHMC-KC. 255
Baptiste Peoria (1800-1874). KSHS. 256
A portion of map *Colton's Missouri* showing the counties of the Platte Purchase and
    Indian lands in Kansas Territory. Published by Johnson and Browning, NY (1859).
    WHMC-KC. 257
Joseph Robidoux III (1783-1868). KSHS. 259
Saint Louis College erected in 1828. St. Louis University Archives (SLU). 261
Brigitte Saucier Chouteau (1778-1829). A 1870s (?) painting after an
    earlier work. WHMC-KC. 262
Kanzas City, Ballou's Pictorial Drawing-room Companion, 4 August 1855.
    Perhaps drawn after an early daguerreotype, represents the Town of Kansas,
    ca.1850. WHMC-KC. 264
Jean Baptiste Valle (1760-1849). Daguerreotype, ca. 1849. DAT 189. [bw detail]. MHS. .. 265
Jeanne Barbeau Valle (Mrs. Jean Baptiste Valle). Daguerreotype of painting, ca. 1850.
    DAT 191. [detail]. MHS. 265
Steamboat *Yellow Stone*. Photograph of painting by Karl Bodmer. WHMC-KC. 268

Foreword

The Chouteau name occupies a prominent place in Missouri history. Members of that influential family helped found the state's two great cities, St. Louis and Kansas City. But the influence of the ubiquitous Chouteaus extended far beyond Missouri's borders. They were instrumental in developing the western fur trade, in establishing commercial relations with key Missouri and Mississippi river Indian tribes, and in initiating a variety of business and financial enterprises.

The activities of the founders of the Chouteau dynasty – Auguste and Pierre and their mother, the indomitable Madame Chouteau – have been well documented. Less well known are the stories of their numerous progeny. Following in the footsteps of their celebrated forebears, the second-generation Chouteaus assumed active and vital roles in the expansion and development of the burgeoning American nation during the first half of the nineteenth century.

Pierre Chouteau's offspring were especially noteworthy – particularly the children of his first marriage to Pelagie Kiersereau: Auguste Pierre, Pierre Jr., Pelagie, and Paul Liguest. The most influential of the lot was Pierre Chouteau, Jr. A man of business who could be as ruthless as the occasion required, Pierre Jr. acquired control of the Western Department of John Jacob Astor's American Fur Company and became a dominant figure in the North American fur trade. He amassed a substantial fortune, and as with many successful frontier entrepreneurs, diversified his holdings with investments in railroads, ironworks, and other ventures. Although less successful financially, his older brother Auguste Pierre (A. P.) was a popular and highly regarded Indian trader and pioneer settler in Oklahoma. Their sister Pelagie married Barthlomew Berthold, who later formed a business partnership with Pierre Jr. Paul Liguest, the youngest child of the Chouteau-Kiersereau union, served as a U.S. Indian Agent to the Osages, operated a trading post on the Neosho River, and mentored his younger half-brothers in the ways of the fur trade.

Following his first wife's death, the elder Pierre Chouteau married Brigitte Saucier, who bore him five additional sons: Francois Gesseau, Cyprien, Pharamond, Charles B., and Frederick. They followed their father and their older siblings into the fur business, but with the exception of Pharamond, who died young, the members of Pierre Chouteau Sr.'s second family abandoned the flourishing entrepot of St. Louis and took up residence in what was then Indian country in the vicinity of the future town of Kansas City.

The trading operations and business ventures of the Kansas City Chouteaus never equaled those of their father and their uncle Auguste, or for that matter, those of their older siblings. Even so, the lives and careers of the disparate members of this extended clan were inextricably linked together, due in large measure to their propensity for keeping business in the family. Francois Gesseau, the most successful of the Kansas City Chouteaus, regularly turned to his father, his older brothers, and his father-in-law, the influential Kaskaskia merchant Pierre Menard, for advice and for assistance. A complicated web of matrimonial and commercial alliances helped keep the Chouteaus in the vanguard of the western fur trade, and the dynamics of their family-run mercantile empire tells much about how the fur business operated.

The letters of Francois Gesseau Chouteau and his wife Berenice Therese, nee Menard, form the core of this valuable study of the Kansas City Chouteaus. All but a few were written in French, and with the publication of this work most of them become available in English translation for the first time. These letters touch upon many significant topics. They amplify the importance of family connections among the French Creole traders who were so influential in the American fur trade. The Chouteaus' intimate associations with native peoples make their observations about the changed circumstances of America's original inhabitants especially useful. Their writings also mirror the difficulties of coming to terms with the realities of a new industrial order that was already transforming the world that they knew. And finally, the reflections of Francois and Berenice about their pioneering efforts in western Missouri and eastern Kansas add important new details about initial settlement in the region. These insightful letters, along with the accompanying annotations and commentaries, clarify and amplify the Chouteau family's important role in Kansas City's early history. This publication augments the work of Louise Barry and Tanis Thorne, among others, and constitutes an important addition to regional history. It deserves a wide reading.

William E. Foley
Central Missouri State University

Acknowledgments

The purpose of this book is to bring the Francois and Berenice Chouteau letters from their quaint French origin to readable English, making available a new resource that otherwise would be difficult for even the most skilled researcher to access. The initial and key task, without which nothing else could have been done, was translating the letters from French to English. This work required hours spent studying microfilm in an effort to decipher difficult handwriting and interpret obsolete vocabulary and faulty grammar, all written on paper aged and often damaged. For accomplishing this Herculean labor, we thank Betty Curtis White, SND, and Marie Dionne Pal.

Katherine Boutros did valuable basic research in the records of St. Louis Superintendency of the Bureau of Indian Affairs, Isaac McCoy papers, and other sources, and we thank her for that productive work and insightful interpretation. From the country of the Osage Indians, Alice Widner of the Trading Post Museum sent maps and information. For encouragement in the early stage of this work, and for sharing his knowledge of Native American tribes of Kansas, we thank Rodney Staab, then curator of Grinter House. We appreciate too conversations with Alan Caldwell who shared his knowledge about the idiosyncrasy of the Missouri River. Also, we thank Barbara Magerl who read and commented on the manuscript, Janice Lee who proofread the manuscript, and Paula Presley for her expert advice and for preparing the index for a very complex text.

Western Historical Manuscript Collection–Kansas City staff members, especially Jennifer Parker, cheerfully went beyond duty to give assistance. Thanks also to the staff of the Special Collections Department of the Kansas City Public Library, who brought the dusty fur trade books from the balcony and also suggested other avenues of research.

We appreciate the valuable assistance of Cheryl Schnirring of Illinois State Historical Library; Chuck Hill, Duane R. Sneddeker, and the other staff of Missouri Historical Society; Alan Perry and the staff and volunteers at the National Archives, Central Plains Region; Bob Knecht and Nancy Sherbert of the Kansas State Historical Society; Kevin Fisher of the Clay County Archives; John Hoffman of Illinois Historical Survey, University of Illinois Library, University of Illinois, Urbana-Champaign; Andrea Bean Hough of Indiana Division, Indiana State Library; John Waide of St. Louis University Archives, St. Louis, Missouri; Isabelle Contant of the Archives des Jésuites à St-Jérôme, Québec, Canada; Robert Matuozzi, Washington State University Library's Manuscripts, Archives, and Special Collections; Shelly J. Croteau, Missouri State Archives; Louis Derbes, C.M., archivist of St. Mary's Seminary, Perryville, Missouri; Morgen MacIntosh, DePaul University in Chicago; and James Goodrich and the staffs of the Western Historical Manuscript Collection–Columbia and the State Historical Society of Missouri. We are also grateful to the late Pauline Fowler for her encouragement and guidance about the history of Independence, Missouri.

We thank Charles Hoffhaus and the Chouteau Society of Kansas City, whose contribution made possible the purchase of the microfilm collection that contained the Chouteau letters.

Funding for the publication of this book came from revenues from the sale of an earlier book, *Legacy of Design: An Historical Survey of the Kansas City, Missouri, Parks and Boulevard System, 1893-1940*. That work was wholly underwritten by the William T. Kemper Foundation, Commerce Bank Trustee, which permitted the income from sales to be accrued in a revolving fund for future publishing projects. We thank the Foundation, and in particular Jonathan Kemper, for their foresight, support, and continued encouragement.

Sylvia D. Mooney, local artist with a deep love for our local history, beautifully designed and painted the original art for our cover.

Additionally, thanks to Dorothy Marra, author, and Marie Pal, translator, who, having invested a small lifetime on this project, viewed the work as community service and are donating back to the Western Historical Manuscript Collection all royalties from the sale of this book. Their generosity will assist in other WHMC-KC publications that hopefully will contribute to the knowledge of our past to the same high degree as their work.

We conclude in the hope that those, named and unnamed, who helped in any way, realize that without their assistance this complex project could never have seen completion. Thank you, one and all.

In preparing this work, we attempted to provide context and explanation for the letters, and in focusing narrowly on them, have of necessity neglected stories and voices that others may think we should have dealt with more fully. We regret that we did not or could not do that within the parameters of this project. Although nearly all the important issues are touched upon in some fashion, we know that the views and experiences of the Native Americans, who were so vital to the Chouteau enterprises, are not adequately represented. We know, too, that the story of early settlement and town-building is not fully explored – after all, Francois Chouteau died too early to be an active participant in the development of the city that grew near his warehouse and home.

Lastly, there are sources that still need mining, and articles and books that still need to be written. We encourage others to build upon the work we have done, much as we have attempted to build upon the excellent research of those who came before us.

David Boutros, Associate Director
Western Historical Manuscript Collection-Kansas City.

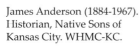

James Anderson (1884-1967). Historian, Native Sons of Kansas City. WHMC-KC.

Louise Barry (1910-1974). Librarian/historian, Kansas State Historical Society. KSHS.

"Aspect general des prairies occidentales de l'amerique – dites vulgairement La Grand-prairie" [General appearance of America's western prairies – commonly called the Great Prairie]. *Père Nicolas Point, S.J., Collection,* Archives de la Compagnie de Jesus, province du Canada frantais.

1 Of Frontier, Furs, and Family

A bitter north wind shrilled through the dense forest that crowded the river bluff, cracking tree branches laden with snow. Wolves atop the precipice howled at a frozen moon. Deer inched through the timber searching for food, their sharp hooves snapping through the crusted snow.

Below the frowning brow of the cliff, log cabins clustered on the riverbank. In one of them, Francois and Berenice Chouteau kept the fire in their hearth burning day and night to ward off the harsh winter, to keep their children warm, and the spark of their hopes alive. Only a few yards from their doorstep, the Missouri River, glinting in the moonlight, thundered past, its channel churning with ice chunks, uprooted trees, and frozen animal carcasses.

Gone are the bluffs where the wolves complained to the moon, and gone are the wolves. The roar of the Missouri River is drowned by the roar of city traffic. The log buildings have vanished and in their stead, towering over the harnessed river, are great skyscrapers housing the commerce of Kansas City that began so humbly almost two centuries ago in the form of a log "outpost" for collecting furs and trading with Indians.

Through the Chouteau letters, the world of pioneer commerce comes alive in the words of Francois Chouteau: the cumbersome modes of transporting goods, problems caused by the turn-around time of communication, shortage of cash and lack of a banking system, and a constant language barrier. Moreover there was the physical strain of living in a wilderness and traveling to branch outlets on horseback or in a boat that depended on human towing power – if there were sufficient water. It was how Kansas City's first CEO operated his business and recorded much of the action in his letters to *Cher Oncle*, Pierre Menard.

The letters of Berenice Menard Chouteau, by contrast, are personal and family centered. They rub the dust of 170 years from the window of her frontier home to give us a glimpse of the domestic scene on the rugged riverbank that became Kansas City. Her letters to Pierre Menard, her *Cher Papa*, depict some of the challenges faced by a young wife and mother who chose to establish a permanent home and raise a family at the westernmost edge of the United States.

Cher Oncle, Cher Papa contains seventy-eight letters: seventy-two written by Francois and six written by Berenice, all originally in French. The letters come principally from the *Pierre Menard Collection (PMC)*, Illinois State Historical Library, Springfield, Illinois. Letters from Francois to his brother Pierre (Cadet) Chouteau Jr. come from the *Chouteau Family Collections*, Missouri Historical Society, St. Louis. Some materials in the appendix come from Letterbook J, *Pierre Menard Collection*, Illinois Historical Survey, University of Illinois Library, Urbana-Champaign. Also consulted were materials from the *Menard Family Papers* in the Chicago Historical Society and the *William Morrison Collection* at the Illinois State Historical Library.

The correspondence spans the years from 1827 to 1840. Berenice wrote other letters to her father during that time, as Francois sometimes alluded to them in his letters. Being of a personal nature, many of Berenice's letters apparently were not saved. Francois's letters, however, documented business transactions and Pierre Menard kept those for future reference. Francois also wrote letters to both Pierre Menard and to his half-brother Pierre Chouteau Jr. that did not survive. Berenice wrote additional letters after the Civil War, in English. This compilation, however, concentrates on the pioneer era, and so Berenice's post-war letters are not included.

Until 1989, researchers in western Missouri knew of only the Francois Chouteau letters at the Missouri Historical Society in St. Louis. Those letters, written to Francois's brother Pierre Chouteau Jr., were thought to be the only ones to have survived. It was assumed that there were no Berenice Chouteau letters, and that perhaps she could neither read nor write. However, in 1989, a team of writers working on the history of the Catholic Diocese of Kansas City–St. Joseph, and tracking early Catholics of the area, followed Berenice Menard Chouteau back to her Kaskaskia home, discovered her father's political importance, and was eventually led to the *Pierre Menard Collection* at the Illinois State Historical Library. The collection is a treasure trove containing, in addition to hundreds of business papers, 2,239 letters, among them the letters of Francois Chouteau and Berenice Menard Chouteau that had never been translated or published.

The task of making these letters available to the public began in 1990 when David Boutros, Associate Director of the Western Historical Manuscript Collection at the University of Missouri at Kansas City, received a donation from The Chouteau Society of Kansas City that enabled him to purchase the microfilm edition of the *Pierre Menard Collection*. The first translation was made by Betty Curtis White, SND, formerly an instructor at Notre Dame de Sion, a Kansas City school once known as the "French Institute."

In 1993, after the first rough translation had been completed, Dorothy Brandt Marra, who had spearheaded the initial discovery of the letters, began the work of making the letters understandable. Shortly thereafter, the search for additional letters was initiated, and more materials were found in collections at the Illinois State Historical Library, as well as at the Chicago Historical Society and the Illinois Historical Survey, University of Illinois Library at the University of Illinois at Urbana-Champaign. Inquiries at other historical societies, archives, and universities in Texas, Oklahoma, and Arkansas yielded no additional material.

Marie-Laure Dionne Pal came to the project in 1994. Pal brought unique qualifications to her task, since her first language is Canadian French rather than Parisian French. (Sister Betty Curtis White and other translators whose French was Parisian were sometimes baffled by the colloquialisms and occasionally rustic nature of the language used in these letters.) Working without reference to the first translation, Pal produced an intelligible translation by filling in gaps and deciphering difficult passages. Both translators worked from microfilm and photocopies. Early in the project, Boutros inspected the originals in the Illinois collections and found little difference between the originals and the microfilms or photocopies.

After completing the second translation of the Chouteau letters, Pal reviewed all letters in the *Pierre Menard Collection* from 1827, the date of the first letter in this work, to December 1840, the date of Berenice's last pre-Civil War letter. This extra effort was undertaken in the hope of uncovering important new information, such as some commercial coup, a definitive statement as to how Francois died, the death date of infant Odile Chouteau, and so on. Nothing of this kind was found, but the secondary letters revealed the identity of several persons mentioned in the primary letters, documented Chouteau travels, and provided, in general, a fascinating enlargement of the original portrait of the early 1800s.

The translation of letters written 170 years ago was complicated by the condition of the letters. Words were faded, entire pages were torn, ink was smudged, and apparently some letters had gotten wet. All suffered from age, but everything considered, the letters could have been in much worse condition. Undoubtedly, the damage to them was sustained before they were archived.

The penmanship of the letter writers presented the second challenge. Francois wrote a neat hand, pleasing to the eye. Unfortunately, he had the habit of re-inking his pen in the middle of a word, thereby leaving a slight gap between the characters and creating the impression that one word was finished and a new one was beginning, whereas actually, he was completing the same word. Berenice's handwriting was difficult to read both in French and in English. (Facsimiles of Francois's and Berenice's letters may be found in appendix 6.)

Both Francois and Berenice took great liberties with French grammar, spelling, and punctuation, but again, Francois was more accurate than Berenice. Often the subject and predicate did not agree; frequently the wrong pronoun or gender was used. Spelling was habitually phonetic, requiring reading aloud to pick up the sound of the intended word. For example, in a letter dated May 26, 1829, Francois wrote that he came to "*flor e sant*," translated as "[where] the flowers are." But on reading aloud, the three words became one: Florissant – the community, now a part of St. Louis, given a bit of charm in the origin of its name. Capitalization was erratic, with personal names often not capitalized while any random word began with an uppercase letter.

Punctuation consisted chiefly of a period now and then, a rare comma, and liberal use of dashes. Paragraphing in Francois's letters was consistent: an opening paragraph saluting Pierre Menard, perhaps apologizing for not writing sooner, and assuring him of the writer's respect and affection. Then followed the body of the letter, containing details of the Indian trade and other business affairs. The closing paragraph was typically of a personal nature. Berenice's letters had no regular pattern.

The editorial goal of the translation was to produce material easily understood and enjoyed by the public, rather than a scholarly verbatim rendition. Nevertheless, the text presented adheres as closely to the original as possible, while being cast into readable form. An effort was made to retain the original flavor or "Frenchness" of the letters. Archaic language was maintained unless it was deemed to be unintelligible to the modern reader.

Original paragraphing, or lack thereof, was duplicated. Punctuation was amended for clarity and ease of reading: periods were added to eliminate the multitude of fragments and run-on sentences, and commas were inserted where needed. French diacritical marks were omitted. Where the text was unintelligible, or missing in part, the translator sometimes inserted words in brackets to suggest the meaning. Names of persons, Native American nations, and place names were capitalized and the spelling corrected.

The challenges of the letters were in both form and content: the condition of the manuscripts; the handwriting; and the grammar, spelling, and punctuation. The content of the letters sometimes bordered on inscrutable, as both the writer and the intended reader were familiar with topics and facts not set forth in the correspondence. In addition, archaic phraseology could cloud the meaning. Despite all of this, however, the marvel is that the message of these letters is still available.

Family relationships were especially important to the French and Creole families who pioneered Missouri. Deference to elders and heads of families, although the norm in that time, was particularly strong among these folk. Francois addressed his letters to Pierre Menard with the salutation "*Cher Oncle*," apparently valuing that relationship more than "father-in-law." Francois never failed to ask about his uncle's health and the health of his wife and family. If Francois had not written for some time, he explained why and expressed his regret. Berenice, being female, was even more deferential than Francois. Her sons, too, wrote letters to their Grandfather Menard expressing great respect for him and promising to do as he wished.[1] After the death of her father in 1844, Berenice transferred her respectful greetings to her half-brother Edmond, who had become head of the family.

These close family ties, extending to second and third cousins by marriage, were the basis of business partnerships and arrangements for buying, selling, and hiring. The French preference for "their own" also reached beyond the family to employees and acquaintances of family and friends. As the commerce of western Missouri developed, Frenchmen from the Illinois country migrated in stages up the Missouri River: from Cahokia to St. Louis or St. Charles, to Rocheport, to Chouteau's Landing. Or they moved across the Ozarks land route from Kaskaskia to Ste. Genevieve or Cape Girardeau, through central Missouri where Indians camped, past Paul Liguest Chouteau's Osage establishment, then either down into Arkansas or Oklahoma, or up to the mouth of the Kansas. These French *engagees* came confident that they would find a French trader who would employ them.

Husband-wife relationships among the French, however, were of a different nature. For that time frame, the French wives behaved in a rather independent way, depending of course, on individual circumstances. A wife's signature as well as a husband's was required on a bill of sale. Berenice apparently traveled as she pleased, for Francois wrote that she had "determined herself" to go to St. Louis.[2]

The French were a social people: they enjoyed conversation, good food and wine, music and dancing. On the Missouri frontier, the long winter months were enlivened by a dance

---

1. See letters from the *Pierre Menard Collection (PMC)*, Illinois State Historical Library, Springfield, Illinois (ISHL): Pierre Menard Chouteau to Pierre Menard, June 24, 1835 (*PMC*, Letter 661); Edmond Francois Chouteau to Pierre Menard, January 15, 1836 (*PMC*, Letter 703). These letters appear in the appendix as items 4 and 5.

2. Francois Chouteau to Pierre Menard, November 25, 1833, *PMC*, Letter 498. For clarity, "determined herself" was translated as "wants to go."

held each week at a different home. A fiddler played and the host provided a large kettle of thick soup called *pot de bouillon* that consisted of game meats, vegetables, and grains.[3] Each guest brought his or her own soup cup. Berenice was so fond of these dances that she fell out of favor with the first Catholic pastor of the Kawsmouth French community, Father Benedict Roux. The conservative French priest considered dancing immoral and wanted his parishioners to give it up.[4] But dancing was something the French Catholics had always done and continued to do, much to Father Roux's dismay.

Their fun-loving nature frequently led the French to give nicknames to each other and to their children. In his letters, Pierre Menard addressed his wife Angelique as *poupon*: little doll. Francois and Berenice often called some of their children by names other than those recorded as official. The oldest boy was called "Gesseau," not Edmond; a child who died was called "little Morgan." Often the second name was the one most frequently used: Francois Gesseau Chouteau was "Gesseau" to his family and friends. Therese Berenice Menard was "Berenice"; Paul Liguest Chouteau was "Liguest"; Pierre Menard Chouteau was "Menard" as a child and "Mack" as an adult.

In the earliest trail-breaking days, the French presence in western Missouri was dominant and continued to be strong until after the flood of 1844 but had almost disappeared by the Civil War. Then the volatile situation on the Missouri-Kansas border, with financial instability and renegades riding roughshod over the citizenry, drove most of the remaining French families out of the Kansas City area to points south and west.

The first three letters of this collection were written by Therese Berenice Menard, married to Francois Chouteau. She was born in Kaskaskia on August 13, 1801, the fifth of six offspring of Pierre Menard and his first wife Marie Therese Godin. These children were Marie Odile, Marie Josephine (died in infancy), Pierre, Hippolyte (died age seven), Therese Berenice, and Modeste Alzire, with whom Berenice maintained an especially close lifelong bond.[5]

Pierre Menard's home, *Illustrated Historical Atlas Map of Randolph County, Illinois*, 1875.

The home into which Berenice was born was comfortable, filled with the sounds of family and domestics going about their daily lives and duties. The varied Menard business interests sustained the family and the extensive Menard establishment. In addition, the large Menard farm consisting of grain fields, orchards, vineyards, berry and vegetable gardens, herb plots, and domestic animals enhanced their lives. Those under the roof of Pierre Menard were well fed, warmly clothed, and securely housed.

---

3. These dances and the soup were described by Father Bernard Donnelly, early pastor of the Cathedral parish, quoted in "When the Indians Danced at Westport," *Kansas City Catholic Register*, 5 October 1916, 1.

4. Benedict Roux to Joseph Rosati, February 12, 1835, Rev. Benedict Roux folder, *Letters of Bishop Joseph Rosati*, Archives of the Archdiocese of St. Louis, St. Louis, Missouri.

5. Berenice's initials were sometimes recorded as B. T. Chouteau or, in error, F. B. Chouteau or B. F. Chouteau. Her correct initials were T. B. Chouteau, though she was called Berenice.

Berenice's father Pierre Menard was well respected and important in the old French town of Kaskaskia. As a businessman he had no peer in the area, and, in addition, he was an influential political figure in both territorial and state governments. Kaskaskia was the state capital of the Illinois Territory, and when Illinois became a state in 1818, Pierre Menard was elected lieutenant governor.[6] Berenice grew up in a home where politics was often the topic of conversation.

Berenice was only three years old when her mother died. Two years later, her father married Angelique Saucier who became little Berenice's stepmother and lifelong friend. Angelique was the only mother Berenice ever really knew, and she called Angelique *mama*. Berenice's devotion to her stepmother was unwavering. Likewise, Berenice doted on her young half-siblings: Francois Xavier, Henri (died in infancy), Jean Baptiste Edmond, Emily (died age four), Matthieu Saucier, Louis Cyprien, Joseph Amedee, and Sophie Angelique. Sophie, twenty-one years younger than Berenice, was a special favorite. Throughout her life, Berenice's letters were filled with questions and sentiments about this second family.

Berenice's education was certainly better than that of most pioneer girls, but not equal to that of young women who spent years in expensive boarding schools. Berenice and her sisters were probably tutored at home, perhaps with the children of other French families in Kaskaskia. This was a common practice at the time. While the Menard sons were sent to costly eastern colleges, extensive inquiry produced no indication that any of the Menard daughters were educated at boarding schools.[7]

In the winter of 1809-1810, Angelique and the Menard children, including Berenice, stayed with the Pierre Chouteau family in St. Louis while Pierre Menard and Pierre Chouteau conducted an expedition for the St. Louis, Missouri Fur Company to the Upper Missouri, reaching the Mandan village. There they returned to his people a Mandan chief who had accompanied Lewis and Clark home to St. Louis in 1806, then went on to Washington City (Washington, D.C.) to see the "great, white father" Thomas Jefferson.

During those months at the Chouteau home, the Menard daughters may have attended the first school for girls established west of the Mississippi. This St. Louis establishment was founded and operated for many years by a Madame Rigauche, who had married into the Pinsonneau family.[8]

Proximity and the long winter months enabled Berenice to become well acquainted with her Chouteau "cousins," all boys, including Francois Gesseau, who was three years older than she. In the large Chouteau mansion they were sharing meals, playing games, and helping each other with the lessons assigned to them by their day school teachers. The education of females in those days included fine stitchery, music, penmanship, and spelling. (Given the translator's difficulties, Berenice may have failed the two latter subjects.)

When Pierre Menard returned from his journey up the Missouri, Berenice returned with her family to Kaskaskia. A fearful episode in that year was the 1811 New Madrid earthquake, undoubtedly felt in the Kaskaskia area, a distance of ninety-four miles from the epicenter.

Therese Berenice Menard and Francois Chouteau were married on July 11, 1819, in Immaculate Conception Catholic Church in Kaskaskia. In the early days of her marriage Berenice prepared to move to the wilderness. Although she was accustomed to the comforts

---

6. Richard E. Oglesby, "Pierre Menard," in *The Mountain Men and the Fur Trade of the Far West*, ed. Hafen, 6: 307-318.

7. Inquiries made to the St. Joseph Academy, Emmitsburg, Maryland; Sisters of Loretto, Louisville, Kentucky; Sisters of Charity, Nazareth, Kentucky.

8. Louis Houck, *A History of Missouri*, 2: 275-276.

Pierre Chouteau Residence, S.W. corner, Main and Washington, St. Louis, Missouri. Ink on paper by Clarence Hoblitzelle, 1897. MHS.

available to her society, Berenice's childhood had prepared her for a pioneer life. She had mastered the techniques of food management, probably learned to operate small boats on the Kaskaskia River that ran in front of her father's house, and was skilled at riding the horses from her father's stable. She had been filled with stories of adventure in distant snow-capped mountains where animals lived in abundance. In addition, Berenice had one asset unusual for her gender and time – she had no fear of Indians. Growing up on her father's Kaskaskia plantation, Berenice had played with the children of Indians camped in the fields; she had seen them walk casually into the Menard house looking for her father. She probably sat with her brothers and sisters around an Indian campfire, eating their food, listening to their songs, and watching their dances. She had always been around Indians – they were neither new nor threatening to her.

Taller than many young women of her day, Berenice was strong and healthy, as the letters attest. Pioneer historian John Calvin McCoy wrote that she was "a great woman. Everything about her testified to the force of her personality and character. She had a zest for living, an ability to adapt herself to her surroundings.... She was not afraid...of anything in life."[9]

So it was that while the wife of neighboring fur trader Joseph Robidoux turned her back on Black Snake Post (present St. Joseph) and remained comfortably and safely in St. Louis, Berenice Menard Chouteau took her two sons, Edmond, barely walking, and Pierre Menard, a babe in arms, and went with her husband to the western Missouri frontier.

While Berenice's preparation for pioneer life was more happenstance than plan, Francois Chouteau, almost from the day of his birth, was groomed for the fur trade. His determination

---

9. "Kansas City's Pioneer Mother Was Wife of First Settler on River Front," *Kansas City Times*, 2 October 1935.

and native intelligence, clearly revealed in his letters, allowed him to branch out into other endeavors.

Francois Gesseau Chouteau was born on February 7, 1797, in St. Louis. His father was Pierre Chouteau Sr. (Jean Pierre Chouteau) and his mother was Brigitte Saucier Chouteau, the second wife of Pierre Chouteau. Francois's grandfather Pierre Laclede Liguest was the founder of St. Louis along with Auguste Chouteau, Francois's uncle.

Francois, being the eldest child of the second family, grew up with his older half-siblings Auguste Pierre (A. P.), Pierre Jr. (Cadet), Pelagie, and Paul Liguest. "Liguest," as Paul was called, was five years older than Francois, and as an adult Francois seemed close to this half-brother who lived about 100 miles south of Chouteau's Kansas City warehouse. Francois's half-brother Cadet figured in these letters as both business associate and family contact in St. Louis. Pelagie was never mentioned and A. P., who was involved in the fur trade in Oklahoma, rarely entered the picture.

As a child, Francois toddled around the Osage villages, playing with small Indian friends. In 1795, two years before Francois was born, the governor of Spanish Louisiana awarded his father, Pierre Chouteau Sr., and Francois's uncle, Auguste Chouteau, a six-year contract for exclusive rights to the Osage trade. To cement the friendly relations they had with the Osages, Auguste and Pierre Chouteau built Fort Carondelet in Osage country (Vernon County) and Pierre took his family there to live. Francois was born during that time, although his mother apparently went back to St. Louis for the birth. When the Chouteaus lost their exclusive rights to the Osage trade in 1802, the family abandoned the fort and moved back to St. Louis.

When Francois was about nine or ten he was apparently sent to a day school in St. Louis, probably the first such for boys founded and operated by French-Canadian Jean Baptiste Truteau, who conducted his school from 1774 until about 1826.[10] It appears that Francois did not receive any advanced education, or if he did, no record of it has been found.[11] Although his limited schooling left his grammar and spelling less than perfect, they served him (and later translators) well enough to let the message of his letters make its way through the murk of time.

After classes and on days when school was not in session, Francois probably edged into the warehouse of his father and his Uncle Auguste to breathe in the musty smells and watch the men stacking bundles of soft, dark pelts for shipment to New Orleans or the large ports of the northeast coast or Canada.

At age fourteen or fifteen, Francois returned to the Osage country to live with his half-brother Paul Liguest and learn the fur business. During this time he renewed childhood ties and forged lifelong friendships among the Osages. When Francois was about seventeen he fathered a son whose Osage mother was named Marie. The baptismal record of Charles de la Croix, a Catholic missionary priest among the Osages, listed the baptism of this seven-year-old boy, James Chouteau, as having taken place in May 1822.[12] As he had spent so much of his young life among the Osages, Francois undoubtedly understood their language and probably spoke it rather well. Whether this would have helped him communicate with the Kansa or the eastern immigrant Indians, it is difficult to say.

---

10. Houck, *History of Missouri*, 2: 275.
11. Inquiries made to the West Point Military Academy; St. Mary's College, Emmitsburg, MD; Georgetown University, Washington, D.C.
12. Louis Burns, *Osage Mission Baptisms, Marriages, and Interments, 1820-1886*, 138. The original *Records of the Catholic Osage Mission on the Neosho River* (St. Paul, Kansas) are in the Diocese of Wichita, Wichita, Kansas, and a microfilm copy may be found at the Kansas State Historical Society (Microfilm roll MS093).

Probably of medium height, as the French were not a tall people, Francois would have been slender and strong in his youth, conditioned by hefting bales of furs, walking and riding miles in heat or cold, and surviving the daily surprises of the wilderness. As early as 1816, Francois and his cousin "Seres" (Gabriel Sylvestre) Chouteau were licensed to trade with the Osages, Kansas, and Pawnees,[13] presumably near the mouth of the Kansas River. In November 1818, factory superintendent George Sibley at Fort Osage reported, "A drove of pack horses passed this way a few days ago on their way up the Kansas River from whence I am told they are to carry goods to trade with the Little Osage. They were owned (or controlled) by Sara [Seres] Chotou [sic] I am informed."[14] Perhaps they were to rendezvous with a boat bringing merchandise from St. Louis that would be transferred to the horses and packed overland to their post of the Four Houses.

In July of 1819, Francois Chouteau and Berenice Menard were married. The wedding trip of legend – bride and groom in a pirogue ascending the Missouri River – if it occurred at all, could have been completed in time for Francois and Seres to get back to the business.[15] In October of that year, Major Thomas Biddle noted from "Camp Missouri" that the Chouteau cousins "have a trading-house not far from the mouth of the river Kanzas, and their capital is about $4,000."[16]

Although Francois and Berenice Chouteau lived in the United States, they were basically French, and their whole approach to life was French: the importance of personal relationships, the honoring of family ties, the recognition of emotions, the appreciation of the joys of life, and the general absence of the stoic approach common to other groups. "Frenchness" was the hallmark of pioneer western Missouri, the core of the early fur trade, and the essence of these letters.

Since 1682, the center of what became the United States had evolved into a virtual French enclave. In that year, French explorer Robert de La Salle had come down the Mississippi from Canada and claimed all the land drained by the Mississippi and its tributaries for his king, Louis XIV of France. He christened the vast territory "Louisiana."

The Missouri River was first documented by Louis Jolliet, Father Jacques Marquette, and five other Frenchmen steering two canoes down the Mississippi River in June 1673. The Indians called the Missouri *Pekitanoui*, meaning "muddy waters," and it was identified by that name on the map drawn by Jolliet and Marquette. They depicted it as a broad river with an uncertain source, emptying into the Mississippi. The banks of the Missouri River were home to several Indian tribes, but the early French, perhaps coming first upon a village of the Missouri tribe, called the river by that name.

Other nations living in the area when the French began to frequent it were the Kansa on the Missouri (and later the Kansas River), the Panis or Pawnee on the Republican fork of the Platte River, and the Osages on the Osage River. Farther up on the Missouri River were the Otoes, the Aiaouez or Iowas, and the Sac and Fox.

The French, however, were not the only ones interested in the center of the vast land. Attempting to extend their influence from the southwest, the Spanish tried to prevent the

---

13. *Territorial Papers of the United States*, 15: 191.

14. George C. Sibley to William Clark, November 5, 1818, 2: 136-137, *U.S. Superintendency of Indian Affairs, St. Louis, 1813-1825* (*SIA*) (MC741), Kansas State Historical Society (KSHS).

15. John C. McCoy also asserted in his reminiscences that Francois and Berenice first ascended the Missouri on this bridal trip to the Black Snake Hills (St. Joseph) where Francois supervised the American Fur Company post. (John C. McCoy Scrapbook, 6, *John Calvin McCoy (1811-1889) Collection* [Native Sons Archives] (KC296), WHMC-KC.) Independent confirmation of this story has not been found.

16. *American State Papers: Indian Affairs*, 2: 202. Camp Missouri was a predecessor to Fort Atchinson, about fifteen miles north of Omaha, Nebraska.

French from establishing permanent settlements in the heartland called Upper Louisiana. In 1720, Antoinio Valverde y Cossio, Governor of Mexico, sent a party of over 100 Spaniards and Indians from Santa Fe on a reconnaissance mission. They were to negotiate with Indian tribes and assess the French presence in the middle of the continent. When the Spanish-Indian explorers were attacked by Pawnees and Otoes near the Platte River, they were unable to defend themselves and over two-thirds of the group was killed.[17] The survivors straggled back to Santa Fe while the French were planning a permanent settlement in the heart of the country.

In 1723, Etienne de Bourgmont and forty Frenchmen traveled up the Missouri and built a small outpost called Fort Orleans near the mouth of the Grand River (Carroll County). Since the French trappers and explorers had already infiltrated Indian lands and villages – de Bourgmont himself had lived with the Missouris for several years – they were tolerated and sometimes even welcomed.

Kansa chiefs visited Fort Orleans and the following spring traded furs to the French. The mission of the Frenchmen at Fort Orleans was to make contact with the Padouca Indians (Plains Apaches) and arrange a peace treaty between them and the Missouri River Indians in order to make the fur trade a less hazardous business. Accompanied by representatives of the Missouri River tribes, bearing gifts and leading horses as presents, the group arrived at the Great Village of the Padoucas in present Saline, or Ellsworth County, Kansas. The Padoucas were cajoled into making a peace treaty and to promising, in addition, to aid Frenchmen trying to reach Santa Fe, twelve days' travel from the Great Village.[18]

Months later de Bourgmont took a party of Indians to Paris, and Fort Orleans fell into disrepair. Its mission had been accomplished and no effort was made to maintain that short-lived French outpost in the wilderness. By 1729 the fort was deserted. The French traffic up the Missouri, however, increased steadily. Risking their lives on the erratic river and at the hands of the unpredictable inhabitants of its banks, the sturdy *voyageurs* pushed forward in their quest for furs. A life lost here, a party killed or drowned in another place – despite these realities, the fur trappers and traders pursued their dreams of wealth.

When American furs became a significant trade commodity in Europe because of a fashion craze for beaver hats and apparel, the French government began to take notice. Word was sent to the Louisiana colony that the trappers and traders on the Missouri should be given protection and encouragement so that more furs could be collected. Consequently, in the spring of 1744, work began on a military fort on high ground overlooking the Missouri River near present Fort Leavenworth, Kansas.

The governor of Louisiana, the baron de Cavagnial, officially chartered Fort Cavagnial in August 1744. A military commandant, Chevalier Francois de Villiers, and a small unit of soldiers took up residence at the fort. Located near the site of present day Fort Leavenworth, the purpose of the establishment was to supervise relations between the Kansa Indians and the itinerant trappers, hunters, and traders. However, neither the French *voyageurs* nor the Indians were particularly eager for supervision.[19]

Around 1750 Fort Cavagnial began to deteriorate. The commandant at the fort complained that the French traders and trappers went up the rivers without stopping and that reaching the relocated Kansa Indian village required a three-day march. When the Indians moved closer to the fort, the outpost was repaired temporarily. Fort Cavagnial was

---

17. A. P. Nasatir, *Before Lewis and Clark: Documents Illustrating the History of the Missouri, 1785-1804*, 16-17.

18. William E. Foley, *A History of Missouri, 1673-1820*, 11-13.

19. Charles E. Hoffhaus, "Fort de Cavagnial: Imperial France in Kansas, 1744-1764," *Kansas Historical Quarterly* 30: 425-454

abandoned when the French withdrew their military presence in Louisiana after their defeat in the French and Indian War. In accordance with the Treaty of Paris, signed in 1763 to end that war, France ceded Louisiana to Spain.

In that same year, a fourteen-year-old boy named Auguste Chouteau began to build the city of St. Louis. He had been given this responsibility by his stepfather and employer, Pierre de Laclede Liguest, who, with Chouteau, had previously chosen the site. Located on a bluff overlooking the Mississippi and just below the mouth of the Missouri River, the new establishment was planned as a trading center for Laclede's New Orleans fur enterprise, Maxent, Laclede and Company, which held the exclusive right to trade with the Indians of Upper Louisiana.[20]

The new city of St. Louis never faltered. Alongside Chouteau's original buildings, new homes and businesses appeared. One cause for the rapid growth of the city was that the agreement that transferred the Louisiana Territory from France to Spain also mandated that Canada and land lying roughly east of the Mississippi be ceded to the British. This meant that the Illinois Territory, heavily settled by the French, was in British control. Dismay swept through the French towns of Prairie du Rocher, Fort Chartres, Ste. Philippe, Cahokia, and Kaskaskia, as well as scattered villages and farms. Many of the French inhabitants packed up their belongings, deserted their lands and homes, and moved across the river to St. Louis. They knew that St. Louis, too, was no longer in French control, but the Spanish – or almost anybody, many Frenchmen felt – were preferable to the British with whom they had been at odds for so long.

As St. Louis thrived, it became a launching site for traders and trappers going up the Missouri River. For a few years the *voyageurs* had it all their own way. They risked encounters with hostile Indians, but they did as they pleased, not especially concerned about licenses and other fine points of Spanish law mandated by a ruling body that was remote and concerned with other things.

The Spanish did, indeed, have their troubles; it took them five years from the time Louisiana was ceded to them to take control in St. Louis. In the meantime, a Frenchman named Louis Saint-Ange de Bellerive comfortably ruled the city on behalf of the Spanish. This pleasant arrangement came to an end in 1770 when Don Pedro Piernas came to St. Louis. For two years previous, a Spanish officer named Captain Francisco Riu had attempted to take command but failed to make a smooth transition, and by the time Piernas arrived, the area was in chaos and near-revolt.

Piernas settled in St. Louis and considered his options regarding the fur industry – the one real source of money in Upper Louisiana. While the isolated *voyageurs* still plied their trade, Laclede almost monopolized the fur business on the Missouri. He sent men with merchandise up the river to trade for Indian furs and encouraged nearby tribes to bring their furs to St. Louis for trade goods and presents. Meanwhile, the number of British traders coming down from Canada had increased, and many furs that had previously gone down to New Orleans were being shipped to Montreal. Both the British and the Spanish/French lured the Indians to their cause with lavish gifts: brandy, tobacco, guns, powder, shot, musket flints, blankets, cloth, shirts, hats, bells, jewelry, medals, ribbons, mirrors, sewing needles, kettles, knives, axes, hoes, and other implements.

In addition to giving the Indians presents, the Spanish government attempted to keep them docile by rewarding friendly tribes with trade opportunities while prohibiting trade with hostile or unruly tribes. None of this worked very well. The Indians took what was

---

20. John Francis McDermott, "The Exclusive Trade Privileges of Maxent, Laclede and Company," *Missouri Historical Review* 29 (July 1935): 272-278.

offered to them and behaved as they desired. If trade goods were not offered, they traveled to where the goods were available and complained loudly about the inconvenience.

In theory, all Spanish subjects, including the French residents, could trade with the Indians. But government officials soon realized that by restricting trade to themselves and their friends, they could make a great deal of money. Securing a trading license became difficult, and in 1769, Maxent and Laclede lost their exclusive trading rights for Upper Louisiana. Maxent sold his portion of the business to Laclede, who moved the firm to St. Louis and made young Auguste Chouteau his partner.

Auguste Chouteau had been serving as Laclede's right-hand man since they had founded St. Louis. Educated in New Orleans, probably at Laclede's expense, Auguste Chouteau kept records, dealt with Indians, and traveled up and down the Missouri and Osage rivers overseeing trade agreements, distributing merchandise, and making friends with influential Indians. The Osage nation on the Osage River was a large tribe and particularly skilled at trapping and hunting. Laclede was eager to trade with the Osages for their many fine furs, but the Indians were inclined to be troublesome, and it was deemed prudent that Auguste Chouteau spend considerable time with them, encouraging them to hunt and determining what merchandise they wanted in exchange for their furs. In this way, Auguste Chouteau established the Chouteau-Osage friendship that was so long-lasting and politically important.

After Auguste Chouteau became Laclede's partner, he delegated the Osage liaison work to his seventeen-year-old half-brother Pierre Chouteau, natural son of Laclede and Auguste's mother, Marie Therese Chouteau.

Marie Therese Chouteau, while living in New Orleans, had been deserted by Rene Chouteau, her husband and the father of Auguste. Inasmuch as she never divorced Rene Chouteau but simply left New Orleans and came to St. Louis with Laclede, her subsequent children all bore the Chouteau name though Laclede was their father.

Both Auguste and Pierre Chouteau, as a result of their long and close contact with the Osages, were fluent in the Osage language and understood and appreciated the subtleties of Osage customs, tribal divisions, and social structure. This friendly relationship gave the Chouteaus a tremendous trade advantage and political clout. It brought them wealth and esteem; the ruling government used the Chouteaus to control the Indians while the Indians made the Chouteaus honorary tribal members, valued their friendship – and also used it to push for special favors.

In recognition of their good influence over the Osages, the Spanish government in 1777 assigned the largest share of the Osage trade to the Chouteaus. Meanwhile, however, Laclede's fortunes and health declined. He died heavily in debt in May 1778, aboard a boat en route from New Orleans to St. Louis. Auguste Chouteau was forced to deal with that portion of Laclede's debt incurred by their business. Chouteau borrowed a small sum, skillfully managed the season's fur crop, and in 1779 finished the year in the black.

The American Revolution distracted the Chouteaus from their fur trade business, as they were forced to face the realities of war. Spain came into the fray, along with the French, on the side of the American revolutionaries. Shortages in trade goods developed in Spanish territory, but the British traders coming down from Canada were well supplied and consequently took over trade that had formerly gone to the French traders.

When the American Revolution ended in 1783 with the signing of the Treaty of Paris, the Chouteaus assessed the new trading scene. It was still difficult to acquire trade goods through New Orleans, so Auguste Chouteau began to deal with Canadian merchants, first in Cahokia and then in Michilimackinac, where trade merchandise was sold at a lower price.

Pierre Chouteau, while working and living at length with the Osages, returned to St. Louis frequently enough to marry Pelagie Kiersereau and father four children. Pelagie died in 1793 and Pierre remarried. His second wife was Brigitte Saucier of a prominent French family in the Illinois Territory. The first of five sons of this marriage was Francois Gesseau Chouteau, born in 1797.[21]

By that time, Pierre Menard had come to the area. Born in 1766 near Montreal, Menard was, like Auguste Chouteau, a child prodigy. He snatched a basic education in Canada and then, at age fourteen, rode down the Mississippi to seek his fortune in the Illinois country. When he was fifteen, Menard was already buying and selling merchandise and giving credit to seasoned traders. A few years later Menard settled in Kaskaskia, Illinois, married, and began his first family, which included daughter Therese Berenice Menard.

Although the Upper Louisiana government had been Spanish for four decades, few Spaniards had followed their officials to the-very-French St. Louis. One exception was an energetic man named Manuel Lisa, who in 1802 wrested the exclusive Osage trading rights from the Chouteaus. However, another political shakeup was about to occur and the fur trade on the Missouri River would enter a new phase.

In 1800, Napoleon finessed Louisiana away from Spain. Shortly thereafter France agreed to sell the land to the United States and signed the Louisiana Purchase, enabling President Thomas Jefferson to proclaim the new government on December 20, 1803. Once more, men in the fur trade kept a wary eye on the political scene.

President Jefferson's immediate goal was to learn whether the river system of the new territory would provide the coveted Northwest water route to the Pacific. To acquire this knowledge, he appointed Meriwether Lewis and William Clark to explore the Missouri River to its source, cross the Rockies, and reach the Pacific Ocean.

Before Lewis and Clark began their sojourn up the Missouri, traders and trappers had already forged well past the Council Bluffs area. But the government-sponsored expedition created a great deal of interest among persons in the fur trade. The St. Louis merchants waited eagerly to learn about many details: how the Upper Missouri tribes reacted to the white explorers, the quantity of game, and most importantly, the number and kind of fur-bearing animals found by the expedition.

Lewis and Clark's report created a stir in St. Louis. In 1806-1807 Manuel Lisa launched his first trading expedition to the Upper Missouri, with financial backing from Pierre Menard and Menard's business associate, William Morrison. Deaths and remarriages brought the Menards and Chouteaus into the same family – both Pierre Chouteau and Pierre Menard lost their wives and married daughters of Francois Saucier.

The St. Louis Missouri Fur Company was organized in 1808-1809, comprised of former rivals Pierre Chouteau and Manuel Lisa along with Pierre Menard and others. In the spring of 1809, they set out for the Upper Missouri in ten boats loaded with merchandise. They reached their destination and unloaded trade merchandise and supplies to support a winter trapping party. Lisa, Chouteau, and two young Chouteaus returned to St. Louis in September, but Menard remained to oversee the trappers. (This was the time when Angelique and the Menard children were staying with Brigitte Chouteau and her children in St. Louis.) It was an experience Menard never forgot and never repeated.

---

21. For a very readable and detailed account of Missouri under the French and Spanish, and of the early U.S. Territorial period, see William E. Foley, *A History of Missouri, 1673-1820*. For more specific information about St. Louis and the early fur trade, see William E. Foley and C. David Rice, *The First Chouteaus*. And for transcriptions of early documents and other research, see Louis Houck, *The Spanish Regime in Missouri*, and his companion three-volume, *History of Missouri*.

Pierre Menard wrote to his new wife with emotional concern for his family and a homesickness that did not end until he was back in St. Louis. Menard had a low opinion of the rough and dangerous wilderness life where he had no control over the elements or the Indians and very little over his own employees. Before and after this wilderness adventure, Pierre Menard was active in Illinois politics, serving as the first lieutenant governor of the Territory. In addition, his business interests were widespread: retail stores, the fur trade, a ferry business, and real estate investments in Illinois, Missouri, and Texas. He was often called upon to mediate government-Indian problems, as his good relationship with the Indians was longstanding and well known. From 1813 to 1833 he was agent for the Kaskaskia Indians, and during the removal of the eastern tribes Menard served as field agent and apparently helped the Indians greatly, for they always considered him their friend.

After the United States government was established in the Louisiana Territory, traders were permitted to do business with the Indian tribes for which they were licensed. In addition, from 1796 to 1822, the government operated a system of factories, or fortified trading posts. Fort Osage in present Jackson County, Missouri, was such a factory, with factor George Sibley in charge. Traders resented the factory system, complaining that the government was usurping private enterprise and creating unfair competition for the traders. In 1822, the government discontinued the factory system.

Licensed traders dealt with government-appointed agents and subagents who operated the Indian agencies. Several agencies were located in a superintendency directed by a superintendent. During the time of these letters, the superintendent of Indian Affairs in St. Louis was William Clark of the Lewis and Clark expedition. He had charge of the tribes in the central United States. The reader of these letters will notice that, for the most part, Francois Chouteau dealt with the agents of the Kansa Agency and of the Shawnee Agency that supervised Indians of many tribes.

"*Keel-boat moving up the Mississippi..*" WHMC-KC.

In 1821, Missouri had become the twenty-fourth state of the union and Francois Chouteau, under a license issued to the French Fur Company (Berthold, Chouteau, and Pratte), began trading on the Missouri River.[22] His post at Randolph Bluffs in Clay County served to lengthen the chain of Chouteau trading posts linking the St. Louis base of operations with western Missouri and Kansas, as well as with the region on the upper Missouri River.

John Jacob Astor formed the American Fur Company in 1826 and created its Western Department by buying the French Fur Company. Francois's half-brother Pierre (Cadet) Chouteau Jr. became leader of the Company's Western Department.

The government began in 1825 to survey and mark the Santa Fe Trail. Trade with Mexico had become a reality, adding another complication to the fur industry and to relations with the Indians. Trail caravans were loaded with goods leaving the United States en route to Santa Fe, and with saddlebags packed with Spanish silver on the return trip. These were tempting treasures and, furthermore, the caravans crossed through lands controlled by several Indian nations. Meanwhile, white settlers moved to the area in increasing numbers. Western Missouri was changing – for the French as well as the Indians.

In January 1825, President Monroe formally proposed the policy of removing the eastern Indian tribes to the territory set aside for them in the West. When the United States adopted the Indian Removal Act (1830), the affected Indians were forced off their valuable lands and sent forth on a journey that would end, years later, in Missouri, Kansas, and Oklahoma.[23] Thousands of disheartened and often angry Indians poured into the area near the mouth of the Kansas River where the fur trade was flourishing. The influx created a situation ripe for discord among the resident Indians being crowded by white settlers and the immigrant tribes from the East.

Transportation and travel methods were primitive and difficult for everyone, on both land and water. The Indians walked or rode horseback on land; on water they were likely to use rafts or canoes. White settlers and merchants on the Santa Fe Trail used covered wagons pulled by sturdy oxen, or horses and mules with packsaddles. On water, the French used large canoes, or pirogues. Large shipments were usually carried on the rough and cumbersome keelboats that gave way to steamboats in the 1830s. These mechanized marvels cut the journey from St. Louis to Chouteau's trading post in present Kansas City from several weeks to a mere ten days or less.

The rapid changes of the years 1825-1838 kept everyone off balance. The U.S. government waffled on its Indian policy; the fur trade executives and post operators pretended supply would always equal demand. Although these traders saw clearly that the supply was diminishing, they never dreamed that the demand would bottom out before the supply. The resident Indians bristled at being pushed by the immigrating eastern Indians. And all these nations struggled to deal with the overwhelming changes to their lives. With this maelstrom propelling them, Francois and Berenice Chouteau settled into their wilderness home and began to raise a family. Although he was only in his mid-twenties, Francois Chouteau had years of experience in the business that would be his life's work.

---

22. Tradition in western Missouri holds that Francois Chouteau built a trading post near Kansas City in 1821. Trading licenses issued in 1822 provide documentation for an 1822 trading post although evidence is lacking for the 1821 date. Nineteenth-century historians, as well as pioneers John Calvin McCoy and J. S. Chick, all maintained that Chouteau came in 1821. The same sources that promoted the 1821 date also said the location of the post was on the south side of the Missouri River. Frederick Chouteau, however, who worked at the post and would have known, indicated it was on the north side. For a complete discussion of these two issues, see Louise Barry, *Beginning of the West: Annals of the Kansas Gateway to the American West 1540-1854*, 102; "Reminiscences of Fredrick Chouteau," *Kansas Historical Collection* 8: 423; and appendix item 1.

23. *History of Jackson County (1881)*, 385-388.

The traditional assumption of Francois Chouteau's role in western Missouri was that he was a manager of a branch operation for the family fur syndicate headed by his older half-brother Cadet Chouteau at the home base of St. Louis. These letters and other supporting documents offer insights into a second, competing interest centered in Kaskaskia with Pierre Menard, whose longstanding trade with the tribes in southeast Missouri transferred to eastern Kansas when those Indians were removed there. Pierre Menard and Cadet Chouteau may have been investors – silent partners of sorts – in Francois Chouteau's frontier venture. Certainly each had an account named "Kansas Outfit" on their books. But that seems too simple a definition for a very complex relationship. It is important to remember that the early nineteenth century was a less formal and regulated time than today. Clearly Francois Chouteau acted on Pierre Menard's behalf in a variety of transactions, including negotiating with Indian tribes, directing employees, purchasing real estate, and collecting debts. It is not clear, however, if he was motivated by profit or because the advantage of a friendly patron in Menard was worth the time and effort of these tasks. At the same time, Francois was also performing many of the same tasks for his brother Cadet and the American Fur Company, a competitor to Menard's business in the area. While there is good evidence of a strong working relationship between Cadet and Menard, there are also indications of a high level of vigilance and distrust that demanded that each warily protect his turf.

So what exactly were the business relationships of Francois Chouteau to his father-in-law Pierre Menard and to his brother Cadet Chouteau? It was certainly not as simple as that of an employee to an employer. Nor was it defined exclusively by familial associations.

Instead, it is better to understand and appreciate Francois Chouteau as a freelance agent – an entrepreneur – walking a fine line between his self-interests and loyalties to longstanding family and social connections. Men on the frontier, such as the Chouteau brothers, Joseph Robidoux, and William Gilliss, were strongly independent. They confronted daily hardships and shifting conditions in the competition for a limited and dwindling resource. They were challenged by an often confusing dynamic among the Indians, government officials, and new settlers. In the end, they always chose strategic solutions that served first to assure their own survival and advancement. They moved in and out of business associations as the needs and circumstances demanded.

Reinforcing this view, some thirteen years after Francois Chouteau's death, Rudolph Friederich Kurz, a Swiss artist who spent six years observing and recording his experiences among fur traders and Indians on the Mississippi and Upper Missouri, wrote about a mature commerce:

> [November 22, 1851]…*Before I knew as much about the fur trade as I now know I was astonished to find prices so unreasonably high, but as I became more and more closely acquainted with the business and attendant expenses I knew that it could not be otherwise. When commodities are obliged to be transported 9,000 miles, nay, some of them halfway round the world, the outlay therefore must necessarily be considerable.*
>
> *Wares are shipped here from Leipzig (little bells and mirrors), from Cologne (clay pipes), beads from Italy, merinos, calicos from France, woolen blankets, guns from England, sugar and coffee from New Orleans, clothing and knives from New York, powder and shot, meal, corn, etc., from St. Louis. The company owns factories both at home and abroad for the manufacture of their staple goods; their trade in furs extends throughout the entire Indian domain from the upper Mississippi to Mexico. Their trading posts are spread along the St. Peters River, the Missouri, Yellowstone, Platte, Arkansas, Gila, Bear River, throughout Oregon, California, Utah, and New Mexico. Trade is distributed through the districts according to the location of navigable streams or some other means of communication: upper Mississippi outfit, lower Mississippi outfit, Platte*

outfit, etc. Members of the company, P. Chouteau Jr., Sarpy, Berthold, O'Fallon, et al., live in St. Louis, where they have their office, an immense storehouse. From there goods are shipped to the various posts, skins and furs are received in exchange, and are sold throughout the world, especially to Russia. In every district there is an agent, employed at a fixed salary ($2,000) and paid in addition certain profits on sales. He has charge of several posts. He orders supplies from the company but is not usually obliged to pay for them in pelts. He is at liberty to dispose of the hides and skins that he takes in exchange in the market where he finds the best prices.

For goods delivered at the factory price plus the cost of transportation agents are required to pay a yearly interest on capital advanced, together with the cost of insurance. He knows, therefore, what the approximate cost of his commodities will be and has only to reckon in addition sums necessary to pay salaries and keep of his employees, and largesse to Indians, in order to maintain his trading post with success.... A bourgeois or head clerk is stationed at each post. He receives a fixed salary of $1,000 and a stated percentage on sales. He buys goods, just as agents do, at the cost price. The bourgeois keeps his own accounts. He orders what he needs from his agent and delivers to him all that is received in exchange for goods sold; whether he makes large profits or suffers losses depends upon how well he knows how to calculate to advantage and to regulate his own expenses.

Agents and bourgeois form, so to speak, a company of their own in so far as they all agree to buy goods from the stockholders at a stipulated price in which is included interest and transportation charges.

If skins and furs bring high prices the agents make a surplus which they divide among themselves and the bourgeois according to the peltry contributed by each. The stockholders assume responsibility for all damages to commodities in transit; agents are required only to answer for goods received at the destination to which they are consigned. All shipments are secured from loss by insurance, the premium on which is quite high for goods sent up the Missouri, because there are such a great number of snags.

The less a bourgeois has to pay for the upkeep of his fort, in salaries for employees, and for skins and furs, the greater will be his profit and that of his agents, who are also bourgeois of a fort. Clerks and engagees are paid on an average the wage they receive in the United States, but they are required to buy everything from the trading post where they are employed and at the price demanded there. Fortunately, they have neither the necessities nor the occasions for spending money that one has in the States; otherwise they would save nothing. The traders, clerks, interpreters, hunters, workmen, and their helpers employed at the forts and who are content to buy on a credit from the company seldom lay by anything for a rainy day. They marry. Indeed, for the purpose of chaining to the fort, so to speak, those who are capable, those who are indispensable, the bourgeois endeavor to bind them down for the next year by advancing sums to them on credit.

For supplies intended for their own use the bourgeois pay the same price that they would be required to pay to the stockholders for the same article, but they demand much more from their employees and the Indians. For a medium buffalo robe they charge an employee $4, for one extra good (prime) $8, for a robe enriched with ornamentation $15; even a higher price than charged in the United States. For the usual robe Indians receive in exchange, for instance, 2 gallons of shelled corn, from 3 to 4 pounds of sugar, or 2 pounds of coffee. The total expense of preparing a buffalo robe for sale, reckoned as one sum, would not exceed $1 gross. In St. Louis these robes are sold at wholesale for at least $2; therefore, the agents and bourgeois can easily realize 100 percent profit if they know the trade. It is not true in every case, however, that a bourgeois is an expert trader; those managers are chosen among clerks who have been trained in this part of the country, and many of them who become efficient clerks under good and careful management are not in every respect competent to conduct a business to the best advantage.

A craftsman or workman receives $250 a year; a workman's assistant is never paid more than $120; a hunter receives $400, together with the hides and horns of the animals he kills; an interpreter without other employment, which is seldom, gets $500. Clerks and traders who have mastered the court language, i.e., the speech of those Indians for whose special advantage the trading posts are established, may demand from $800 to $1,000 without interest. All employees are furnished board and lodging free of charge; that means, engagees are provided with nothing but meat, a place to sleep, and one raw buffalo hide. Hunters and workmen eat at the second table, i.e., meat, biscuit, and black coffee with sugar. Clerks are served with the bourgeois at the first table, which is, on an average, a well-furnished table for this part of the country. We have meat, well selected, bread, frequently soup and pie on Sundays. Everyone must furnish his bedclothes; however, one may borrow two buffalo robes from the storehouse.

If an employee has a mind to save he can under certain conditions put aside almost his entire income. In that case he must have on hand a supply of clothing, must be content with the fare at the fort, indulge in no dainties or feasting, and never allow himself to come within 10 feet of the Indian women.

As these employees are not stimulated to greater exertions by increases in pay or percentages, it is hardly to be expected that they will work harder or make sacrifices for a company that is accumulating great wealth and, at the same time, charging them such extortionate prices. Independently of the equal salaries they receive, head clerks have advantages over traders that inspire them to greater zeal and more willing sacrifices. Clerks and traders, both at the forts and at their winter quarters, are continually beset by begging customers of the company they serve. They are in no sense obligated to give away their small earnings merely for the purpose of procuring a greater number of buffalo robes for their agents, but the bourgeois not only like for them to be generous with the customers but, on the other hand, either directly or indirectly require it of them. Mr. Denig came near getting a sound beating a few years ago because of some such unreasonable demand that he made of one of his clerks. He fled to his bedroom!...[24]

A spring day at Francois Chouteau's warehouse in the early 1830s, on the site of present Kansas City, was a hustle and bustle of pioneer commerce. Indians and French *voyageurs* arrived with their winter harvest of furs. The men came on skinny horses or in canoes or mackinaw boats, looping short ropes around bank-side willow trees just a few yards from Chouteau's impressive warehouse.

Inside the building, Chouteau stood behind a long counter with his account books, recording the number of furs turned in and the amount of merchandise given as payment. He ran a practiced hand over each pelt, feeling its thickness and texture; his eyes took in every detail of the appearance of every fur, as Chouteau was selling to the very particular fashion industry of London and Paris. Behind him the wall was ranked with shelves holding the merchandise that drew the Indians like a magnet: red calico cloth, beads, brassware, tools, knives, guns, and powder, in addition to much more. Perhaps there were also silver bracelets with small engravings or blankets with decorative stitching around the edges.

---

24. Myrtis Jarrell and J. N. B. Hewitt, eds., "Journal of Rudolph Friederich Kurz: an Account of His Experiences Among Fur Traders and American Indians on the Mississippi and the Upper Missouri Rivers During the Years 1846 to 1852," in Smithsonian Institution, *Bureau of American Ethnology Bulletin* 115, 234-237.

Chouteau employees, young French *engagees* and several black slaves, carted off the fur pelts to a far corner of the large room, where they were sorted, pressed, and tied into packs. From the Shawnee trading post on the Kansas River, where Cyprien Chouteau was in charge, came a barge with the furs he had collected from the Shawnee and Delaware tribes, as well as from the newly arrived eastern nations: the Weas, Peorias, Piankeshaws, and Kaskaskias. On another barge from farther up the Kansas River came the fur harvest of the great hunters and trappers, the Kansa Indians. The pelts brought in by the Kansa usually numbered more than those of all the other tribes combined. These furs from the branch posts had already been made into packs and needed only to be counted and stored to await shipment down river.

Before the tribes left for the hunt, Francois made a "treaty" with the leaders. These "treaties," much discussed in Chouteau's letters, were business agreements and must not be confused with the political treaties between the U.S. government and the Indians. Making a fur trade treaty probably entailed ceremony, with Francois promising to pay well (in merchandise) and the Indians promising to bring in what Francois desired – many beaver one year, many otter at another time.[25]

Sometimes the Indians did not have enough furs to pay for everything they needed or wanted, and in that case, they often asked to buy "on credit." Francois would then check his records and decide if he would comply. A perennial theme in these letters is Francois's complaint that the Indians were not paying their "credits."

The ice on the Missouri was gone, and steamboats were already making their scheduled runs from St. Louis to Council Bluffs. Some vessels built with a shallow draft would push all the way to the Yellowstone River with their cargo of goods, returning with a bonanza of furs. Going up the river, the steamboat would stop at Chouteau's to unload bales of merchandise and allow passengers to disembark. On the return trip, the steamboat would stop again to pick up passengers and the fur packs destined for the St. Louis shipping house.

The fur trade must have been a stressful business – so dependent on the weather, the water conditions, the whim of the Indians, and coordination with government agents who might or might not wish to make things run smoothly. Sometimes the government Indian agents arrived early and paid the Indians money promised by treaty (their annuities) before Chouteau had received the bulk of his merchandise from his St. Louis suppliers. This meant that the Indians, if they did not wish to wait for Chouteau to receive his shipment, went out to bargain with the smaller, independent merchants who were settling in Independence and elsewhere.

As spring eased into summer and the influx of furs tapered off, the warehouse was manned each day for sales to white settlers and to Indians crossing the area. After the spring runoff, the water level in the Kansas River went down and often was unnavigable. Thus, it was imperative to get the furs down and the merchandise up to the outposts before midsummer. What was left to be transported had to be carried on horseback.

By late summer business was slow and Chouteau could travel out to the Indian villages to renew his friendships with Indian chiefs and tribal leaders. There was time to take a trip to St. Louis to see his family and to Kaskaskia to see Berenice's family, especially her father Pierre Menard, who was Francois's business associate. However, this was the season of malaria, and the Chouteau letters document too many deaths in that dangerous time of year.

---

25. The agreements were apparently verbal, though the Pierre Menard correspondence indicated that some treaties were written and signed, as stated in Menard's letter in appendix item 3e, page 210. Other specifics may have been reflected in Francois's account books.

Autumn brought cooler weather and "the fever" disappeared. The Indians set out on their autumn hunt, garnering fur pelts and buffalo hides. They dried the meat for winter use, and while the men hunted, the women and children gathered seeds, berries, and roots to carry them through the long winter months.

Chouteau's warehouse was once more a lively place by late fall or early winter, as the fall fur harvest arrived. There would be no more furs until spring, but the fall harvest kept a few workers busy through the winter. Traveler and writer Jim Beckwourth wrote that he spent the winter and spring of 1825-1826 packing furs at Chouteau's warehouse.[26]

Then spring came and the cycle began anew. Some years were good; some were bad. The Chouteau family grew, the business expanded, the wilderness surroundings changed. And Francois and Berenice, taking quill pens in hand, wrote the letters you will now read.

American Fur Company Warehouse, 1835. North side of Walnut Street between Main and Levee Streets, St. Louis, Missouri. Ink on paper by Clarence Hoblitzelle, 1897. MHS.

---

26. Delmont R. Oswald, "James P. Beckwourth," in *The Mountain Men and the Fur Trade of the Far West*, ed. Hafen, 6: 42.

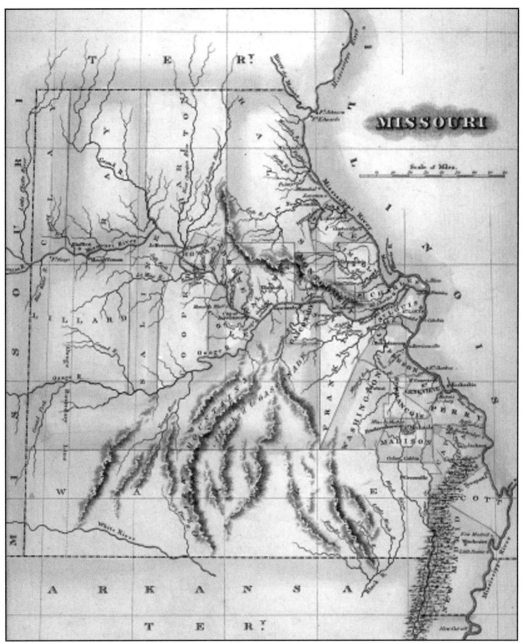

Second map of the State of Missouri. Drawn and published by F. Lucas Jr., Baltimore, 1823. Western Historical Manuscript Collection-Kansas City.

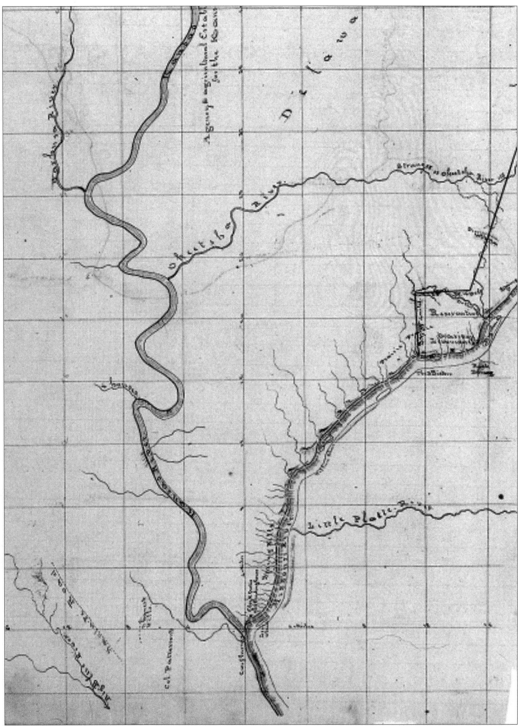

Portion of map drawn by Isaac McCoy, ca. 1830, showing the mouth of the Kansas River. North is to the right and the grid marks four-mile squares. Shown on the map are 4-houses Creek, the Curtis and Eley post, and the Shane and Wells post near Westport. The last was at or near the Shawnee Agency. *Isaac McCoy Papers*, Kansas State Historical Society.

"*Barge du Fort Louis*" [Barge of (from) Fort Lewis]. *Père Nicolas Point, S.J., Collection,* Archives de la Compagnie de Jesus, province du Canada frantais.

2 "Filled with Respect and Affection": The Early Letters

Francois Chouteau's first fur trading post in the area that became metropolitan Kansas City stood on a muddy bank across the river at Randolph Bluffs, and it was there that he and his new wife, Berenice, began life in their frontier home. Earlier modest operations had come and gone, but it was Francois Chouteau who stayed the course: he set up shop, built a home for himself and Berenice, and raised his family in future Kansas City.

The Chouteau post, or warehouse, provided a spacious, dry enclosure for collecting, sorting, packing, and shipping furs; and for trade, exchanging merchandise brought from St. Louis for pelts and skins: beaver, raccoon, otter, bear, and deer. The location of Chouteau's first warehouse was a few miles below, or east of, the mouth of the Kansas River, on the north bank of the Missouri at Randolph Bluffs, slightly to the west of the Chouteau Bridge.[1] The present community of Randolph is farther east from its nineteenth-century location at

---

1. For discussion of Chouteau posts locations, see appendix item 1, page 191.

the north end of the bridge. Modern downtown Kansas City sits diagonally across the Missouri River about three miles west of the original Chouteau establishment.

Francois and Berenice, legend says, selected this site on their wedding trip up the Missouri River to the present St. Joseph in 1819. (Francois's father, having spent the winter of 1790-1791 with the Kansa Indians, was familiar with the region and probably put his stamp of approval on the site before one log was erected.[2]) John Calvin McCoy, who came to western Missouri in 1830, said that in 1821 the French Fur Company with whom Francois was associated sent an advance team of workmen led by Grand Louis Bertholet. The men constructed one cabin on the south side of the Missouri (Jackson County) before being forced to abandon the site by a band of Sac Indians. They removed to Clay County, built a fortified building, and awaited Chouteau's arrival the following spring. McCoy asserted that Francois Chouteau negotiated permission to settle on the south bank in 1822 and his men constructed six buildings not described by contemporaries, but which probably consisted of a large warehouse or depot for the fur operation, a cabin of more than one room for the Chouteau family, and outbuildings for domestic help and livestock.[3] All were made of timbers cut from nearby abundant forests. It was to this enclave that the Francois and Berenice Chouteau household came from St. Louis on keelboats loaded with Indian trading goods, domestic supplies, and livestock. The company of people included, in addition to Francois and Berenice, their two young sons Edmond and Pierre Menard, business employees, and slaves.[4]

According to an affidavit given by Berenice in 1887, the year she and her children came to western Missouri was 1822.[5] The year 1821 is commonly accepted for the establishment of the post based upon McCoy's information, but his knowledge was second-hand, as he was not on the scene at the time. Although sixty-five years after the event, Berenice's memory may have been accurate for an 1822 arrival. However, she was in St. Louis for the birth of her second son Pierre Menard on April 28, 1822, and for his baptism on June 4th of that year.[6]

In 1819, Francois Chouteau and a cousin, Gabriel Chouteau (called Seres or Cerre), built the first fur trading post along the Kansas River. It was located where Cedar Creek enters the Kansas River, about two and one-half miles east of present DeSoto, Kansas.[7] This post was called the "Four Houses" because it consisted of four log buildings arranged in a square with their corners adjoining to create an enclosed courtyard. The "Four Houses" post was used for trade with the Kansa Indians until a new establishment was built in late 1828.

---

2. William E. Foley and C. David Rice, *The First Chouteaus*, 49.

3. Notwithstanding McCoy's colorful narrative, Frederick Chouteau, who worked at the Randolph Bluff post, clearly placed it in Clay County.

4. John C. McCoy Scrapbook, 31, (KC296), WHMC-KC.

5. Sworn affidavit by Berenice F. Chouteau dated October 26, 1887, recorded May 28, 1890, Book B423, page 404 (no. 150360), Jackson County, Missouri. The issue related to the church land acquired by Rev. Benedict Roux.

6. *Guide to the Microfilm Edition of the Pierre Menard Collection*, 30.

7. An untitled and undated map drawn by Isaac McCoy in the early 1830s labeled Cedar Creek as "4-Houses" (*SIA* (MC741), 1: 36, KSHS); Surveyor Angus L. Langham, on August 28, 1826, also registered the location of Cedar Creek as "Mouth of *Quartier Maison* (Four Houses) heads south," 2096.4 chains [26.205 miles] from the mouth of the Kansas. (William Clark to Thomas McKenney, April 29, 1828, *St. Louis Superintendency, 1827-1828,* Letters received by the Office of Indian Affairs, 1824-1881 (OIA), Records Group 234, Microfilm roll 748, National Archives and Records Administration (NARA)).

Trade at the Four Houses may never have been brisk. In 1821 or 1822, it came to the attention of Pierre Chouteau Jr. (Cadet) that there was not enough business to support two traders. Perhaps Francois had pointed this out to him. Francois may have been feeling the pressure of family obligations and was not realizing sufficient profit from his newly opened Randolph Bluffs post. As a half-brother to Cadet, Francois had a stronger claim to the trade of that area than did his cousin Seres.

In July 1822, Cadet wrote a letter on behalf of the fur trading company of Berthold, Chouteau, and Pratte that employed both Seres Chouteau and Francois. (For complete text of this letter, see appendix item 2, page 205.) Cadet presented to Seres several options. He could go to the Upper Missouri and open a post for Berthold, Chouteau, and Pratte, or stay in the region of the Kansas and Missouri rivers. A third choice was to move to some other place but still associate with the company. If Seres stayed on the Kansas and Missouri rivers, Cadet pointed out, his would be a "fourth" post in the area. The other three were apparently Andrew Woods, on the Missouri River about a mile above (north) of the mouth of the Kansas on the west side; Curtis and Eley, located near to Woods' post; and the post operated by Francois at Randolph Bluffs. Seres opted for the Upper Missouri. He and Francois apparently parted on good terms, for in a letter dated July 14, 1837, Francois referred to Gabriel S. Chouteau as "friend Cerre."

The central warehouse in the area that was to become Kansas City was referred to in Francois's letters as "my trading post," but to avoid confusing it with the Chouteau posts in Indian Territory (Kansas), it will be referred to as a warehouse (either Randolph Bluffs warehouse or Kansas City warehouse). Working as an associate for the St. Louis-based company, Chouteau initially found the fur supply plentiful. In 1824, an astounding harvest was gathered into the Randolph Bluffs warehouse. The following tabulation was gleaned from shipping records:

> 26,732 shaved deer skins (at 40 cents each), 1,218 deer skins (37 and a half cents each), 501 blue deer skins, 132 inferior deer skins (15 cents each), 120 inferior bear skins (75 cents), 26 cub skins (50 cents each), and 57 inferior cub skins at three for a dollar.... pelts of these 29,666 animals [were valued by the Chouteaus] at $11,735.71.[8]

In the autumn of 1824, before ice closed the Missouri River, Berenice loaded her two sons into a pirogue paddled by one of her husband's employees, and rode down to St. Louis where she awaited the birth of her third child. The ample courage she displayed in coming to live in the wilderness did not extend to delivering a child without the comfort of female relatives and domestics well experienced in the skills needed to give assistance. Berenice and the two small boys spent the winter in the commodious *maision* of Francois's father, Pierre Chouteau. A son, Louis Amadee, was born on February 16, 1825.

Sometime before 1825 (perhaps as early as 1822), Francois's brother Cyprien came to work at the Randolph Bluffs warehouse. Five years younger than Francois, Cyprien was then twenty years old. Their fifteen-year-old brother Frederick joined the two in 1825. He was thirteen years younger than Francois.

Disaster struck the small Randolph Bluffs settlement in the spring of 1826. Abundant snowfall in the mountains of the Upper Missouri caused a heavy spring runoff as huge snowdrifts melted into cascades and rivulets running into small streams that emptied into

---

8. Rodney Staab, "The Kansa Indians of Wyandotte County" in *The Ethnic History of Wyandotte County*, 2: 295-298. For additional research done by James Anderson, and transcriptions of Francois Chouteau-related accounts and documents found in the Missouri Historical Society's collections, see "Fur posts at Kawsmouth," Chouteau's (Topical) Scrapbook [17.1], *Native Sons of Kansas City Scrapbooks* (KC395), Western Historical Manuscript Collection-Kansas City (WHMC-KC).

tributaries of the Missouri River. By the time its boiling, muddy waters crashed through the bend where the Kansas River joined it, the Missouri River was out of its banks, charging across green fields and challenging hills.

Francois Chouteau's establishment had been built close to the river so that boats could easily be loaded and unloaded. When the floodwaters hit Randolph Bluffs, the log buildings of Chouteau's settlement were crushed and swept away without leaving a trace. Probably the Chouteaus had been warned of the onslaught, for everyone escaped. As John McCoy recounted years later, the settlers made "a hasty retreat to the hills of Clay County."[9] After the flood, some writers maintained, Francois took his family twenty miles up the Kansas River to live at the Four Houses post.[10]

Perhaps the Chouteau family did live at Four Houses during the summer months of 1826, but shortly Francois, Cyprien, and Frederick established a new warehouse on the south bank (Jackson County side) of the Missouri River, most likely near the foot of today's Gillis or Harrison Streets. Meanwhile, by autumn of that year Berenice and the three small Chouteau boys, Edmond, Pierre Menard, and Louis Amadee, were in St. Louis. It was there that, in October, the one-and-a-half-year-old Louis Amadee died of undocumented causes. (Perhaps malaria, as it was an autumn scourge.) His funeral was held on October 25, 1826, in St. Louis. He was buried in the pioneer cemetery next to the Old Cathedral on the banks of the Mississippi.[11]

The three letters of Berenice Menard Chouteau that appear first in the chronological sequence of this collection were written while she was in St. Louis during the winter and spring of 1827. Her letters differ dramatically from most of her husband's correspondence. Berenice wrote in an emotional way about very personal concerns. Her first letter reflects her grief at the recent death of the toddler Louis Amadee, her fears about her impending confinement, and her anxiety about her husband who, with his brothers Cyprien and Frederick, had remained on the frontier to receive and bundle furs and skins brought in by the resident Indian tribes at the end of the fall and winter hunt.

In the French towns and villages such as old St. Louis, Ste. Genevieve, and Kaskaskia, New Year's Day was celebrated in grand style. Young people and children spent the day visiting the older generation – parents, aunts and uncles, good friends – bringing gifts and hearty wishes for a healthy and a happy New Year. The host families in return provided music, dancing, games, and a regal feast of food and drink. If distance separated families, respects were offered in a written greeting, as shown in the following letter from Berenice to her father.

Nineteenth-century manners and the mores of her culture dictated that Berenice show her *papa* deep respect, and in her case, it was combined with almost child-like affection. Although Pierre Menard's letters reveal him to have been a devoted family man who genuinely cared for his wife and children, they also show that he was a controlling person who would easily have inspired the feelings expressed by Berenice.[12]

Born near Montreal, on October 7, 1766, throughout his lifetime Pierre Menard exhibited determination, confidence, and a natural ability to succeed in business. Menard received some education in Canada, for he was literate, but at the age of fourteen, he left home, headed south into the United States, and entered the commercial world of the new country. Wasting no time, the youth began trading and extending credit to men twice his age. He

---

9. John C. McCoy Scrapbook, 31, (KC296), WHMC-KC.
10. *History of Jackson County (1881)*, 378.
11. *Guide to Menard Collection*, 30.
12. *Guide to Menard Collection*, 1-5.

lived for a time in Vincennes, Indiana, but by 1791 had settled in the Illinois Territory in the French community of Kaskaskia on the east bank of the Mississippi River, fifty-two miles south of St. Louis. Menard acquired commercial licenses and became a leading citizen of the community. His barges traveled up the Ohio to Pittsburgh and down the Mississippi to New Orleans, carrying bundles of furs he had gathered through purchase or trade. These he exchanged for merchandise to be sold in his Kaskaskia store. He invested money in fur hunting and trading ventures, and involved himself in local and territorial politics. Menard befriended Indians residing in his area or traveling through, and they often came to him in times of need. From 1813 to 1833, Pierre Menard served as subagent for the Kaskaskia Indians, and as field agent assisted the eastern tribes in their enforced journeys to Indian Territory.

In June 1792, Pierre Menard married Marie Therese Michelle Godin in Kaskaskia. She died in 1804, leaving him with five children, Berenice among them. After two years as a widower, Menard married Angelique Saucier of the well-known Sauciers of Cahokia, Illinois. This marriage brought Menard into family ties with Francois Chouteau's father, Pierre Chouteau Sr., who was married to Brigitte Saucier, Angelique's half-sister. Pierre Menard and Angelique Saucier had eight children.

Both Berenice and Francois usually ended their letters by sending compliments to or from "my aunt" or "my uncle," giving the impression that they were both part of the same family. Francois and Berenice were not blood cousins, but rather legal cousins related through marriage.[13]

When Berenice wrote the emotional letter of January 25, 1827, her father was dealing with the problems of the Shawnee tribe emigrating from Wapakoneta, Ohio. In a January 17, 1827, letter to Shawnee agent Richard Graham, Menard reported that there were 255 emigrant Shawnees camped on the east bank of the Mississippi.[14] As the Indians moved on toward Indian Territory, white settlers along the route of the migrants refused to sell food to them or demanded such exorbitant prices that the Shawnees literally sold the clothes off their backs to obtain it. Tensions ran high between the settlers and the Indians, who were still waiting for the promised government compensation for the improvements they had left behind on their Ohio land. The settlers were anxious about their safety and protective of their livestock. It was Menard's task to mediate the disputes while also providing humanitarian aid to the suffering travelers.

Although Pierre Menard may have wished to be with his daughter in St. Louis to give her moral support, it was virtually impossible, both because of his Indian obligations and the hazard of sailing on the ice-filled Mississippi River.

Berenice's affection for her husband is evident in all the letters she wrote during his lifetime. She consistently expressed concerns for "my dear Gesseau," the name by which Francois Gesseau Chouteau was known to family and close friends. (Americans on the western frontier called him "Colonel" Chouteau, an honorary title bestowed on respected and wealthy men who had served in the military in any capacity for however brief a time.[15])

The letter that follows opens a window onto the world of worries Berenice took upon herself as a concerned daughter, an anxious wife, and a distraught mother.

---

13. See the glossary entry for Berenice Chouteau for an explanation of this relationship.

14. Pierre Menard to Richard Graham, January 17, 1827, *Richard Graham Collection*, Missouri Historical Society, St. Louis (*MHS*).

15. Francois Chouteau was appointed 3rd Lieutenant in the 1st Company, 1st Battalion, 1st Regiment of the Missouri Militia on March 26, 1816 (Sere was a 2nd Lieutenant in the same company at that time). A year later in April he was promoted to 2nd Lieutenant in the 3rd Company. (*Territorial Papers of the United States*, 15: 189, 277.)

St. Louis   January 25, 1827[16]

Cher papa,

I take advantage of this opportunity to write to you and to wish you this New Year as happy as it is possible to be. At the same time, to ask you to pardon my great negligence. I believe, however, dear papa, that you do not believe me indifferent. I assure you that I am full of affection and of respect for you and mama. The cause that I do not write to you more quickly is that we have been expecting you since last month. I desire to see you very much. However, I will not ask you to come while the Mississippi is frozen and also the ice is very bad.

I have had no news from my Gesseau and from Alzire for a long time – with this in mind, that worries me a little. I am on the verge of delivering which torments me much. I'm worried about death on account of my little children. If God wants it this way. In this way, I recommend, dear papa, to you as well as my dear mother, my little Menard. I do not desire for him to go to anyone except to your house. Perhaps God will allow me myself to raise my children, but at last I take the precautions necessary so that this poor little children [sic] may be happy. Recently, several women in my condition have died. I have nothing new to tell you. Tell mama that I am unhappy not to have succeeded to find an occasion to send her bonnet and several other little things. And my dear little Sophie her little cradle. Kiss the whole family for me. I beg of you to believe me for life, your very affectionate and submissive daughter,

Berenice Chouteau

My aunt and my uncle join me to extend to you their compliments, as well as to mother.

Berenice's quaint French phrase "I profit of the occasion" has been converted to "I take advantage of the opportunity" wherever it was found in these letters. Other conversions will be duly noted as they occur.

The three 1827 Berenice letters that precede Francois's business correspondence were written while she was in St. Louis. As noted, in the early years of her married life, Berenice returned to St. Louis for the birth of her children. During the long months living at the home of her husband's parents, Berenice had ample time to reflect on life's vicissitudes, as reflected in her letter.

Berenice's fourth son, Louis Sylvestre, was born on February 16, 1827. Following that event, Berenice wrote the second letter of this collage, addressed to her stepmother Angelique Saucier Menard. Despite Berenice's fears, as expressed in her previous letter, she had survived childbirth and had apparently recovered quickly. In the following letter, she recounted going about St. Louis to conduct business errands for her father and shop for Angelique.

---

16. Letter 203, *Pierre Menard Collection (PMC)*, Illinois State Historical Library, Springfield, Illinois (ISHL). [Hereafter the letters will be referenced only to their letter numbers, with additional mailing and note information given.] Envelope: [To] Col. Pierre Menard, Kaskaskia, Illinois. [From] St. Louis; 10 cents postage.

St. Louis   April 18, 1827[17]

Cher mama,

With pain I learned that you were not better. I hope, however, that if you would put all your faith in Roi, that you will quickly recover, as I assure you that Pharamond was very pleased with him, that he took his prescribed remedies, he no longer has a fever. I have done my errands. I gave the letters to Mr. Renard. He told me not to worry, that it is with pleasure he takes on the responsibility and that he will have it put back in order whatever happens. Papa tells me he will be pleased to have Charles. I talked about it to my uncle, and he decided to send him. We are recommending him to you also, to ask Mr. Raphael to teach him the ways of behaving in the store. I assure you, dear mother, that Charles is a good boy, that he only needs to get away from the paternal house. It will give me much pleasure to see that it is papa who is giving him a start and that I am persuaded that Charles will be grateful to him. And I am happy that you will know that you are the one who encouraged him [Pierre Menard] to be happy about it.

Mme. Acades sends you three hairpieces, one veil, a bonnet, and begs me to assure you of her friendship as well as my aunt who would be well except for her foot which is always aching. Tell Virginia that I am eager that she would come to spend a few days with me before too long. Remember me to my little brothers. Tell little Sophie that her sister thinks about her every day. If you see Edmond, hug him and tell him that he is very lazy not to have answered the letters that I wrote to him.

I have no news to tell you. Give my respects to all those who ask about me. We are all well and we hope that the present will find you the same. I am always awaiting my dear Gesseau. Farewell, dear mother, for life, one of your most affectionate friends and stepdaughter.

Berenice M. Chouteau

The Mr. Renard to whom Berenice gave letters may have been an accountant or an attorney. This specific person has not been identified. Renard family members were not listed in the U.S. census for Missouri in 1830, but were listed in the 1840 census as living in St. Louis. The shopping errands for Angelique suggest that fashionable merchandise was more available in St. Louis than in Kaskaskia. The Mrs. Acades mentioned must have been a milliner but she was not listed in the census or in the St. Louis Directory.

Berenice's letter introduced new family concerns: the illness of her stepmother Angelique Saucier Menard, and the father-son discord in progress at the Pierre Chouteau mansion in St. Louis.

The illness that Angelique suffered was not clearly documented at the time this letter was written. However, Angelique's son Francois Menard (Berenice's half-brother) wrote to his half-brother Pierre Menard Jr., or Peter, in November 1828 and mentioned that his mother's illness was of long duration. He specified that the problem was an abscess or boil on her leg from which two gallons of infected fluid had been drained![18] Letters exchanged between Berenice's brothers reported that when Berenice was in St. Louis, she traveled

---

17. *PMC*, Letter 213. Envelope: Madame P. Menard, To Kaskaskia.
18. *PMC*, Letter 272.

often to Kaskaskia to assist in the care of Angelique. For a solution to the problem, Berenice's suggestion was one she often made: seek the advice of a good French doctor in St. Louis. In the case mentioned in her letter, Berenice's brother-in-law Pharamond Chouteau, Francois's younger brother, had done so. Born in 1806, Pharamond was apparently not robust. He died in 1831 at the age of twenty-five, four years after this letter was written.

The Charles Chouteau discussed in this letter was Francois's brother, eleven years younger than he, born in 1808, of Pierre Chouteau's second marriage. When this letter was written in 1827, Charles was nineteen years old and had apparently not launched into a career. This probably grated on old Pierre Chouteau, as the other sons of his second marriage – Francois, Cyprien, and Frederick – had left home around age fifteen, and were well established in the fur trade by Charles's age.

That Pierre Chouteau Sr. had a volatile personality is amply reported in song and story. John Calvin McCoy passed along a tale that put a pregnant Berenice, her two small sons, her elderly father-in-law Pierre Chouteau, and an incompetent boatman in a pirogue heading downstream to St. Louis. If there is any truth to the story, this must have been the autumn of 1824. That would have been when Berenice was returning to St. Louis to await the birth of her next child.

On their first day of the voyage, the boatman made a serious navigational error and almost upended the open boat on a large rock. Such an accident would have dumped an expectant mother, two small boys, and an old man into the rushing torrent of the Missouri River. "*Au terre, au terre!*" shouted Chouteau in a rage. "To land! To land!" (That is, "Go to the shore!")[19]

The boatman paddled furiously and struggled to steer the craft towards land. Imploring Heaven to pour down on the head of the boatman every evil known to mankind, Chouteau reached under his seat and pulled out a gun. Apparently he had every intention of shooting his employee.

Berenice, however, saw immediately what he was about. She grabbed the gun and held it fast, the drama probably accompanied by screams from the little boys. Meanwhile, the boat bumped ashore, and once the family was safely on solid ground Chouteau's anger subsided and he settled for a few more curses.

In the preceding letter, Berenice had taken on a characteristic role, striving to strengthen family ties and promote peace and harmony. Attempting to resolve the difficulty between Charles Chouteau and his father, she had asked Angelique to intercede with Pierre Menard, gaining his consent to bring Charles to Kaskaskia, away from the heavy hand of his father. Pierre Menard was apparently in St. Louis at the time this letter was written, as Berenice wrote that she "talked" to him. Under the guidance of Pierre Menard's trusted assistant, Raphael Widen (Wyden), Charles Chouteau was to learn how to work in the Kaskaskia Menard and Valle store.

Berenice, then twenty-six, had already established her lifelong devotion and loyalty to her extended family. Her half-brother Edmond, to whom in this letter she sent a hug, was fourteen years old and attending The Asylum, a Ste. Genevieve boarding school for boys. The school was an experimental establishment in which the students worked on the school farm, caring for livestock, planting, tending, and preparing produce for sale. In this way, the school reaped financial benefits while the students gained a practical knowledge of farm life.[20] As Kaskaskia was directly across the Mississippi from Ste. Genevieve, it was possible for the Menards to visit their son when the river was navigable.

---

19. John C. McCoy Scrapbook, 35, (KC296), WHMC-KC.
20. Gregory M. Franzwa, *The Story of Old Ste. Genevieve*, 77; *Historic Ste. Genevieve*, 12.

Berenice's third letter, dated May 19, 1827, was written to her only living full-brother, Pierre Menard Jr., called Peter, four years older than she. At the time, Peter was ill and staying at his father's home in Kaskaskia. Berenice again recommended the services of a good French doctor in St. Louis. Peter may have taken her advice as, in the early autumn of that year, he wrote letters from St. Louis.[21]

St. Louis   May 19, 1827[22]

Cher frere,

I learned with pain that you were still ill. I wish to receive news of you upon the next occasion and I advise you to come to St. Louis to consult a French doctor who is here. Gesseau has arrived and we await Cyprien who will be here in a few days to take us to Kansas. I have received news from Alzire through Mme. Kennerly. She did not write because she plans to be here within two or three weeks. My compliments to grandmother, to Odile.

Believe me for life, your affectionate sister,

Berenice Chouteau

Apparently Peter Menard shook off this illness, as the United States Indian Department appointed him to be subagent for the Potawatomi Indians at Peoria from 1828 until the tribe was removed to Indian Territory (Kansas) around 1829.[23]

Peter was subject to depression and his work with the Indians seemed to aggravate his condition. In April 1828, Peter wrote to his father about how unhappy he was.[24] Pierre Menard replied in a touching letter, gently chiding his son, offering the simple solutions of the times. All one needed to be happy, Pierre Menard told Peter, were honesty, a good reputation, a good morale, a good wife, children, good food, some courage, and good friends![25] It took Peter five more years to find the "good" wife, but other letters indicate he remained emotionally fragile.

A year after the exchange described above, Peter wrote to his father that he had been beaten by the Indians because they were unhappy with the terms of their treaty.[26] Yet the young Menard, instead of feeling resentment or fear of the Indians, was sympathetic to their plight, pointing out that they were being deprived of what "God and nature" had given them and felt injustice as deeply "as the whites."[27]

Berenice also mentioned that Mrs. Kennerly, the mother-in-law of her sister Alzire, had relayed the news that Alzire would soon be coming to St. Louis. Alzire was married to George Hancock Kennerly, sutler of Jefferson Barracks in St. Louis. Alzire often traveled

---

21. *Guide to Menard Collection*, 116.
22. *PMC*, Letter 214. Envelope: [To] M. Peter Menard, Son, Kaskaskia; [filing note] 1827, Berenice Chouteau.
23. William Clark to Thomas McKenney, April 24, 1827, *St. Louis Superintendency, 1827-1828, OIA*, RG234, Microfilm roll 748, NARA; "United States Indian Agencies Affecting Kansas: Superintendents, Agents, Subagents, Millers, Blacksmiths, Interpreters, etc.," *KHC* 16: 723-724.
24. *PMC*, Letter 246.
25. *PMC*, Letter 247.
26. *PMC*, Letter 300.
27. *PMC*, Letter 361.

with her husband and that worried Berenice, especially if considerable time had elapsed since her last news about or from Alzire.

Berenice's thoughts of family were reflected in the "compliments" she sent to her older sister Odile and to "grandmother," who was probably Angelique's stepmother, Francoise Nicolle Lefevre. This woman was a widow who became the third wife of Francois Saucier, Angelique's father. Angelique's mother, Angelique Roi *dit* Lepensee, died in 1787 when Angelique was four years old. In 1793, Angelique's father Francois Saucier married Francoise Lefevre, who became Angelique's stepmother. From ten years of age until she was twenty-three and married Pierre Menard, Angelique was mothered by Francoise Lefevre Saucier. Angelique must have called Francoise "mother" just as Berenice addressed her, Angelique, as "mother." Hence, Angelique's "mother" (i.e., stepmother) was "grandmother" to Berenice and her brother Peter, to whom she was writing.

Berenice and Francois, with their three sons Edmond, Pierre Menard, and the newborn Louis Sylvestre, and accompanied by Cyprien Chouteau, returned to "Kansas," as they often referred to western Missouri. Although their mode of travel was not specified, they almost certainly traveled by keelboat rather than a horse and wagon bumping through the trackless forest. As it was May, they would have been battling a strong current in the Missouri River. The heavy keelboat would have been hauled by ropes looped around bank-side trees, and pulled hand over hand, making progress measured in inches, not miles. In some spots, the boat could be pushed forward with long poles jammed into the muddy river bottom. Day and night, the newly hatched mosquitoes and other insects bedeviled them all. Daunting though the task was, sturdy crewmen were employed for just that purpose, and, using their skill and muscle, they brought the Chouteaus back to their home in western Missouri.

Berenice's preceding letter was kept and filed with Pierre Menard's business papers. This is evident from the fact that it survived, and also from the filing note written on the envelope: "1827, Berenice Chouteau." Pierre Menard or his assistant Raphael Widen noted on the envelope the date a letter was received and the name of the person who had written it before filing the correspondence. Sometimes the date recorded was the date the letter was written.

When Berenice settled back into frontier life, she immersed herself in the role of wife and mother. Her husband Francois often sent news of her and the children in his letters to Berenice's father, Pierre Menard. Berenice wrote additional letters – Francois sometimes referred to them – but they apparently did not survive. The next Berenice letter in this collection was from the "Kansas River," dated February 3, 1831.

Francois Chouteau's 1828 letters to "*Cher Oncle,*" spelled out the details of his struggle to run a profitable business amid the most adverse conditions. He traveled endless miles on horseback in all kinds of weather, visiting Indian villages and encampments to freshen friendships and arrange business deals. He sought out the government Indian agents, offering his services, making his presence felt. He watched the Missouri River, wondering if his merchandise would arrive on time; he studied the water level in the Kansas River, hoping it would be sufficient for transport and travel. And all the while, he tried to best his competitors, fend off infringing traders, and care for his family.

Chouteau's life was often complicated by government regulations. At the time of the earliest of these letters, the Office of Indian Affairs (OIA) was in its infancy, having been established in 1824, subject to the authority of the War Department. The OIA divided the country into geographical regions called superintendencies. In control of each was a superintendent whose staff included agents and subagents. An agent was in charge of several neighboring or related tribes and usually did not live among the Indian people but in a nearby settlement. A subagent working with one significant tribe or several smaller ones reported to an agent and was expected to live at the agency, the regional headquarters for the administration of Indian affairs. He was assisted by an interpreter, a blacksmith, and an agriculturalist. The agency was supposed to be located near the village of its Indians.

The Indians with whom Francois Chouteau traded lived in the St. Louis Superintendency with William Clark, of Lewis and Clark fame, as superintendent. An exception to the usual chain of command affected the subagent for the Kansa Indians, who reported directly to Superintendent Clark in St. Louis rather than to Agent John Dougherty at Fort Leavenworth. Another tribe important to Chouteau at this time was the Shawnee. One agent handled the affairs of the Shawnee Nation, although it was split into groups: those still in Ohio, others en route to Indian Territory (Kansas), and still others who had already arrived. Subagents worked with the separate groups until they were all reunited on their reservation in present Kansas.

Since the old patronage days of Spanish and French rule in Upper Louisiana, the Chouteaus had held Indian trade licenses as required by the government. After the Louisiana Purchase in 1803, the United States government had continued the previous licensing system based, as before, on patronage. Since at least 1777, Chouteaus had been in the Indian trade – at that time, it was Francois's uncle and father, Auguste and Pierre Chouteau, trading among the Big Osages. Although the Upper Louisiana, or "Missouri country" as it was then known, had been under Spanish control from 1762 until 1770, the Iberian officials tarried in New Orleans, enjoying the good life, while Frenchman Louis Saint-Ange de Bellerive, with Spanish consent, did their work for them up in St. Louis. One thing he did was award the most lucrative trading rights to Frenchmen, while the Spanish traders had to paddle their own canoes.

A license to trade with various Indians had been in Francois Chouteau's possession since he was nineteen.[28] As each license expired, he applied for another. At the time the following letter was written, Chouteau was in the process of setting up a new post and it, too, would be licensed by the Office of Indian Affairs. Having a long and clean track record, and still observing the government regulations, Chouteau was disturbed that everyone else, as he saw it, played fast and free. The American spirit of free enterprise was emerging, and with it the widespread practice of undercutting the competition and hoodwinking the customer into buying shoddy merchandise. At first the Indians were gullible and accepted anything, but as these letters show, they learned fast. Francois Chouteau, however, still lived – or desired to live – in a business world based on patronage, family ties, and favors given and received.

Before the era covered by the letters in *Cher Oncle, Cher Papa*, trade with the Indians was partly controlled through a "factory" system. In 1796, Congress approved funding to set up a chain of fortified trading houses, or factories, to provide the Indians with good merchandise that would be priced fairly and exchanged for the fur pelts the Indians were selling. This did not affect the Missouri country until after the Louisiana Purchase in 1803.

One such factory was Fort Osage, forty miles by river below the mouth of the Kansas River, the westernmost government trading post built in the Louisiana Purchase land. William Clark chose the site as he and Meriwether Lewis took their "Corps of Discovery" upstream in 1804. Originally called Fort Clark, it was erected in 1808 on a high bluff overlooking the Missouri River.

The factory system proved to be ineffective because the government failed to put teeth into the regulations. Instead of monopolizing trade with the Native Americans, taking sole and total control of the fur trade, the government continued to issue licenses to private

---

28. *Territorial Papers of the United States*, 15: 191, 378.

traders. The traders proceeded to locate themselves near their Indian customers and undercut the factory prices. The factories were located far from the Indian villages, and it was usually easy for the traders to lure the Indians away from the government trading houses. In 1822, the government gave up and the factory system was discontinued, leaving a wide-open field in which the traders, both licensed and unlicensed, engaged in a no-holds-barred trading battle that lasted until the fur trade dried up around 1840-1844.

However, in the late 1820s and the decade of the 1830s, there was still a great deal of money to be made in the fur business, with everything depending on the collection of furs. The Kansa Indians, with whom Francois Chouteau traded for nearly twenty years, were superior hunters and trappers. They carried a map of the Midwest in their heads and knew every stream and rivulet where beavers lived.

The Kansa Nation was a resident tribe in the area of the Missouri and Kansas rivers, having, by 1830, lived on the banks of these waterways for more than 100 years. Probably two centuries before the time of these letters, the Kansas, a Siouan-language tribe, inhabited a region near the Great Lakes. Gradually they drifted southwest, and by the late 1600s, were living beside the Missouri River. As the fur trade developed, the Kansa people moved farther west, nearer the beavers and the vast buffalo herds that supplied them with meat and hides.

The Kansas lived in extended family groups led by a chief they considered worthy or whose ideas they shared. Probably no formal vote was taken to elect a chief, but rather he was selected by consensus, a very democratic process. A powerful chief and his followers lived in their own separate village. From approximately 1790 to 1829, the Kansas occupied one large village of 125 lodges on the Kansas River at the mouth of the Big Blue, two miles east of present Manhattan. By 1829 or 1830, the Kansa Nation had abandoned the large village and moved eastward, dividing into three groups: Fool Chief's village was north of the Kansas River and six miles west of Soldier's Creek; Hard Chief's village was on high ground near the Kansas River, about seven miles west of Fool Chief. American Chief's village was located in the bottomland on the west side of Mission Creek west of Topeka.[29] These villages were situated on the reservation set aside for the Kansa Indians in the Treaty of 1825. It was this treaty that caused much dissension among the Kansas, and resulted in their dividing into separate groups. In that treaty, the Kansa Nation gave up fifteen million acres in Missouri and Kansas for a reservation 30 miles wide and 200 miles long, running east and west, beginning 20 leagues (60 miles) west of Kansas City.[30]

In November 1825, the first contingent of Shawnees, the Missouri group numbering 1,383, ceded their Cape Girardeau lands to the United States in exchange for a tract in Indian Territory (Kansas) that was to be shared with an 800-member group of Ohio Shawnees. During November 1827, a Shawnee speaking to Superintendent William Clark described their journey:

> ...we went to see the Kanzas River and the lands of which you spoke.... After we passed the Delaware towns on our way, we traveled three days through prairies and I thought we were near the place of the great Spirit, for we could see nothing but what was above us and the Earth we walked upon, until we came near where [Paul Liguest] Chouteau lives.... [We] reached the [Missouri] state line and followed the blazes to [the] mouth of the Kanzas where it empties into the Missouri River. We then went up the Kanzas about

---

29. Louise Barry, *Beginning of the West*, 166-167.
30. William E. Unrau, *The Kansa Indians: A History of the Wind People, 1673-1873*, 107; *American State Papers: Indian Affairs*, 2: 589-590. Also in Article 8 of the Treaty, Francois G. Chouteau was named to receive $500 from the United States Government to liquidate a debt owed him by the Kansa tribe.

eighteen miles and camped on good land.... the good land and timber would continue until...Soldiers creek and above that was nothing but prairie and poor land.[31]

This route through south-central Missouri was the one taken by most of the Shawnees. Indian Field Agent Pierre Menard arranged for the Ohio Shawnees to be ferried across the Mississippi River at either Cape Girardeau or Ste. Genevieve. The Shawnees then made their way, as described above, toward their new land. The Indians, however, were not rigidly organized and some groups may have followed a path along the Missouri River. The Shawnees, migration into Kansas was not complete until 1833.[32]

When Chouteau wrote the letter that follows, some of the Shawnees had arrived and were settling onto their new land west of the Missouri state line and south of the Kansas River. The Shawnee Chief Mayaweskata "marked the place of my village on several trees" and the Shawnees began to build their houses about three and one-half miles west of the "Big Line that...is to divide us from your white children" and about five miles from where Shawnee Chief "Perry marked the place for his village...."[33]

Baptist missionary Isaac McCoy was an early and active proponent of removing the Indians from the lands east of the Mississippi. In addition to his missionary work, McCoy was paid by the government to survey the Indian reservations set aside for the incoming eastern Indians. In 1828, observing the newly arrived Shawnees setting up their villages on their new reservation, he wrote that they were putting up "with their own hands very neat log cabbins."[34] A large group of these Shawnees was led by Chief Fish (William Jackson), a white man raised with the Shawnee tribe.[35]

In Francois's first letter of this collection, he mentioned a Mr. "Chaine," who became prominent in these letters. This man was Anthony Shane of the Shane and Wells trading post near Westport at the state line. Chouteau's phonetic spelling of the name was consistent, always "Chaine." In a letter of January 17, 1832, Chouteau identified Shane as "the underagent of the Kansa." Anyone who worked at the government Indian agencies seemed to be an "underagent." Actually, Anthony Shane was an interpreter for the Shawnees from 1830 to 1834.[36]

Shane was well known on the frontier, and perhaps had something of a chameleon personality. John C. McCoy recalled an incident in which the corpulent Anthony Shane was attempting to cross the Kansas River on horseback, but kept falling off, sputtering, in the river.[37] Indian agent George Vashon, however, seemed to value Shane's services. In October 1829, he wrote to President Andrew Jackson to recommend that Shane be given a raise in salary, and that the government pay for the education of Shane's son Charles.[38] In August of

---

31. November 7, 1827, *St. Louis Superintendency, 1827-1828*, OIA, RG234, Microfilm roll 748, NARA.

32. Grant W. Harrington, *Historic Spots, or Mile-stones in the progress of Wyandotte County, Kansas*, 14-15; Barry, *Beginning of the West*, 128.

33. December 1, 1827, Talk in Council Room, *St. Louis Superintendency, 1827-1828*, OIA, RG234, Microfilm roll 748, NARA.

34. Lela Barnes, "Journal of Isaac McCoy for the exploring expedition of 1828," *Kansas Historical Quarterly* 5: 260.

35. Ed Blair, *History of Johnson County, Kansas*, 27.

36. Richard W. Cummins to Lewis Cass, November 7, 1831, *OIA, Fort Leavenworth Agency, 1824-1836*, M234, Microfilm roll 300, Frame 255. "United States Indian Agencies Affecting Kansas," *Kansas Historical Collection* 16: 724, 725.

37. John C. McCoy Scrapbook, 59, (KC296), WHMC-KC.

38. George Vashon to Andrew Jackson, October 27, 1829, *Isaac McCoy Papers*, Microfilm roll 7, Frame 230, KSHS.

that year, Shane was a witness, with Vashon, to a talk of the Kickapoo at "Indian Agency South Kansas River."[39] At the time the following letter was written, Shane and Chouteau were on good terms.

10 miles from the mouth of the River   November 5, 1828[40]

Cher oncle,

 I received your letter today through Cyprien which pleased me greatly. I should have written you previously but I did not know when you would return. I gave to the Shawnee their money and their thousand dollars in merchandise I gave on credit to Fish's band. If they make a hunt, I hope to be paid. As to their money, I was unable to have it. They wanted to have the merchandise about at cost price at St. Louis. They used a part of it at a store that there is in Independence and the other part to purchase animals and foodstuff from the farmers. There is a group of Shawnee who are building for themselves at the present and that makes me believe that they will not do much [hunting] this fall but I hope to carry on business this spring. The greater part of the village of the Kansa has gone into the wilderness. I believe they will catch beaver. At least I will do what is possible to encourage them in the affair. I hope that the Kansa will do well enough. This year they are not sick. I handed over to Mr. Chaine and to old Louis [Bertholet?] the articles that were put aside for them in good condition on board ship. With much difficulty I took the barge to the place where I would spend the winter. Since my arrival many things have gone wrong, but I hope that things will turn out better at the end. Blando is negotiating with the Kansa. There is near to his abode seven or eight lodges. That does not appear to conform to the arrangements that were made. I also believe that Mr. Ogle will carry on trade with the Shawnee if he is able. There is a band that has gone hunting on the Marais des Cygne. I will carry out with Mr. Chaine that which you recommend if the affair pleases him. Mr. Kennerly has arrived here the second of this month. He has sent for Mongren Noel among the missionaries to go with him as guide. Nothing else of which to inform you at present.

 I beg you to give my love to my good aunt and to tell her that I learned with much joy that she is recovering from the recurence of her sickness.

I am with gratitude and respect
Your Nephew
Francois Chouteau

 I beg of you to extend my compliments to Mr. and Mrs. Valle as well as to all the family.

---

39. August 15, 1829, *OIA, St. Louis Superintendency, 1829-1831*, M234, Microfilm roll 749, Frame 800, NARA.

40. *PMC*, Letter 271. Envelope: [To] M. Pierre Menard, Kaskaskia.

By way of apology for tardiness in writing, Chouteau explained that he was uncertain when Pierre Menard would return. The trip, in this case, was to Wisconsin, where Superintendent William Clark said Colonel Menard was to join General Lewis Cass at Green Bay.[41] Francois seldom failed to express great respect for Pierre Menard, as well as affection and gratitude. Very probably Francois had good reason to be grateful; the letters bear witness to Pierre Menard's having considerable control over the Chouteau operation in western Missouri. Almost certainly Chouteau's *"Cher Oncle"* and father-in-law provided a portion of the merchandise and money needed to start business at the Randolph Bluffs and then the Kansas City warehouse. Menard and Chouteau were in some kind of a financial partnership, perhaps, as in the Menard-Valle arrangement, an unwritten "gentleman's agreement."

In his letter, Chouteau commented that the Indians were not sick that season. The Kansa suffered smallpox epidemics in October 1827 and April 1828, so some developed immunity. In subsequent letters, Chouteau anticipated, based on past experience, that the Indians would not be sick for several years after an epidemic. Observation had evidently provided some concept of immunity, since vaccination for smallpox was not offered to the Indians until 1832.[42]

The store in Independence to which Chouteau suspected the Shawnees sometimes took their fur pelts and money, may have been operated by J. Lemme (or Lemi, Lemai, Leme, Lemmau). A Joseph Lemai was listed as a resident of Carondelet in 1794.[43] In 1829, Isaac McCoy identified J. Lemme as a merchant in Independence.[44] Having come from Carondelet to Independence, by 1830 the wanderlust overtook Lemme again and he joined a hunting expedition comprised of "Chemie, Picotte, Pascal, Lemi and P. D. Papin," who hoped they would "do better next season."[45]

Chouteau introduced a topic he explored in almost every letter through the early 1830s: the encroachment of other traders on his licensed turf. The manner in which these traders were mentioned suggests that Chouteau knew these men. The Blando who was "negotiating with the Kansa" was Maurice Blondeau, who was in the Michigan fur trade around 1805. Zebulon Pike hired Blondeau to take a lost soldier down the Mississippi to catch up with his unit heading into the Rocky Mountains in 1806.[46] In 1824, Blondeau was in Keokuk, Iowa, running a tavern next to an American Fur Company trading post, surrounded by an encampment of Sac-Fox settlers of mixed blood.[47] By 1828, he had apparently taken to trading among Chouteau's tribes.

Another man who had moved into Chouteau's territory was John Ogle, formerly a trader in the central Ozarks. There he alternately competed against and worked with William Gilliss. When Ogle was on the White River, apparently both he and Gilliss received merchandise from Pierre Menard.[48] While Blondeau and Ogle were interlopers in Chouteau's licensed Kansa and Shawnee trade, both were, like Chouteau, selling their furs to the

---

41. William Clark to Thomas McKenney, Director of Indian Affairs, August 2, 1828, *OIA, St. Louis Superintendency, 1827-1828*, RG234, Microfilm roll 748, NARA.

42. Barry, *Beginning of the West*, 214-215.

43. Louis Houck, *History of Missouri*, 2: 65.

44. Isaac McCoy's Correspondence List, February 24, 1829, *Isaac McCoy Papers,* Microfilm roll 7, Frame 103, KSHS.

45. P. D. Papin to P. M. Papin, July 28, 1830, *Chouteau Family Collection*, MHS.

46. David Lavender, *The Fist in the Wilderness*, 60-61.

47. Tanis C. Thorne, *The Many Hands of My Relations*, 142.

48. Pierre Menard to John Ogle, September 30, 1829, Letterbook J, [9/1829-2/1834], *Pierre Menard Collection*, Illinois Historical Survey (IHS), University of Illinois Library, Urbana-Champaign.

American Fur Company, generating Chouteau's complaint, in the preceding letter, that the situation did not "conform to the arrangements that were made."

Mr. (George Hancock) Kennerly, Chouteau's sister-in-law Alzire's husband, then at the Chouteau post, was preparing to escort an expedition into an unidentified region where he would need a guide. For that purpose, he had sent for "Mongren Noel." Mongren Noel was actually Noel Mongrain, an interpreter and guide among the Osage and Kansa Indians. In 1820, nine children of Noel Mongren (French) and M. Paku Shan (Osage) were baptized in St. Louis.[49] The missionaries mentioned here were the Presbyterians of Harmony Mission for the Osages, located on the Marais des Cygne River in Vernon County, Missouri, about a mile and a half northwest of present Papinsville.[50]

In many of his letters to Pierre Menard, Chouteau sent greetings to Mr. and Mrs. Jean Baptiste Valle. Pierre Menard and Valle had been partners in a store in Ste. Genevieve since 1820. Jean Baptiste Valle founded the Ste. Genevieve business and when his son, Felix, reached maturity, Felix managed the operation. Pierre Menard's store in Kaskaskia eventually became a Menard and Valle business. Both stores sold retail goods to the townspeople, but the primary purpose of the Ste. Genevieve store was to sell merchandise to traders who in turn sold or traded goods to the eastern Indians migrating westward to Indian Territory (Kansas). Pierre Menard was Field Agent for these Indians, but "conflict of interest" was an issue rarely raised in those days.

The "10 miles from the mouth of the [Kansas] River" dateline location of the preceding letter was the first reference to Francois's new Shawnee Post, described in detail in the following:

From the house of Mr. Chaine   December 2, 1828[51]

Cher oncle,

I am on the road to the Kansa trading post in order to carry an order of merchandise. I wanted to write to you through Major [Agent Richard] *Graham but he left without my being informed. Clark and Doorty, Iowa Indians who must pass by your place, will carry this to you. Mr. Chaine assures me that he believes the Indians will pay me the credits that I made to them. I believe that they had deposited* [i.e., left or spent] *a small part of their money at Independence where there was a store in a small town which is ten to twelve miles from here. But Mr. Chaine tells me it is not so, that they* [will] *pay their debts they contracted here, as I know that they still have some of that money. Fish's band hasn't yet returned from the hunt. I believe they will do something. I believe I'll get along better with this band than with the other. The Kansa are in the wilderness in many bands. A good part of them have gone. They haven't returned. There is also a band near the River* [....] [....] *that trades with Ogle. I will try to attract them here as much as possible. The Shawnee think that we sell a bit high, and that they are able to buy cheaper at Independence, but they will not consider, or pretend not to consider, that our*

---

49. Louis Burns, *Osage Mission Baptisms, Marriages, and Interments, 1820-1886*, 137.

50. [Joseph Tracy], *History of American Missions to the Heathens, from Their Commencement to the Present Time*, 171, 229. For a more complete history of the mission, see Doris Denton, *Harmony Mission, 1821-1837*. James Chouteau, Francois Chouteau's son with Marie of the Osage, attended the school at Harmony Mission in 1823. (*American Missionary Register* 6: 273, cited in Denton, 32.)

51. *PMC*, Letter 273. Envelope: M. Pierre Menard, Kaskaskia.

merchandise is infinitely superior to what is found elsewhere. For their annuities they got cheaply made [goods] and you will see in the end that we did not overcharge them. They doubtlessly recognize good merchandize, but too much opportunity is offered to them to learn all the prices. I read to the chiefs the letter of Michel Menard, and Mr. Chaine interpreted what I said and I also said to Mr. Chaine that if he needed a house you would authorize me to build it for him and that I would take the necessary means for that. He said he was well enough housed for this winter and that he would have no need. Gilliss has just arrived and his Indians are on the other side of Independence and he went to see Major Campbell at Madame Vasquez' home. I did not see Gilliss. It is Mr. Walls who tells me of his arrival. Now I have three good houses [posts] made. My situation is not very comfortable but I believe that for the business that I could not choose a better location. I am exactly across from the Shawnee village, [a] distance of about six or seven miles, near the Kansas River. It is a very elevated point. Water has to rise more than 40 feet to endanger us. There is a good port and a good place for the barge. On the other side across from our establishment, it is a beautiful side, rolling low land where we gather stone when we are in need. Major Graham tells me that Colonel Leavenworth has the intention of cutting a road from the fort all the way to the Kansas River. And he believes that at our establishment will be the best spot suitable to cross over. I am almost in a straight line with the fort and the landing on the two sides of the river is very good. And if the transaction is completed, that could be an advantage for our place [....] [....] If the Kansa do any hunting we will probably sell to them. You will have the kindness to tell my brother Cadet that there are twenty-seven guns charged to our expedition that we have not yet received. I've been told that they were transported to the fort when they paid the balance of annuities to the Kansa. Mr. Doorty must know that we still have almost all our guns and carbines. We need none for the next year probably. Here is a bit of news that circulates – some 1500 [....] on the Santa Fe road to [....] and the whites. I presume that you know that already. And that news causes here a bit of consternation. If the Pawnee begin war again, the Kansa and the Shawnee will not do much [hunting] this spring. I assure you that I fear for Mr. Kenerly and his party if they go as far as the Arkansas River. It seems to me that the agents, especially Doorty, should have taken the necessary means to warn Mr. Kenerly of that. That is all I have to say to you at present. As soon as the Indians return I will write to you. That will be in about fifteen days. That will also be the time of my return from among the Kansa. I assure you, my uncle, that I do not write you really as often as I desire, but do not believe me ungrateful for that. I had much trouble and vexation since my arrival. I was delayed in my building by having remained three or four weeks with Mrs. Vasquez in mending the cabins to hold the merchandise. I unloaded the whole barge and unwrapped all the merchandise to pay the annuities to the Shawnee and I think also to have a part of their money and at the end of the time, repack, reload the boat again and I came to where I am now with sails and ropes, that is to say, I carried the goods loaded in a pirogue and then I directed after that I immediately put all my people to work. I was near them almost always, guiding [....]. At the present we have housed the merchandise in a good store well set up. Finally we are well enough set up at present. The hatchets that I took at Ste. Genevieve are useless, they are almost all broken. Out of a dozen I have only four or five that can be used.

Give my compliments to my good aunt and to Peter as well as also Mr. and Mrs. Vallé and the family, my respect and friendship. I wish you good health and I am with respect, your nephew,

Francois Chouteau

This lengthy letter was written in Francois's usual fashion, skipping from one topic to another and then returning to the original subject, without benefit of paragraphing or adequate punctuation. It was sent by couriers "Clark and Dooty" who were Iowa Indians (not to be confused with William Clark, Superintendent of Indian Affairs in St. Louis, or John Dougherty, Agent of the Upper Missouri). The point of origin, "the house of Mr. Chaine," was the Shane and Wells place, located, as noted, south of the mouth of the Kansas River, near the state line.

As Chouteau informed Pierre Menard in the first sentence, he was en route taking merchandise to the Kansa Post. The articles were to be exchanged for furs and skins the Indians would bring in after their fall and winter hunt. The old Kansa Post at the Four Houses had been abandoned and a new one built at Horseshoe Lake, on the south bank of the Kansas River about seven miles west of present Lawrence. Chouteau expected to return from "among the Kansa" in about fifteen days.

The post that Chouteau described at such length was the new Shawnee Post, not the new Kansa Post. (The Kansa Post was intended to be temporary, as will be discussed later.) The Shawnee Post was, as Francois wrote, "across from the Shawnee village" – that is to say, across a portion of land, not across the river. The Shawnee village was on the south side of the Kansas River in present Shawnee Township.[52] Chouteau's post was "near the river," also on the south side, a distance of six or seven miles from the Shawnee village. The new post was on high ground, forty feet above the river. Chouteau, no doubt well remembered the flood of 1826. Located about twelve miles from the mouth of the Kansas River near present Turner, Kansas, this establishment later became known as "Cyprien's Post" and in modern times has been referred to as the "Turner Site." The post conducted business chiefly with the Shawnees, but also with the Delawares, and probably some Kansa as well.

A Catholic priest, Rev. Joseph Anthony Lutz, who hoped to evangelize the Kansa Indians, in November 1828 described the construction: "Messrs. Francis, Cyprien and Frederick Chouteau have begun to erect at the Kanzas River a large building which will soon be looked upon as a sort of emporium for the sale and exchange of goods among the Shawnees and Kanzas Indians."[53] Francois (and perhaps also his brothers) was to spend the winter at the new post while Francois's family was in St. Louis, where Berenice awaited the birth of their fifth child.

The Indian money that Francois mentioned was the cash given in annuity payments that were distributed periodically as compensation for rights, lands, and improvements surrendered to the United States according to a treaty agreement. The annuity payment varied according to the value of the Indian rights and the intensity of the government's desire to have them. Many Native Americans came to rely on these cash payments to buy

---

52. Anna Heloise Abel, "Indian reservations in Kansas and the extinguishment of their title," *Kansas Historical Collection* 8: 78-79; J. J. Lutz, "The Methodist Missions Among the Indian Tribes in Kansas," *Kansas Historical Collection* 9: 162-163.

"goods" they had learned to love: red cloth, beads, blankets, sheets, metal cooking pots, knives and hatchets, guns, powder, and lead.

Before the immigration of the eastern Indians, the Kansa people had the Kansas and Missouri River area much to themselves. Little attempt was made to control their affairs until Baronet Vasquez was appointed in 1825 to be the first Kansa subagent. He hired Francois Chouteau to build him a house to serve as Kansa Agency and living quarters for the Vasquez family. Apparently, as Chouteau later wrote that he mended "cabins," the Vasquez establishment consisted of more than one building. It was on the south riverbank at what is the foot of Gillis Street in present Kansas City. The location of the Kansa Agency was not convenient for the Indians, who lived about seventy miles up the Kansas River, but it was very convenient for Vasquez, who owned a farm in Jackson County. Often the Indians clustered in camps around the Agency, waiting for their annuities or for some decision or solution.

Vasquez died of cholera in August 1828 while en route from St. Louis in a buggy, escorting Rev. Joseph A. Lutz to western Missouri. Lutz, an idealistic young German priest, intended to establish a mission in the Kansa village, as requested by Kansa Chief White Plume himself in an interview with Superintendent Clark.[54] (It did not work out and Rev. Lutz returned to St. Louis.)

After Vasquez died, the American Fur Company purchased the Kansas City buildings from Vasquez' widow, who planned to return to St. Louis. While Chouteau was repairing the Vasquez buildings, a boatload of merchandise arrived and the Shawnees wanted to examine the goods. And so, as Francois wrote, he "unloaded" and so forth. He and his crew then wrestled the boat up the Kansas River to the site of the new Shawnee Post. At last the Chouteaus were able to finish building that establishment, then unload the merchandise again, and stock the shelves. They were then, it seems, "well set up."

A man named Dunning McNair[55] was appointed interim Kansa subagent, pending a permanent replacement for Vasquez. McNair handled routine duties, but important matters such as the payment of the annuities were reserved for his superior from the St. Louis Superintendency, John Dougherty, agent for the Upper Missouri since 1827. Dougherty lived at Fort Leavenworth and required that the Indians under his jurisdiction travel there to receive their annuities. After a new subagent was appointed, as noted, John Dougherty was no longer involved in Kansa affairs, as the subagent reported directly to William Clark.

Major John Campbell, subagent for the newly arrived Shawnees, was at the Vasquez residence when William Gilliss came to see him. Chouteau heard of Gilliss's arrival through a third party. In this and subsequent letters, William Gilliss was mentioned frequently as Chouteau described their encounters.

Born in Maryland, William Gilliss ran away to sea as a lad, fought in the War of 1812, and eventually settled in Kaskaskia, Illinois. There, probably through his French mother, he became acquainted with the town's leading citizen, Pierre Menard. With trade goods supplied by Menard and Valle, Gilliss followed migrating Indians across central Missouri and

---

53. Letter, Rev. Joseph Anthony Lutz to Bishop Joseph Rosati, November 12, 1828, cited in Gilbert J. Garraghan, S.J., *Catholic Beginnings in Kansas City, Missouri*, 32. The original letter written in Latin is in the Rev. Joseph Anthony Lutz folder, *Letters of Bishop Joseph Rosati*, Archives of the Archdiocese of St. Louis, St. Louis, Missouri.

54. May 17, 1827, White Plume visit to Superintendent William Clark, *OIA, St. Louis Superintendency, 1827-1828*, RG 234, Microfilm roll 748, NARA.

55. Dunning was the older brother of Missouri's first governor, Alexander McNair, who following his term, was appointed Agent to the Osages until his death in 1826. The brothers often associated in mercantile ventures.

established a successful trading post on the Upper James River near a Delaware Indian settlement. Gilliss was so closely associated with the Delawares that they were called "his" Indians. When the Delawares removed to the lands reserved for them in Indian Territory (Kansas), William Gilliss went with them.[56]

As in the case of Blondeau and Ogle, Gilliss was moving onto Chouteau's preserve. Accustomed to being his own boss, Gilliss did not take kindly to the notion of answering to Chouteau, although Francois had official status, prior claim, and seniority as a trader at the mouth of the Kansas River. As Menard's nephew and son-in-law, Chouteau would have been expected to have an edge over Gilliss; but whatever Gilliss's infractions as reported in Chouteau's letters, Menard never distanced himself from Gilliss.

By the time the 1828 letters were written, Fort Leavenworth had become a significant presence in the region. Founded in 1827 by Henry Leavenworth as a cantonment, or temporary troops quarters, the establishment was installed to protect wagon trains on the Santa Fe and other trails. In 1832 Cantonment Leavenworth became Fort Leavenworth. Personnel at the fort attempted to enforce laws and regulations that had been ignored for years. (They enforced, especially, the prohibition against selling whiskey to the Indians, to be examined in connection with Francois's letter to his half-brother, Pierre Chouteau Jr., written September 24, 1829.)

Francois's account of the incident on the "Santa Fe road" referred to a series of events that began in mid-August 1828. Traders traveling from Santa Fe to Missouri with twelve hundred (not fifteen hundred) head of livestock were ambushed by Pawnee Indians, who killed two white men. Later, a group of white men took revenge by slaying several Pawnees. The Pawnees retaliated by mounting attacks against the whites.[57] Chouteau was none too happy to realize that when George Kennerly departed from Chouteau's Shawnee Post, he was headed into the region of unrest.

While the preceding letter gave Pierre Menard full details about the operation of their business, the reference to Francois's half-brother Cadet signaled the beginning of a new supply line. In addition to merchandise from Menard and Valle in Kaskaskia or Ste. Genevieve, Chouteau apparently began to receive some quantity of his goods from the St. Louis-based operation of the Western Department of the American Fur Company of which Cadet was in charge.

Three weeks later Francois wrote from the "Shawnee establishment" and the envelope showed that the letter was posted from Independence. Probably Chouteau wrote the letter in one place, that is, the new Shawnee Post, and then mailed it from Independence.

Shawnee establishment   December 22, 1828[58]

Cher oncle,

For some time I have been back from my trip to the Kansa. It seems that, from the information that I was able to obtain from those who arrived and who brought in quite a

---

56. Lynn Morrow, "Trader William Gilliss and Delaware Migration in Southern Missouri," *Missouri Historical Review* 75 (January 1981): 147-167.

57. William Waldo, "Recollections of a septuagenarian," *Glimpses of the Past*, 5: 59-94; Barry, *Beginning of the West*, 150-151.

58. *PMC*, Letter 376. Envelope: [To] Monsieur Pierre Menard, Kaskaskia; [from] Independence, Mo., December 25, 1828; [filing note] Francois Chouteau, December 22, 1828, Received January 18, 1829, answered January 20.

few pelts, that the others had a successful enough hunt. I believe that they will all be back the first days of January. So that I am not able to write to you the results as yet, but you will be informed through my next letter. The Shawnee did not go hunting and we have given them about 1000 dollars in credit, including the band of Fish. I believe that the latter will pay us well. These are Indians much more unbearable than the Kansa to ask continually for credit. And I believe they pay no better than the Kansa. I told them that I will give them nothing until the first credits are paid. We sold some of our horses. That is a good merchandise among the Kansa, because they are glad to pay at the time of the purchase. As for the Shawnee, they want to buy on credit. But I told them "no" in no uncertain terms. There were four or five of these horses, untamed, that were worse than the devil. So much so that we were not able to sell them along with the others. The Kansa are divided into many bands. They stayed a few days at Mr. Ogle's and probably they also traded with the Shawnee who were on that side then. And Blando on the Missouri, carried on business with a small tribe of Kansa that had been hunting around there. I was informed and even I believe that he is trying to lure those that are here on this side. I learned from Major Campbell in person that Gilliss had the goods, and that his intention was to cross the [state] line and to build a house on the Shawnee Territory, to gather their credits and to deal with these latter as much as possible. So you see regarding us, that we have validated this information from other sources. The Kansa tell me that Blando gives them a better deal, therefore, he must be a fool who wastes the merchandise of the company. I believe that if you had a small store at Independence in Jackson County that would be to your advantage. The Indians go there often, especially when they have money. We could also make out pretty well with the whites because the land is well settled. There is a small store where goods are expensive and where business is carried on at a good pace. There are several people in that area who encourage me to set up a store there, who did not doubt that I would do well, saying to me, "let us know the price at which you value this fur, so that we are able to set the cost for ours." Three Little Osages approached me to ask that I send goods to the Marais des Cygnes. I told them I was unable to do that, that it was forbidden. They then told me that Mr. Ogle had sent two bundles of merchandise to them and they traded right away. Then I told them that if Liguest did not have merchandise to sell to them, if they came here to carry on business, that would be suitable, but that I did not want to send goods to them. The Marais des Cygnes has dried up pretty much this year. And the Osage Tribe tell me that they destroyed all the [beaver] lodges in front and killed all the [beaver] inhabitants. I have been told that a few days ago a peddler came into the village of the Shawnee with a small wagon of merchandise. That is just about all the news that we have to present to you.

I beg of you to assure my good aunt of my sincere affection. Give my compliments to Mr. and Mrs. Valle, as well as to all the family.

I am with respect and gratitude
Your nephew,
Francois Chouteau

Three days after this letter was written, Berenice gave birth to another son in St. Louis. Benjamin F. Chouteau was born on December 25, 1828, and was baptized in that city in July 1829. Francois may not have known about his new son for several weeks, as news traveled slowly in winter; with no navigation on the Missouri River, mail service was poor, and few couriers made the hazardous overland trip.

So, when Francois wrote the preceding letter, business was uppermost in his mind, namely, protecting his licensed rights as trader to the Shawnee and Kansa Indians. Gilliss and Ogle had continued trading with the Delawares as they moved from south-central Missouri onto their land in Indian Territory. The two men then began to trade also with the Shawnees, ignoring Chouteau's status as the official trader. Blondeau, meanwhile, was freelancing among the Kansa, while a traveling salesman went into the Shawnee village. Gilliss, Ogle, and Blondeau were, as noted, all loosely associated with the American Fur Company, a situation that Chouteau found nearly incredible.

When Gilliss moved from the James River to Indian Territory (Kansas), he brought along his trade goods, as Francois mentioned, most of which had come from Menard and Valle. Subagent John Campbell, knowing about Gilliss's activities, complained to his superior Richard Graham that Gilliss had commandeered Indian ox-carts for his personal use, and thus slowed the progress of the Weas and Piankeshaws to their reservation in Indian Territory.[59] Later Gilliss delivered to Francois Chouteau merchandise that must have been Menard's, as Francois reported the delivery to him. Gilliss then began to operate as he pleased, independent of government bureaus and agents, to the consternation of the American Fur Company and traders like Francois Chouteau, who held licenses to trade where Gilliss was setting up shop.

As to infringing on others' licensed trading rights, Chouteau himself could have played at that game, but he chose to abide by the rules. The Osages from the Marais des Cygnes came to Francois's Kansas City warehouse, asking him to send them merchandise. Although he had strong and intimate ties with the Osages that dated back to his childhood, Francois declined to encroach on his half-brother Paul Liguest, who was entrenched as trader and subagent to the Osages.

Given Francois's background with the Osages, it was not surprising that they were eager to do business with their friend Francois Chouteau, as he reported. The Indians, like the French, put great stock in loyalty to time-tested relationships. Francois, on his part, would have profited; everyone coveted the Osage trade, as, of all the tribes in present Missouri and Kansas, they brought in the finest pelts of every variety.

Amid the confusion of the eastern Indians arriving on their new lands, along with the entourage that followed them, the year 1828 ended.

---

59. John Campbell to Richard Graham, December 3, 1828, *Richard Graham Papers,* MHS; for reply, see Richard Graham to John Campbell, January 20, 1829, *Richard Graham Papers*, MHS.

"Filled with Respect and Affection": The Early Letters

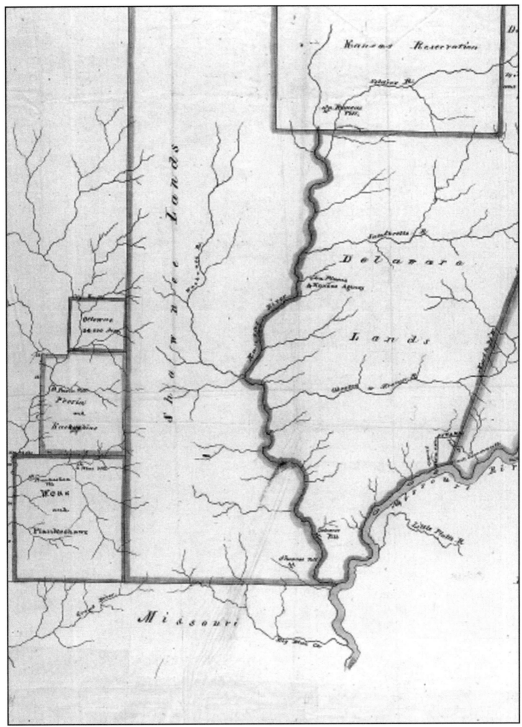

Portion of map drawn by Isaac McCoy, 1830, (west at top) showing the locations of the various tribal lands in the vicinity of the mouth of the Kansas River. *Isaac McCoy Papers*, Kansas State Historical Society.

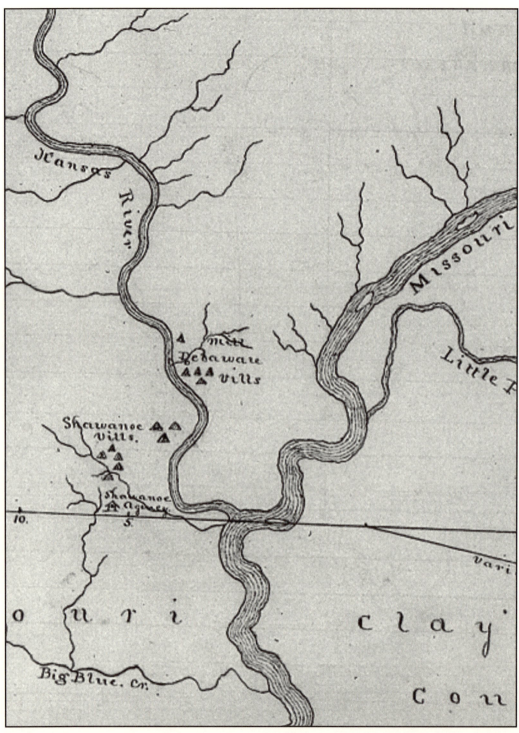

Portion of map drawn by Isaac McCoy, 1839, (west at top) showing the locations of the Shawnee and Delaware villages and the Shawnee Agency. *Isaac McCoy Papers*, Kansas State Historical Society.

"Presse des ballots" [Press of the packages (packs of furs)]. *Père Nicolas Point, S.J., Collection,* Archives de la Compagnie de Jesus, province du Canada frantais.

3 Gains and Losses: A Balance Sheet

In nearly every fur trading post, the credit-debt merry-go-round had riders who did not know how to dismount. The Indians, only having recently learned to manage their lives in a cash-based economy, sometimes bought frivolous items with their furs or annuity cash, then were forced to ask for credit for necessities. Although Francois Chouteau was part of the industry that fostered this system, he personally came to the conclusion that it was not especially desirable. (In his letter of November 30, 1831, he announced to Pierre Menard that he had brought the Indians "back from the abuse of heavy credit.") This topic arose often during the 1830s, and in the letter that follows, Francois aired his worries about the debts owed by the Indians.

It was common practice to use the word "treaty" to designate a business rather than a political agreement. Before each hunt, a new "treaty" or business agreement was made with the Indians.

River of Kansas   January 12, 1829 [1]

Cher oncle,

    We have just about finished our Fall Treaty which is a small thing. The Shawnee have done nothing. If they had accomplished as much as the Kansa, we could have made out all right. And what upsets me with them all the more is that they do not pay their credits. I assure you that if I had known them to be as irresponsible as they are, they would not have received a single penny of the credits. The Kansa are more honest than they are. At any rate, those to whom I gave credit paid us. There is a part of the band of Fish who have not yet returned. I presume they have gone to carry on business on the side of the river the Osage were on. Those that came have brought a few fur skins they traded somewhere, I believe, but I am not able to know yet, because I notice that they are great liars, just as the Kansa are. Really, there is no difference. I am unable to tell you how many deerskins we have. There is a band of Kansa of ten lodges who have not yet arrived. We're expecting them in a few days and I believe that the band of Fish will give us more skins upon their arrival. These ten lodges of Kansa are the last to arrive. The others have all arrived. I am informed that this little band had a good hunt. I believe that with the Kansa we will make up this fall about 100 packs. The Shawnee, about from 25 to 30, and I believe that if the Kansa had good shotguns they would come up with more furs than the Shawnee. The villages of the Kansa and the Shawnee that are here are about the same size. We have about 400 pounds of beaver, 200 otter and 1000 raccoons produced by the Kansa. I wrote to you, I believe, that it would be advantageous to have a store at Independence, because the annuities that the Indians will receive always for the most part, will go there. I want to know what you think about that and even commerce with the whites will be considerable. If your intention is to have merchandise in that place, it would be good to have a house set up and to carry out the necessary preparations. I beg of you to let me know the value of the skin of a rare red beaver, the otter, raccoon, [musk] rat, so that we can settle when we buy these. I will send out the boats probably in the month of March, with the packs that we will have ready. I have not seen Mr. Chaine for some time. I believe he is a good man, but I also believe he is very indifferent towards those who render kindnesses towards him. I presume that old Campbell has written to you concerning Gilliss. He carries on business in the state without a permit and even a county license.

    Frederick has gone to the Kansa and I expect him within a few days. Cyprien is well and is joining me to wish for you as well as to my aunt a good year and good health. I beg of you to convey my friendship to Mr. Valle and his family.

I am with respect your nephew,
Francois Chouteau

---

1. *PMC*, Letter 279. Envelope: [To] M. Pierre Menard, Kaskaskia; [from] Independence, Mo., 25 [cents postage], January 15, 1829; [filing note] Francois Chouteau, January 12, 1829, answered February 10.

This letter, written from "River of Kansas," was the first of many to carry that heading, indicating that Chouteau was writing from the Kansas City warehouse built to replace the Randolph Bluffs establishment destroyed by the 1826 flood. No later than the fall of 1826, Chouteau had a new business site across the river from his original location. His building on the south bank of the Missouri River was about two miles below the mouth of the Kansas River, near present Troost or Harrison Street.[2] In late October 1826, a Colonel John Glover traveled from Kentucky to western Missouri to scout the land, apparently with a mind to settle there – although he never did. In a short diary, he recorded where he went, at whose house he stayed, and how much it cost him, along with comments on the land. He wrote of going south from Liberty, crossing the Missouri River on a ferry and traveling in the "Blue country," land of the Big and Little Blue rivers. "Traveled on and came to Shotoes [i.e., Chouteau's] Trading house 1 mile below the Kaw river on the Missouria."[3]

John McCoy placed the new Chouteau post or warehouse at Harrison, and recalled that "At that time, three others were located at this point, viz., Daniel Morgan Boone, a son of the famous pioneer, Gabriel Philibert, and Benito [sic] Vasquez...." Those three, all connected to the Kansa Agency, moved west when the new agency was established, but meanwhile, others came. "...Quite a little village grew up at the new Chouteau location.... Louis Roy had a cabin and clearing at Oak and Second Street, Louis Uneau at Main and First where he ferried people across the river on a frail contrivance made of two canoes with a platform deck thereon, and Calise Montardine [Montardy, Montardeau] had his cabin...and a few acres cleared on the hill between Main and Wyandotte streets."[4]

By 1828, Francois was adding to his establishment on the south bank of the Missouri River. His brother Frederick claimed in an 1880 interview that "My brother Francis...built his home at what is now Kansas City in 1828 – a frame house – where he lived with his family."[5] As Francois recognized the uncertainties of the fur trade, he developed "one of the largest and best farms in the county, with a steamboat landing [built in 1832, perhaps near what is now Olive Street, Kansas City, Missouri], warehouses, and costly dwellings, and outhouses...."[6] Most of this farm lay in what became known as the East Bottoms.

Being "indifferent towards those who render kindnesses toward him," as Francois wrote of Shane in the preceding letter – was no small matter to him. Francois Chouteau grew up in a culture based on good feelings among business associates. One person performed a "kindness" for another, and that person was expected to return the favor in kind when the opportunity arose. These Frenchmen in the fur trade along the Missouri and its tributaries knew each other personally or by hearsay. They routinely exchanged favors and employment. Shane's Anglo-American approach to business, in which "kindnesses" did not count, annoyed and possibly offended Francois.

Since the preceding letter was written at the "River of Kansas," meaning the Kansas City warehouse, Francois must have then carried the envelope to Independence to post it. Sending a letter from Independence to St. Louis by way of the U.S. postal service in 1829, as the envelope documented, cost 25 cents. Apparently the prior letter dated December 22, 1828, was the first one Chouteau entrusted to postal service, rather than a courier. The service had been in place since 1827, when the town was established. Mail pick-up and delivery began in Westport in 1832, but in neither location was this a daily service, and it

---

2. Gilbert J. Garraghan, S.J., *Catholic Beginnings in Kansas City, Missouri*, 28-30.
3. Marie George Windell, "Westward Along the Boone's Lick Trail in 1826, The Diary of Colonel John Glover," *Missouri Historical Review* 39: 195.
4. John C. McCoy Scrapbook, 31, (KC296), WHMC-KC.
5. "Reminiscences of Frederick Chouteau," *Kansas Historical Collection* 8: 425.
6. John C. McCoy, "Forty years ago," *Kansas Monthly* 2 (June 1879): 83.

was – the current postal promise not yet having been declared – very much affected by rain, sleet, snow, and ice in the Missouri River.

Independence, as a trailhead for the Santa Fe trade, was a fast-growing community in the late 1820s. Founded in 1827 to serve as the seat of the newly established Jackson County, the first lots in Independence were sold in July of that year, and the town began to take shape with the building of stores, a jail, and a courthouse. In 1831, Blue Mills Landing was established on the Missouri River to serve Independence. After that, much of the overland Santa Fe trade that had been starting from Franklin, Missouri, came by boat to Independence and began the overland journey from there. The town seethed with activity until Westport and the Town of Kansas (sometimes derisively called Westport Landing) rose to prominence in the 1840s. At the time of these letters, however, Chouteau saw Independence as a place of opportunity.

Although the postal service was available, Francois, as seen in the following letter, continued to send his correspondence by courier when one was available. This demonstrated either the French preference for the personal touch, or a distrust of the postal system. (By 1835, Chouteau was bemoaning the performance of the postal service, as expressed in later letters dated May 5, 1835, and January 28, 1838.)

The opportunity to have his letter hand-carried to St. Louis prompted Francois to pen a report on the autumn hunt.

River of Kansas February 15, 1829[7]

Cher oncle,

I received your letter dated January 20, which gave me a real pleasure. I write this one to you through the Shawnee smithy who is going to St. Louis. His name is LaLiede and probably you know him. We have finished for the time being our fall treaty and I am going to take the necessary measures to settle the Kansa and to make them set out for the spring hunt. Several of the chiefs have come to visit me and they seem in a good disposition for that. I also plan to speak to the Chief of the Shawnee to send their young men for a month on the hunt. If I can succeed, I believe they will pay the greater part of their debt. About the last ones mentioned, they wish to grow a lot of corn but that will not pay their credits. That is why I'm going to do my utmost to have them go on a hunt for one month, after which they will still have time to grow their corn. They owe us about 800 dollars. I assure you that if I did not believe I would be blamed, that Mr. Ogle would not have made 60 to 80 packs with the Osage, but Cadet informed me that each one has to remain at his post and not to spoil things among the other Indians. I could have sent there easily but I do not want the American Fur Company to say that I had disobeyed the order that I had received. The Osage came twice to ask me for some merchandise. I told them that my orders were to trade at my post. Major Graham has encouraged the Shawnee a lot to trade in Independence with Mr. Leme and also told them that he could pay them their annuities in good merchandise and very cheap. He promised to little Wells to be assistant agent of the Shawnee. I do not know what interest he can have to show himself such an enemy to us. The hired hand of Gilliss, Mr.

---

7. *PMC*, Letter 281. Envelope: [To] Monsieur Pierre Menard, Kaskaskia; [filing note] February 15, 1829, F. Chouteau.

> *Mairs, has been here for some time now. He has about 15 packs of deerskins and raccoon. He asked me whether I could bring them down in a boat. I answered him that I could. And he will probably come down himself. Dagenai is here also. His Indians have not yet gone on the Marais des Cygne. They will go as soon as the weather is good enough to get there. Nothing else for the moment. Be assured that I do everything that depends upon me to make our business succeed. I am short of porcelain, a very good article. About them, I was only given a very small quantity, saying that Mr. Ogle needed a lot. We have a lot of silverware and we can do without it for the present.*
>
> *Give my love to my good aunt, and tell her that I am very sorry about the long sickness that she has undergone. But that I hope that the good weather will be favorable to her and will put her back on her feet. And extend my friendship to Mr. and Mrs. Valle and to the whole family.*
>
> *I am with respect, your nephew,*
> *Francois Chouteau*

With the arrival of the Weas and the Piankeshaws in 1828-1829, there also came the usual interpreters, government employees, and traders. The "Mairs" identified as an assistant to Gilliss was William Meyers, who had traded in the central Missouri Indian camps. The hiring of William Meyers sheds some light on the business relationship between Pierre Menard and Francois Chouteau. Menard wrote Francois on September 30, 1829, informing him that "William Meyers is the person that I appoint to trade with the Piankesaws, Weas, and Peorias."[8] Francois accepted Meyers as he understood that Meyers knew the Wea language because of his previous association with them. On that same day, Menard also wrote to Meyers (who was apparently then on the White River):

> *Sir, you will proceed without delay to the establishment of M. Fr. Chouteau and the Kansas River and there you will receive an assortment of goods suitable for the Piankesaw, Wea, and Peoria with whom you are to trade this coming winter. I have written to Capt. Vashon in order to obtain the license. You will inform me immediately of the place selected by the agent as the trading place for those Indians. You will conform yourself to the rules and regulations of trade in that section of country and by no means violate the laws regulating trade and intercourse with Indians.*[9]

Though Meyers complied with the instructions and went to the Kansas River region, apparently the establishment of the Wea Post did not occur until later. In October 1832, a trading license was issued to the American Fur Company for Francois Chouteau to establish a post for the Weas, Piankeshaws, western Missouri Kickapoos, and Peorias. The trading post was to be located on a branch of the Marais des Cygne in what is now Miami County. (The county name is a reminder that these people were sometimes call "Miami Indians.")[10]

The name "Dagenai" was first mentioned by Chouteau in the preceding letter, as he remarked that the man was there with "his Indians" who had not yet gone to the Marais des Cygne. In a letter of March 3, 1829, Chouteau referred to the same man, but spelled his name "Dajane." (Other contemporaries spelled it Dajanai, Dagnet, or Dashney.) Dajane was

---

8. Pierre Menard to Francois Chouteau, September 30, 1829, Letterbook J, *Pierre Menard Collection*, IHS. (Letter is reproduced as appendix item 3a on page 207.)
9. Pierre Menard to William Meyers, September 30, 1829, Letterbook J, *Pierre Menard Collection*, IHS.
10. *H. Doc. No. 45*, 23rd Cong., 1st sess. (Serial 254): 2.

mentioned in connection with William Meyers. A letter from subagent John Campbell to his superior, Agent Richard Graham, shed some light on this Dajane. Campbell, whose English spelling was every bit as erratic as Chouteau's phonetic French, wrote that "Noel Dashney" (or Dashnay) was employed by the Department of War (Indian Affairs) as an interpreter and that he was insubordinate. "Dashney" was not dismissed from his position, Campbell explained, because his service as translator was needed until the Indians reached their lands.[11] Since Campbell was subagent for the newly arriving Weas, Piankeshaws, and Peorias, as well as the Shawnees, it seems reasonable to assume that these were "Dagenai's Indians." This is further confirmed by the location of the Wea village, near the Marais des Cygne in present Kansas.

Yet another spelling of the man's name appeared in the letter Graham shot back to Campbell telling him that "As to Dagenet, complaints are useless. When he refuses to obey you within the line of his duty, employ for the service some one else for the object you want, whose pay shall be deducted out of his [Dagenet's]."[12]

The "little Wells" of the previous letter was probably the Wells who was a partner in the Shane and Wells trading post located near the state line north of Westport during the 1830s. The "Walls" Chouteau mentioned in the following letter was perhaps the same man. A few years later, a J. B. Wells was growing timothy and fescue on contract for Fort Leavenworth.[13] Other men named Wells appeared in the region much later.

In the following letter, Chouteau showed a good deal of satisfaction that the fall shipment contained valuable furs. This success enabled him to approach the coming months with more than modest expectations.

River of Kansas   March 3, 1829 [14]

Cher oncle,

I received your letter dated January 20 where I see that the furs seem to be worth something. We accept all that the Indians are bringing to us and paid them accordingly. I spoke to the Shawnee and Kansa chiefs a few days ago to encourage them as much as possible to make their people hunt this spring. The Kansa left well disposed for that. The Shawnee talk about planting a lot of corn, but I believe they will also do a little hunting. I spoke to the Kansa to obtain from him the favor that he will allow to go with them this spring, a few men of the band of the old Fish. There is no doubt that they will capture beaver and that they will give them an idea of the land that they wish to know as they tell me they still do not know the good places to hunt beaver. I propose to leave shortly to get the packs that we have among the Kansa, that is to say, at our trading post. I will go up on the boat probably if the river permits it, and upon my return I will send out the boat with all the furs that we will have. I will put on board the packs of Gilliss. Mr. Meyers proposes to come down with the barge. I offered to assist him as well as Dajane in whatever they might need. I also offered to Mr. Chaine, after your

---

11. John Campbell to Richard Graham, December 3, 1828, *Richard Graham Papers*, MHS.

12. Richard Graham to John Campbell, January 20, 1829, *Richard Graham Papers*, MHS.

13. *S. Doc. No. 200*, 25th Cong., 2nd sess. (Serial 316): 352, 353, 360.

14. *PMC*, Letter 282. Envelope: [To] Mr. Pierre Menard, Kaskaskia; [from] Independence, Mo., March 5, 18 3/4 [postage]; [filing note] Francois Chouteau, March 3, 1829.

recommendation, to give all the assistance in my power that he needs. I also advanced him a little money which he needed. I think that the Kansa trading post at the River of Kansas will be expected to produce a lot of furs next year. There are many reasons to make me believe that. I propose to write to you by way of the barge when it sails, if I do not descend on her. I do not have a man upon whom I can rely to command it. And I know that the Missouri River is always to be feared a little. However, I have Big Baptiste who informs me that I can rely upon him for that. That's just about all I have to tell for the time being.

I was informed, with pleasure, by your letter that my aunt was beginning to get better. I hope that that will continue. Pass on to her my heart-felt wishes, as well as to all your family.

I beg of you also not to forget for me Mr. and Mrs. Vallé and all the family. I wish you good health, as well as the recovery of my aunt.

I am with respect your affectionate nephew,
Francois Chouteau

[Note on envelope] *10th of February 1829. I gave $100 to Gesseau for Dogeen* [?] *Mongren. Reminder: some bracelets for the Pawnee by the Yellow Stone, one and one-half inch wide with little engravings.*

The preceding letter brought to an end the series of "compliments" and "regards" sent to Mr. and Mrs. Vallé. Following a visit to St. Louis, Francois no longer mentioned Mr. and Mrs. Vallé. He wrote three consecutive letters to his half-brother Cadet, all containing specifications for orders and other business information. It seems that Francois and Pierre Menard had transferred their merchandise orders to Cadet Chouteau's American Fur Company wholesale warehouse. As Menard was still in partnership with Vallé, perhaps Cadet Chouteau instigated this new arrangement.

The $100 referred to in the note written by Pierre Menard or his clerk, Raphael Widen, may have been sent by courier to western Missouri, as Francois (Gesseau) Chouteau was not in Kaskaskia or St. Louis in February 1829. Francois wrote from Kansas City on March 3 and again on March 31. There would not have been time for him to make a round trip to St. Louis, and in addition, travel on the Missouri River during the winter months rarely was attempted.

The "Dogeen" Mongrain for whom the money was intended has not been identified, but he must have been one of the large Mongrain clan associated with the Osages, serving as interpreters, guides, and couriers.

The Pawnees were not among the Indians with whom Chouteau usually traded, so the bracelets mentioned in the note may have been gifts, tokens of respect from the Chouteaus or the American Fur Company to the restless Pawnees. The Indians did not forget who gave them gifts.

This jewelry was to be shipped aboard the *Yellow Stone*, meaning the keelboat *Yellow Stone Packet*, as the steamboat *Yellow Stone* arrived on the scene two years later. The first steamboat appeared on the Missouri in 1819 when *The Independence* made its way from St. Louis to Franklin, Missouri. In August of that same year, the steamboat *Western Engineer*, masquerading as a dragon of the deep, steamed past the settlement around Chouteau's warehouse, belching black smoke from its smokestack mouth, terrifying the Indians, as it was intended to do.[15] By the late 1820s, steamboats ran regularly on the Missouri River, with their arrivals, departures, and cargo printed daily in the St. Louis newspapers.

Chouteau's preceding letter reported that he spoke "to the Kansa," meaning a Kansa chief. Prominent at that time were Fool Chief, Hard Chief, American Chief, and White Plume, whose settlement was the nearest one to Chouteau. In addition to proximity, the Chouteaus had another connection with Chief White Plume. The chief's daughter (or niece?) had married Frenchman Louis Gonville, and their daughter Mary Josephine, or "Josette," was raised in the home of her baptismal godparents, Francois and Berenice Chouteau.[16]

Although it is unclear which Kansa chief Chouteau meant, the outcome of the talk plainly demonstrates the esteem and respect accorded to Francois Chouteau. Using all his charm and powers of persuasion, he induced the Kansa men to take their competitors and erstwhile enemies, a Shawnee band led by Chief Fish, with them on the spring hunt so that the Shawnee hunters could become familiar with the hunting grounds of the unfamiliar land.

Shipping the furs to St. Louis should have been a simple business, but as Chouteau admitted in his preceding letter, "the Missouri River is always a little to be feared." There was something prophetic about that remark.

River of Kansas   March 31, 1829[17]

Cher oncle,

It is with the greatest sorrow that I inform you of the loss of the keelboat Beaver, loaded with 200 packs on the way to St. Louis. She hit a rock about 10 feet from her stern and she sank in less than three minutes. Two men drowned and Madame Baronet and her family who were going down as passengers, escaped as by a miracle. This poor woman had on board a little money and her little household. I fear she lost all. Frederick, to whom I had entrusted the responsibility of disembarking, saved himself by swimming, as well as those who knew how to swim. Mr. Dougherty was a passenger who was taking eight Indians of the principal chief of the Kansa to St. Louis. They tell me that the stubbornness of Baptiste Datchurut whom I had hired, was for a great part the cause of the misfortune for not having wanted to withdraw from that rock when he was advised to, and when he wanted to, the current threw them in spite of the oars. I had just come from a trip from the Kansa village with that same boat. I had carried the merchandise for the spring treaty and brought back 84 packs that we had made up at that place. I had the packs from the Shawnee that we had at the post and I had the barge repaired. I had a large oar attached instead of a small rudder. That was more prudent for going down the Missouri. She left from here the 27th. The boat was docked at my place where Baronet was. We loaded Mrs. Baronet and 20 packages that [s]he had, and passengers, and she [the boat] perished near the coal shed around 4:00 in the afternoon. As soon as I heard of the misfortune, I sent Cyprien with some men,

---

15. "Post of St. Louis Steam Boat Intelligence," *St. Louis Enquirer*, 15 June 1819, 3.

16. Frederick Chouteau Letters, May 6, 1880, General (series B), Kansa (subgroup 9), *Indians History Collection*, (MC590), KSHS.

17. *PMC*, Letter 283. Envelope: [To] Monsieur Pierre Menard, Kaskaskia, Ill.; [from] Independence, Mo., April 2nd 18 3/4 [postage]; [filing note] F. Chouteau, March 31, 1829.

implements and what was necessary to save the best goods from the accident. Not being able to go myself because of the frostbite that I got on both feet in my last trip to the Kansa, and which cause me to suffer much. I hope that in a few days, I can travel there. You can judge of the terrible situation in which I find myself at present and the continual reflection that I make concerning this wretchedness. To sum it up, I am almost discouraged. After another long absence from my family, after so much pain, so much work, running around and having been sent hither and thither, so much trouble and vexation with the Indians in order to obtain what the boat contained, and to see, after that, all my labor lost in an instant, makes me doubt for hope in the future. However, that will not stop me from working, nor from accomplishing what my duty demands of me. I am unable to say what has been lost. I have not received news since the departure of Cyprien. Here is what was on board the barge:

15 thousand deerskins
400 pounds of beaver
1500 muskrat
400 otter
2 thousand raccoons
2 barrels tallow
Ditto of wax
45 bear skins

I should have gone down on the boat. I cannot say that this would have prevented the misfortune. Having consulted with Cyprien, it was thought that it was best that I remain in order to see to the business and that Frederick would go down in my place for the disembarking of the boat.

All of that takes away my inclination to set up a store in Independence. I will tell you the motives which hindered me from writing you on this subject upon my return to St. Louis.

Tell my aunt hello. I am respectfully your affectionate nephew.

Francois Chouteau

The twelve miles separating Francois Chouteau from the scene of the accident kept him in despair longer than would have been necessary. Those on the scene, however, were too busy dealing with the emergency to let him know what was happening.

Francois's brother Frederick Chouteau, twenty years old at the time of the wreck, recalled in an interview in April 1880 the sequence of events in the sinking of the keelboat *Beaver*:

Mrs. Vasquez with her children took passage on this boat. There were four children, all small, the oldest not over ten or twelve years. The following persons were on board to go down to St. Louis. Mr. Hughes and John Dougherty, Indian agents; two pilots and a daughter of one of them; Mrs. Vasquez and her four children; eight hands; ten Kaw Indians, and myself – twenty-nine in all.

My brother had hired an old mulatto pilot, named Baptiste Datchurut, to pilot the boat. The boat was all loaded and Baptiste was drunk and could not be found; so I hired his brother pilot, Frank Zabette, also a mulatto, to take the steering oar and steer the boat.

> *Two miles above Prime's ferry, where Independence now is, the old rascal* [Datchurut] *overtook us in a canoe, with a discharged soldier by the name of Kennedy. He showed me his papers, and says he, "Your brother sent me to take charge of the boat." I said, "I am very sorry; I wish you had not overtaken us."*
>
> *The wind was blowing very hard from the south, so that we laid by for a while against the southern shore, and when we started again we kept as near the southern shore as we could. Between the place where we were detained by the wind and Prime's ferry was a large rock, which was in the bank at low water, but was out in the current in high water, as it was now. I saw that we were running towards the rock. I told the men to row away. They did, and threw the bow of the boat away out from the rock; but the old man was not stout enough as the brother was, to throw the stern out, and the boat struck its side against the rock, breaking the side in. We turned right toward the shore, but the boat began to sink fast. We threw the anchor but it would not catch. The seven hands and myself jumped in and swam ashore. Three of the hands, Kennedy and two Canadians, were drowned. Myself, Frank and three of the hands got safely ashore. The others remained on the boat. The boat's anchor soon got a hold and stopped the boat.*
>
> *I hastened to Prime's ferry, a mile below, and got a flatboat and went to the rescue of the party remaining on the keel-boat. I got them all off in safety.*
>
> *Next day we got all of the packs out. We cut a hole in the deck. Joe Lulu dived down and brought out all the packs, one at a time, and we took them ashore and dried them.*
>
> *Mrs. Vasquez lost $300, which she had in the little cabin that I had made for her near the stern of the boat.*
>
> *Kennedy's body I found three or four days after, and had the men bury it. I paid them five dollars which I found in his pockets. Prime's landing was Independence landing, twelve miles below Kansas City. We hauled all the pelts up to Kansas City, where my brother* [Francois] *had a house, and packed them again and shipped them on a steamboat.*
>
> *Mrs. Vasquez went down on the steamboat with Mr. Doughtery.*
>
> *Joseph Lulu, a mulatto who belonged to my father, took the peltries out of the keelboat, diving down in the water for every pack, except a few which we could get out when we first cut the hole in the deck. He went under water no less than 375 times, taking out a pack each time. He was worth his weight in gold.*[18]

Francois's devastation over this accident was so great that he saw that he would have to force himself to carry out his duties. He lost his appetite for additional responsibilities, such as opening a store in Independence. No doubt he was somewhat consoled when he learned that the keelboat's cargo had been salvaged, but the loss of life remained, and he held himself responsible. Chouteau wrote that two men had been drowned, whereas Frederick recalled that three had perished. Perhaps at the time Francois wrote the letter he knew of only the two men who had worked for him, and had not heard of the soldier, Kennedy.

In the following letter, Chouteau mentioned a coal shed. This was a part of the system used to provide fuel for steamboats on the Missouri River. An enterprising individual made arrangements to provide a bank-side coal supply so that a steamboat could refuel en route to its destination. In the preceding letter Chouteau cited the location of the keelboat accident in relation to a coal shed near Independence. In a subsequent letter, dated February 24, 1832, Chouteau told of putting "steamboat wood" on a point of land where the steamboat could pick it up. When steamboats had no prearranged fuel deposits, the crew was obliged to disembark and cut wood from the forests along the riverbank.

---

18. "Reminiscences of Frederick Chouteau," *Kansas Historical Collection* 8: 424-425.

Francois's next letter to Pierre Menard was written after Francois arrived in St. Louis, bringing with him a load of furs. This cargo, too, had a brush with disaster as a boiler on the steamboat exploded near Florissant. (Could it have been the same cargo that was raised from the sunken keelboat?) Chouteau decided to strike out across country. He wrote that he disembarked at *flor e sant* – the flowering place – thus sketching a charming image as well as suggesting the origin of the name Florissant, now a St. Louis suburb.

When Francois composed the following letter, his children and Berenice were in St. Louis, where Berenice had given birth to their son Benjamin on the previous Christmas Day. This letter reveals a different Francois – a man no longer concerned with delinquent debts, infringing traders, or even a sunken keelboat. Personal loss had changed his perspective.

At St. Louis, May 26, 1829[19]

Cher oncle,

I take advantage of the occasion of Dougherty who leaves today to go to Kaskaskia to inform you of my arrival. Instead of the joy that I anticipated at my arrival among my own, I find that I lament the loss of my dear and good mother. I assure you I find an immense emptiness in the house in not seeing her whom I loved so much. Papa is not well. My arrival renewed his sorrow and his pain in all its force. But I hope that for now I can console him little by little. Berenice also to you as well as to my aunt sends her compliments, and I, likewise. I arrived in the steamboat Duncan that burst one of its boilers in arriving at the coal shed of papa. I came from that place on foot to Florissant where I mounted a horse and I arrived on the night of the 23rd at home. I send you two letters and I received them from Meyers and Dougherty.

I am with respect,
your nephew,
Francois Chouteau

I brought the fur pelts and left all the deerskins at the Kansas River, in good order, 155 bundles.

Francois's mother was Brigitte Saucier, born in 1777, probably at Prairie du Rocher, Illinois. Brigitte's mother, Marguerite Cadron, was the first wife of Brigitte's father, Francois Saucier. Marguerite died young, and by 1779 Francois Saucier had married Angelique Roy (Roi) and was living in Cahokia, Illinois, where Francois's father, Gabriel Saucier, had settled in 1760.[20] This second wife was the mother of Brigitte's half-sister, Angelique Saucier Menard.

Francois Saucier's second wife, Angelique, died in 1787, and he then married Francoise Nicolle Lefevre, a widow with eight children. Francois and Francoise themselves added eight more to the family. Four of Francois Saucier's daughters married men prominent along the Mississippi: Brigitte married Pierre Chouteau of St. Louis; Angelique married

---

19. *PMC*, Letter 291. Envelope: [To] Mr. Menard, Kaskaskia; [filing note] May 26, 1829, Frs. Chouteau.

20. John Francis McDermott, *Old Cahokia, A Narrative and Documents Illustrating the First Century of its History*, 51.

Pierre Menard of Kaskaskia; Emily married James Morrison, a wealthy businessman in St. Charles; and Eleanor married James Morrison's brother, Jesse.[21]

Francois Chouteau's letter documented that Brigitte Saucier Chouteau died in May 1829, cause of death not recorded. Berenice's letter of April 8, 1827, contained a statement that her aunt, that is, Francois's mother, Brigitte, "would be well except for her foot which is always aching." Otherwise, there was no mention of Brigitte being in poor health. She was fifty-two when she died.

As the mother of Pierre Chouteau's second family, Brigitte probably experienced some heartache on behalf of her children, all sons. Pierre Chouteau expended none of the energy or money on Brigitte's offspring that he had invested in the children of his first wife Pelagie Kiersereau, who, before her death in 1793, had borne four children: Auguste Pierre (A. P.), Pierre Jr. (Cadet), Pelagie, and Paul Liguest.

The apparent disparity of treatment was not necessarily rooted in a lack of feeling on the part of Pierre Chouteau. He probably cared for both his wives and their children. However, at that time, marriages among the French were carefully considered mergers designed to connect two families, with advantage to both.

Pelagie Kiersereau was a sixteen-year-old orphan of considerable wealth when Pierre Chouteau married her. They had been married only ten years when she died. Undoubtedly her fortune subsidized the education of their first-born, Auguste Pierre (A. P.) at West Point Military Academy, although it was his father's influence that secured his appointment. A. P. Chouteau graduated from West Point in 1806, but followed a military career for only a short time before he resigned his commission to enter the fur trade.

The second son of this marriage, Pierre Chouteau Jr. was born in St. Louis in 1789 and was widely known by the nickname "Cadet." This French word meaning "younger brother" was originally bestowed on Pierre Sr. to point out his relationship to his famous older brother, Auguste Chouteau. Pierre Jr. was, like his father, a younger brother. His elder brother, A. P., ironically, never matched the success of the younger Cadet.

Cadet was educated in St. Louis day schools and like his father seemed to have the golden touch. He was heir apparent to the Pierre Chouteau Sr. enterprises, probably from an early age, as he displayed aptitude and interest, while his older brother A. P. went off to West Point. Cadet married Emily Gratiot, and they had five children. After John Jacob Astor established his American Fur Company in St. Louis in 1826, Cadet Chouteau became head of the Western Department of that company. In that capacity he traveled widely, engaging in financial and political matters. He and Emily made extended visits to Washington City (Washington, D.C.) and New York City. Apparently, they even considered moving to the East. When Astor wanted out of the fur business in 1834, Cadet bought the Western Department.

The last son of the Pierre Sr.'s first marriage was Paul Liguest, who apparently had some schooling in St. Louis, then learned the Indian trade in the Osage village. Later he became both Osage agent and trader on the Marais des Cygne.

Brigitte Saucier, Pierre Sr.'s second wife, did not bring wealth to her marriage, but rather a respected family name and desirable connections. Having no maternal money behind them, her sons apparently were expected to start earning their keep at an early age.

The boy Francois, as explained, attended school in St. Louis. Francois's brother Cyprien probably received an education comparable to that of Francois, but Frederick, in the opinion

---

21. For a comprehensive genealogy of the Saucier family and its connections, see Walter Saucier, *Gabrielle's People*.

of Kansas City pioneer J. S. Chick, was an uneducated man.[22] His school was the warehouse at Randolph Bluffs and his teachers were his brothers, Indian agents, and the Kansa people.

Pierre Chouteau's efforts to promote the careers of the sons of his first family consisted of wielding influence as well as providing money. His considerable prestige with the Osage Nation was a lever he almost certainly applied in getting his eldest son Auguste Pierre (A. P.) appointed to West Point, and Paul Liguest named Osage agent. Especially in the late 1700s and early 1800s, government officials (Spanish, French, and U.S.) relied on the Chouteaus to negotiate with the powerful Osages.

By the time Francois was ready to establish himself in business, Pierre Chouteau was sixty years old. For whatever reason, he basically left Brigitte's sons to fend for themselves. Francois's marriage to Berenice Menard drew her father into the picture. Pierre Menard apparently furnished the merchandise needed to get the posts in western Missouri started. Internal evidence warrants this assumption: the constant reporting of financial details to Pierre Menard and the relaying of information about the progress of fur collection. In addition, there were Francois's constant assurances that he would do as Pierre Menard desired, as well as Francois's direct reference to "our business" in letters dated February 15, 1829, and May 12, 1837.

As for Cyprien and Frederick, it was up to their elder brother Francois, under the auspices of Pierre Menard, to give them a start, enabling them eventually to have trading posts of their own in Indian Territory.

Of Brigitte's other two sons, Pharamond worked briefly in the fur trade with Francois, but was never in good health and died in 1831 at the age of twenty-five. As Berenice's letter of April 8, 1827, revealed, Charles was in conflict with his father, and after Berenice's successful negotiations, he went to Kaskaskia where Pierre Menard gave him a position in the Menard and Valle store.

Having presented all this, it is still safe to say that there was a strong family bond between Francois and his St. Louis family. During her extended visits to St. Louis, Berenice and her children stayed at the commodious Chouteau mansion, often during an entire winter, while Francois was on the frontier collecting furs. Francois demonstrated a genuine affection for his father. When writing business letters to his half-brother Cadet, Francois seldom failed to send greetings to *papa*. Nonetheless, for all his traveling to St. Louis and back, Francois had anchored his future to western Missouri, independent of the St. Louis Chouteaus. He bought land, enlarged the scope of his warehouse, cultivated his farm, and became the leading citizen of the community.

It is unclear whether Cyprien or Frederick had deep feelings for their St. Louis family. Cyprien went to St. Louis on business during the lifetime of Francois, but settled permanently in western Missouri. Frederick apparently never looked back to the place of his birth. He left St. Louis when he was fourteen, established himself in business in Kansas, and was a local legend by the time he died there in 1891.

Brigitte Chouteau died in May 1829, and Francois's next letter was written in early August, immediately after he and Berenice returned from St. Louis with their sons Edmond, Pierre Menard, and baby Benjamin, then nine months old. For some reason – perhaps to console an ill and grieving old Pierre Chouteau – Francois and Berenice had remained in St. Louis during the summer of 1829, and Benjamin was baptized that July. During the same month, two-and-one-half-year-old Louis Sylvestre died. He was buried in the new Catholic cemetery on St. Charles Road, since the old burial ground on the Mississippi riverbank had been closed in 1828.

---

22. "Joseph S. Chick interview," October 19, 1908, General (series A), Kansa (subgroup 9), *Indians History Collection*, (MC590), KSHS.

Francois and Berenice and their three sons were back in western Missouri when Francois wrote his next letter, this time to Cadet.

River of Kansas   August 10, 1829[23]

Cher frere,

We arrived in this place without accident, and all our effects in good condition.

I beg you to pay Mr. Steele 217-70 sol – for the freight and my passage. I am unable to return to you the rifles at present. The boat leaves as soon as our effects are unloaded. I learned that the annuities of the Kansa have been taken to the agency, but I do not know if the Indians have received them. That is what I shall give my attention to immediately.

Give our compliments to papa. Tell him that I will write to him at the next occasion – no other news at present.

Your affectionate brother,
Francois Chouteau

Berenice asks Cyprien to bring her two bottles of olive oil and a little wash-hand basin.

The store operated by the Western Department of the American Fur Company under the control of Cadet Chouteau apparently carried a running account for Francois, the sum of which was deducted from the payment due him from the fur sales. Most of his purchases were for the business, but he probably also "charged" items for domestic use, and justified the bill periodically. The sum added to Francois's account in the above instance was very little – a *sol* was approximately one cent.

The Kansa Agency mentioned in connection with the annuities was on the north bank of the Kansas River, about seven miles upriver from Lawrence.[24] The death of Kansa Subagent Baronet Vasquez in August 1828 had given Superintendent of Indian Affairs William Clark the opportunity to move the agency site from its Kansas City location to a place more convenient to the Indians the agency served.

Another letter to Cadet kept the St. Louis business up to date on activities on the frontier.

River of Kansas   August 25, 1829[25]

Cher frere,

The Indians want to have everything on credit, the Kansa as well as the Shawnee, and I will give it to them [and] give to the Kansa all the guns that are here. I will try to fix them as well as possible so that they may have a good hunt, so as to make up for our loss last year.

---

23. Francois Chouteau to Pierre (Cadet) Chouteau Jr., August 10, 1829, *Chouteau Family Collections*, MHS. No envelope.

24. William E. Unrau, *The Kansa Indians*, 114-115; Louise Barry, *Beginning of the West*, 138.

25. Francois Chouteau to Pierre (Cadet) Chouteau Jr., August 25, 1829, *Chouteau Family Collections*, MHS. No envelope.

> *The chiefs of the Shawnee came to see me upon my arrival and ask me if I had brought their annuities. I told them "no." Captain Vashon took two thousand dollars to them. They have taken a thousand of them* [the dollars]. *They took a thousand and a thousand was reserved for Mr. Menard. I would have been very pleased if you could have given or told me the prices for which we can give the merchandise for annuities, even though I do not have here at present what they need. I have only sheets and blankets. They presume* [expect] *to get their merchandise for the annuities at a very low price. Mr. Vashon told them that he had the prices of all the merchants in St. Louis and he could get them their merchandise at the best rate. I would like for our merchandise to arrive as soon as possible and that Cyprien would come also. The Indians have promised me to await their arrival. Captain Vashon and Chaine* [Anthony Shane] *and several chiefs are leaving tomorrow to go on the White River. He says he wants to send for the Loups, etc. The merchants of Independence have given the Indians merchandise at St. Louis prices – and even several things cheaper. Next month I want to have our deerskins bundled to send by the first occasion. They hardly suffered from moths but there was a little damage from the rain. I would like to know the price of the articles that I bought at the store of Pratte and Co. Do tell Cyprien to ask Charles to send me my newspaper to Independence.*
>
> *Berenice joins me in sending our greetings to you as well as to your wife. I also ask you to give our regards to papa and Mr. Menard.*
>
> *Your affectionate brother*
> *Francois Chouteau*

While Francois was in St. Louis in June 1829, George Vashon had been named Indian Agent to replace Richard Graham, who was discharged for questionable management and recording of financial matters dating back several years. Graham devoted a great deal of time and energy trying to vindicate himself, but to no avail. After his dismissal, he entered the fur chase in the Rocky Mountains and then journeyed to California during the Gold Rush. Rather than seek the elusive golden specks, he set up a sawmill and made a fortune.[26]

George Vashon's position as Indian Agent made him responsible for the Delawares, Shawnees, Kickapoos, Piankeshaws, Weas, and Peorias residing in Missouri and Arkansas, and the territory west of Missouri.[27] He did not dwell among these Indians, but relied on subagent John Campbell to handle day-to-day affairs, as Campbell lived at the Shawnee Agency in present Johnson County, Kansas, near the state line. Vashon, however, as agent, distributed annuities and made the important decisions.

The journey mentioned in the letter as being undertaken by Vashon and interpreter Anthony Shane (Chouteau's "Chaine") was to the White River area of the south central Missouri Ozarks. This was the region of the White, Current, and James rivers where some of the eastern Indian tribes had lived from approximately 1804 to 1828. William Gilliss's trading post, as noted, had been near the Delaware settlement on the James River before he moved with them to their land in present Kansas. Probably a few of the Delaware-Loup Indians had remained behind while the rest of the group moved to their reservation in Indian Territory, and Vashon was going to get them. Chouteau's letter of October 15, 1829,

---

26. For an overview of the progression of his activities see the *Richard Graham Papers*, MHS.
27. Barry, *Beginning of the West*, 156.

to Cadet mentioned that Vashon had fetched the six Loup men and was escorting them to the reservation to show them their new land.

The most widespread understanding of "Loup Indians" is that they were a band of Pawnees from the Loup Fork of the Republican River in Nebraska. These Pawnee-Loups ranged far and wide, and could easily have passed through Chouteau's country. Basically, however, they lived about 200 miles from Chouteau's Kansas City warehouse. Francois, Cyprien, and Frederick had no licenses to do business with the Pawnees. They may have, on occasion, given them gifts or purchased furs from them, but they did not trade with them on a regular basis.

Chouteau's correspondence presents strong internal evidence that the Loups of these letters were a band of Delawares – not the Pawnee-Loups. To begin with, Francois made clear that Major Cummins, who followed Vashon as Shawnee agent, was the person in authority over the Loups. Cummins's charges did not include Pawnees, but did include Delawares. Moreover, constant reference to daily happenings at the Loup village – deaths, illnesses, Gilliss carrying whiskey to them on Christmas Day – indicates that the village was close, and their news spread quickly to Chouteau's Landing. More specifically Francois in his letter of February 12, 1833, to Pierre Menard concerning a new post among the Loups, made the observation that the distance from the Loup village to Fort Leavenworth was twenty-five miles, while the distance was three miles from the Loup village to the Chouteau post, probably meaning the Chouteau-operated Shawnee establishment. This three-mile distance placed the Loups squarely in the Delaware reservation.[28]

Pratte and Company (or Berthold, Chouteau, and Pratte) was the St. Louis operation that in 1826 became the Western Department of John Jacob Astor's American Fur Company. The establishment was, as noted, run by Cadet Chouteau to sell merchandise wholesale to traders or retail to the general public. When the Indians wanted goods at "St. Louis prices," they referred to wholesale prices in stores like Cadet's before the cost of shipping had been added.

Keeping accounts was a tricky business, these letters imply; in the preceding letter, Francois knew neither the price of what he had purchased (several articles at Pratte's store), nor the price of what he was selling (the deerskins, identified by the French as *chevreuil*, or dwarf deer).

Cyprien Chouteau, still in St. Louis, received instructions from Berenice in the previous letter, and from Francois in the following one. The "Charles" Francois mentioned was Joseph Charless, editor of the *Missouri Gazette,* an English-language paper that, among other news items, carried records of legal transactions such as land sales, foreclosures, bankruptcies, shipping information, and the like. As Francois matured and developed his commercial skills, he apparently recognized the possibility of using business news to his advantage. Hence, his request for the newspaper. Although Francois's native tongue was French, he must have been fluent in English, as he dealt constantly with English-speaking Indian agents

---

28. Beyond a general consensus among some scholars that the French in Missouri routinely referred to the Delaware as the Loups, the internal rationale for this assumption is quite strong: the Delawares (who called themselves "Lenape") were divided into three sub-tribes. One of these three was the "Minsi," meaning "people of the mountain." This referred to their origin in the hills near the mouth of the Delaware River. (The Delaware word "Minsi" or "Mincie" has survived as "Muncie," the name of a small town that has become part of Kansas City, Kansas.) Also, the totemic animal of the Minsi people was the wolf (William E. Connelley, *History of Kansas*, 1: 226-232.) It is likely these Native Americans took pride in this wolf symbol, and may have identified themselves as "wolf" people. And *loup*, of course, is the French word for wolf. What was happening was that the Indians were being quite specific as to who they were – not just Delawares, but Minsi; not just Minsi, but wolf, that is, Loup. Having no written language, of course, the Indians left no documentation for this.

and non-French traders and businessmen on the frontier. (Berenice's English, on the other hand, may have been slower to develop, while the children, running from their home to the warehouse, probably spoke English and French equally well.)

Francois's later letter to Pierre Menard, dated September 24, 1829, reveals that Cyprien did not return on the steamboat with Francois and family, but remained in St. Louis to purchase horses that he drove overland to western Missouri. He must have paused frequently so that the animals could graze and rest, for Cyprien arrived at his brother's Kansas City warehouse with the animals in good condition, ready for resale to the settlers or Indians.

Francois's letters to Cadet became more frequent in the year 1829. Francois was definitely in the shadow of this illustrious older half-brother, but his letters are straightforward, matter-of-fact, and in no way obsequious. Francois told Cadet plainly what he needed for the western Missouri posts, and when things went awry – such as merchandise arriving late – he made sure that Cadet knew about it.

The following lengthy letter to Cadet is the quintessential business correspondence, filled with discussion of supplies, money received or expected, and the merits or faults of personnel. But it is a French business letter of the early nineteenth century, and thus must close with the personal touch.

Kansas River September 24, 1829 [29]

Cher frere,

Since my arrival in this place I have had a lot of worry and trouble with the Indians. I gave [things] on credit to the greater part of the village of the Kansa. They are now very well fixed to make a good hunt which I very much hope. I paid the rest of the annuities to the Weas and Piankeshaw, according to the letters that Mr. Menard wrote to the chiefs of these bands. The chief of the Peorias was not here. I will pay him upon his arrival. He went with Captain Vashon to the Arkansas River. This agent is not at all esteemed in this country. He has made many enemies since his arrival. He claims that every one sells whiskey to the Indians and that they have always been cheated by those with whom they had business, that he came here to see that justice is done towards them, that he knows the price of all the merchants of St. Louis and that he can get them merchandise at a cheaper price than anyone at all. I got this from Major Campbell and several other persons told me almost the same thing. He has sued several persons as venders of whiskey. He has always been the dupe, never being able to show sufficient proof. I will try to pay the Shawnee upon the arrival of the barge, a thousand dollars of the annuity which is coming to them. As for the annuities of the Kansa, I assure you that if I had been here, they would not have taken them, but I hope that is all that they have – old Clark – the agent of the Kansa, and well loved here, as much by the whites as by the Indians. I am very disappointed to know that there is no powder or lead on board the barge. At present we lack these two articles which we cannot get along without. Nevertheless, I will see if I can buy some here. If not, I will let you know right away. I did not think that we would have needed so much. I send you the account of the

---

29. Francois Chouteau to Pierre (Cadet) Chouteau Jr., September 24, 1829, *Chouteau Family Collections*, MHS. No envelope.

provisions [?] *with which I have furnished Mr. Lamonte. I will send Kennerly's* [account] *by the mail. Clement wishes for you to send him his detailed account and that you let him know the money you paid for him. He is finding mistakes in that business. Send to him, I beg you, what he is credited with, so that I can be paid. Mark the time when you withdrew these appointments* [i.e., when you no longer did business for/with this person] *until you have stopped this or finished.*

Berenice joins me in wishing you, as well as your wife, good health and all possible happiness.

Your affectionate brother
Fcois Chouteau

I will write you as often as possible and I beg you to write me sometimes. I do not always have time to do it. I am obliged to be here and there and I often miss the mail days. I had asked you to tell Cyprien to ask Charless to send my newspaper to Independence. I think you forgot.

Writing from his Kansas City warehouse, Francois outlined the status of the Indian annuity payments. Apparently the Weas and the Piankeshaws had traveled to Chouteau's central location for the "payment" of their annuities. Probably only the chiefs made the journey from the land where they had recently settled, south of the Shawnees. As the tribes mentioned, the Weas and the Piankeshaws, were small, Chouteau probably had enough merchandise in his warehouse to "pay" them, that is, to provide them the merchandise equivalent of the money due them.

The Weas, whose name Chouteau wrote "wias," although typically mentioned as a separate tribe, were actually a band of Piankeshaws. For many years they lived in the area of present Chicago. Some time after the seventeenth century, pressure from the Potawatomis forced the Weas to move to Ohio, then to Indiana. Between 1827 and 1830, having lost their lands in the United States, they were removed to Indian Territory (Kansas), where they lived with other Piankeshaws, the Peorias, and the Kaskaskias.

The Shawnees, being a large tribe, were not to be "paid" until the arrival of the barge bringing a new supply of goods from St. Louis. Native Americans like the Shawnees, who had years of exposure to manufactured goods, were familiar with the variety of items available, and wanted to have a wide selection from which to choose. Hence, they waited for the barge.

The chief of the Peoria, who was not "here," and was to receive his allotment "upon his arrival," was Baptiste Peoria, well known in Missouri and Indian Territory. He served as interpreter, guide, and courier, as he was geographically savvy and spoke several languages. Francois Chouteau, as his letters testify, put great trust in Baptiste Peoria, and sought his help in negotiations, in carrying letters and sums of money, and in providing information and news.

The reference to the Kansa annuities probably meant that the Indians had accepted merchandise from someone other than Francois Chouteau, and that party had received their annuity money. Chouteau was especially irritated by this, as the Kansa owed him for outfitting their last hunt.

Until around 1829, few if any Midwestern tribes received their annuities in cash payments. Instead, they were given the equivalent in merchandise according to arrangements made between the Indian agents and the traders. If the merchandise was bought at too high a price, obviously, the annuity money did not purchase much merchandise for the Indians. By late 1829 and the beginning of the next decade, the Indians were detecting some flaws in this system.

Rumors shadowed new Indian Agent George Vashon as he made his first visit to the Indians in his charge, and his own subagent, John Campbell, was apparently helping to spread the gossip. Campbell was subagent at the Shawnee agency from 1825 to 1833. He had been with the tribe when they lived in south-central Missouri and assisted them on their journey to set up their village south of the Kansas River in present Johnson County, Kansas. Major Campbell was a genial, talkative old gentleman who, as Francois admitted in his letter of September 24, 1829, perhaps did not "always tell the truth."

Vashon's charge that everyone was selling whiskey to the Indians undoubtedly galled Francois. One of the federal regulations most flaunted during the pioneer era was the prohibition against selling liquor to the Indians. There are endless tales of the tricks wily traders perfected in order to get their spirits past Fort Leavenworth inspectors. Francois Chouteau, as far as can be determined, made no attempt to bootleg whiskey to the Indians. His letters from the late 1820s through the 1830s catalog the tragic results of alcohol use by nearby tribes.

The whiskey problem worsened in the Missouri-Kansas area as the number of traders increased. Wanting to capitalize on the swelling population of Native Americans, some of the traders sold the Indians whiskey that almost certainly was nothing but raw alcohol. The federal law prohibiting the sale of liquor to Indians dated back to 1825, but was not enforced. In 1833 Congress issued a mandate to enforce the law, and the militia at Fort Leavenworth began to inspect cargo on steamboats moving up the Missouri River. The vessels were permitted to carry enough liquor for the "personal use" of the crew and the employees of the upriver posts. This loophole was notoriously abused. On occasion, a conscientious officer questioned whether "personal use" could require such vast quantities. Some traders circumvented the law by transporting liquor by an overland route where there was no inspection, or by distilling liquor in the wilderness and then carrying it to the posts where the Indians traded.

While the United States prohibited sale of liquor to Indians, the British fur enterprise, the Hudson Bay Company, located within easy travel of the Upper Missouri Indians, issued whiskey and other spirits to the Indians without restriction. The Chouteaus and other representatives of the American Fur Company complained that they were at a disadvantage because the Indians took their furs to the British posts, where they would be feted with liquor, rather than to the American posts where, because of the federal law, the liquor supply was erratic.

As furs became increasingly difficult to get, liquor was used to induce the Indians to bring their peltries to a post where they would receive whiskey. By 1833, American Fur Company employees in the Upper Missouri country thought they had endured enough of the British trade advantage created by their liberal alcohol policy. Distillery equipment was smuggled into the remote posts and shortly thereafter – never mind the aging process – the liquor pipeline to the Indians was open. Someone, however, carried the news of the distillery back to Superintendent William Clark, and by early 1834, Cadet Chouteau was writing urgent letters to his employees to cease and desist immediately, or risk the loss of all their licenses. The stills were destroyed and the status quo was reestablished.[30]

In the valleys of the Kansas and Missouri rivers, ferment was also brewing between the government's Indian agents and the traders over the use of whiskey to influence the Indians.

---

30. Hiram M. Chittenden, *The American Fur Trade of the Far West*, 1: 355-362.

In 1843, Shawnee Agent Richard Cummins complained in a letter to the Office of Indian Affairs that some early settlers of Kansas City, especially Milton McGee, had been selling whiskey to Delawares and Shawnees since 1830.[31]

Unfortunately, the whiskey problem was never resolved. The government tried, to some extent, to prevent alcohol from reaching the Native Americans, but geography made this almost impossible. If the traders or traveling salesmen in Indian Territory did not provide liquor to the Indians, dram shops right across the state line in Westport, Town of Kansas, and Independence sold it to them by the glass or by the gallon.

By the time the preceding letter was written, trappers and hunters going to the Rocky Mountains had learned that they could get hunting supplies and other necessities from Chouteau's Kansas City warehouse. The man Chouteau furnished with provisions was Canadian Daniel Lamont, a partner in the Columbia Fur Company, a mostly British operation that originated in the Upper Mississippi. During the late 1820s, that company moved into the Upper Missouri and, with Kenneth McKenzie at the helm, provided some stiff competition for the American Fur Company.[32]

This letter documents the beginning of a trend in Chouteau's business affairs that was leading him into a kind of "pioneer banking." On behalf of merchants in St. Louis and Kaskaskia, Indians, Indian agents, government employees, and settlers, Chouteau served as a financial middleman. He loaned money, collected debts, distributed funds, and, in general, was the man people consulted about money matters. Probably he received a commission for his services, but there is no way of knowing. From the late 1820s until the end of his life, Francois's letters chronicled this kind of activity.

Clement, who in this letter wanted his account straightened out, was Clement Lessert, an interpreter for the Kansa Indians from 1825 to perhaps as late as 1847. He may have been in need of funds, as he had recently married Julia Roy (Roi) in Jackson County. By 1840, Lessert had purchased land in Kansas City and was a member of the Catholic parish of Father Nicolas Point.[33]

The vacancy in the position of subagent for the Kansa Indians that had been created by the death of Baronet Vasquez was temporarily filled by Dunning McNair. In March 1829, Marston G. Clark was appointed to the position and took up his duties in May of that year. He was a general during the Indian wars in Indiana, and cousin of William Clark, Superintendent of Indian Affairs. (This generates some confusion since both Clarks were called "General Clark.")

True to his usual letter-writing pattern, Chouteau kept his personal comments and news until last. In this letter, he asked Cadet to give regards to his wife, Emilie Anne Gratiot. In addition, Francois asked his half-brother, who ran a large business in St. Louis and was involved in international trade as well as Washington affairs, to write to him, assuming that Cadet had more opportunities to write letters than he did! Francois was very conscious of the unproductive time he spent on the back of a horse, or hauling a boat up the nearly dry Kansas River, as he made his way among the trading posts and his Indian customers.

The name of the courier for the following letters was deciphered as "Calais," Francois's phonetic spelling of "Calice," whose last name was Montardeau, Americanized as "Montardy." This man operated a ferry across the Missouri River near the mouth of the

---

31. R. W. Cummins, *OIA, Fort Leavenworth Agency, 1824-1851, 1843-1848*, RG234, Microfilm roll 302, NARA.

32. Ray H. Mattison, "Kenneth McKenzie," in *The Mountain Men and the Fur Trade of the Far West*, ed. Hafen, 2: 218; Chittenden, *The American Fur Trade of the Far West*, 1: 326, 388.

33. "Clement Lessert notes," Fur Trade Biographies, Chouteau's (Biographical) Scrapbook [17.2], (KC395), WHMC-KC.

Gains and Losses: A Balance Sheet

Kansas River.[34] Chalifoux (Shallford) is a variant reading of this almost illegible word. A Marie Louise Chalifoux was married to Joseph Roy (Roi). The Roys were great river men and perhaps a Chalifoux in-law carried the letter to St. Louis. Francois Chouteau had a vast acquaintance along the Kansas and Missouri rivers and down into Osage country: trappers, traders, government officials, military men, Indians, settlers, merchants, and river men. This network also stretched eastward into western Illinois. Chouteau could and did call on any one of them to carry a letter or do other favors for him, as he frequently did for them.

River of Kansas   September 24, 1829[35]

Cher oncle,

I write a few lines to you through Calais[?] who is going to St. Louis. I paid the Weas and the Piankeshaws the sum that came back to them from their annuities indicated in the letters that you wrote to them. The Peorias are awaiting the flatboat to bring what is coming to them. I sold the goods a bit higher than you had marked it to give them. I will endeavor to keep it the same. Otherwise, I will give them at the going price as indicated. There are 1000 dollars to be paid to the Shawnee in merchandise towards the money that the agent [Vashon] brought in for them. I will endeavor to please them all, if I am able. I am told that Captain Vashon is a very difficult man. He is held in esteem by no one here from what people tell me. He said to an Indian that up unto the present, we have always cheated them, but that things will not be the same with him. He said he was certain to lead all the Loups here in the same way. I was so informed by Campbell. Perhaps he does not always tell the truth. I extended credit to almost all the village of the Kansa. I believe they will have a successful hunt. The credits that I have extended to the Kansa consist in gunpowder and bullets, and no merchandise. The Shawnee are frankly real rascals who have come to buy on "charge account" with us, and who take their money, their fine pelts to Independence, so as not to pay their credits. The Kansas River is very low. I do not know how to carry the merchandise into the village of the Kansa. However, I have to find a means. I have repaired the building that the [American Fur] company has purchased from Mme. Vasques and put everything in order. It is a very nice place to store things but I have been informed that a man from here has purchased the land. If that is so, he will claim the building along with the rest. Nothing more to tell you for the time being. I took the merchandise from Gilliss. I do not have a bill, but I think that Meyers gave it to you. I left with papa the receipt of the money that I gave to Loret for you. Cyprien arrived the 23rd with all his horses in good condition.

We are all in pretty good health and I hope that it is the same for you and your family, too. We are satisfied with our situation here and we would be happy if we had our dear little Morgan that we cannot forget. Gesseau goes to school in Independence at Mr. Dogles.

---

34. "Calise Montordeau notes," Chouteau's (Biographical) Scrapbook [17.2], (KC395), WHMC-KC.
35. *PMC*, Letter 303. Envelope: [To] Monsieur Pierre Menard Sr., Kaskaskia, Illinois; [filing note] Francois Chouteau, 24 Sept. 1829.

Berenice joins me to assure you, as well as my aunt and all the family of our sincere affection.

I am with respect,
Your nephew,
Francois Chouteau

Chouteau's letter to Pierre Menard contained basically the same information that he had written to Cadet on that same day, with the additional news that William Gilliss had left merchandise with him, Francois. This, as previously pointed out, was merchandise Menard had supplied on consignment for Gilliss to sell at his post on the James River near the Delawares. Inasmuch as Gilliss was establishing himself as an independent trader in his new location at the Kansas and Missouri rivers, he returned the Menard and Valle goods to Chouteau, who was still associated with Menard.

The Vasquez house mentioned in the preceding and later letters, was "a good-sized comfortable sort of building...[that] stood on the south bank of the Missouri just below the mouth of the Kaw, probably at what is now the foot of Gillis Street in Kansas City [Missouri]."[36] Francois had built the structure for Baronet Vasquez to serve as his home, as well as the subagency for the Kansa Nation. Whether it had survived the flood of 1826 or was not constructed until afterwards is not clear. Frederick Chouteau, however, remembered that Vasquez was at Randolph at his brothers' post.[37]

When Vasquez had contracted for the house to be built, he probably did not register or enter a claim for title of the land, but merely settled there and built what he needed – a common practice at the time. After Vasquez's death, his widow sold the building(s) to the American Fur Company, but she had no right to sell the land. In any event, Francois reported that the Vasquez place would serve as a good warehouse, and in his letter of November 3, 1829, indicated that he and his family lived there during the winter of that year. However, the preceding letter reported that the land on which the house stood had been purchased by someone who would undoubtedly claim the building when he took possession of the land.

Frederick Chouteau, in his 1880 reminiscences, said that Francois had, in 1828, built a house for his family on the south side of the Missouri River. This was to replace the dwelling destroyed by the flood of 1826. Perhaps Frederick meant that the house was started in 1828 but not necessarily finished in that year. When the preceding letter was written, the new house may not have been livable. This would account for the Chouteau family spending the winter of 1829 in the Vasquez house. Francois and his family were certainly living in the new house at the Chouteau farm by the time their first daughter, Mary Brigitte, was born in 1835, as her birth was registered as taking place in Jackson County at the Chouteau farm.

In his personal closing, Francois provided a rare glimpse into his home. He and Berenice and their three sons were comfortable and healthy, housed securely and warmly as the winter approached. Their food storage bins were filled with harvest enough for all their household. Berenice, perhaps, sat in a rocking chair before the fireplace, lulling baby Benjamin to sleep while Edmond and Pierre Menard played on the floor. And they would all have been happy, as Francois wrote, except that they could not forget their "dear little Morgan." It is interesting that Francois expressed this heartfelt sentiment to Pierre Menard, not to his brother Cadet.

---

36. Garraghan, *Catholic Beginnings in Kansas City, Missouri*, 28.
37. "Reminiscences of Fredrick Chouteau," *Kansas Historical Collection* 8: 423.

"Dear little Morgan" must have been Francois and Berenice's two-and-one-half-year-old son, Louis Sylvestre, who had died in St. Louis the previous July. Given the French penchant for nicknames, the Chouteaus may have called the child "Morgan" in honor of Daniel Morgan Boone, son of Daniel Boone. From 1827 to 1831, Daniel Morgan Boone was agriculturist for the Kansa Indians. Francois, being so closely associated with the Kansas, would have known Boone well. That the Chouteaus and the Boones had a close relationship was documented by the baptismal records of Father Benedict Roux, the first Catholic pastor of present Kansas City. In 1834, Berenice was godmother to Elizabeth Boone, grandchild of Daniel Morgan Boone. In 1835, Francois and Berenice's young son Benjamin was godfather to Eulalia Boone, another grandchild of Daniel Morgan Boone.

"Gesseau," who was going to school in Independence, was Edmond Francois, the eldest son of Francois and Berenice. Francois's middle name, "Gesseau" (Gesso) was Edmond's nickname, not a given name.

The "Dogles" (Douglas) school must have been a subscription school since there were then no public or church-sponsored schools in Independence. A Mr. Thomas Douglas was a trustee at the Six Mile Academy near Independence in 1841, and possibly, at this earlier date, he was conducting the school mentioned here.[38]

Subscription schools were private institutions financially dependent on the families of the students. Sometimes a group of families banded together to hire a teacher and provide a space for the school. At other times, a teacher came into the district, established himself (never herself, at that time) in a school, and solicited students.

The following letter sent word to Cadet that the barge his workers had loaded and launched from St. Louis had arrived at Chouteau's Landing. No doubt it was greeted by a throng of eager customers, anxious to see what the barge had carried up the river to them.

River of Kansas October 15, 1829 [39]

Cher frere,

Chartran has just arrived with the barge in fairly good condition. It should have been keeled before leaving as it is an old barge and always ships water. I will try to fix it.

I have drawn an order against you in favor of James Aul [sic] of Liberty for a hundred thirty three dollars for some powder and lead which I bought from him. I did not think that we would have run out of these articles in view of the quantity that was left at the trading post. Perhaps I still will have to buy more.

The Kansa, Peoria, Weas, and Piankeshaw are very well equipped for the hunt and have all left. Only the Shawnee remain who have not left yet. I will try to pay them their thousand dollars annuity as soon as the agent [Vashon] gets here. He has returned from the White River with six Loups whom he took to see the area which they are to occupy.

I saw Mr. Owens and I spoke to him about your claim against Vasquez. He tells me that he will write to you on this subject, so that you may send him the substantiated accounts as proof because of the formalities which the court requires. I gave Chartran a rough plan and a canoe which he will give you.

---

38. *History of Jackson County* (1881), 231.
39. Francois Chouteau to Pierre (Cadet) Chouteau Jr., October 15, 1829, *Chouteau Family Collections*, MHS. No envelope.

Give papa our best compliments and receive our kindest regards.

F. Chouteau

The Kansas River is very low. We will have trouble in getting the barge and the merchandise to their destination, that is, to the village of the Kansa.

The man to whom Cadet had entrusted the barge may have been a St. Louis resident at that time. There were also Chartrans in St. Charles and Kaskaskia, including Joseph Chartran (Chardon) who traded in the Upper Missouri.[40] Apparently Chartran was skilled enough to bring a leaky boat up from St. Louis, but Francois was quick to point out to Cadet that the vessel should have been repaired in St. Louis. He did not say so, but in St. Louis there were skilled workmen and plentiful materials, whereas both were in short supply around Chouteau's Landing.

Francois kept the barge, so Chartran was returning to St. Louis in a canoe that he was to give to Cadet, along with a "rough plan" that was probably an estimated inventory of the American Fur Company goods for which the Vasquez estate was liable. Francois was in western Missouri in November 1828, a little over two months after Vasquez died, so he may have had some knowledge of what Vasquez had. In fact, he probably supplied the annuity merchandise to Vasquez. The list Francois compiled would be compared to Cadet's records, and from the two, Cadet would produce the document needed by the Jackson County Probate Court.

Samuel Owens, to whom Chouteau had spoken, was the first clerk of Jackson County. During the raucous trailhead days in Independence, Owens was a well-known figure. In addition to his position in city government, he was a prominent businessman. Owens purchased one of the original lots sold in 1827 by Independence, and was also one of that city's first merchants. Owens supplied merchandise to the Kansa Agency in 1832-1833 when Marston Clark was subagent there.[41] Owens, like Francois Chouteau, was often called upon to deal with documents and financial matters, as there were no professionals available for these tasks. Owens later was one of the fourteen members of the Town Company for the Town of Kansas.

The patchwork financial system was in use again as Chouteau wrote that he had "drawn an order against you in favor of James Aull of Liberty...." In other words, he had written a "check" against Cadet's business account to James Aull for $133.00 to pay for gunpowder and lead. The next time someone from the Aull company was in St. Louis, he would collect either money or merchandise from Cadet in the amount cited.

Although the American Fur Company steamboats made frequent trips to Chouteau's Landing, sometimes Francois used independent freighters such as the Aull brothers. A letter dated October 5, 1833, from the Aull enterprise's manager, Samuel Owens, to Cadet Chouteau

---

40. The Chartran or Chartrand family in Missouri (including Joseph, Amable, and Thomas) was originally from Canada, moved to Kaskaskia, and then to St. Louis and St Charles. (Louis Houck, *History of Missouri*, 2: 22, 54, 55, 66, 92, 96, 199); A Joseph Chartran was an employee of B. Pratte & Company in 1826. Chartran joined Joseph Nicollet's 1839 expedition to the Upper Missouri which, among others, included John Fremont, Charles Geyer, Etienne Provost, and Jacques Fournaise ("Old Pino"). (Edmund C. Bray, and Martha Coleman Bray, eds. *Joseph Nicollet on the Plains and Prairies: the Expeditions of 1838-1839 with Journals, Letters, and Notes on the Dakota Indians*, 28.)

41. *H. Doc. No. 490*, 23rd Cong. 1st sess. (Serial 259): 75.

documented the shipment of a sum of money from Francois Chouteau via J & R Aull on the steamboat *John Nelson*.[42]

The Aull brothers, John, James, and Robert, were freighters on the Missouri River during the 1830s and 1840s, reaping fortunes from the expanding demand to move cargo from St. Louis to western Missouri that was being created by the steady influx of new settlers. James Aull, like Samuel Owens, bought one of the first lots sold in Independence. The brothers operated stores in Liberty, Independence, Richmond, and Lexington, their original location. In the late 1840s, John and Robert Aull owned a mill on the Little Blue River. John Calvin McCoy stated that James Aull and Samuel Owens sought protection during an overland journey to Santa Fe by joining Alexander Doniphan's regiment en route to Mexico, and that Owens was killed on Christmas Day in 1846 by the first volley of Mexican fire in the battle on the plains of Sacramento, a short distance from Chihuahua. A few months later his partner James Aull was robbed and murdered by bandits in his store in Chihuahua.[43] However, Susan Magoffin, telling substantially the same story in her diary, confirms February 28, 1847, as the date of the three-and-one-half-hour battle.[44] Writing to *Cher Oncle* on November 3, 1829, Chouteau's first topic was the whereabouts of "our Indians," the Kansas, Shawnees, Weas, Piankeshaws, and Peorias.

River of Kansas   November 3, 1829[45]

Cher oncle,

Our Indians at the time being are all well outfitted for their hunt and have almost all left. The Shawnee told me that they will be hunting no longer than a month. The Kansa will not return until around Christmas. I have paid the Shawnee the 1000 dollars of the annuities and Captain Vashon returned the money to me. I had lent him 300 and he gave me an order on General [William] Clark and told me he would need more. I paid the Shawnee 80 after having been much pestered by Cornstok and Perri. They claimed 40 pairs of blankets from their annuities of last year. If Chaine [Shane] had not pushed them to ask that, they would not have done it. But he told them before me and Vashon that you had told them it was your intention to give the 80 and that he was making himself responsible for what he was telling me. The Weas, Piankeshaw, and Peoria have been paid. Afterwards, I paid according to the requirement of Captain Vashon 70 dollars to Andre and to Madeline – 40 to the first and 30 to his wife. Campbell tells me that is their part of annuities. I was unable to obtain a license to trade at the Marais de Cygne. Captain Vashon tells me that he is unable to give a license for the Weas, Peoria and Piankeshaw because these Indians will not go to take possession of their lands. And that

---

42. Samuel C. Owens to Pierre (Cadet) Chouteau Jr., October 5, 1833, *Chouteau Family Collections*, MHS.

43. John C. McCoy Scrapbook, 127, (KC296), WHMC-KC; An entry on the inside cover of one of his company's account books states, "James Aull was killed in Chihuahua on the 23rd June 1847 at night by four Spaniards and robbed of about $5,000." (Daybook, 1840-1847 (v. 15), *Aull Family Business Records, 1830-1862* (C3038), Western Historical Manuscript Collection-Columbia).

44. Stella M. Drumm, "Down the Santa Fe Trail and into Mexico: the Diary of Susan Shelby Magoffin, 1846-1847," 220-222.

45. *PMC*, Letter 307. Envelope: [To] Monsieur Pierre Menard, Kaskaskia, State of Illinois; [from] Independence, Nov. 12, 1829; [postage] 18 3/4; [filing note] Francois Chouteau, November 3, 1829.

it is uncertain whether they will establish residence at that place. So upon seeing that, I thought it would be preferable to retain Meyers with us as he knows these Indians pretty well and we do not know them. He could draw up a treaty with them at the post and assist us with the other treaties as I presume that they will come out to here. I am giving him 300 for this year to negotiate when it is necessary. I thought it would be difficult to send him away after having come from so far. And as recommended by you, I believe he is a young man, very honest and who will not get in our hair here. I have to oversee everything. I am not for long at the same place. Tomorrow I leave to go to the village of the Kansa to take the necessary merchandise for the post and to repair the buildings that are in bad condition. The river is very low and my intention is to draw up the boat in order to avoid the trouble of doing so this spring. Because as soon as the river is open, the barge can take down the fur pelts. Berenice will spend this winter at the house of Baronet that I set up nicely and in the spring I propose to move from that place as it is unhealthy, however, we have not been ill. The old General Clark, agent for the Kansa, is a fine man I believe. He gave me all the offers in his power. I hold him in high esteem. I found Captain Vashon much better than people had presented him, although he is a bit too talkative – freely at times. I had the occasion to tell him my opinion in the same way as at the trading post. And we are good friends. I only wish for that. I have no other news for now. An Osage, one of my friends, came to find me in order that I might send merchandise to the Marais de Cygne. One also came who said to me they will come again to trade after the hunt. I invited the Osage to come to the post to discuss it, not being able to send the merchandise to them.

Berenice joins me in sending you, as well my aunt, our sincere affection.

I am with respect,
your nephew,
Francois Chouteau

By Loret I sent to Valle 30 dollars – that is to say, he must have given it to Raphael for Valle. I beg of you to find out if he has received it.

The Kansas River is very low. We will have trouble in getting the barge and merchandise to their destination, that is to the village of the Kansa.

From among the crowd of new faces in Indian Territory, names and personalities began to emerge and were duly mentioned in Chouteau's letters. Cornstok (Cornstock) and Perri (William Perry) were Shawnee chiefs who had arrived in Indian Territory (Kansas) by 1828.[46] Another prominent Shawnee chief was the "old prophet" Tenskwatwa, the brother of Tecumseh. In 1832, another group of Ohio Shawnees came to Indian Territory. Among them was Chief John Perry, the brother of Chief William Perry, and also a chief named Peter Cornstock – Chouteau's "Cornstok," referred to in the preceding letter, who had probably returned to Ohio to assist another group of his people in their migration to Indian Territory.[47]

Andre and Madeline, who received individual annuity payments, were apparently Shawnee Indians, as the government officials mentioned were associated with the Shawnees

---

46. McDermott, "Isaac McCoy's second exploratory trip in 1828," *Kansas Historical Quarterly* 13: 442.
47. Barry, *Beginning of the West*, 223.

– George Vashon as agent and John Campbell who, as subagent, was living on the Shawnee preserve.

The note on the bottom of the letter regarding the thirty dollars sent to Valle via Loret (who remains unidentified) made reference to Widen. This was Raphael Widen, Pierre Menard's right-hand man and the "Mr. Raphael" who, in her letter of April 18, 1827, Berenice hoped would instruct Charles Chouteau "how to behave in the store," when that young man moved to Kaskaskia from his father's house in St. Louis. Raphael Widen spoke and wrote both English and French, and took over business affairs for Pierre Menard when he was absent from Kaskaskia.

A second note pointed out that the Kansas River was quite low. In the letter itself, Francois had written that he would "draw up the barge," meaning that, as there was so little water, the boat or barge would be dragged by ropes looped around trees on shore, and pulled every inch of the way. Chouteau always wrote "I," which conveys the image of Francois himself performing these Herculean tasks. The fact was that he had a crew of several men who were doing this manual labor, with possibly an occasional helping hand from Francois. Chouteau's role was to supervise, shout encouragement and perhaps threats, and take on all the worries of the low-water voyage.

The preceding and following letters were primarily business correspondence and were, therefore, filed for future reference. The letters kept by the St. Louis Chouteaus and now found in the Chouteau Collections typically have no envelope, while those in the Menard collections usually do have envelopes. The Menards were confirmed savers. They meticulously recorded correspondence in letter books; the microfilms of various Menard papers contain reproductions of lists on torn scraps of paper, notes written on used envelopes, and the like. Paper was expensive and they valued it, but the real reason for keeping every written letter, note, or scrap that came into the Menard establishment was that any or all of it might be needed in future court actions.

Perhaps one cold and rainy November day followed another and provided Francois the opportunity to catch up on his correspondence. The day after he had written to Pierre Menard, Francois wrote to Cadet a letter containing much of the same information.

River of Kansas   November 4, 1829 [48]

Cher frere,

All the Indians of this post have left for the hunt. There should be a good deal of furs because they are well outfitted for that. I leave tomorrow to go to the Kansa post to take the necessary merchandise for the trade and to repair our houses which are in bad shape. I can't predict when I shall return from that place as I am the one who gave credit to the greater part of the Kansa and I must be there. I paid the thousand dollars annuity to the Shawnee – and received the money. I lent three hundred to Captain Vashon. He gave me an order on General Clark which I will send you at the first opportunity. He told me that he would still need from four or five hundred. I will give it to him and I will send you the drafts. I presume that Mr. Owens will have written to you concerning the Baronet's business. He promised me he would do it – I have not been able to obtain a license for the Marais de Cygne, that is, for trading with the Weas, Piankeshaws, and

---

48. Francois Chouteau to Pierre (Cadet) Chouteau Jr., November 4, 1829, *Chouteau Family Collections*, MHS. No envelope.

Peorias. Captain Vashon tells me that he cannot do it because these Indians will not take possession of their land. The Osages have also come to see me in order to get merchandise. There are thirty to forty lodges on the Marais des Cygne. I think that a few lodges will come to trade at the post – some Sacs came to trade for powder and lead. They tell me that they will come to see us when the hunt will be finished as I suppose some Kansa will go to trade at the Black Snake. I fear that they will take my credits over there – but I will do everything to prevent them from it.

The horses which Cyprien brought are at present in good condition, but we have a great deal of trouble in getting them together because of the wild horses which sweep them off in every direction. If the Kansa go hunting, I believe that we shall sell them well. Baronet's settlement is at present in good order, as well as that of the Shawnee which I put in good condition. I don't think I will have returned from my voyage to the Kansa before the month of January. In that case I will write to you upon my return, the result of the autumn trade, etc. – We are all in pretty good health. Berenice as well as I send you our sincere friendship.

Your affectionate brother
Fcois Chouteau

 Regards to papa for us.

Although each nation had its assigned trader, the Indians were curious about merchandise and prices offered at other trading posts. Hence, the Osages from south of the Marais des Cygne came to Chouteau's establishment at Kansas City. (North of the Marais des Cygne were the Weas, Piankeshaws, Peorias, and Kaskaskias.) The Osages were attracted by the presence of their longtime friend Francois Chouteau, and hoped to do business with him. Perhaps they thought he would give them a better deal than they were offered at their post, operated by Francois's half-brother, Paul Liguest Chouteau.

The Sacs and the Foxes also came, although Joseph Robidoux at Black Snake Creek (present St. Joseph) was their trader. By the same token, the Kansa, though the Chouteaus were their assigned traders, often decided to check out the competition at the Robidoux post. The Shawnees sometimes bypassed their designated post and took their cash to Independence.

As Francois wrote the following letter, he and Berenice were at home in the Vasquez residence. Adjacent to the house were other structures that he used for storage and probably the cabins of workers and other settlers – hence the reference to a "settlement." The location may have been low and damp, a situation considered unhealthy, even if not associated with the mosquitoes bred there.

Village of the Kansa December 12, 1829 [49]

Cher frere,

 I write by Clement who is going to St. Louis. I have been here for a month. I have given a lot of credit to the Kansa and I am remaining here to recover it. If I am paid we

---

49. Francois Chouteau to Pierre (Cadet) Chouteau Jr., December 12, 1829, *Chouteau Family Collections*, MHS. No envelope.

will do fairly good business at this post as, according to the information which I have been able to get, they have lots of furs and I have no doubt that we are going to pay the annuities this time. I have already spoken to the chiefs on this subject and I propose to speak of it again when they are all assembled and I will send you a memorandum of the merchandise which will be necessary for that, etc. I get along very well with the old agent here but he is going to St. Louis. I would have preferred that he not go, but that won't make any difference. Try to make his acquaintance. He is a good old fellow. He is a novice at all business affairs. If the chiefs tell him that they wish me to pay the annuities he will consent. I believe that it would be wiser for you to make arrangements with the steamboat Duncan to take down the deerskins. It will probably come up early in the spring. As the barge is old and worthless, it is better for it to remain here. It is all we need to travel on the Kansas River. We always are needing it to carry merchandise to the post. Clement will see you. I presume that you will let him know where the treasure has passed that he had confided to you. He has no money at present. On the contrary, he owes a lot, but I am sure that he will pay well. He is mixed up with a card player but he tells me that he is certain that you are fair. He is a good young man. He will immediately understand what you will say to him on this subject. I will try to have his orders when his debts are paid. He gave me two orders on you, one for 82 or [8]3, and the other for 25. The latter he owed me personally. You could not have paid him for me. Please write to me. You will know by my next letter the result of the autumn trade and I will send you a memorandum of the articles that you must send early in the spring, as I believe that we shall lack merchandise for the other trade. The payment for the annuities that [we] made has made us very short. I did not expect that when I left St. Louis, we needed more blankets and other articles.

We are all in good health and I hope that it is the same with you and your family.

Your affectionate brother Francois

The Chouteau post for the Kansa Nation, as noted, was then at Horseshoe Lake, about seven miles west of present Lawrence on the Kansas River. Ordinarily, in the winter months there would be no opportunity to send a letter from that location to St. Louis, and Francois had indicated in his previous letter to Cadet that he would not be able to communicate again until he returned from Indian Territory. However, he had a bit of luck. Clement Lessert, interpreter at the Kansa Agency, happened to be at the Kansa Post and was soon to travel to St. Louis. Possibly the winter had been mild, in which case Lessert canoed down on the Missouri River, but more than likely he was forced to travel by horseback over the rough and frozen trail alongside the river. At any rate, he became Francois's courier.

Chouteau's explanation about Lessert's finances and his defense of the young man are somewhat unclear; "where the treasure has passed that he confided to you" can be read as "what happened to the money that he gave you." That Lessert had a gambling habit was divulged using the French phrase *embrouillie pour un cartier*. Literally, this translates as "a maker of cards," but the meaning is "a card player."

Because communication was slow and uncertain, Francois continuously tried to schedule shipments of furs and merchandise well in advance of the need. In the preceding letter, he wanted the deerskins to be taken to St. Louis in the spring by the steamboat *William D. Duncan*, a side-wheeler that began regular voyages between St. Louis and Franklin, Missouri, in April 1829. This ushered in the era of regular steamboat travel on the Missouri River.[50] By the spring of 1830, the *Duncan* was apparently coming up at least as far as Chouteau's Kansas City warehouse.

At this point, Chouteau still had a good rapport with Marston Clark, the "old agent" who was, in reality, the Kansa subagent, appointed in March 1829. As previously mentioned, the subagent of the Kansa Nation reported directly to Superintendent William Clark rather than to the agent of that region – in this case, John Dougherty at Fort Leavenworth. Hence, it seemed that the Kansa subagent was his own boss, since he answered to no one on the frontier. On the other hand, Campbell, subagent of the Shawnees, answered to Agent George Vashon who was frequently in the area.

The trip Marston Clark was making to St. Louis alerted Chouteau's business instinct; he knew not why, but it made him uneasy. To forestall any problem, Francois encouraged Cadet to make Clark's acquaintance and treat him to a little of the Chouteau charm. Clark apparently went to St. Louis to price merchandise; he was developing ideas of his own about how annuity goods should be handled. Perhaps Clark was not really such "a novice at all business affairs" as Francois supposed.

As the decade of the 1820s drew to a close, Francois may have taken stock of the past ten years. In the business world, despite many reversals, Francois Chouteau was at the top of the fur trade in western Missouri. He had helped two of his younger brothers, Cyprien and Frederick, get started at outposts that would eventually become their own. But it was never easy. Francois had seen his thriving Randolph Bluffs post crushed to matchsticks and sent swirling down the Missouri River. During 1829, he had lost the keelboat *Beaver* in the Missouri River, with three persons drowned. The fur cargo had been lost and then recovered. Other developments were not catastrophic, but were constant irritations: the infringing traders, problems with the government regulations, and difficulties collecting debts.

In his personal life there were also losses and gains. He and Berenice were comfortably established in their wilderness home. They had three sons who seemed destined to survive. But they had lost two small boys and buried them in St. Louis, one of whom, "our dear little Morgan," they could not forget. Francois had also lost his mother, Brigitte Saucier Chouteau, who had recently died.

Although rapid political and social change was taking place on the western frontier, Francois's major concerns were still the fur trade, the Indians, and government officials, over and above the constant worry about health, the weather, and all the unpredictable elements of pioneer living. Would there be so little snow that the Kansas River would have insufficient water for barge travel? Would the Indians remain healthy and eager to go hunting? And in far-off Europe, would the fashion of wearing beaver hats stay in vogue, thus sustaining the demand for beaver pelts? As 1829 ended, events over which Chouteau had no control were changing his life and the character of western Missouri.

---

50. Louise Barry, "William Clark's Diary, May 1826-February 1831," *Kansas Historical Quarterly* 16: 284, 285; Barry, *Beginning of the West*, 158.

"*Free hunter*," drawn by Nicolas Point, S.J., Folder 4, *Pierre Jean De Smet (1801-1873) Papers*, Manuscripts, Archives, and Special Collections, Washington State University Libraries.

4   New Faces on the Frontier

    New people, new technology, new businesses were all rushing into western Missouri as the 1830s began. The frontier population was no longer predominantly French. Americans of British and Irish descent were streaming into the area. Immigrant Indian tribes from east of the Mississippi were settling onto their lands, much to the discomfort of the resident Kansa and Osage nations. Steamboats were becoming commonplace on the Missouri River, changing the way a manager like Francois Chouteau conducted his business.
    Superficially, the fur trade seemed healthy. It was the major industry in the valley of the Missouri and Kansas rivers. Indian, French, and American hunters and trappers carried their pelts from the Upper Missouri, the Rocky Mountains, the plains of Kansas, and parts of Missouri to Chouteau's warehouse, where the furs were inspected and sorted, repacked, and shipped to St. Louis.
    In fact, however, the fur trade was already in decline. The century-long harvest of fur-bearing animals had thinned their ranks and hunters were obliged to go farther and work harder. Competition for the pelts was becoming intense. From his vantage point, Francois Chouteau must have seen this development for he increasingly spread out his resources. From the earliest days of government land sales, Chouteau had purchased (patented, entered)

large tracts of land in the area that became Kansas City. As the fur trade became a less reliable source of income, Francois increased his investment of effort and capital in building up his farm in the East Bottoms.

By the beginning of the 1830s, according to John Calvin McCoy, Francois was developing his farm "with costly buildings about one mile below the city upon what is now known as the Guinotte tract [East Bottoms]. He owned about 1200 acres and the only warehouse and steamboat landing up to 1839 between Wayne City and Fort Leavenworth."[1]

During the mid-1830s, after all the government land had been sold, Chouteau sold some of his acreage and bought other plots. In addition, he was increasingly involved in financial transactions. His letters suggest that, had he lived longer, he might have gone into banking, as lending and collecting money began to occupy a great deal of his time.

Francois wrote the following letter from the comfort of his Kansas City home, after spending long weeks at the Kansa Post.

River of Kansas   February 15, 1830[2]

Cher oncle,

I have not written to you for some time because of my absence from home. I have returned from among the Kansa only a few days ago. I have almost always remained at the post because I saw that there we would bring in more pelts. I was not mistaken in my calculation. I have put up here 150 packs of handsome deerskins, 20 bundles of good raccoons, 3 bundles of beaver, and 350 otter of the first quality. The Shawnee: 50 packs of deerskin, 5 of raccoons, 100 beaver, and 150 of otter. The Kansa have pretty well paid their credits and owe us about 300 dollars. I suppose they will have a good enough hunt, all being in a good mood for that. They have in mind to go to the branches of the Kansas River and they tell me that there is still a lot of beaver. I presume that we will also pay them the annuities this year. I wrote to Cadet for the necessary merchandise and I hope he will send them as soon as possible. I spoke with the different chiefs of the nations. They all agree to receive their annuities from me, saying to me that our merchandise is infinitely superior to that they were given last year for their annuities. They are still displeased regarding the payment. We presume that Mr. [Marston] Clark, the agent, had made some arrangements in St. Louis for this business. In any case, if I receive the merchandise that I'm asking for on time, I will be finished with it. I have sent to Cadet the receipts of the annuities paid to the Peorias, Weas, and Piankeshaws as well as two drafts of Captain Vashon on General [William] Clark for the money that I sent to him. Charles Chaine [Shane] has changed the horse that you lent him to come here, and he gave to me an old one in its place. I sold it recently to the Kansa. I think he must have come out ahead. About the merchandise that Gilliss left here – there were 140 dollars taken off his order. The rest I had sent to the trading post and clumsily, we used it before taking inventory. So that I do not know the sum total of what remained. We have a lot of merchandise left over. What I'm asking of Cadet is to bring those we have left over,

---

1. John C. McCoy Scrapbook, 3, (KC296), WHMC-KC.
2. *PMC*, Letter 317. Envelope: [To] Pierre Menard, Kaskaskia, Illinois; [from] Independence, Mo., Feb. 20; [postage] 18 3/4.

then we would have a nice assortment. In the fall we will see again what we will need for the trade as well as for the annuities. We also have left fourteen horses that I expect to sell this spring.

Berenice joins me to wish you as well as my aunt good health and all the possible happiness. Give our love to Peter Menard and Francis.

I am respectfully your affectionate nephew,
Francois Chouteau

While Francois's letters rarely mentioned anyone in his household other than Berenice or the children, several other persons lived there. The 1830 U.S. census for Missouri listed the members of the Chouteau household: 1 male, age 1-5 (Benjamin, age 2); 1 male, age 5-10 (Pierre Menard, age 8); 1 male, age 30-40 (Francois, age 33); 1 female, age 1-5 (who?); 1 female, age 20-30 (Berenice, age 29). Slaves: 1 male, age 36-55; 1 female, age 1-10; 1 female, age 24-36.

The listing for "male, age 5-10" should have listed two boys, Edmond, then nine years old, as well as Pierre Menard. However, Edmond was not included because he was not at home. Edmond had been sent to St. Louis for schooling (more about this later). The female child, age 1-5, may have been one of the many frontier girls who grew up in Berenice's care. The female slave child under the age of ten was probably the child of the female slave whose age was listed as "24-36."

"Pay the annuities," as has been pointed out, was Chouteau's way of saying that he would supply merchandise that the Indians would receive instead of cash for their annuities. The government would then pay Chouteau for the merchandise. New Kansa subagent Marston Clark called this arrangement into question and started to make difficulties for the Chouteaus' trade with the Kansa Indians. Francois was beginning to recognize this, as shown in the preceding letter. He spoke to the Kansa chiefs and they agreed to take their annuity merchandise from him. In the previous annuity payment, Marston Clark had managed to "pay" the annuity merchandise to the Indians while Francois was not on the scene. (Chouteau expressed his indignation about this in a letter to Cadet, September 24, 1829.)

Charles Shane was the son of Anthony Shane, government interpreter and a self-employed trading post operator. Charles apparently borrowed a horse from Pierre Menard so that he could get back to his father's house in Indian Territory (Kansas) without waiting for the navigation season to open. (George Vashon, as previously noted, recommended that the government pay for the education of Charles Shane as a bonus to Anthony Shane for his services.)

River of Kansas   April 22, 1830[3]

Cher oncle,

It's true, there was a bit of negligence on my part for not having written to you more often, although I have almost always been absent from home and also because of the lack of postal delivery days. However, I am here since three weeks. At this time we have almost finished our treaty. The Kansa, as well as the Shawnee, have all come back from the hunt and you will see the good results of our treaty: there are 236 bundles of deer

---

3. PMC, Letter 323. Envelope: [To] Monsieur Pierre Menard, Kaskaskia, State of Illinois; [from] Independence, Mo., May 1; [postage] 25; [filing note] Francois Chouteau, 22 April 1830.

skins, the weight will be roughly 25,000 lbs.; 50 packs of raccoons containing 100 skins in a pack; about 500 beaver skins, 800 otter, 500 [musk]rats, and 2 bundles of bear skins. And really, these skins are superb. I sent a part of these bundles by barge and I put on board the steamboat Globe, 81 packs. And still about 40 remain. I did not dare to load the barge fully because it is not worth a thing. I am going to send the balance of the skins on the first safe occasion. We here bought some very nice beaver skins from the Loups by giving them a little money with the merchandise. I received by the Globe steamer merchandise that I'm applying to pay the annuities of the Kansa. The Indians who had learned of the arrival of the boat are all here at this time telling me that they will accept no other merchandise but mine. The agent [Subagent Marston Clark] [....] unhappy with them for that but they told him that last year they had received too little, and of too poor a quality. That it will not be that same way this time. At this moment I am having the merchandise taken to the trading post. I am going to unpack and let them see everything. I am sure they will be very satisfied. The agent told them that we had probably already bought their annuities in St. Louis. All the chiefs were on my side and no one on his side. In such a way that I believe that he is angry to see that the Indians are showing me consideration and confidence. And he would like [....] [....] all that would be for him alone. I saw Captain Vashon about Connor's order on Marshall's behalf. He informed me he would pay as soon as he has the money, that he is expecting it every day. And I told him that a draft on General Clark would be the same thing. But he said he had made a rule not to draw from the [government] funds before giving notice. As soon as he shall have paid, I will inform you.

We are all in good health. Our children are very well. Our little Benjamin walks all over and begins to speak French and English.

Berenice joins with me and wishes you as well to all your family, all possible happiness.

I am, with respect,
Your nephew
Francois Chouteau

Subagent Marston Clark's objection to the Chouteaus supplying annuity merchandise to the Kansa Indians created friction that was still heating up when this letter was written. Francois, with his valid trading license, battled to protect what he considered his right – to provide annuity merchandise for the Kansa Nation. Probably to his way of thinking, his longstanding Kansa trade license meant that neither agents nor other traders should be offering merchandise to "his" Indians. (He may have been remembering the old days of exclusive trade rights, such as his Uncle Auguste and his father, Pierre Chouteau, had enjoyed with the Osage Nation.) But the scene on the western frontier was changing. New settlers became merchants, opened stores in Independence, and came at the invitation of the Indian agent to offer their merchandise to the Indians.

On another topic, the Connor mentioned in this and later letters was Jim Connor, a Delaware Indian and an interpreter for the Delawares from 1828 to 1833.[4] At the time of this

---

4. "United States Indian Agencies Affecting Kansas," *Kansas Historical Collection* 16: 724-726.

letter, Connor was trying to secure government money to pay William Marshall, who with William Gilliss, had been a trader in the central Ozarks when the Delawares lived there. Connor figured as a robbery victim, as recounted in a letter from Francois's half-brother, Paul Liguest Chouteau, subagent of the Osage Agency. The following letter to Francois Chouteau was dated April 30, 1831:

> *Dear Brother, The Little Osages have stolen some beaver, otter, etc. from some Delawares immigrating to Kansas River. I have paid them here all the money I had and have been compelled to give Jim Connor, one of them, an order on you for Fifty Five dollars and also an order on you in favor of Nee-te-me-threen (a Delaware Indian) for Ninety five dollars. You will be sure to find out if the last named one presents the order himself as I have sent it to him and they may attempt to cheat him. Arrange with them for money or goods as you can, and charge me. P. L. Chouteau*[5]

In 1836, Connor's name appeared on the roster for the last time, as an interpreter at the North Agency, Western Territory.

In May 1830, Paul Liguest Chouteau was promoted from subagent to agent of the Osage Agency in present Neosho County, Kansas. In late July 1834, the position of agent of the Osages was discontinued, and Paul Liguest Chouteau accepted the position of subagent.[6]

Francois's next letter described, with increasingly heated rhetoric, the latest episodes in the dispute with Kansa subagent Marston Clark. Not everything that was happening, however, was revealed in Francois's letters. Subagent Clark set forth his complaints in a letter to Superintendent of Indian Affairs William Clark, in July 1830. He had reduced them to three: the methods used to purchase annuity merchandise, the location of the Kansa Post, and the excessive influence Francois Chouteau had with the Indians. Superintendent William Clark, in forwarding a copy of the letter to John Eaton, Secretary of War, wrote extensive comments that, while not rancorous, agreed with Marston Clark: "He [Agent Clark] complains, as most of the Agents do, of the interference of the Traders. I have for some time perceived that great efforts are made by some of the Traders (particularly those residing with annuity-receiving Tribes) to acquire influence over them; so much so as to induce the Indians to receive their goods at the highest prices."[7]

The debate over the annuity merchandise has been explored in connection with Francois's letter to Cadet Chouteau, dated September 24, 1829. Marston's second complaint was about the Chouteau post for the Kansa Indians. Clark maintained that the post was too close to the Kansa Agency that was located on the north bank of the Kansas River, between present Topeka and Lawrence. The site had been chosen in 1827 by Kansa leaders and the Kansa subagent at that time, Baronet Vasquez.

Frederick Chouteau, under the supervision of Francois, had apparently been using the old Four Houses as a Kansa Post until the autumn of 1829, when he, Francois, and Cyprien with their work crew, built a post on the south side of the Kansas River. This was at Horseshoe Lake, about a mile from the Kansa Agency, and on the opposite bank.[8] The trading license issued to the American Fur Company, that is, to Francois Chouteau, in October 1831, specified

---

5. Paul Liguest Chouteau to Francois Chouteau, April 30, 1831, *Chouteau Family Collections*, MHS.
6. Louise Barry, *Beginning of the West*, 272.
7. William Clark to John H. Eaton, Secretary of War, August 31, 1830, *OIA, St. Louis Superintendency*, 1829-1831, M234, Microfilm roll 749, Frame 1025-1033, NARA.
8. William E. Unrau, *The Kansa Indians*, 143-144.

a site for the Kansa Post "between the two upper villages of the Kanzas, on the Kanzas river."[9]

Frederick, however, tarried at his Horseshoe Lake location until 1832. The Chouteaus wanted their post where the Indians would come, and that meant near the Kansa Agency. Although the purpose of the Agency was to serve the Indians, Subagent Clark did not want the Indians to come to his Kansa Agency too frequently. In a letter to Francois, Clark objected to the proximity of the Kansa Post to the agency, claiming that it was "bringing down on this agency, large bodies of Indians to the great annoyance of the few whites at this place by killing their stock, crowding their houses and begging for provisions...."[10]

The third point, that of Chouteau's influence with the Indians, is too nebulous to merit discussion. Francois probably thought of that complaint as a compliment. In the final analysis, it was the assertions of the Clark cousins against the assertions of the Chouteau brothers, and both adversaries stood to gain financially by a clear-cut victory. If either Subagent Clark or Francois Chouteau could purchase the annuity merchandise at a low price, then convince the Indians to accept it at a higher price, the annuity money left after the merchandise cost was deducted could result in a tidy profit. It is interesting, however, that Clark did not make this an issue in his list of complaints. The truth of the matter must have been hard to come by, and in addition, the names of both combatants carried considerable weight in Washington. Probably no official wanted to be in the awkward position of supporting one against the other: Clark was the name of an American hero, and Chouteau was a name both influential and respected. The Chouteaus and the fur company were, as far as can be ascertained, never reprimanded or warned.

Nonetheless, this controversy was all very unsettling to Francois, as his agitated letters demonstrate. He could not always be at the Kansa Post, and he had to leave much to his twenty-year-old brother Frederick, who may not have been as judicious as Francois. Francois did his best to keep matters under control, as his letters document his constant visits to the Kansa Post and villages. For the most part, he held himself responsible for what went on there in his absence.

The disputes between government officials and the traders, with all their ramifications, contributed to general unrest in the Kansa Nation. By 1829, the Indians had deserted their one large village near the Big Blue River in Kansas and divided into three groups, each following the chief of its choice. Fool Chief's village was north of the Kansas River and six miles west of Soldier's Creek; Hard Chief's village was on high ground near the Kansas River, about seven miles west of Fool Chief. American Chief's village was located in the bottomland on the west side of Mission Creek west of Topeka.[11]

These villages were situated on the reservation set aside for the Kansa Indians in the Treaty of 1825. It was this treaty that introduced dissension among the Kansas, and ultimately resulted in the splintering of the nation. In the 1825 treaty, the Kansas ceded fifteen million acres in Missouri and Kansas in exchange for an annuity, various government assistance, and a reservation beginning sixty miles west of present Kansas City.

The Indians knew not what course to take: they were pushed by the traders to go hunting and pulled by the government to the farm fields. They undoubtedly preferred the hunt, with its instant rewards of excitement, plentiful meat, and pelts to trade for merchandise. Farming had always been considered "women's work," and the Kansa men may not have recognized its long-term benefits. The turmoil culminated in a murder, and the three chiefs

---

9. Marston Clark to William Clark, October 4, 1831, *SIA* (MC741), 6: 303, KSHS; *H. Doc. No. 104*, 22nd Cong. 2nd sess. (Serial 234).

10. Marston Clark to F.R Chouteau, December 20, 1831, *SIA* (MC741), 6: 413, KSHS.

11. Barry, *Beginning of the West*, 166-167.

accused of being involved broke away from the main tribe. A confrontation between the two groups seemed a prelude to civil war in the Kansa Nation. When the estranged group threatened unarmed warriors, women, and children, Marston Clark stepped in, and, according to his report to William Clark, put his life on the line and brought an end to the crisis.[12] Marston Clark tried to settle the blame for all of this squarely on the Chouteaus.

However distressing the local happenings, the most disruptive event in the lives of the Kansa Indians, beside which all others paled, was the displacement and confinement they experienced as they were forced onto a reservation by the influx of eastern immigrant Indians. The Kansa Indians, the wind people, had roamed at will, past where the eye could see, following the setting sun. Now they were told that they could only go so far and no farther. The newcomers, of course, could not be held responsible. They had been negotiated out of their lands, and had themselves been pushed out by others. The tragic sequence had been set into motion and was playing itself out on the plains of Indian Territory. The Kansa people were not alone in their misery, for it was shared almost equally by hundreds of their brother and sister Native Americans.

River of Kansas   June 6, 1830[13]

Cher oncle,

I received from Captain Vashon the money for Connor's order. I'm sending you 133 dollars. He [Vashon] paid to the Kickapoos 2000, that is to say, since there is only half of the Indians here, he paid them a thousand and gave me a thousand so that I might pay the band who is on the River of the Osage upon their arrival here. Out of the 2000 that he had paid, we received 500. And I presume that we will still have two or three hundred more. He sent for the Weas, the Peorias, and the Piankeshaws to pay them also. I will do all I can to catch all that I can; these three still have 365 coming to them. Captain Vashon will depart from here as soon as it is paid which will be about toward the 10th or 12th of the present. He carries with him 5500 for the annuities of the Loups and 1500 for those of the Weas who are down below. I will do everything in my power to have the larger amount of money to be paid here – although we are coming out of this pretty well. I've been told that Boggs is to bring two wagons of merchandise to Fish's village to try to attract a part of the annuities, but I will be on the lookout for him. There are three stores in Independence, and they all have a little Indian merchandise, but ours are infinitely superior. Then we have the competition of the whiskey that a great many of the local rascals among the inhabitants sell to the Indians at night and on the sly. The villages of the Kickapoo were drunk from the day they received their annuities. The agents were making a lot of noise about the principle of the whiskey, but now they say nothing because they almost got beat up for that. About the annuities of the Kansa, it is the greatest theft that one can ever see on the part of the Department at St. Louis. And the behavior of the second-in-command [Marston Clark] in that respect is no less knavish. The principal chiefs asked me last winter to make out a list of the merchandise

---

12. Marston G. Clark to William Clark, July 28, 1830, *OIA, St. Louis Superintendency, 1829-1831*, M234, Microfilm roll 749, Frame 1027-1033, NARA.

13. *PMC*, Letter 327. Envelope: [To] Pierre Menard, Kaskaskia, State of Illinois; [filing note] Franc. Chouteau, June 6, 1830.

for their annuities. I did so and forwarded it immediately to St. Louis. And I received everything I asked for. As I offered the merchandise at the St. Louis prices, the Indians were very pleased with the conditions. But Mr. Clark didn't want to accept the merchandise saying he was going to St. Louis to find a better deal. He was warned by the chiefs not to bring merchandise because they would not accept them. Finally he brought their annuities, trying to force them to accept whether they wanted or not. The Indians were outraged and said that they wanted their money to buy themselves that which they needed. We have about 1800 dollars of the one-half paid to the Kickapoo, Weas, Peorias and Piankeshaw. There were three stores represented at the agency the day of this payment and with us made four. I beg of you to please give me a word [let me say a word] *about a horse about which Cyprien* [Chouteau] *already has written to you. There is a woman here who gave a part of the money to Meyers and who will pay the balance on the arrival of the horse if you can take care of this. This is the second time I have written to Sarpy and to my brother about the little box for Meyers which is at Ste. Genevieve and which should arrive here. The steamboat has come twice and it was not sent. Meyers wrote to Felix Vallé to send it to Sarpy and he* [Meyers] *did not get an answer either. He sent a small memo for the medication and it was not sent either. From time to time he has fever. He is a charming young man, who works with all possible courage and who is very good with the Indians here. I desire that he be sent what he asks on the next delivery.*

We are in good enough health for the moment. Berenice joins me and wishes you as well as my aunt, all the possible happiness – and our affection to all your family –

I am with respect and gratitude –
your nephew,
Francois Chouteau

This letter was [....] [given?] *to Cyprien by the clerk of the J. B. Globe who had given a receipt for the money that he* [Cyprien?] *owed.*

				Handed	out	
17	May	[17?]	1 good one	1	1	
		19	11 ditto	6	5	Seneca
		21	[....] ditto	2	3	Seneca
		21	1 ditto	15	17	ditto
		24	1 ditto	1	1	Miami [Piankeshaw]
		25	1 ditto	5	7	
		27 [?]	1 ditto	2	11	Assinboni
		30	1 ditto	3	2	Weas, Wakiow [Kiowas]
	June	11	1 ditto	5	5	Weas
		12	1 ditto	3	4	Weas
		13	1 ditto	2	1	Weas
		16	1 ditto	2	2	Shawnee
		24	1 ditto	6	8	Kiowa, Shawnee, Seneca [?]
				43	46	[....] [....]

This memo was scribbled on the bottom of the second page of Francois's letter. Several letters in this collection were recycled in this way. Although this cryptic list was included in this compilation, it may have no connection to the Chouteau-Menard correspondence. What items were "handed out" was not stated. Clearly documented, at any rate, was the fact that on May 17, someone received "one good one!" The memo was not in Francois Chouteau's handwriting; the notation could have been made by Pierre Menard or Raphael Widen, or someone else. Chouteau's letter probably happened to be nearby when a piece of paper was needed, and the memo was a record for the Menard operation and Francois probably never saw it. As Menard was an Indian field agent and dealt with traveling Indians, a logical hypothesis is that these items were given out to relieve the needs of these travelers who stopped at Menard's establishment in Kaskaskia. Perhaps he gave them blankets? A horse? A wagon? A cooking pot? Some measure of a food staple? One can only guess.

Most of the Indians mentioned were moving to new homes in Indian Territory. The Senecas came from Sandusky River, Ohio, and completed their migration to their reservation in present southeastern Kansas by July 1832. The Kiowas were better known as the Kiowa Apaches in the southwest. Pawnees lived in the Platte valley in Nebraska, but they were great travelers and well known around the Missouri-Kansas area. The Assiniboines were a Siouan language nation of the Upper Missouri that traded with the American Fur Company. Their name means "people who cook with stones." Some band of these Indians was apparently in the Midwest at the time of the preceding note; in 1837, the tribe was almost destroyed by smallpox.[14]

The origin of the Weas was explored following Francois's September 24, 1829, letter to Cadet. As pointed out, these Indians, mentioned so frequently in Chouteau's letters, were probably a band of Piankeshaws who came from the Great Lakes region, near present Chicago. The tribes lived in harmony with their other close relatives, the Peorias and the Kaskaskias. The Weas, Piankeshaws, and Peorias were also known as Miami Indians. They all spoke an Algonquin language and were farmers as well as hunters. Eventually these tribes and the Kaskaskias banded together into the Peoria Confederacy.

The letter introduced several new names: Boggs was probably Lilburn W. Boggs, who opened a store in Independence in 1826 and was engaged in the Santa Fe trade in 1832-1833. He was also treasurer of Jackson County in 1827 and served as governor of Missouri from 1836 to 1840.[15] Another possibility might be Lilburn's son Thomas Boggs, a freighter on the Santa Fe Trail.[16] Other men named Boggs in the area were Angus G. Boggs, who signed as witness to a treaty with the Shawnee and Delaware Indians in 1836,[17] and three men named Joseph Boggs.[18]

Around this time, the Indians began to realize they could strike a better bargain for merchandise if they had cash in hand and freedom to do some comparative shopping. When the chiefs first insisted on receiving money instead of merchandise, the annuity money was given to the Indian nation and the chiefs made the purchases for their people. As time went on, however, some chiefs began to distribute the cash to individual families so that they could trade or bargain for themselves. The concept of private ownership was new to Native Americans, and tended to erode their ancient cultures.

---

14. Barry, *Beginning of the West*, 324.
15. "Reminisces of William M. Boggs, son of governor Lilburn W. Boggs," *Missouri Historical Review* 6: 86.
16. Barry, *Beginning of the West*, 132.
17. *SIA* (MC741), 1: 262, KSHS.
18. See Glossary entry for Boggs for a more complete explanation of these possibilities.

In previous letters Francois often sent his compliments to Mr. and Mrs. Valle. The Felix Valle mentioned in the preceding letter was the son of Jean Baptiste Valle and his wife, Jeanne Barbeau. Felix operated the Ste. Genevieve Menard and Valle store that provided merchandise for traders and sold retail goods to settlers and townsfolk. "Sarpy" was Jean Baptiste (J. B.) Sarpy, manager of the American Fur Company's store in St. Louis. This store sent Francois the merchandise he had ordered through his brother Cadet. Francois sometimes called Sarpy "cousin," the relationship coming through Francois's cousin, Marie Pelagie Labbadie, who had married Gregorie Sarpy, J. B.'s father.

Francois's overpowering message in the next letter was anger toward Marston Clark.

River of Kansas   July 15, 1830 [19]

Cher oncle,

I write to you by way of Captain Vashon who is going to St. Louis. I wrote you via the steamer Globe and in the letters I put some money that I withdrew on the order of Connor. I presume that it has been given to you. We have a few furs here and 2000 dollars in money that we made through annuities that have been paid recently. We have competition from all the merchants in Independence, who were invited to the agency by Captain Vashon and they took from us about 1500. But I assure you they did not make any profit and that they will not come again another time. I did not know that an agent could grant permission to come to trade at his agency. Our post was the only one designated to make treaties. However, we must not complain of Captain Vashon; he is still worth much more than all the rascals, the underagents who are stationed at these posts here. The Kansa left to hunt buffalo after having taken the merchandise of Mr. Clark without knowing either the price or the quantity, like a band of wild animals. I did all I could to stop them from taking it so that they could compare their merchandise with mine. But those monsters from Kansas cannot resist when they see loot, good or bad. I believe that this underagent of the Kansa [Marston Clark] *is a famous rascal. Upon arrival at his agency he opened a box and showed to White Plume a pair of superb blankets with a yellow stitching near the edge, saying "you certainly see that I have beautiful blankets" and he* [Clark] *replaced them immediately in the box, and the other blankets were very inferior with no yellow stitching. He said in Independence that he had written to the president to remove me from here, as I was very hard to get along with, contrary to the Governor's ideas about the happiness of the Indians. If he did that, I promise you, he will pay for it as I can find proof to put him in the most difficult situation in the world. Everybody with whom he has done business have become his enemies. Several whom I know have threatened to beat him up. It is very disagreeable for me to carry on business with such a scoundrel and to see such little good faith in that kind of behavior.*

We are all in good enough health. Berenice must have written to you. I beg you to extend my affection to my aunt and because she is able to believe that we have forgotten

---

19. PMC, Letter 330. Envelope: [To] Pierre Menard Sr., Kaskaskia, State of Illinois; [filing note] Francois Chouteau, 15 July 1830.

her, to tell her that we speak often of her. Menard is growing much, and little Benjamin speaks French and English and runs everywhere. Give my love to Peter and to Francis.

I am with respect, your nephew
Francois Chouteau

The most remarkable news in this letter was that Marston Clark claimed he had written to the president asking for Chouteau's removal. President Andrew Jackson, in office at the time, would have passed the letter to the Office of Indian Affairs, under the authority of the War Department, namely Secretary of War Eaton, who was already familiar with the problem. This chain of command was in effect until 1849 when Indian Affairs was transferred to the newly created Department of the Interior. Apparently, the letter generated no action. The OIA must have received stacks of letters complaining about the traders, and other stacks complaining about the agents.

In the preceding letter, Chouteau reported with disgust that Clark had succeeded in getting the Indians to accept his merchandise. Although Francois was upset about losing the business, his letter suggests that he was equally disturbed by the ill will and the attack on his good name.

Kansa Chief White Plume was also known as Monchonsia, or Nampawarah.[20] The government and the agents considered him the most important tribal leader for many years. White Plume lived in a two-story stone or brick house adjacent to the "half-breed tracts" east of Topeka. Superintendent William Clark wrote to Samuel Hamilton of the Indian Affairs office in Washington City (Washington, D.C.), that building the house for White Plume was not a provision of the Treaty of 1825, but "a promise made to build him a house when he chose to have one."[21]

The Kansa "half-breed tracts" lay east of present Topeka, with the Kansa Agency east of the last plot, and White Plume's house near the agency. These twenty-three "half-breed" plots were set aside for mixed-blood Kansa Indians in the Treaty of 1825. Four of the plots went to White Plume's grandchildren. The name Gonville is often associated with these grants, as White Plume's daughter (or niece?), married Frenchman Louis Gonville, and their "half-breed" children were awarded tracts.[22]

Francois's personal remarks referred to Menard, then eight years old, and Benjamin, two and a half years old. The eldest son, Edmond, called "Gesseau," as previously explained, was attending school in St. Louis.

For the first time Independence appeared as a place of origin in the following letter. Perhaps Francois was writing from his Jackson County farm, instead of from his Kansas City warehouse.

Independence   September 18, 1830[23]

Cher oncle,

I am writing to you via Major [Richard] Cummins an agent of the Shawnee who is going to St. Louis. We are much grieved over the sickness of poor Francois that you told

---

20. Barry, *Beginning of the West*, 357.
21. William Clark to Samuel S. Hamilton, Indian Department, November 22, 1830, *OIA, St. Louis Superintendency, 1829-1831*, M234, Microfilm roll 749, Frame 1097-1098, NARA.
22. Charles J. Kappler, *Indian Affairs, Laws and Treaties*, 2: 222-225.
23. *PMC*, Letter 336. Envelope: [To] Mr. Pierre Menard, Esq., Kaskaskia, State of Illinois; [filing note] Francois Chouteau, 18 September 1830.

us about in your last letter. We had hoped to see him here with papa who is going to come soon. I believe that traveling slowly would do him good. Berenice is thinking about going to St. Louis this Fall. She is eager to see all of you. The Indians are getting ready to go hunting. The Kansa have almost all departed. The Weas, Peorias, and the Piankeshaws are asking us to send them some goods to their camps, to their village near to Marais des Cygne. I asked for a license from the agent. But since he is going to St. Louis, I am writing to Cadet to pick up the license from him for this post here. And he [Cummins] can bring it back to me upon his return. Here I have about 20 bundles of deerskins and some old skins that I would like to send upon the first occasion. The Kansas River is very low. I do not know how we will manage to transport our goods. It may be necessary to carry everything overland. We have no other news for now. We have had hardly any sickness this summer. However, fever is beginning to spread a little.

Berenice joins me in sending much love to you as well as to my aunt and to the whole family.

*I am with respect your devoted nephew
Francois Chouteau*

I will charge 35 dollars to the Indians for the horse that you gave them down there.

The good fortune to be healthy was something Francois never took for granted, as his correspondence shows. The letter opened and closed with remarks about health. Berenice's half-brother Francois Menard was the "Poor Francois" who Francois and Berenice had hoped would accompany Pierre Chouteau when he came to visit them. (Was Pierre Chouteau coming to throw his considerable influence on the side of Francois and Frederick in their embroilment with Marston Clark?) The climate of western Missouri, drier than that of St. Louis and Kaskaskia, was always considered by Francois to be healthier than the Mississippi River environs. Both of Francois's and Berenice's infant sons – Louis Amadee and Louis Sylvestre – had died while in St. Louis.

Francois Menard was attending school in Bloomingdale, New York, when he wrote to his parents that he was suffering from a chest malady and was coughing up blood.[24] He probably had developed tuberculosis, for which there was no known treatment except moving to a warm, dry climate.

The fever that was "beginning to spread" was probably either malaria or typhoid, both of which were earmarked by high fever. While the settlers had no concept of germs, bacteria, or illness carried by insects, they did notice that low-lying damp (and hence mosquito-infested) areas were associated with illness. Francois's letter of May 20, 1832, informed Pierre Menard that cholera victims who died aboard the steamboat *Otto* had been thrown into the water. Did Chouteau think this was terrible? Perhaps, as he knew the river water was used by many for household needs.

The following letter written by Berenice was considered important enough to be filed with the Menard business papers. The last Berenice letter kept was written in May 1827. The other letters she wrote to her father, and sometimes mentioned in Francois's letters, were personal and not retained for future reference. Perhaps the little Menards were allowed to draw on the back of Berenice's letters with pieces of charcoal raked from the kitchen hearth.

---

24. *PMC*, Letter 294.

Modeste Alzire Menard Kennerly, to whom this letter was written, was Berenice's youngest full sister. Alzire, as she was called, often traveled with her husband, Captain George Hancock Kennerly, a supply officer at Jefferson Barracks in St. Louis. This letter, addressed to Alzire in St. Louis, may have gone to Jefferson Barracks or to the home of Captain Kennerly's mother who lived in St. Louis. By what piece of fortune the letter survived is not known. Perhaps Alzire kept the letter to recall this time of personal loss, and it was found by her heirs after her death in 1886.

River of Kansas   February 3, 1831 [25]

Ma chere soeur,

I did not receive your letter dated the 25th of December until the last of January. Also, since then I learned of the cruel loss of our brother Francois and that of your little son. I consider the death of your little one and of my own very difficult for us but that loss is nothing in comparison to that of our very dear and good father and mother. I do not doubt that the death of our good brother is cruel for them and for all of us because he was made to be loved by all those who knew him. And when I learned the unhappy news, I tried to write to our beloved father but I was unable to finish because what consolation was I able to give him, as well as to you, my beloved Alzire. I suffered this pain twice and I know well that nature will take its course. That's life. I beg you, my good friend, to bear up as much as it is possible. I beg of you to give me news of our very unhappy father and mother, as well as of all our family. I beg of you to give me news of my boy as I have had none for a very long time. That fact causes me much worry regarding his fate. The only reason that keeps me from going down this Fall is the health of my poor Gesseau that is very bad which means that I couldn't resolve myself to upset him [by leaving]. I don't expect to deliver until next month after which I will write to you. I beg you to give our brother-in-law, Kennerly, love from me and Gesseau and to embrace your dear children.

Goodbye while awaiting the pleasure of seeing you. Believe me your affectionate sister

Berenice Chouteau

I was planning to go down [to St. Louis] *on the first occasion before the death of our very dear brother whom I have in my prayers but now I do not expect to* [....] *down below before June or July.*

Berenice's twenty-four-year-old half-brother, Francois Xavier Menard, died January 8, 1831. He was six years younger than Berenice. Francois Menard was nineteen when he traveled to Auburn, New York, to attend St. Mary's College, a Catholic boarding school for young men. The letters he wrote from college to his father and mother expressed deep affection for family, and a determination to master the studies he was undertaking. In

---

25. *PMC*, Letter 345. Envelope: [To] Madame George H. Kennerly, St. Louis, State of Missouri; [from] Independence, Missouri, Feb. 5; [postage] 18 3/4.

November 1826, he expressed a desire to go to Montreal, his father's birthplace, to visit Menard relatives, but apparently that never came to pass.

Looking for a more suitable academic program, Francois Menard transferred to a college in Bloomingdale, New York, in December 1827. He wrote regularly about his classes, asking advice on whether he should study Spanish, and the like. Eventually, however, the harsh climate of upstate New York, the cold buildings heated only by inadequate fireplaces, and his delicate constitution combined to bring on his fatal illness.[26]

While infant death was common in the early 1800s, many parents felt the loss deeply. Berenice and Francois Chouteau had lost two sons, and this letter revealed that Alzire had also recently lost a baby, her eleven-month-old son, George Hancock Kennerly Jr., born February 21, 1830, died January 15, 1831. The news of this death traveled quickly, as Berenice's letter was dated only two weeks after the event.

"My boy," about whom Berenice inquired, was her oldest son, Edmond Francois (Gesseau), then ten years old and attending St. Louis College (present St. Louis University) in St. Louis. St. Louis College, a Catholic boarding school for boys, was then the equivalent of a high school. The school was founded in 1818 by the Jesuits (Society of Jesus), a Catholic religious order for men. Gesseau was not only enrolled at St. Louis College, but doing quite well.

An 1831 awards program listed Edmond Francois Chouteau's name twice: First Premium in Grammar (French? English?) and Second Premium in Parsing (Latin?). In 1832, he took a First Premium in Spelling and a First Premium in Profane History. Slightly prophetic was his selection of a reading for the 1832 commencement. The name of the poem was "Ode on Rebellion." Exhibiting a flair for the dramatic, Gesseau played the part of Gessler in a scene from *William Tell* that was part of a commencement program in August 1833.[27]

If Gesseau's Grandfather Menard had been in St. Louis, he almost certainly would have sent news of his grandson. Grandfather Chouteau, who lived probably no more than a mile from the school, apparently did not send word that he had seen the boy. Berenice, as she wrote, would have gone to St. Louis but for "the health of my poor Gesseau that is very bad...." This was the first mention of Francois Chouteau's health problem.

Francois's next letter referred to Berenice's decision to stay at home only in the remark, "but then she didn't want to go."

River of Kansas   March 20, 1831 [28]

Mon cher oncle,

I received your letter dated February 22 which pleased us greatly and grieved us much at the same time although we already knew the sorrow that you had undergone. It is true that I have neglected for some time to write you but I assure you I did not forget you for that. The sad and painful situation which I know you were in is the cause of it. And I was aware that the business could not interest you at that time. I wrote to papa a few times when I always spoke of you and of my poor aunt. I know that your sorrow is

---

26. For a list of the Francois Menard letters, 1826-1829, see the *Guide to the Microfilm Edition of the Pierre Menard Collection*, 110.

27. *Catalogue excerpts*, 42, 60, 74, University Archives, St. Louis University.

28. *PMC*, Letter 349. Envelope: [To] Monsieur Pierre Menard Sr., Kaskaskia, State of Illinois; [filing note] Francois Chouteau, 20th March, 1831.

very great, because I myself have some experience in that area since [also]. *But our dear uncle, we have to console ourselves — for those who remain with us. I received the letters for the Indian chief and for Baptiste. I will do what you recommend in that regard. A week ago, Baptiste was here. He came to pick up a load of corn to eat and to feed the horses that are very thin because of the hard winter that we had. I have never seen so severe a cold spell and as much snow since I have arrived in this area. The Loups have lost more than 200 horses, the Kansa have lost a good half of theirs. Even several Indians died during the winter. Right now we are in the middle of loading the barge for its departure to St. Louis. It will carry 250 packs. We were unable to send all the fur pelts on the boat. Regarding the improvements that we purchased from Mme. Baronet — is about 350 acres, very mediocre. The land is very undulating, a lot of hills. It is a fine place for a warehouse but we could have a piece* [of land] *near there that would be just as good to build a warehouse. I do not have the right to preempt. It is a person named Hunot* [?] *who began to settle that place. Berenice was to go to St. Louis last fall. I offered to take her at the time she had planned but then she didn't want to go. She as well as the children enjoyed very good health since we've been here. Our children are much healthier here than in St. Louis. For the time being, she is awaiting the birth of the child. I have taken all the possible precautions to give her all the possible assistance. And as soon as her delivery, I will write you.*

Frederick and Meyers arrived from their wintering place two or three days ago, in good health. And give you their respects as well as to Cyprien [Menard].

Berenice joins me to wish you, as well as my aunt and your family health and happier days.

I am respectfully
Your affectionate nephew
Francois Chouteau

After he had returned from college in New York, Francois Menard spent two years as an invalid in his father's house at Kaskaskia. His parents Pierre and Angelique Menard, having watched helplessly as he declined and died, were deeply grieved. That Pierre Menard wrote to Francois Chouteau concerning their business, and sent a letter for an Indian chief, indicated that he was trying to pull himself back to society. And so, Francois replied in kind, passing along to" his *Cher Oncle"* the details he liked to receive.

"Baptiste" was a name common among the French, and, hence, also common in the Indian families that were connected or related to the French. Mentioned in these letters were several men with the name "Baptiste." Baptiste Peoria, as noted, was a leader among the Peorias, Weas and Piankeshaws, as well as an interpreter at the Shawnee Agency. Usually, when Francois used only the first name "Baptiste," he referred to Baptiste Peoria. Baptiste Datchurut ("Big Baptiste") was the boatman mentioned in Frederick Chouteau's "Reminisces," quoted at length following Francois's letter of March 31, 1829. According to both Frederick, and Francois, Baptiste Datchurut was responsible for wrecking the keelboat *Beaver*. In the last months of Datchurut's life, Frederick Chouteau took him in and cared for him. Baptiste Pascal was mentioned in several Chouteau letters of a later date. In the early 1830s, an Indian named Pascal (no first name or tribe given) traveled with Lucien Fontenelle and Andrew Drips to St. Louis. In April 1831, Pascal was still with Fontenelle and Drips, then on an expedition in Wyoming.²⁹ Baptiste Pascal may have been the same person, or a member of the same family.

The American Fur Company's purchase from Mrs. Vasquez, mentioned again in the preceding letter, was indeed of the improvements or buildings only.³⁰ Francois could not claim the land and was therefore quick to point out its disadvantages. Scoured by three major floods in the intervening years, and attacked by countless shovels and bulldozers, all that remains of the topography Chouteau described as "undulating" is a gentle slope to the river. The name of the claimant to the Vasquez land is difficult to decipher; it appears to be Hunot (also spelled Uneau, Euneau, Uno.) A family named Uneau lived at the foot of Main Street during the 1830s, and operated a ferry across the Missouri River. Hunot may not have had clear title either since the land would later be part of the Gabriel Prudhomme estate that eventually became the core of the Kansas Town Company purchase.

As had his brother Francois before him, Frederick Chouteau had spent the winter in a location convenient for the Indians to bring pelts from the winter trapping. He and William Meyers were probably at the Kansa Post, though it is possible they had hibernated in the area of the Indians Meyers knew, the Weas. Frederick and William Meyers were apparently great pals. In 1830, Frederick married a Shawnee woman whose name was either Nancy Logan or Elizabeth Tooley, and named his first child William Meyer Chouteau.³¹

While the Chouteaus were all healthy, such was not the case in the Indian communities where, Francois reported, several Indians had died. Among the fatalities was "Captain" Johnny Quick, who in September 1829, had been one of the group of Delawares at the Council Camp on the James fork of the White River to sign a supplemental article to the Treaty of 1818.³² In 1830, the Delaware Nation appointed Quick to accompany Isaac McCoy on his expedition to survey the Delaware lands.

Francois's next letter carried the glad tidings that Berenice had safely delivered another child.

Independence   April 16, 1831 ³³

Cher oncle,

It is with great pleasure that I announce that my Berenice gave birth, the 14th of this month, to a plump son without accident, and I hope, within 8 to 10 days, she will be well. Menard is very pleased by the fact that his little brother resembles him, and he thinks he is very handsome. I have been here now for two weeks to give my Berenice the care of which she is in need. I am writing you a short letter, having no other news of which to inform you at present. Since the departure of the barge we have prepared 30 bundles of furs and skins of roe deer. I hope we will assemble more. The Kansa lost a part

---

29. Lyman C. Pedersen Jr., "Warren Angus Ferris," in *The Mountain Men and the Fur Trade of the Far West*, ed. Hafen, 2: 144.

30. See also appendix item 3c on page 209, Pierre Menard letter to Francois Chouteau, February 22, 1831.

31. Oliver H. Gregg, *History of Johnson County, Kansas*, 45; William E. Foley and C. David Rice, *The First Chouteaus*, 215.

32. John Campbell to Isaac McCoy, January 14, 1831, *Isaac McCoy Papers,* Microfilm roll 7, Frame 574, KSHS.

33. *PMC*, Letter 353. Envelope: [To] Monsieur Pierre Menard Sr., Kaskaskia, State of Illinois; [from] Independence, Mo., April 16th; [filing note] Franc. Chouteau, 16th April 1831.

of spring by going to war with the Pawnees. We are very desirous of seeing you here and the Indians share the same feelings.

Cyprien, Frederic, and Meyers are at the trading post. We await our merchandise so that we can take care of the annuities. It seems that the Indians from here are close to agreement to receive their annuities in money. Berenice joins me and sends to you as well as to my aunt all the possible love while awaiting the pleasure of seeing you all.

I am respectfully your nephew
Francois Chouteau

The son whose birth on April 14, 1831, was announced in the letter was Frederic Donatien Chouteau, the first of the Chouteau children born on the frontier. When Francois wrote this letter, his brothers Cyprien and Frederick, along with William Meyers, were at the "trading post," meaning the Kansas City warehouse, as his next sentence specified that "we" were waiting for merchandise to arrive so that they could take care of the annuities. Probably most of the Indians came to the Kansas City warehouse, as there they could see the variety of merchandise offered. A quantity of goods would have been transferred to the other posts after the initial trading in Kansas City.

Berenice's father, Pierre Menard, actually did come to western Missouri to visit his daughter and son-in-law, as Francois in his letter of October 27, 1831, to Cadet wrote of "M. Menard's departure." In addition to visiting family, Menard probably also called on the immigrant Indians he had assisted in western Illinois and eastern Missouri – the Weas, Piankeshaws, Peorias, and Kaskaskias. Pierre Menard was sixty-six years old in 1831, and as subsequent letters indicate, was becoming less willing to make long trips.

Francois's usual news about the Indians, the annuities, and the fur collection was augmented by a weather report in the following June 1831 letter:

River of Kansas   June 3, 1831 [34]

Mon cher oncle,

I received your letter dated from May 19, informing me of the arrangements made with the American Fur Company. Gilliss arrived here the first of the month with a wagon and in company of Philibert and Saucier. Gilliss is to give me the merchandise that he brought. I will pay an accurate bill of all the articles and I will give to him a receipt, as well as for all the other things that he might give me. I will do things as you wish. There remains at the establishment of Gilliss one load of merchandise. I have observed to him that it would be good to have this here as soon as possible. He tells me that the season is at present very bad. The rivers have all gone down and there is much time [spent traveling] in the prairies and the animals would not be able to survive. And this is so true. So we must wait for a more favorable time. They tell me that Marshall will be here in 10 or 12 days. I told Gilliss to let me know if he accepts the work that was offered to him so that I can get myself ready for that. I will tell the same thing to Marshall upon his arrival. I could employ them at the Loups as we will need a trading

---

34. *PMC*, Letter 359. Envelope: [To] M. Pierre Menard, Kaskaskia, State of Illinois; [from] Independence, Mo., 4 [....]; [filing note] F. Chouteau, June 3, 1831.

post in their village for the treaty and the convenience of the Indians. There are the annuities that will be paid soon. We don't have enough merchandise. I am angry that they didn't send me all that we asked. Sarpy tells me that he will do it at the first opportunity. Gilliss's merchandise arrived. About the Weas, the Sioux, Kickapoo, Loups, and Kansa – they are receiving all their annuities in money this year. Berenice proposes this year to come down in the company steamboat with the children and I would have gone down also if I did not have to stay for the annuities. As soon as that is done, I will go to St. Louis.

You have heard, no doubt, of the accident that happened to the furs that we had loaded on the steamboat Missouri. I am angry about that as it was a great part of the furs sorted – in all, 57 bundles, beavers, otter and raccoons were all first quality. I received 20 dollars from Perry for your horse. He is supposed to give me the remaining $10 soon. I will send them to you. This is about all the news.

Berenice joins me to assure you of our love as well as for my aunt that we hope to go see soon.

I am with respect your affectionate nephew,
Francois Chouteau

The agents have not yet received the money to pay the Indians. The Missouri is low on all sides and this is unusual for this time of year. I am afraid that Cadet will not get up to the Yellowstone.

The drought of the spring and early summer of 1831, mentioned by Francois, complicated both water and land travel. The river was too low for Gilliss to transport his goods, and the plains were too dry to support animals pulling loaded wagons. On the Santa Fe Trail, Comanches killed legendary mountain man Jedediah Smith when he separated from the pack train in an attempt to find water for the desperate men and animals.[35]

On the Missouri River, the American Fur Company's steamboat *Yellow Stone* set out on her maiden voyage to the Upper Missouri in June 1831. This was the vessel that Berenice hoped to take down to St. Louis on the return voyage. Before that, however, the new ship had leagues to sail.

The *Yellow Stone* steamboat was the pride of the American Fur Company and of Cadet Chouteau, who had encouraged the company to build the boat, and then arranged for its construction in Louisville, Kentucky.[36] Cadet must have paced the deck with pride tempered by anxiety as the craft puffed up the Missouri River. She must have docked ceremoniously at Chouteau's Landing before becoming the first steamboat to travel past Council Bluffs. The boat churned toward the Upper Missouri to gather the winter harvest of furs from the company's remote posts.

Although the *Yellow Stone* was built with a shallow draft for navigation in the often inadequate channel of the upper river, the hull sometimes dragged over the riverbed, rock, sand, and mud, while the steam power pulled and pushed the vessel forward. In the summer of 1831, as Francois feared, the lack of water cut short the voyage at Fort Tecumseh in present South Dakota. In the summer of 1832, there was enough water for the *Yellow Stone* to reach its namesake, the Yellowstone River.

---

35. Barry, *Beginning of the West*, 202.
36. Donald Jackson, *Voyages of the Steamboat Yellow Stone*, 1-2, 159.

Not owned by the American Fur Company, the steamboat *Missouri* was built around May of 1828, sank in September, and was recovered in November.[37] The event that Francois noted was when the *Missouri* hit a snag at Bonnots Mill (east of Jefferson City) on May 1, 1831.[38] No lives were lost and the vessel may have been raised again, but it is not clear what became of the cargo, particularly the valuable Chouteau furs.

Mishaps on the treacherous Missouri River were common. Often boats were snagged by the uprooted trees that lay just below the surface of the water. Other times the problems were manmade and involved an exploding boiler. Steamboat captains sometimes overheated boilers in an effort to increase speed. The result could be loss of life and merchandise. Such incidents inspired Cadet Chouteau, as head of the Western Department of the American Fur Company, to build and operate steamboats so that the company would have greater control over the system.

Joseph Philibert was one of the men who arrived from the James Fork area with Gilliss and his wagon of merchandise. Philibert worked as gunsmith at the Ozark establishment, then became Gilliss's clerk and business associate. Saucier was probably one of the numerous descendants of the three Saucier men of Cahokia, Illinois. Apparently he was well known to Francois Chouteau, whose mother and aunt were Sauciers.

The preceding letters documented that Francois was then receiving his merchandise for the Indians from the St. Louis American Fur Company warehouse, supervised by Cadet Chouteau and with J. B. Sarpy in charge of daily operations. Francois's orders from Menard and Valle in Ste. Genevieve declined, probably because shipping from St. Louis was less expensive and quicker.

The following letter was sent to Cadet in St. Louis, then passed on to Pierre Menard in Kaskaskia, where it was filed and eventually became a part of the *Pierre Menard Collection*. Note the straightforward approach Francois used in writing to his brother, contrasted with the convoluted, extremely respectful phraseology in letters to Pierre Menard.

River of Kansas   *October 27, 1831*[39]

Cher frere,

I have arrived at this place after eleven days of traveling. The Loups have got the small pox. Fifteen have died since Mr. Menard's departure and the others have dispersed in different directions in an endeavor to avoid it. That will cause confusion for the hunt. I found M. Gilliss had built at the Loups. Upon my arrival here he told me that he received permission from Mr. Menard and also permission to take some money from us when he needs some. He says he has the order to build a good, well-made house. I made the suggestion that you told me to make regarding the subject of salary of 600 dollars a year. He considers that salary much too low. He told me that he expected to receive the amount that was given to him by Menard and Valle, without informing me what the amount was and, moreover, he informed me that he would not consent to serve for that salary without having an assistant with him. He named M. Philibert as a suitable man,

---

37. *Missouri Republican*, 4 May 1828, 3; 2 September 1828, 3; 4 November 1828, 3.
38. William M. Lytle and Forrest R. Holdcamper, *Merchant Steam Vessels Of The United States, 1790-1868: The Lytle-Holdcamper List*, 282.
39. *PMC*, Letter 366. Envelope: [Forwarded to] Mr. Pierre Menard, St. Louis, State of Missouri, [....] AM Fur Company; [filing note] F. Chouteau to his brother Pierre, October 27, 1831.

who will demand, I suppose, three or four hundred dollars. He told me he would write to Mr. Menard later about the proposition that I had made to him and he will [not] *begin work until the answer came. I believe he is a good negotiator for the Loups because of his long familiarity with that nation and because he speaks the language. However, it appears he wants to do as he sees fit and not to be under the direction of anyone here. At least I think this. I would like for you to see Mr. Menard as soon as possible to give me an answer right away. I do not know who to put in that post in case the conditions of Gilliss do not suit you. Regarding the piece of land at the entrance of the Kansas River — when Mr. Menard was here, he talked about entering it. Gilliss told me he had entered it in his* [Gilliss's?] *name as Mr. Menard had not already entered it.*

Berenice joins me and conveys to you as well as your wife our sincere affection.

Send me the license for the Kansa if you haven't already done so. For the Loups and the others I will make application to Major Cummins.

Tell papa hello for us.

Your affectionate brother,
Francois Chouteau

Regarding Saucier, I believe he could be useful to us. He also wrote to Mr. Menard. He appears ready to work hard.

Francois's letter was sent to Cadet, who forwarded it to Pierre Menard so that he, too, would have the information it contained. Francois probably wanted Cadet to apply for the Kansa license in St. Louis so that he, Francois, would not have to deal with Marston Clark. Perhaps Cadet Chouteau went directly to Superintendent William Clark, who was indebted to the Chouteaus for many favors. Francois was content to apply to Major Cummins, the new Shawnee Agent, for the other permits.

River of Kansas   November 30, 1831 [40]

Cher oncle,

If I have not written to you, you must not attribute that to my lack of affection. I supposed after what was related to me, that you would leave shortly after me to visit Wichita. Gilliss was not satisfied with the proposition that I was charged to make to him. He said he was going to write you on that subject. He is asking for an increase in salary and an assistant for the treaty and many hired men. As soon as your [....] *here, he began building among the Loups without the approval of Major Cummins, without notifying him of it. The latter was displeased and upon my arrival here he came to discuss it with me and asked me if it was upon my order that Gilliss was building among the Loups. I answered "no" — who would think that I would have acted as I already did, by seeking a license and designating a location. He answered he never doubted that and that perhaps Gilliss took it upon himself. Gilliss says it is upon your order. Major Cummins*

---

40. PMC, Letter 369. Envelope: [To] M. Pierre Menard, Kaskaskia, State of Illinois; [from] Independence, Mo., [postage] 18 3/4; [filing note] F. Chouteau, March 30, 1831.

tells me that he doesn't believe anything at all and that you know the business better than that. I wish that Gilliss were employed if arrangements can be agreed upon on both sides. He knows the Loups well and he speaks their language. But I am told that he doesn't wish to be under the direction of anyone here; that he has no need for anyone to show him how to trade nor when to give credit, that he knew as much and more than most people about that. And finally that he has no need of an overseer. You see then if it is like that, I have no doubts that he will not conform to our plans for the treaty as well as for giving credit. In some respects we have brought the Indians back from abuse of heavy credits. And I believe it will be prudent to continue the plan. We have paid 50 dollars to Jean for the little daughter of Lorimer while still keeping something of the total to dress her as she will be sent to school soon. I do not believe we will do much trading this winter. We received our merchandise too late. The sickness among the Indians is the main cause. For there are some who are saved from the pox who have not yet returned. Regarding the silver which we spoke about your sending; to send you a memorandum: we have enough for the present. I will let you know when we need some and then you can send it to us by the first occasion, twelve [....] extra large and twelve brooches. Berenice wants me to ask you to inform her of the price of the little mulattress of Valle and she will write you whether she wants her or not. We have received through Philibert the balance of the merchandise that comes from White River as well as the wagon with six horses. I will have the horse Tim evaluated and I will send you the bill for all.

I have asked Gilliss to send me the ox cart and other articles which belonged to Menard and Valle and he didn't do any of it. There are still, I believe, a few horses with the ox cart.

I beg you to send my sincere love to all the family.

I am with respect your affectionate nephew,
Francois Chouteau

I would have written you through Baptiste Peoria if I had been at home.

The smallpox epidemic of the summer of 1831 took a heavy toll among the Native Americans in the region of the Missouri and Kansas rivers. The Shawnees were stricken first, and then the disease spread to the Delaware-Loups. They, like the Kansas, sought refuge in the wilderness. Isaac McCoy reported that nine Shawnees had died and fifteen Delaware-Loups. Dr. Johnston Lykins, accompanied by Subagent John Campbell, began to vaccinate Shawnee Indians in the summer of 1831.[41]

In May 1832, Congress provided funds for a vaccination program for the Indians. Doctors were sent to John Dougherty's Upper Missouri Agency to vaccinate the Pawnee Republicans, Sac, Fox, and Sioux tribes; to Paul Liguest Chouteau's Osage Agency to vaccinate the Big and Little Osages; and to Richard Cummins's Shawnee Agency to vaccinate the Shawnees, the Kickapoos, "and others," presumably the Weas, Peorias, Kaskaskias, and Piankeshaws.[42]

---

41. Barry, *Beginning of the West*, 207-208.
42. Barry, *Beginning of the West*, 214-215.

In late December 1832 and January 1833, the Kansa Indians in the lower village were vaccinated by a Dr. Crow, accompanied by Subagent Marston Clark. They sent a message to the upper village of the Kansa, requesting that the Indians delay leaving for their hunt so that they could be vaccinated. The Indians waited two or three days, but because they were in a starving condition, they left on their hunt in order to find food. It was five or six more days before Dr. Crow and Marston Clark arrived at the upper village. The Indians were gone.

Marston Clark accused Frederick Chouteau of influencing the Indians to leave and avoid being vaccinated. Frederick denied the charge, but as the issue was a matter of life or death, the Office of Indian Affairs authorized an investigation. Neither the testimony of the Indians nor the sworn statements of the two Kansa interpreters, Clement Lessert and Pierre Ravelette, implicated Frederick Chouteau, and eventually the matter was dropped.[43]

Although only partially completed at that time, the vaccination program, along with acquired immunity, combined to reduce the number of smallpox victims, and in his next letter Francois supposed "there will not be much sickness among the Indians."

The "Jean" (John) to whom Chouteau paid fifty dollars must have been, in some way, responsible for "the little girl of Lorimer." This was probably a child of mixed blood, who very likely was being cared for by the Chouteaus until she was sent to school. The Lorimers were a well-known family from Cape Girardeau. Louis Lorimer Sr. was a member of the Court of Common Pleas and Quarter Sessions in 1805.[44] Later, he and his son Louis Jr. built a trading post near the Delaware village in south-central Missouri. In 1822, they sold the post to William Gilliss.

Pierre Menard frequently assumed responsibility for the education or training of children or youths who in his estimation needed assistance. His daughter Berenice took on something of the same role, as her later letters document. She secured class schedules and tuition information, and offered her service as chaperon to take girl students to St. Louis for convent education.

River of Kansas   January 17, 1832 [45]

Cher oncle,

I take advantage of the occasion of Toiniche who leaves tomorrow to give you news of us. Our treaty will not be noteworthy, but there is room to hope that this year will be advantageous for the fur trade and that we will make many bundles. And I don't believe I will be very mistaken. I suppose that there will not be much sickness among the Indians. I'm making our preparations early by giving credit to the Indians as necessary for the hunt. We may presume that our different posts will give us many bundles. I believe that the Kansa are well equipped and will produce as many pelts as the Loups and the Shawnee together. I am going to have that experience this year. The establishment of Gilliss among the Loups has remained there. You know he went to work there without notifying Major Cummins, nor asking him where the trader would be

---

43. Accusation, denial, and sworn statements may be found in *OIA, Fort Leavenworth Agency, 1824-1836*, M234, Microfilm roll 300, Frame 375-387, NARA.

44. Louis Houck, *History of Missouri*, 2: 384.

45. *PMC*, Letter 371. Envelope: [To] M. Pierre Menard, Kaskaskia, State of Illinois; [filing note] January 17, 1832, F. Chouteau on the subject of the wagons.

located and that displeased the agent who came to discuss it with me. I told him that I had nothing to do in the affair and that I didn't know if M. Gilliss was authorized to set up trading houses among the Loups. He said that you had authorized him to build and to draw upon us for the money that he will need. He asked for 300 dollars and he didn't get anything. I said I had no money and that was true, but even if I would have had some to dispose of, I surely would not have given him any without an order from you or from Cadet. When you will have learned of the conduct of Gilliss and Saucier, you will be astonished to see that they are real cheats and scoundrels. They do not deserve any work or protection. I am going to collect the money that Baptiste Peoria owes you as soon as he has it as well as a small bill that he has with Valle. I am unable to send you the receipts of Joel Walker because I have not seen him to have him sign. He lives far from here. As soon as he signs them I will send them to you. I paid the order that you drew on behalf of Mr. Chaine, the underagent of the Kansa and the biggest scoundrel that I have ever known. There are few worse than he is. And he is a coward, a scoundrel who puts up with all the insults we give him. He detests us unto death. And why? Because we discovered he was a rascal and that I can prove that through very good evidence.

I am going to build a fine trading post for Meyers and for Frederick. The location has been established but a short time ago.

The children all have whooping cough but that cannot hurt them much. Berenice is very anxious to have Menard back again and if old Loumus leaves the school – she says he is too young to go out alone. About that, do as you think appropriate. We hope without a doubt to see you this spring. Berenice joins me and wishes you as well as my aunt all good health.

I am with respect, your affectionate nephew
Francois Chouteau

Berenice has a beautiful bedspread for my aunt and for myself, I will send her a good barrel of deer fat to make candles. I had fifty dollars from Baptiste Peoria for you. I will have him pay the balance when he receives his next quarterly payment. I received an estimate on the two wagons by the experts: the horse wagon and its paraphernalia = 350; the ox cart = 80.

Toiniche, though not identified, was more than likely in the fur trade. In May 1838, Paul Liguest Chouteau wrote a letter to J. B. Sarpy saying that Toiniche was claiming a debt that Paul Liguest said he had paid in 1833. Liguest wanted Sarpy to check his records to see if he could document the payment.[46]

What exactly Francois could prove against "Chaine," that is Anthony Shane, was not revealed. Chouteau identified Shane as an "underagent of the Kansa," but he was actually an interpreter. (Perhaps he also had other duties.)

Mountain man and Santa Fe trader Joel Walker, mentioned in the preceding letter, was one of many legendary figures (among them, Bridger, Fontenelle, Sublette, Bent) who stepped

---

46. Paul Liguest Chouteau to J. B. Sarpy, May 1838, *Chouteau Family Collection*, MHS.

through the door of Chouteau's Kansas City warehouse during the 1830s. If these men were associated with the American Fur Company, Francois was called upon for supplies – in small amounts at first, but as the 1830s progressed, in larger quantities. However, the receipts that Joel Walker was to sign may not have been connected with the Chouteau and Menard business, but only to Pierre Menard.

Francois and Berenice's second son, Pierre Menard Chouteau, called "Menard," was attending St. Mary's of the Barrens, a Catholic boarding school for boys located in Perryville, Missouri. Although Menard was only ten years old, he joined a student body of other boys as young as he. His older brother, Edmond, or Gesseau, had also been sent to St. Louis College, also when he was ten. Berenice, however, was uneasy – perhaps she had heard that Menard was unhappy. She wanted "Loumus" (unidentified, but probably a servant or slave) to bring Menard home.

The wagon and cart mentioned at the end of the letter were the ones Chouteau had previously asked Gilliss to bring to him, as reported in his letter to Pierre Menard of November 30, 1831. The denomination of money used to estimate value of these items was the American dollar.

River of Kansas   February 24, 1832 [47]

Cher oncle,

I received your letter dated the 8th of the present where I see that you did not get two letters that I had written to you since the first of the month of November. I assure you that I have written you about all that you inquired of in your last letter. And that when I am at home, I never cease doing what you wish of me. As for Mr. Chaine, your order was paid immediately, 31.50. About Joel Walker I informed you in the letter that you didn't receive that I was unable to see that man to have him sign the receipts. Baptiste didn't see him and gave back the receipts and the money to Mr. Samuel Owens who had promised me that as soon as the man would come into town, to have him sign them and to forward them to you. I am surprised that you received the letter of Berenice and that you didn't receive mine which is from the same date and that was sent by the same express. Meyers also sent you the papers that you had asked of him two months ago, through Joseph Philibert and he cannot conceive for what reason Philibert did not send them to you. He suspects that it is not impossible that this was done on purpose. I told this to you in my letter about Gilliss. I also told you that my opinion regarding them is not much and when I see you and I tell you how they conducted themselves, you will not be able to do otherwise than approve of what I'm telling you. Again I tell you that Gilliss says that he needs no advice [....][....] It is possible that regarding the salary of Gilliss that I made a mistake, that could easily happen. But also I will remind Cadet that it is he who drew up a memorandum of salary and who said to me that if Gilliss doesn't find the salary sufficient, to put another in its place. I assure you that Gilliss does not have the intention of acting in agreement with me, that he does not consider the expense

---

47. PMC, Letter 372. Envelope: [To] Col. Pierre Menard, c/o R. Weden [Raphael Widen], Kaskaskia, Illinois; [from] Independence, Mo., February 26th; [postage] 18 3/4; [filing note] February 26, 1832.

and then, instead of doing the work with our people, which was surely the most economical plan, he sent almost all the work to the Americans in the country, payable in silver. He drew upon Cyprien for 300 dollars. We had no money, but even then if we would have had some, surely I would not have given him any without an order from you or from Cadet. I will not give a dollar to anyone unless I am advised. Again Gilliss, who was beginning to gain favor, caused the agent [Richard Cummins] to turn his back on him for having had 7 gallons of whiskey carried to the Loups on Christmas day, and for having had Saucier frolic with them. Major Cummins was informed of this immediately by the same chiefs to whom he [Gilliss] had given the whiskey.

It is with sorrow that we heard of the long and painful sickness that you have suffered. But I hope that you have completely recuperated. You may write me upon the reception of this letter and I am ready to do all that will please you.

With respect,
Your nephew,
Francois Chouteau

We are all well enough and also wish you as well as my aunt, good health. Tell Menard that his mother and I hug him tight and that she wishes to see him very much even though I am happy to know that he is learning well and that his teacher at school is happy with him. Give my love to Edmond [Menard] and the whole family. Berenice asks me to give you as well as my aunt and the whole family her love. F. Chouteau.

Meyers made a treaty with the Weas, Piankeshaw, and Peoria as usual and is here at the present time. I can't tell you the quantity of packs that we have. They are not all put together, but we do not have as many as last year. I hope that we will trade again this spring. I collected from Baptiste [Peoria] a part of what he owes me. I will have him pay the rest as soon as practical.

I entered the piece of land at the entrance of the Kansas River for the company and put on the point ten cords of steamboat wood for the Yellow Stone.

This letter repeated much of the information given in the two letters that Pierre Menard had not received, and that were dated November 30, 1831, and January 17, 1832. The missing letters did eventually reach Pierre Menard, as they are in the collection. It is unclear how Francois's correspondence came into Pierre Menard's hands. Perhaps, as Mr. Menard had been quite ill, Francois's letters actually had arrived but were kept in the office because they contained business information; whereas Berenice's personal letter was delivered without delay and taken to Pierre Menard's sick bed. Later, when Mr. Menard returned to his desk, perhaps he found Francois's letters, containing all the familiar material, buried under his paperwork.

William Gilliss's behavior as described in Francois's letters suggested that he was distancing himself from his French connections – he returned the supplies from Menard and Valle, hired workers other than the French crews employed by Francois, and most emphatically, did not want to answer to or take advice from Francois Chouteau. Gilliss was not, however, above trying to borrow money from Francois's brother Cyprien.

The agent mentioned in the preceding letter was the new Shawnee agent, Richard W. Cummins, replacement for George Vashon, who was transferred to the Western Cherokee

Agency in Oklahoma. Cummins remained in his position until 1849, when he, like Graham and Campbell, was "removed."[48]

The "point" of land at the mouth of the Kansas River where Chouteau placed ten cords of wood for the American Fur Company steamboat *Yellow Stone* has long since been carved away by flood waters and the shifting Missouri River channel.[49] However, in the 1830s it was a convenient pick-up site for steamboat fuel and sometimes fur packs.

Six months elapsed before the date of Chouteau's next letter, written after the family returned from a visit to St. Louis and almost certainly to Kaskaskia.

River of Kansas   August 12, 1832[50]

Cher oncle,

We have arrived here in good order after nine days of travel. On board we were in a very good company of men and women. In such a way that our trip was one of the most pleasant that I have ever made for a long while. Mme. Sams arrived safely and was very happy to reach her destination. You were aware that I was to go down on the boat on its return. My desire was to go spend the winter in New Orleans, but Father's doctor told me that this country wasn't one bit good for me and advised me to go farther on. But I do not like to go to distant lands where I know no one and especially in circumstances such as these where the cholera can show up from one day to another. So I decided to remain here again this winter. I wrote to Mr. Siloqua that I was displeased not to have seen him, because he is the one in whom I have the greatest confidence. I wrote to papa to have his letter sent to him right away so that if he sends me some medicine, I could receive it by the boat that will come back soon. Ligueste left here yesterday for his post. His wife has stayed with us for as long as the month of September. Berenice sends to my aunt a pair of Indian moccasins and three pairs for each of the little boys at the Barrens.

Mme. Meyers has left the River of Kansas never to return, from what she says. Since my arrival, two Loups have died here due to liquor. One drowned while crossing the river and the other had his chest crushed against a tree by a horse.

Cyprien, Fredrick, Berenice, all the children are well. We wish you good health.

I am with respect, your nephew
Francois Chouteau

Francois and Berenice's son Menard may have come to Kaskaskia, or the family may have gone to Perryville to see him. Something happened to relieve Berenice's anxiety about Menard, for he did not return with them. The three pairs of moccasins sent to St. Mary's were for Menard and two of his young uncles. Matthieu Saucier, Louis Cyprien, and Joseph Amadee Menard were in and out of St. Mary's during the early 1830s.

---

48. Barry, *Beginning of the West*, 895.
49. The Certificate of Patent 2069 was issued from Washington, D.C. on December 5, 1833 to Francois Choteau [sic] for the southwest quarter of section 31, Township 50 north, Range 33 west. Today the entire north half of the quarter section is under the Missouri River.
50. *PMC*, Letter 392. Envelope: [To] M. Pierre Menard, Kaskaskia, Illinois; [filing note] F. Chouteau, August 12, 1832.

The "Mme (Madame or Mrs.) Sams" mentioned in the preceding letter was almost certainly Mrs. Samuel Owens. Francois usually referred to married women of status using the husband's first name after the title, as in "Madame Baronet" (Vasquez) and only rarely as "Madame Vasquez."

The wife of Francois's half-brother Paul Liguest was his second spouse, Aurora Hay. Liguest's first wife, Constance Dubreuil, had died in 1824. Aurora apparently found the people and activity at Chouteau's settlement on the Missouri something of an attraction compared to the wilds of the Osage country. At any rate, she planned to stay with her in-laws for another six weeks.

This letter provides a clear picture of the seriousness of Francois Chouteau's illness. Perhaps the recent trip to St. Louis was made specifically for Francois to consult a doctor there. Apparently his doctor of choice was a man named Siloqua who happened not to be available. Francois's father's doctor recommended that Francois spend the winter in a warm climate, but not New Orleans, a place notoriously disease-ridden.

The warm climate of the Caribbean was thought to cure many illnesses. Later, Berenice's brother Cyprien Menard suffered from a chest disease similar to the one that killed their brother Francois Menard. In the winter of 1839-1840, Cyprien Menard wrote letters from New Orleans, Havana, and Matanzas, Cuba.[51] The warm climate may not have been a factor, but Cyprien Menard did conquer his illness and lived until 1870.

The following letter shows that Francois, like many of his contemporaries, was fascinated by the miracle of the 1830s – steamboat speed. While in the early 1820s keelboats took as long as three months to struggle up the Missouri River from St. Louis to the mouth of the Kansas, the steamboat bringing Francois's merchandise had made the journey in five days and ten hours!

River of Kansas   September 7, 1832[52]

Cher oncle,

We received our merchandise by the Yellow Stone that made the trip from St. Louis to the River of Kansas in five days and ten hours. We do not have enough blankets but my brother Cadet said he wrote to you to have some. We are now drawing up a treaty for the annuities for the Indians and there is no lack of concurrence [competition?] *even though they* [his competitors] *are making very little because they do not have merchandise suitable for the Indians, or at least they only have very little. I believe that we will make approximately five thousand dollars with the Loups and probably three thousand with the Indians that remain to be paid. We have made 40 packs of deerskins since my trip to St. Louis. The Loup tribe drinks a lot at the present and often many die. Not a day passes that at least 30 gallons of whisky is not brought to the village. In five years from now, I presume that they will be almost all destroyed if they keep on at that pace. In three days Major Cummins will pay the Kickapoo and then the Wea and then Piankeshaw. I spoke to Major Cummins about the complaints that Gilliss brought to you against me and he said it was false; that he had never had such a conversation with*

---

51. Cyprien Menard to Pierre Menard, December 1839-May 1840, *PMC*, Letters 1023, 1028, 1031, 1035, 1038, 1048, 1055, 1061, 1069.

52. *PMC*, Letter 399. Envelope: [To] M. Pierre Menard, Kaskaskia, State of Illinois; [from] Independence, Mo., Sept. 8th; [filing note] September 7, 1832, F. Chouteau.

anyone whatsoever and that Gilliss was very light on belief [you can't always believe him] *and that I could not have told him* [Cummins] *anything about this whiskey business since he knew of it before me.*

We had some children sick with a disease of the mouth that was catching here and that was very bad. Measles has killed many children in the country and apparently it is of a bad variety. Tell Menard that his mother as well as myself beg you that if the cholera comes to St. Louis, to have Gesseau leave college and to put him at the Barrens with Menard.

Berenice writes to you. I wish to you, as well as my aunt good health. Give my love to the entire family and tell Peter [Pierre Menard Jr.] *to come to see us. I am still suffering from chest pains and that makes me almost unable to see to the business.*

I am respectfully, your affectionate nephew,
Francois Chouteau

Francois was only thirty-five years old but in the predicament of being in a stressful business that involved long hours and extensive travel requiring physical endurance, while his affliction made him almost unable to "see to the business." His sons, unfortunately, were too young to be of help. Francois's brothers, then, were called on to shoulder more of the load. Cyprien, thirty years old, with maturity and years of experience, assumed responsibility for the Shawnee Post from this time, it appears, as Francois seldom mentioned further duties connected with that establishment. Perhaps he finalized this arrangement while in St. Louis and Kaskaskia.

Frederick, then twenty-three and well established at the Kansa Post, still seemed to need assistance, partly because he was in continuous conflict with Kansa subagent Marston Clark. Francois needed help at the central, or Kansas City, warehouse, and while he had many employees, Francois apparently had no one who could take charge and manage the business for him.

In addition to his duties in the fur trade, Francois continued to collect debts, arrange loans, and secure signatures on documents (when he could track down the wanted party) – all services that required time and travel, and that would have been performed by bankers, accountants, or lawyers had there been any. Meanwhile, Chouteau sold and bought real estate, and worked to increase the size and prosperity of his farm, almost certainly foreseeing the day when the fur trade would no longer provide a living or that he would simply decide to get out of it.[53]

The abrupt appearance of cholera was something that worried Francois, as expressed in his letter of August 12, 1832. So it was that, as he reported in the preceding letter, he took the precaution of suggesting to Pierre Menard what should be done if the sickness appeared in St. Louis, where Gesseau was in school.

Safety from cholera, Francois thought, was more likely to be found in a small town like Perryville than in the booming town of St. Louis. The school, St. Mary's of the Barrens, was established in 1818 as a seminary for students studying for the Catholic priesthood. The Vincentian fathers, a religious order for men, operated the institution. In 1822, St. Mary's began accepting younger boys in addition to the seminarians. Perryville's rather isolated location, eighty-seven miles south of St. Louis, and not on the river, made it less likely that cholera would appear there.

---

53. "Land Data notes," Chouteau's (Topical) Scrapbook [17.1], (KC395), WHMC-KC.

The following letter was written after Francois returned home from the Kansa Post.

River of Kansas   December 12, 1832 [54]

Cher oncle,

I have neglected a little long to give you news of me since my arrival at home. The Indians haven't yet returned from the hunt. They had a beautiful autumn for that. I presume they will bring in many pelts, especially the Kansa to whom we gave about 100 guns on credit. The Shawnee and the immigrating Ottawas arrived here about the first of the month. They come to see us from time to time and always bring a little money. I paid to the Loups their order of 250, and also that of Mr. Chaine 150. And we will also pay the one from Nancy Jones for 40. Likewise we have paid about a thousand dollars for the Company to two men from the mountains, LaLiberte and Dupuis.

We have presently a good trading post built among the Kansa, between the two villages, very well stocked with merchandise and provisions for the winter. We also have among the Weas a fine trading post, built and arranged for what is necessary for trade. Meyers is there at the present time. Finally, I hope that we will be able to make lots of packs this year.

Everybody of our establishment is in good health. There is nobody sick here. As for myself, I am about the same as I was when I was in St. Louis. Old John has died a few days after my arrival home from St. Louis. He and two others as a result of liquor.

Berenice sends you her love as well as to my aunt and to all the family.

I am with respect, your affectionate nephew,
Francois Chouteau

Give my love to Charles and tell him to write to me.

The mountain men of the preceding letter had probably just returned from the Rocky Mountains and were paid $1,000 for their fur pelts. Pierre LaLiberte was one of the original landowners in Kansas City. His property lay atop what became Quality Hill. In 1834, LaLiberte sold forty acres to the first resident Catholic priest of the area, Rev. Benedict Roux, for a grand sum of six dollars. On this land was built "Chouteau's Church," later called St. Francis Regis, the forerunner of the present Catholic Cathedral of the Immaculate Conception at 11th and Broadway in Kansas City.

LaLiberte's fellow trapper, Dupuis, has not been identified, although a Paul Dupuis was known to be in the Missouri-Illinois state line area around 1800. Like Dupuis, Nancy Jones will be remembered only for having been paid and duly recorded in this Chouteau letter. Otherwise, she is unidentified. "Old John," also unidentified, may have been a member of one of the nearby tribes, as he was grouped with the two Indians who died as a result of liquor.

The Ottawa Indians who, as Chouteau wrote, were immigrating into Indian Territory, came from east of the Mississippi and arrived at the Shawnee Agency in November 1832.

---

54. *PMC*, Letter 413. Envelope: [To] M. Pierre Menard, Kaskaskia, Illinois; [from] Independence, Mo., Dec. 15; [postage] 18 3/4; [filing note] F. Chouteau, Trader, [....][....] Received 29 and answered January 7, 1833.

John Calvin McCoy had surveyed the 34,000-acre reservation set aside for them. The Ottawa land lay south of the Shawnees and west of the Peorias, Piankeshaws, Weas, and Kaskaskias.[55]

Frederick's new post among the Kansa was licensed on October 18, 1832. The location was described as "On the Kanzas river between the two present [upper] villages of the Kanzas [i.e., Hard Chief's and American Chief's towns] on their lands....", not far from present Valencia.[56] Again, there were two viewpoints about this relocation. Francois indicated that he and Frederick had been waiting for a new location to be designated, and when it was, they built the new post and moved from the Horseshoe Lake post.

Marston Clark, on the other hand, took Francois to task for not moving the post immediately upon receipt of their new license in October 1831. The Chouteaus seemed in no hurry to prepare the buildings in the new location until, Clark further charged, they were certain that William and Thomas Johnson would establish a Methodist mission near the Kansa villages. In this way, the new Kansa Post could sell not only to Indians, but also to the pioneers who would settle near the school. This dual purpose was a practice Clark deplored.

While Clark dressed down the Chouteaus, he subjected himself to criticism from other sources. At the time of the Clark-Chouteau wrangling, a contemporary observed that while the Indians suffered, their agent Marston Clark was "living like a patriarch, surrounded by laborers and interpreters, all snugly housed, and provided with excellent farms."[57]

Francois seems to have resigned himself to a permanent state of conflict between himself and Marston Clark. Chouteau was no longer unduly agitated, but rather simply disgusted with the whole affair. It was apparent by this time that Marston Clark was unable to inflict a mortal blow to the Chouteau brothers' business. However, Clark continued to maneuver against them behind the scenes.

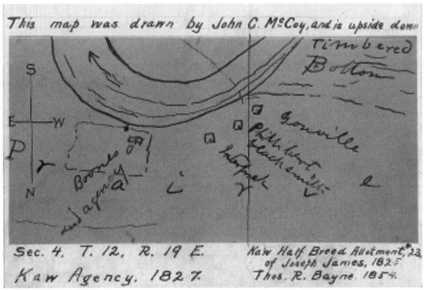

Map drawn by John Calvin McCoy of the Kansa Agency (1827-1834). KSHS.
For another view of this site see the illustration on page 244.

---

55. Barry, *Beginning of the West*, 217, 223.
56. *H. Doc. No. 45*, 23rd Cong. 1st sess. (Serial 254): 2.
57. Unrau, *The Kansa Indians*, 141.

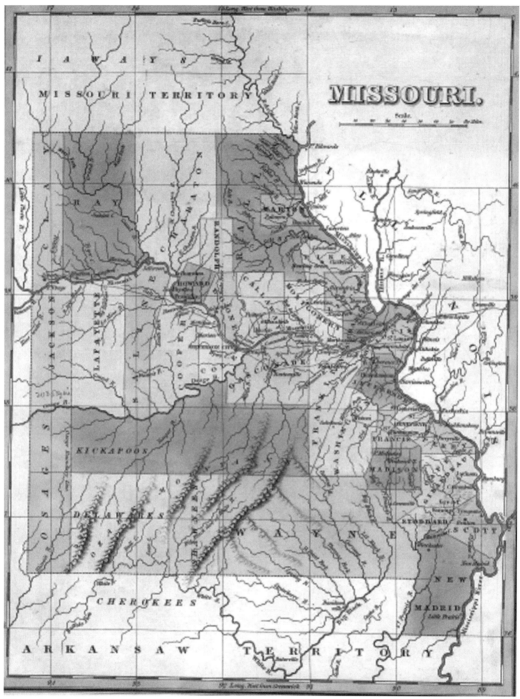

Missouri, published by A. Finley, Philadelphia, 1831. Note the road from St. Louis to Liberty. Also the locations of the Osage, Delaware, Shawnee, and Kickapoo lands in the southwest. Lastly that Jackson County extends from the Missouri River to the Osage River. Western Historical Manuscript Collection-Kansas City.

"*Vue de la premiere hutte des Kants avant d'arrivier a la riviere du meme nom. Village des Kants*" [View of the first hut of the Kansas before the arrival at the river of the same name. Village of the Kansas]. Drawn by Nicolas Point. *Pierre Jean De Smet (1801-1873) Papers,* Manuscripts, Archives, and Special Collections, Washington State University Libraries.

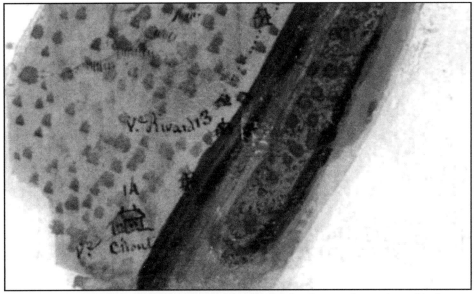

A section of Nicolas Point's *"Plan de Westport (Missouri)"* with the Chouteau home pictured in the lower center. *Père Nicolas Point, S.J., Collection,* Archives de la Compagnie de Jesus, province du Canada frantais.

5   At Home on the Chouteau Farm

The New Year of 1833 began with hopes and frustrations, as well as with debts carried over from the previous year. Francois and Berenice, with their children Menard, Benjamin, and Frederic Donatien, were at home on the Chouteau farm. Their oldest son Gesseau was still in school in St. Louis. Francois's brother Cyprien was keeping the Shawnee Post and Frederick was hunkered down at the windswept Kansa Post. In the following letter, Francois sent his first report of the New Year.

River of Kansas   February 12, 1833[1]

Cher oncle,

I received your last letter dated from the month of December, and I am a little late in answering you, in order to give you more information. All the Indians have just come out

---

1. *PMC*, Letter 430. Envelope: By Mr. W. Myers [To] Monsieur Pierre Menard, Kaskaskia, Illinois; [filing note] February 12, 1833, Francois Chouteau.

from the hunt. I thought we would have 300 bundles but will have about 280. I had written to Cadet that we would have 300 bundles. We would have made them and maybe more if the Kansa Indians had been hunting this spring. But their horses were so thin when they came back from the fall hunt that, after having paid their credits and treaties, all the villages of the Kansa went to Missouri to fatten the horses in the prairie. The Kansa have made more skins than the Loups, the Shawnee, the Piankeshaw, Peorias, and Weas all together. You recommended to me to have a trading post among the Loups. I am going to make an observation to you and then you can judge better than I what has to be done. It seems to me that our post of the River of Kansas does not give enough profits to increase the expense. We must try to economize on the expenses as much as possible. A post among the Loups will not give us any advantage with them and the annual cost and expenses for that place will be almost as high as for my establishment. The distance from here to them is so small that it cannot make the least difficulty.

At the present they have a boat at their establishment and we always have some canoes to take them across when they come to discuss business. It is necessary to trade with some of them at the fort [Leavenworth] but some of these drunks go there with the intention of getting whiskey as they always get some every time they go to that place. And with us, we never give them any [whiskey]. So you see that when they make 25 miles to go to the fort rather than three to come to us, even if we had a post with them, it would not stop them from going to the fort. There are some of those rascals who have taken credit with us, and in order not to pay here, they go to the fort. I think you already have enough people employed to carry on your business at the Kansas River with all the Indians. Cyprien and Meyers are of the same opinion. Now I will await your orders in order to do as you judge suitable. I presume that our pelts will be all prepared at the mouth of the river around the 20th of the month of March to put aboard the first ship that will come up.

Here we have paid about 1000 dollars on the order of Cadet and by you and I think we have just as much left. I have received a horse that you had lent to an Indian and who returned it to me. Meyers, having completed the treaty and having nothing more to do at his post for some time, asked me to go to visit his family.

Berenice is near the time of delivery. I will write you again as soon as possible. I am expecting Frederick around the end of the month with his furs, 150 packs. He would be here already if there had been enough water.

Berenice joins me to give you her love as well as to my aunt, and to all the family. She will write you soon as that is possible. Menard is attending class at Mr. Johnson's.

I am respectfully your affectionate nephew,
Francois Chouteau

Francois's lengthy reasoning against a trading post among the Delaware-Loups did not include the salient factor, namely, that William Gilliss already had a corner on that market. The financial liabilities of such a post were more than Francois wanted to assume. In addition, the potential customers, the Indians, were inclined to go to Fort Leavenworth – where, ironically, at that government installation, they were more likely to get whiskey than at Chouteau's posts.

William Meyers, the young trader among the Weas, was reported by Francois as having left his post because, Meyers said, there was no more business to be done. Meyers was apparently eager to go to Ste. Genevieve where his wife was. As Francois relayed to Pierre Menard in his letter of August 12, 1832, Mrs. Meyers was the woman who had stated so emphatically that she was leaving the "River of Kansas, never to return."

Chouteau made several shipments of fur packs each year, the largest being in early spring, resulting from the accumulation of furs received during the winter. The furs were packed at the outer posts and, in the spring when the ice melted, brought down the Kansas River to the Kansas City warehouse where Francois counted and stored them until a steamboat came up from St. Louis. When the water in the Kansas River was low in the spring, Francois and Frederick had their share of trouble.

The fur packs from Francois's warehouse were delivered to Cadet Chouteau's American Fur Company warehouse in St. Louis. From that depot the furs were sent to either the East Coast or New Orleans for shipment overseas, chiefly to London, to be made into garments and hats for the continental fur markets.

Apparently Cadet had sent Francois cash to pay a variety of American Fur Company debts. As currency was in short supply on the frontier, a great deal of bartering went on. However, cash was always in demand. The Chouteau letters documented many requests for cash – some refused on principle, others refused because there was no money, and some acceded to, with the recipient writing a draft or check on his source of finances in St. Louis. Chouteau then sent the draft to Cadet, who collected the money. The Indian agents in particular seemed to be in the position of often needing cash in advance of the government supply.

The preceding letter revealed that Menard had come home from Perryville and was "attending class at Mr. Johnson's" school. Rev. William Johnson and his brother, Rev. Thomas Johnson, had come to the Missouri-Kansas region in 1830 to establish Indian missionary schools. Rev. Thomas Johnson was the prime mover behind the Shawnee Mission Indian Manual Labor School. In the fall of 1831 or early in 1832, under the auspices of the Delaware Methodist Mission, William Johnson had established a school near Delaware Chief William Anderson's village on the Kansas River.[2] Menard, then eleven years old, may have ridden a horse to school daily, or perhaps some arrangement was made for him to stay with the Johnsons, especially in bad weather.

The letter that follows was another birth announcement:

River of Kansas   February 25, 1833[3]

Cher oncle,

I'm writing a small letter to you to inform you that Berenice had another big boy the 23 of the present month and that she is pretty well.

---

2. Louise Barry, *Beginning of the West*, 210; Perl Wilbur Morgan, *History of Wyandotte County, Kansas, and Its People*, 55.

3. *PMC*, Letter 437. Envelope: [To] Mr. P. Menard Sr., Kaskaskia, Ill.; [from] Shawnee, [Jackson County] Mo., March 5; [postage] 18 3/4; [filing note] Feb. 25, 1833, F. Chouteau. [Note: *Guide to the Microfilm Edition of the Pierre Menard Collection*, page 88 mistakenly dates this letter February 28, 1833.]

> *I was obliged to have Fredrick go this morning to the Meyers post. He did not arrive here until five or six days ago from among the Kansa with all the furs. My friend Meyers was in too much of a hurry to leave his post to go to St. Genevieve where he had nothing to do. He told me that there was nothing more at all to do and after that I had all the merchandise brought back as well as his packs. But I observed to him that it would be bad to bring back this merchandise if he had any hope of making a profit, that our expenses were already committed and it would be very inappropriate to incur double expense. The Indians [Weas] who arrived at his house among the Indians to trade and having found Meyers gone, they came here to ask me for some merchandise, that they were unable to carry the furs here, that their horses were too skinny. So, you see that it's making me do double expense where the costs were already set. He arrived here the 10th of February. He should have remained at his post until the end of March.*
>
> *I am with respect your nephew*
> *Francois Chouteau*

The newborn Chouteau boy was named Benedict Pharamond. The infant was given the name Pharamond in memory of Francois's younger brother Pharamond Chouteau, who had died in 1831. The name Benedict was probably added when the Reverend Benedict Roux came to western Missouri. He baptized the baby in February 1834. Benedict Pharamond was the second child of Francois and Berenice born in Jackson County and the first to be baptized on the frontier.

The return address on the envelope of the preceding letter was "Shawnee," which was located in Jackson County, Missouri, not Kansas. The Shawnee Post office was established in June 1832, with Johnston Lykins as postmaster. After the founding of Westport in May 1834, the post office name was changed to "West Port." John Calvin McCoy was then appointed postmaster.[4]

Francois, in the following letter, recounted more of the Marston Clark involvement and had more to say about "friend" William Meyers:

> *River of Kansas April 16, 1833* [5]
>
> *Cher oncle,*
>
> *Major Cummins has no instructions from the commissioner to pay Mr. Marshall $1225. If he receives the order for that, I will let you know. I will also see about the business of the Coups and of the Kickapoo. I haven't seen Gilliss since last fall in St. Louis, but I will see him about that business. Our merchandise hasn't yet arrived and Clark is paying the annuities of the Kansa the 18th of the present month. We are missing many very important articles, such as blanket[s], 3 pint boiler[s], small box[es], and many other thing[s]. Competition will be as usual, and they will have the advantage over us because they have received their merchandise. You see how Clark is a rascal. He sent*

---

4. Barry, *Beginning of the West*, 261.
5. *PMC*, Letter 445. Envelope: [To] Monsieur Pierre Menard, Kaskaskia, Illinois; [from] Shawnee, Mo., April 16, 1833; [postage] 18 3/4; [filing note] Francois Chouteau, April 16, 1833; Received the 30th and answered the 5th of May.

an express letter to Independence to invite all the merchants, and to the fort, also. He took all the precautions so that we would not know anything. He sent his express [letter] more than five miles away from us.

Meyers would have made 20 bundles more, if he had wanted to remain at his post. Indians often come to trade here. Not having anyone at the post, they are going to carry on business at the blue water [Blue River?] *with a whiskey salesman who catches* [gets] *all the raccoons and otters. If my friend* [Meyers] *does not want to remain at his post, he would do better not to come among the Indians. He hasn't collected his credits.*

Berenice joins me to wish you good health, as well as to my aunt.

*I am with respect,
Your nephew
Francois Chouteau*

The large sum of money that Francois mentioned in the letter was the amount of the debt owed by the Wea Indians to William Marshall, who, as previously explained, was a trader in eastern and central Missouri among the emigrating Indian nations, the Weas being one of them. The Weas had left Indiana in the fall of 1830 and, probably encouraged by Marshall, some of them had spent the winter trapping in the swamps along the Mississippi River.[6] Marshall sold to these people a considerable amount of merchandise on credit but was unable to collect the money. Evidently the trapping expedition in the swamps had been a failure.

The Weas journeyed on toward Indian Territory (Kansas) where they joined their relatives, the Piankeshaws, on their reservation near the Marais des Cygne in present Miami County, Kansas. Marshall, Menard, and Francois Chouteau wanted the Weas to allow Marshall's debt to be deducted from their annuities. But the Weas refused to release any money to Marshall until other matters were settled. Eventually Pierre Menard paid Marshall with the understanding that the Weas would repay him. Later letters related more on this subject. The debt originally owed to William Marshall (then to Pierre Menard) dragged on and was still unsettled in August 1836 when Pierre Menard wrote to Francois about it. (See also appendix item 3g, page 212.)

The "business of the Loups and the Kickapoo" was probably in some way connected to William Gilliss and a result of the previous Gilliss-Menard and Valle association. The details, however, were not recorded in the letters, and the whole affair was apparently settled in person.

The "blue water" of the preceding letter was almost certainly the Blue River that begins in Johnson County, Kansas, meanders through Missouri, and empties into the Missouri River. The Big Blue River in Kansas near present Manhattan was probably too far from the Wea Indians who would have traded at Meyers's post if he had been there. In addition, as the sale of liquor to Indians was prohibited in Indian Territory, a whiskey salesman was more likely to ply his trade in Missouri.

Francois never failed to notify Pierre Menard of the shortcomings of anyone who could affect the profit line of the Menard and Chouteau business – whether these men were his own workers or others, even though they were Pierre Menard's protégés, as in the case of William Meyers. (For Menard's reaction to the Meyers affair, see his letter to Francois Chouteau, appendix item 3f, page 211.)

---

6. Barry, *Beginning of the West*, 183.

River of Kansas   May 20, 1833 [7]

Cher oncle,

I have received your letters dated 6 and 7 of the present through Meyers, where I see that you told me to give him the sum of $1769. I would have given him that money, but I had already sent it to St. Louis through Capt. Shalcross. However, I will try to get it here if that is possible and I will give it to him and I will send the merchandise to the Indians and we will leave to arrive there about at the same time. But I am obliged to await the arrival of our merchandise as we are so under-stocked that we don't have what we need to make the payments. I spoke to Gilliss about the business of the Loups and of the Kickapoo as your letter of February 20 mentioned. He promised me he would help as best he could to try to make the Indians acknowledge their debt and to have them sign the agreement. We have notified the four Kickapoo chiefs to come to see us. As soon as they arrive, we will carry out the transaction.

Meyers apparently has no desire to continue among the Indians although you offered to increase his salary by 100 a year. I believe he sees he has become unpopular among the Indians. And indeed the natives let it be seen. And then he is observing that it is hard on the women to remain in that country.

Frederick remarked to me that since the company offered Meyers 100 more a year that he believes, with justice, that we should give him the same offer. The post of Meyers produces 50 to 60 bundles; that of Frederick produces 150 to 160 and almost always, about $2500 in annuities. You see that the total sum of Frederick is much larger than that of Meyers. Frederick collected the credits for 80 guns granted to the Kansa, or about that. Meyers didn't collect at the most a fourth of his and the rest is very risky.

Your Indian shoes are well stitched by Mrs. Prudhomme but we have no ribbon with which to trim them. We will have some soon and I will send them to you immediately. I will try to send Menard to you this fall if I do not go myself. He learns very well at Mr. Johnson's school. He says he has enough ability so he will be able to go to the Barrens this fall.

Everyone in the establishment is in good enough health. The steamboat Otto passed yesterday on its way to the fort. They have cholera on board and some of them have died on the way and they throw them into the water.

Berenice joins me to express to you as well as to my aunt, the expression of our love and wishes you good health. Tell Charles that I wish him all the possible happiness. And Frederick tells me he is angry with himself for not having gone to see him.

I am with respect your affectionate Nephew,
Francois Chouteau

We have sent 315 packs, $1000 in money. Here we have 15 packs of 120 otters, 50 lbs. beavers.

---

7. PMC, Letter 454. Envelope: [To] Monsieur Pierre Menard, Kaskaskia, State of Illinois; [from] Independence, Mo., May 22; [postage] 18 3/4; [filing note] Francois Chouteau, May 20, 1832, answered June 13.

[Menard's reminder to himself] *I'm telling him to take care of it.* [....] *Meyers and* [....] *Cadet find* [....] *for the Kickapoo. That he knows better than I which deal to make them and I remitted* [....] *to Major Cummins.*

Steamboat travel on the Missouri increased rapidly through the decade of the 1830s. The captain or master of a steamboat was more educated than most of the population and generally inspired some respect. He was often entrusted with money or letters to be delivered. Captain John Shallcross, mentioned in the preceding letter, was apparently held in esteem by Chouteau, as he trusted the captain to deliver a sum of money when his steamboat, the *Diana,* docked in St. Louis.

In November 1832, the Kickapoo chiefs signed a supplemental article to the Castor (Beaver) Hill Treaty that had been signed a month earlier. The addendum established the boundaries of the new Kickapoo reservation in Indian Territory (Kansas). The Kickapoo reservation lay north of the Delaware reservation, fronting the Missouri River.

Two of the principal signers for the Kickapoo Nation were Pashachahah, or Jumping Fish, and Kennekuk, the Kickapoo prophet.[8] Pierre Menard wrote to Francois about this affair on February 20, 1833 (See appendix Item 3e, page 210). The Kickapoos had apparently taken goods on credit from four traders, and the traders, in turn, owed Pierre Menard for this merchandise. (So it was actually Menard who was out of pocket.) At the time of these letters, the Indians were making arrangements to pay the debt through deduction from their annuities. Usually in these cases, the original debt was considerably reduced. Gilliss agreed to intervene on behalf of Menard, while Francois was to exert the influence he was said to have among the Indians.

When the chiefs arrived to confer with Francois, the meeting would have been filled with ceremony – the giving of gifts to the chiefs, the smoking of the ceremonial pipe, and the sharing of food, and no doubt both the Frenchmen and the Native Americans made long and indirect speeches that circled before directly facing the matter at hand.

From time to time either Francois or Berenice sent "Indian shoes" as gifts to family and friends in St. Louis or Kaskaskia. Already at this date, the Indians were far enough removed from the eastern part of Missouri that it was difficult for people of that region to obtain these soft and comfortable, finely made "Indian shoes."

Mrs. Prudhomme, who stitched the moccasins, was a Native American of the Cree Nation of Montana. This Susan Prudhomme was the widow of Gabriel Prudhomme, who was killed in a tavern brawl in November 1831.[9] In 1829, Gabriel, who had been trapping in the Upper Missouri, came down to the mouth of the Kansas River and entered a land claim. This same property was sold in 1838 by the Prudhomme estate to the Town of Kansas, and eventually divided into lots that formed the original town site of Kansas City.[10]

---

8. Charles J. Kappler, *Indian Affairs, Laws and Treaties,* 2: 365-367.

9. Violence on the frontier was not uncommon. To mention a few episodes, Cyprien Menard, in 1840 visiting his sister Berenice Chouteau at the Town of Kansas, wrote of three young men wrestling over a knife. In the struggle, one of them, an Indian, was cut so badly that he died of his wounds. (Cyprien Menard to Pierre Chouteau, July 16, 1840, *PMC,* Letter 1089.) White settlers and Native Americans often ran afoul of each other. Francois Chouteau wrote to Pierre Menard of an action on the Grand River involving Iowa (?) Indians and resulting in the death of two Americans. (Francois Chouteau to Pierre Menard, July 18, 1836, *PMC,* Letter 737.)

10. "Life Tales of Early Days: Kansas City's First Baptismal and Marriage Records," *The Kansas City Star,* June 5, 1898, 12; Theodore Brown, *Frontier Community, Kansas City to 1870,* 31-33. For additional information about the formation of the Town Company and the men involved, see *Kansas Town Company Records* (KC352), WHMC-KC.

Rev. William Johnson, in his capacity as teacher, assured Francois that his son Menard "had enough ability" to return to school at the Barrens, where he had a brief stint a year earlier. At that time, Menard was apparently not doing well at the school, and as Francois pointed out, Berenice was unhappy about her ten-year-old son being away from home.

The William Meyers story continued to unfold in the preceding letter as Francois explained additional details: credits that may never be recovered, Indians being disappointed with Meyers, and, as previously pointed out, Mrs. Meyers's refusal to return to the wilderness of the Wea Post. Located within a few miles of present Paola, Kansas, the frontier trading place was certainly remote, and evidently too rugged for the wife of William Meyers.

Francois Chouteau may have been counting his own blessings if he recalled that his wife had taken her place in the wilderness at a time when comforts at that place were few, although the assistance of company workers and the companionship of one or two female slaves eased Berenice's burden. Nevertheless, she had left what could be called luxury behind in St. Louis and Kaskaskia, and, three-hundred miles and at least thirty days away from civilization, she had taken on the responsibility for the health and well-being of her husband and her children.

The following letter documented that the meeting with the Kickapoo chiefs had the results desired by Pierre Menard and Francois. Gilliss, taking advantage of the opportunity to improve his standing with Mr. Menard, was delivering the good news.

River of Kansas   June 17, 1833 [11]

Cher oncle,

I am writing to you through Gilliss who will bring to you the papers signed by the chiefs of the Kickapoo. Also I handed over to Meyers the money to pay to the Peoria and the Kaskaskia. I borrowed the money and I drew on Cadet for the amount, with the exception of about 500 that the Indians paid to Gilliss. I presume that we did business not far from the others. The Kickapoo asked for a trader among them. I wrote to Cadet about that. Gordon wanted to pay them 6000 in merchandise. They will not consent to that — that is to say, 4000 in merchandise and 2000 in money. That is what the Prophet [Kennekuk] told me to say. He said that his father, General [William] Clark, told him that he desired his happiness and that he will be paid in merchandise or in money as he wished, and that he was offered merchandise but that he turned it down and that money suited him much better, in that he could divide it in a more satisfactory way among his nation. And afterwards, these folks would trade for goods as they will judge appropriate. He says that he cannot divide merchandise to please these folks, that he will give to one man a piece of merchandise of which he will have no need and because of that this man is [....] satisfied.

Gordon also brought merchandise for the Loups. I presume these last mentioned will take the merchandise. Perhaps they have agreed about that in the treaty that was drawn up in St. Louis.

By Gilliss you will receive the Indian shoes that you have asked for. Meyers told me that with regards to his family he would prefer to leave the Indian trade. And he said to

---

11. *PMC*, Letter 459. Envelope: [To] Pierre Menard, Kaskaskia, Illinois, favor of Mr. W. Gilliss; [filing note] F. Chouteau, 17 June.

Frederick that if the company desired to give him 1000 dollars and a clerk that he would be trader for the Kickapoo. But I was informed also that my friend Meyers was unhappy with me for having written to you that he had left his post and because of that we lost 25 bundles also and certainly the truth is that I was obligated to send Frederick to his post and because of that I was required to make expenses that had already been incurred.

Thus you see that the reason of my friend bore no weight. I bought his [Meyers] mulatto. I gave him an order of credit for 550 from Cadet. He [the slave] is very expensive but he is skillful and a good farmer and we have the greatest difficulty obtaining men here. We have only four men and this is not enough for our different [....] we will do as we can. Berenice sends a pair [....] to Sophie. Everybody here is well. [....] suffer from my eyes.

Berenice joins me to wish you as well as my aunt and the entire family good health. Give my love to Charles. He never writes to us.

I am respectfully your affectionate nephew
Francois Chouteau

The original letter was badly torn, resulting in the gaps near the end. The Gordon mentioned was William Gordon, a special agent for Superintendent of Indian Affairs William Clark. Gordon "came to 'Kansas' in May or June 1833 to distribute annuity merchandise."[12]

The following letter, along with other topics, continued the story of the battle against cholera. Diarrhea and vomiting, typical cholera symptoms, appeared with sudden violence. Usually the victim either recovered or died within one to five days. The several strains of cholera caused by a variety of bacteria often spread along well-traveled routes both on land and water.

Independence   Aug 12, 1833[13]

Cher oncle,

We have about finished the payment of annuities except for the Loups who haven't been paid yet but who are going to be in five or six days. We have $10,000 in cash and I hope to have had three thousand more. If our merchandise had been as good as usual we would have discouraged much more the competition which we always have against us. The wife of Marshall is asking if you will advance 100 dollars on her husband's money. The Loups are not drinking as much this summer as customarily. I attribute this to the fact that they haven't received their money yet.

The Yellow Stone brought in cholera very close to our settlement and eight died from Independence to the River of Kansas. I have just seen a letter at this moment from Fort Leavenworth which says that several people have died from cholera at Council Bluffs at the agency of Dougherty. Among the seconds in command Bitchum [?] said that the

---

12. *S. Doc. No. 512*, 23rd Cong., 1st Sess. (Serial 247): 522-525.

13. PMC, Letter 467. Envelope: [To] Monsieur Pierre Menard Sr., Kaskaskia, Illinois; [from] Shawnee, Mo., Aug. 18; [postage] 18 3/4; [filing note] Aug. 12, 1833, Fs. Chouteau, Received 24 and answered 25 of the same month.

sickness was in the merchandise which the Yellow Stone had unloaded at this spot. As for us, up until the present, we've had the luck to escape from that wretched sickness.

I'm afraid, however, that some boats will end up bringing it to us here. There is more sickness than ordinarily around here and this fact has been brought about by the quantity of unripe fruit.

Cadet speaks to me of sending Abadie Beral to replace Meyers among the tribes Weas, Piankeshaws, and Peorias. It would be fitting to send him quickly. I believe he will fit the post well. And if no one is installed, others will do the trade for us.

Meyers made Cyprien pay him for the entire time [....] to [....] of his post without informing me, saying that you had promised him that he will be repaid as if he had remained at his post the whole time. I told Cyprien that if you had promised him that it was fine.

I sent the rest of the pelts by the Yellow Stone and I am eager to find a good occasion to forward the money that I have in hand which will amount to 13 or 14 thousand dollars.

Everyone at home is well.

Berenice joins me to send you as well as my aunt our sincere love.

I am with respect your nephew
Francois Chouteau

John Dougherty, Indian agent at the Council Bluffs Agency, was stricken with cholera and almost died. In connection with that, no one by the name of "Bitchum" has been identified. Possibly the name should be "Pilcher." Joshua Pilcher operated an American Fur Company trading post near the Council Bluffs Agency at this time.[14] In April 1837, he became agent of the Upper Missouri Agency for the Sioux of the Missouri, Cheyennes, and Poncas.[15]

When word came to a community that cholera was aboard a particular ship, that vessel was prevented from docking – if the captain had attempted to do so. Francois, being on the alert for news of cholera aboard any ship, would have taken a firm stance when necessary. Although the concept of contagious germs was unknown, both the Indians and the settlers understood that cholera and smallpox were spread from person to person. (Note how the Indians fled into the wilderness to escape disease.)

The suggested replacement for William Meyers among the Weas, Piankeshaws, and Peorias, was "Abadie Beral." "Beral" may have been a nickname, but "Abadie" was almost certainly a corruption of the name "Labaddie." Francois's aunt Marie Pelagie Chouteau, the sister of Francois's father, was married to Sylvestre Labaddie, and A. P. Chouteau, Francois's oldest half-brother, was married to Sophie Labbadie. The man mentioned here was probably in some way connected to the St. Louis Labaddies.

The following letter bore testimony to Berenice's basically strong constitution, a particular advantage in her wilderness life.

---

14. Ruben Golden Thwaites, "Maximilian, Prince of Wied's Travels in the Interior of North America, 1832-1834" in *Early Western Travels, 1748-1846*, 24: 14.

15. Barry, *Beginning of the West*, 321.

River of Kansas   September 9, 1833 [16]

Cher oncle,

I write to announce to you that I nearly lost my good Berenice. She had a serious illness, a fever, biliousness with a strong inflammation. She suffered for five days the most unbearable pain. And I expected to see the end from one moment to the other. I lavished upon her all the care within my power and all that I could bring from elsewhere. And thanks to God, she is beginning to gather strength, but one would say she emerged from the tomb.

I am going to arrange for Gesseau and Menard to send them down to school. I wish to find a suitable occasion for that. I beg of you to place Menard at the Barrens as soon as he arrives. And I do not know whether Gesseau would not be better off at the Barrens than at St. Louis where he is too much exposed to bad companionship. It appears to me that at the Barrens he could have no chance for bad companionship or debauchery. He's growing up. And I hope to make of him and of his brother nice boys. It seems to me that the College in St. Louis is too near to the world and all sorts of things. I beg of you to speak of this with papa and to tell me your opinion about that.

I have here 14 thousand dollars of the company that I wasn't able to send for lack of a good occasion with the rest of the pelts. Pinnsonneaux is here and the other returned to St. Louis. I made the necessary arrangements at his [Pensineau's] *arrival here to go immediately to construct his trading post among the Kickapoo. But first of all, I went to advise the agent* [Cummins] *who told me he had to see the place to designate it and make his report on it to Gen.* [William] *Clark. He promised me he would go to see the place in 2 or 3 days. But he fell very ill and he is not yet over it so you see how all these formalities slow us down. Frederick left a few days ago with the merchandise for the village of the Kansa. A few days ago a Kansa went to the fort and he left sick. Upon arrival at his lodge, he died. And 12 to 15 died in the space of two or three days. One supposes it was he who gave the illness to them. I do not believe it was the real cholera but it was something like it. They have all abandoned the village and ran away to the prairie.*

I wish you good health, give my love to my aunt.

I am with respect, your nephew,
Francois Chouteau

This letter took an unusually personal tone as Francois reflected on the gravity of his wife's illness. Berenice's brush with death was, in Francois's opinion, somehow related to the liver or gallbladder. Her illness was painful, but she survived. The Kansa Indians, however, were not so fortunate, as at least fifteen perished from a variety of cholera.

Life went on, however, and Francois considered the alternatives for the education of his sons. Gesseau had been home on holiday, and now the question was, should Gesseau go

---

16. *PMC*, Letter 473. Envelope: [To] Monsieur Pierre Menard Sr., Kaskaskia, Illinois; [from] Shawnee, Mo., Sept. 10; [postage] 18 3/4; [filing note] Sept. 9, 1833, Fs. Chouteau.

back to St. Louis College or should he join his brother Menard at St. Mary's of the Barrens in Perryville?

Gesseau's Chouteau grandparents as well as many cousins were in St. Louis. In addition, Gesseau was familiar with the St. Louis school and had performed very well there. But Francois was looking at the advantages of St. Mary's of the Barrens as he considered Gesseau's future. The school's Perryville location was close to the Menards, who were educating their own sons at the Barrens and would certainly extend their solicitude to Gesseau and Menard.

As frontier parents, Francois and Berenice had no choice but to send their sons to boarding school, as opportunity for education near home was limited. The "Mr. Dogles" school that Gesseau had attended for a while, as well as Mr. Johnson's Methodist Mission School where Menard attended classes, probably both offered only the basics of reading, writing, and arithmetic.

In the late 1830s, St. Mary's of the Barrens was offering a classical program that included Latin and Greek, and a commercial program that omitted those two languages but emphasized math and science. Both programs included chemistry, astronomy, algebra, geometry, surveying, moral and natural philosophy, and the modern languages of French, Spanish, German, and Italian.[17] St. Louis College was offering a similar schedule through the decade of the thirties.[18]

In relation to the fur business, Francois confirmed that the trader for the Kickapoos, Laurent (Laurence) Pensineau, had arrived, and that "the other" – William Meyers, who applied for the job – had returned to St. Louis.[19] Pensineau was probably a member of the family of that name that came from New Orleans to St. Louis in the late eighteenth century.[20] The wife of that Pensineau (then Pinconeau) founded the first school for girls in St. Louis that Berenice may have attended. In October 1833, Laurence Pensineau was granted a license to operate the American Fur Company trading post among the Kickapoo. The post was located approximately two miles south of Weston on the Kansas side of the river. Pensineau apparently also operated a ferry at the site.[21] As subsequent letters show, Francois was no longer responsible for that trade.

After the onset of Francois's poor health, he seldom mentioned the Shawnee Post in his letters, as his brother Cyprien was apparently in complete charge there. Frederick, at the Kansa Post at Mission Creek, was being given more responsibility: Frederick collected the credits; Frederick took the valuable merchandise up the Kansas River and brought down the furs. Francois's youngest brother was then twenty-four, and had been in the fur trade for nearly ten years.

The following letter conveys some idea of the complications caused by the lack of a banking system in western Missouri. Did Francois hesitate as he handed nearly $14,000 of the company's money to Sam Owens?

---

17. "The Metropolitan Catholic Almanac and Laity's Directory, for the year of Our Lord, 1839," in *Sadliers Catholic Directory, Almanac and Ordo*.

18. *Catalogue excerpts*, 70-73, University Archives, St. Louis University.

19. Barry, *Beginning of the West*, 248; Gilbert J. Garraghan, S.J., *Catholic Beginnings in Kansas City, Missouri*, 53, 54.

20. Louis Houck, *History of Missouri*, 2: 275.

21. George A. Root, "Ferries in Kansas, Part I – Missouri River," *Kansas Historical Quarterly* 2: 23.

Independence   September 22, 1833 [22]

Cher oncle,

I received your letter dated August 25. Today I brought here 13,800 dollars that I entrusted into the hands of [....][Samuel?] Owens to be sent to St. Louis by the steamboat Otto on the way to that place and 1000 that I kept to pay to Giraud by the order of Cadet.

With regards to Meyers, Cyprien informs me that he has paid 66 dollars for the time that he was absent last spring and not for the time that he was in the swamps. I believed Cyprien told me 100 at first, but I made a mistake. It was only 66. I did not see Major Cummins lately, but Mr. Chaine [Shane] told me that he had the money for the Kaskaskia tribe who had not yet arrived, but who should have by now. I received the two bills that you sent, one for 10 and the other for 45 that we will collect upon the first occasion. With regards to the sickness, it begins to diminish. In the country there was an outburst of very bad bilious fever. Almost all my children were ill, but they are better at present. Berenice is not yet on her feet, although she is much improved in every way from what she was. She suffers still a little and gets strong very slowly.

Cyprien and Frederick were well. Frederick went to his post among the Kansa with the merchandise. I am going to send Gesseau and Menard upon the first good opportunity, in order that they can start school at St. Mary's. [....][....].

It was the greatest sorrow when we learned of the death of the unfortunate Maxwell and the desolation in which the poor Odile must find herself. I can imagine the sad situation with her numerous family on her hands. She could not have suffered a greater loss. Her sister [Berenice] is sincerely afflicted. Divine Providence sends us blows very often which seem beyond endurance.

Extend the expression of my love to all the family. Berenice unites herself with me to wish to you as well as my good Aunt – good health.

I am respectfully,
Your affectionate nephew
Francois Chouteau

The death of Hugh Herbert Maxwell grieved Francois and Berenice and aroused sympathy for Berenice's eldest sister Marie Odile Menard Maxwell. When her husband died in September 1833, Odile was left with twelve children – the "numerous family." She lived in Kaskaskia, and it is likely that her father, Pierre Menard, helped her raise her children.

Maxwell's name lives on in the Southwest in the Maxwell Land Grant involving Herbert Maxwell's son, Lucien. Santa Fe's notable Charles Bent, in the 1840s, convinced territorial governor Armijo that he could promote settlements and lucrative cattle ranching by providing land grants to investors. The Maxwell Land Grant (also called the Miranda) consisted of 1,714,000 acres, the largest land grant in the history of the United States.

---

22. *PMC*, Letter 478. Envelope: [To] Monsieur Pierre Menard Sr., Kaskaskia, Illinois; [from] Independence, Mo., Sept. 25; [filing note] Sept. 22, 1833, Fs. Chouteau.

Francois's letters show that he found the Meyers incident a continued aggravation. As instructed by Mr. Menard, the Chouteaus paid Meyers for the time he did not spend at the post, but did not pay for the time Meyers spent at the post, that is, in the swamps near the Marais des Cygne. (Meyers had already been paid for that time, apparently.)

The Giraud to whom Francois was paying $1,000 was Michel Giraud, who was on the payroll of the Osage Agency of Paul Liguest Chouteau from October 1831 to September 1832 for carrying annuities. By 1839, Giraud was in present Linn County, Kansas, operating a trading post that had been licensed to Cadet Chouteau, serving the "newly arrived" Potawatomis. Located about three miles west of the Missouri state line, this became the town of Trading Post.[23]

The new steamboat *Otto* made its first run to the Kansas River in April 1832 with James Hill as master. The greater number of steamboats on the Missouri was changing the way Chouteau ran his business – steamboat transportation, while more reliable and faster, was more costly. Passengers quickly took up steamboat travel, and slowly but surely, the old pirogues and keelboats began disappearing from the river.

The letter that follows passed on to Pierre Menard a few business details and the latest family news. Francois conjured up the delightful image of himself and Berenice traveling about the rugged countryside, breathing the fresh air, and enjoying the sights of hills, trees, streams, and wild animals.

River of Kansas   November 25, 1833[24]

Cher oncle,

I received your last letter by the steamboat John Nelson where I see that you were at St. Louis with two of your sons and that you were to take Menard with you to enroll him in college at the Barrens. I would have wished that Gesseau had gone with his brother, but since papa did not so wish, I do not desire to hurt him, or to distress him in any way.

Berenice wants to go to spend the winter in Kaskaskia and I engaged her to come down with the little boys but she did not want to go before the return of the same ship that was to return right away. But the water was so low that the ship did not come all the way to us and I would have come down with her. She had a relapse of her sickness but at present she is better. And I hope that the change of seasons will put her back on her feet little by little. I left the house for a month to take her on a tour of the surrounding prairie and of Independence. That did her a lot of good. The rest of the family is fine. I suffer from time to time from chest trouble.

The Kickapoo post is now established. As soon as I was able to obtain a location and a license from the agent, I took the measures in such a way that the post could be built in a short time. It is four miles from the fort, in a beautiful location, that is to say, above the garrison and in the sight of the Missouri.

---

23. Barry, *Beginning of the West*, 376.
24. *PMC*, Letter 498. Envelope: [To] Monsieur Pierre Menard Sr., Kaskaskia, State of Illinois; [from] Shawnee, Mo., November 26; [postage] 18 3/4; [filing note] November 24, 1833, Fs. Chouteau.

> *Andre is our trader this year among the Wea and the Peoria, and I am very sure there are many whites who are not as good as he is. In any case, Frederick is at his post among the Kansa and all the Indians are hunting.*
>
> *Berenice and I wish good health to you as well as to my aunt and extend our love to all your family. Tell many things to poor Odile whom we remember with much concern. Berenice will write to you by the next mail. Liguest was here three days ago and he came ahead of Mr. Ellsworth who returned from among the Pawnees and who is taking 40 men to make peace with the Osage. Mrs. Ellsworth passed by here and expressed her desire to know all the Chouteaus.*
>
> *I am with respect, your nephew*
> *Francois Chouteau*
>
> *At the present we have here a Cure, Mr. Roux who desires to remain in our country. I believe he is a worthy man. We intend to build a small church for him. All the French families here are well disposed to supply, according to their ability. Berenice assures me she intends to put in a contribution. You, papa, and Cadet, you are able to judge better than I that the thing cannot be anything but advantageous. We will then later on certainly have a small group of fine people. The riffraff perhaps will improve as this will be a cause of betterment for the area. F. C.*

A note of excited optimism crept into Francois's postscript announcing the arrival of the Catholic priest, Rev. Benedict Roux. Chouteau used the form of address common at that time: "Mr." before the surname, rather than "Reverend." The title "Reverend" was not used consistently in the early 1800s, and many persons addressed a priest or clergyman as "Mr." Most of the French pioneers around Chouteau's Landing were Catholics, but few of them would have been able to offer financial support to the church. The Chouteaus were probably the one frontier Catholic family that could realize the building of a church.

Father Roux was an idealistic Frenchman who came to America in 1831 to evangelize the Native Americans. He was scholarly, slight of build, and spoke only French and Latin. The St. Louis bishop in charge of Catholic activities in a huge area of the Upper Louisiana Purchase was Bishop Joseph Rosati. Rosati recognized that Father Roux was not suited to Indian mission work.

Father Roux, however, plagued Bishop Rosati until the prelate finally agreed that the priest could establish a parish for the French Catholics near the mouth of the Kansas River. In November 1833, Father Roux arrived at Chouteau's Landing, having traveled by horseback through Liberty and Independence. In April 1834, Father Roux purchased the forty acres previously mentioned. A log church was built there in 1835, and the importance of Francois and Berenice to this project was evident; it was called "Chouteau's Church," while the rugged thoroughfare on the south side of it was called Chouteau's Street. (Present 12th Street.)

The steamboat *John Nelson* that brought the letter that Francois answered was another American Fur Company steamboat built to ride high in the water for navigating the often-inadequate depths of the Missouri River. Even so, the next time the *John Nelson* came up from St. Louis, the ship was unable to reach Chouteau's Landing and probably turned around at Franklin. Although Francois "had engaged," that is, made a reservation on the vessel for Berenice and the two little boys (Benjamin, five years old, and Frederic Donatien, two), they were unable to go to Kaskaskia at that time.

The uncertainty about where Francois and Berenice's oldest son Gesseau was to attend school seemed to have been settled by the boy's Chouteau grandfather, who wanted Gesseau to attend St. Louis College. Francois's wish for his son to go to Perryville was probably supported by the warm and slightly overbearing Pierre Menard in an appeal to Pierre Chouteau. Nevertheless, it seemed that when Pierre Menard left St. Louis, he would be escorting his sons and only one grandson, Pierre Menard Chouteau, back to St. Mary's of the Barrens in Perryville.

Pierre Menard probably was making his last autumn visit to St. Louis before ice began to develop on the Mississippi, leaving navigation to only the foolhardy. The Menard sons in St. Louis with their father were two of the three younger boys: Saucier, Cyprien, or Amadee. The older sons were occupied elsewhere, with Pierre Jr. serving as Indian agent in Peoria, Illinois, and Edmond in college at Georgetown University, Washington City (D.C.).

The fall of 1833 had been a busy time for Francois's fur trade business. A new trader had to be found to replace Meyers at the Wea Post. Or, as Chouteau had remarked in his letter of August 12, 1833, "others will do the trade for us." The Andre sent to the Wea Post has not been identified, but was apparently a mixed-blood French and Indian, or a mulatto, as Chouteau commented that there were many "whites" not as good as he.

The Kickapoo post, four miles above the garrison of Fort Leavenworth and within sight of the Missouri River, was ready for Laurent Pensineau to begin business. As for the proposed post among the Delaware-Loups, it seemed that Pierre Menard took Francois's advice and abandoned the idea.

The Ellsworth party mentioned in the preceding letter was led by Henry Ellsworth, one of three commissioners appointed by President Andrew Jackson to investigate the condition of immigrant and resident tribes in the "Far West." Ellsworth and his wife came from Connecticut. Members of the group of about thirty persons traveling with Ellsworth apparently came and went in random fashion. Some of the notables riding part of the distance were a young Swiss count, the English traveler Charles Joseph Latrobe, and writer Washington Irving.[25]

Ellsworth was in Missouri and the Indian country from the autumn of 1832 until the end of 1833. He traveled from one Indian village to another, trying to make peace between warring tribes and negotiating land agreements and concessions from the Indians. He met with chiefs, Indian agents, military commanders, and traders. From the Osage to the south to the Otoes in the north, he visited them all.

Although Ellsworth and the two other commissioners, Montfort Stokes and Rev. John Schermerhorn, had been appointed partially for humanitarian reasons, in the end they were bargaining and trying to push the Indians to other locations in a tragically familiar pattern.

---

25. Descriptions of the trip can be found in *The Western Journals of Washington Irving*, edited and annotated by John Francis McDermott, and *Washington Irving on the Prairie; or, A Narrative of a Tour of the Southwest in the Year 1832*, by Henry Leavitt Ellsworth and edited by Stanley T. Williams and Barbara D. Simison.

Scene of St. Francis Regis – "Chouteau's Church" – and to its right, the rectory cabin. Behind the church was the Catholic cemetery. *"Depart de Westport,"* drawn by Nicolas Point, S.J., Folder 1, *Pierre Jean De Smet (1801-1873) Papers*, Manuscripts, Archives, and Special Collections, Washington State University Libraries.

6

"We Have a Lot of Disappointment This Year...."

Chouteau's challenges on the frontier had an element of sameness, with some variations from day to day. The following letter responded to another family sorrow as well as new complications in the fur trade.

River of Kansas   January 15, 1834 [1]

Cher oncle,

I received your last letter of the date of December 4 where you say to me that my two boys are at school together at the Barrens to my great satisfaction.

---

1. *PMC*, Letter 522. Envelope: [To] Monsieur Pierre Menard Sr., Kaskaskia, Illinois; [from] Shawnee, Mo., January 17th; [postage] 18 3/4; [filing note] January 15, 1834, Received the 5th of February and answered the 7th of the month, F. [....].

The package of which you speak to me is a box sent to my aunt by Berenice. It contained a large bedspread and a ball of yarn to make a rug. I had written the name of my aunt on the box but I suppose it had been erased. I gave the letter to Helen Decoigne and I read it to her. She told me to inform you that she does not want to sell her land for the time being. McLaine has died and she is very unhappy. She wishes to be paid by Lorimer and to withdraw the little credit that she had made at Kaskaskia.

The two bills that you sent me, I hope that we can get the payment out of them. I gave the one for 40 to Pinsoneau to collect and the one for 10 against Marie I propose to collect myself when she receives the annuities.

It is with much sorrow that we learned that poor Odile lost her daughter Lucretia which is a new cause of sorrow for her. That poor unfortunate person has suffered rude attacks. We had not heard of this last bad news prior to reception of your letter.

I am unable to inform you yet of the result of the treaty. There are many Indians who have not yet come out and our treaty is not yet finished. The season was very favorable for the hunt. I have just arrived from among the Wea and the Piankeshaw where I have been since the month of December to collect the debts. The Kansa, I believe, will have a successful hunt and will pay off their debts well, although we have the competition of Morgan against us. I do not know why the company furnishes merchandise to this man who, afterwards, comes to oppose us among all the Indians. It seems to me that it's not a good understanding of one's own interests – it's just fighting among themselves.

Berenice is much recovered from her illness. There only remains a little weakness. The children are well as everybody else.

Give our love to my aunt.

I am respectfully your nephew
Francois Chouteau

We wish you a good and a happy New Year.

This letter confirmed that both Gesseau and Menard were in school at St. Mary's of the Barrens, and Francois acknowledged that it was "to my great satisfaction." So, it seems Pierre Menard did not rest Francois's case but convinced Pierre Chouteau that his grandson Gesseau would best be sent to St. Mary's, in accordance with his father's wishes.

Berenice's recently widowed sister, Odile Maxwell, lost her seventeen-year-old daughter Marie Therese on November 9, 1833. As the French so often bestowed nicknames on their children, the girl must have been called "Lucretia" in honor of some person dear to the family.

Collecting debts owed to Pierre Menard or the American Fur Company occupied an increasing amount of Francois Chouteau's time. The "Decoigne" mentioned in the preceding letter possibly should read "Le Coigne." A Le Coigne was one of the persons representing the Peorias and Kaskaskias at the signing of a peace treaty on November 12, 1833.[2] Helen

---

2. Louise Barry, *Beginning of the West*, 251.

was probably a member of that extended family and would have been acquainted with Pierre Menard because of his long association with the Peoria and Kaskaskia Indians. If she had lived for some time around Kaskaskia, that would explain how she came to own land there that Pierre Menard was interested in purchasing. (To "withdraw a credit" meant to pay a bill.)

The death of a man named "McLaine" was making this Helen unhappy, according to Chouteau, but that person has not been identified. The name "McLean" did appear in connection with the Piankeshaw bands, and it is possible that Chouteau's phonetic rendering was "McLane."

"Marie," from whom Francois promised to collect a ten-dollar debt, also has not been identified. Francois consistently used first names only when referring to Native Americans; since this woman was called "Marie," she was very likely a Native American, who owed money to Pierre Menard.

Francois had previously complained about the American Fur Company's having more than one trader competing for the same territory. In this letter, he broached the subject again. An Alexander G. Morgan was sutler to Fort Leavenworth in the fall of 1834. Perhaps he ran a trading operation on the side, especially when he knew the Indians had cash to spend.

Pierre Menard himself had tried to do something about a similar situation in 1829, when two traders, John Ogle and William Gilliss, were in a trading war on the James River. Menard wrote two identical letters to Ogle and Gilliss, chiding them for competing against each other by paying high prices for fur pelts and charging low prices for the merchandise. The Indians enjoyed a brief bonanza until Ogle and Gilliss finally understood the message.[3]

The next letter was written in St. Louis. The Chouteau family group included Francois, Berenice, and their sons: six-year-old Benjamin, three-year-old Frederic Donatien, and one-year-old Benedict Pharamond. The summer voyage east provided the opportunity to see family and friends in St. Louis and Kaskaskia. In addition, Francois would have had business to take care of, and Berenice would have shopped. Pierre Menard was apparently in St. Louis at the same time as Francois and Berenice. The proximity to Perryville makes it probable that either the Chouteaus went to Perryville or Gesseau and Menard came to St. Louis or Kaskaskia to see their parents.

St. Louis   July 21, 1834 [4]

Cher oncle,

It is with pleasure that we learned of your arrival home with Peter in good health. We are all well enough, the last one to be sick was one of my children. The steamboat Assiniboine hasn't arrived yet, on which we were counting on going home. However, it is possible we will return in from six to eight days on another ship. We always have hope to see you before our departure. Berenice tells my aunt she has purchased articles for the nuns at as good a price as she could find. There are no more small all-white handkerchiefs. She was unable to find any. The music notebook is not exactly what she would have wanted, but

---

3. Pierre Menard to John Ogle and Pierre Menard to William Gilliss, December 24, 1829, Letterbook J, *Pierre Menard Collection*, IHS.

4. *PMC*, Letter 578. Envelope: [To] Monsieur Pierre Menard Sr., Kaskaskia, Illinois; [filing note] July 21, 1834; F. Chouteau.

she presumes they will serve the purpose. I have no news deserving of your attention for the moment. It appears that there is no, or very little, cases of disease in St. Louis at the moment. Give our love to my aunt, say "hello" to Peter for me and that we want to see him badly.

I am with respect your affectionate nephew
Francois Chouteau

The American Fur Company steamboat *Assiniboin* that Francois and Berenice hoped to ride home was named in honor of the Assiniboin Indians of the Upper Missouri. Like other American Fur Company ships designed for the Upper Missouri, the *Assiniboin* was built with a light draft. As Francois and Berenice knew, steamboats going all the way up the Missouri could not be relied on to meet a schedule, as the variable water level affected their progress.

"Peter" was Pierre Menard Jr. During the late 1820s, he had served as subagent for the Indian Department in Peoria, Illinois, but Peter no longer held that government position because the Indians had been removed. From April-August 1832, Peter Menard had fought in the Black Hawk War. Perhaps at the time of the preceding letter he was unoccupied and making a long visit to family in Kaskaskia.

While in St. Louis, Berenice indulged in some city shopping, something she apparently enjoyed. In her letter of April 18, 1827, to Angelique Menard, Berenice wrote of shopping errands. Although by 1834 St. Louis offered a wider variety of stores, Berenice was unable to find what she needed. The nuns for whom she sought the white handkerchiefs were the Visitation Sisters, an order of Catholic religious women who, with financial assistance from Pierre Menard, established a convent and school for girls in Kaskaskia in 1833. The flood of 1844 destroyed their establishment and the sisters moved to St. Louis. It was this Kaskaskia convent school some writers have erroneously maintained that Berenice attended. Any roster listing a "Berenice" must have referred to Berenice Maxwell, the daughter of Odile Maxwell, Berenice Menard Chouteau's sister. By 1833, when the Kaskaskia convent school opened, Berenice Menard Chouteau, mother of five, was long past her school days.

That Berenice would be shopping for a music notebook contributes to the lore of her love of music. Legend has it that Madame Chouteau brought the first piano to western Missouri, tied to the deck of a rocking keelboat. Local tradition also attributes to Berenice a great fondness for the fiddle music played in rousing fashion by the Rivard brothers at the dances organized around Chouteau's Landing during the long winter months. Berenice was so enamored of these "balls" that she had a serious clash with the pastor of the Catholic parish, Father Benedict Roux, who considered dancing a moral hazard.[5] The opinion of the prim French priest differed dramatically from that of his successor, Father Bernard Donnelly, who recalled that he never saw anything more proper than the "balls" of the little French community.[6]

Two weeks after the previous letter, the Chouteaus were still in St. Louis, waiting for a steamboat to take them home.

---

5. Benedict Roux to Joseph Rosati, February 12, 1835, Rev. Benedict Roux folder, *Letters of Bishop Joseph Rosati*, Archives of the Archdiocese of St. Louis, St. Louis, Missouri.

6. "When the Indians Danced at Westport," *The Kansas City Catholic Register*, 5 October 1916, 1.

St. Louis   August 4, 1834[7]

Cher oncle,

I received your last letter, dated July 29. I did your errand for Roland and Auguste. Peter has left for the Illinois River the day after you left St. Louis.

Berenice is much better as well as the children. Our steamboat hasn't yet arrived; we await it from one day to another. As soon as it arrives, we will be ready to go. There is a small mill in the store at St. Charles that I would have liked to have very much to grind the corn meal. I am angry [with myself that] *I did not take it while I was there to take back to Kansas.*

I beg of you to give our love to my aunt and to all your family.

I am respectfully, your affectionate nephew,
Francois Chouteau

While Francois and Berenice were yet in St. Louis, they saw Peter Menard depart for the "Illinois River," meaning Peoria, Illinois. Among frequent travelers of water routes, it was common practice at that time to identify a town by the river on which it was situated. Francois and Berenice both, for many years, identified their location as "River of Kansas."

The "Roland" for whom an errand was accomplished was probably John Ruland, who after 1826 was a special subagent for Superintendent of Indian Affairs William Clark.[8] "Auguste," though not identified with certainty, was probably A. P. Chouteau, Francois's half-brother, who had been with the Ellsworth party. Auguste could not have been Francois's uncle, Auguste Chouteau, as he had died in 1829. Another relative with the first name of Auguste was Francois's cousin Auguste Aristade, but he also was deceased.

Francois's description of the "small mill" for grinding cornmeal can only suggest that, although he did not ask him to do so, Francois hoped that Pierre Menard or one of his employees would purchase the device for him. While the letters contain nothing more on the topic, perhaps the "little mill" was delivered to Chouteau's Landing within the next few weeks.

The long delay in St. Louis, as the following letter announced, had a sad finale:

St. Louis   August 16, 1834[9]

Cher oncle,

We had the sorrow to lose our poor little last one. He died the 6th of the present. I always fear such a misfortune while spending the summer here. I would have liked to send you better lard than that which you have gotten, but the ones I brought and [....] *that, I believe that Sarpy has charged you for* [....] *two barrels.*

---

7. *PMC*, Letter 583. Envelope: [Stamped] St. Louis, Aug. 4, Missouri; [postage] 10; [to] Monsieur Pierre Menard, Kaskaskia, Illinois; [filing note] August 4, 1834, F. Chouteau.

8. Louise Barry, "William Clark's Diary, May 1826-February 1831," *Kansas Historical Quarterly* 16: 4.

9. *PMC*, Letter 587. Envelope: [Stamped] St. Louis, Aug. 18, Missouri; [postage] 10; [to] Monsieur Pierre Menard Sr., Kaskaskia, Illinois; [filing note] The carrier also carried for Gesseau a towel and some soap; August 16, 1834, Fs. Chouteau.

The money which Berenice advanced to the nuns she wants you [when they repay it] *to give it to my aunt in order that she distribute it from time to time to our boys in college, Gesseau and Menard. We have all been sick since your departure from here. At present we are better. I presume that we will leave next Thursday on the Galena that is going to Independence.*
Give our love to my aunt.

I am with respect your nephew,
Francois Chouteau

The "little last one" who died on August 6, 1834, was eighteen-month-old Benedict Pharamond Chouteau. The child was buried in St. Louis. Although no cause of death was given, the late summer date suggests that what had affected the entire family was a kind of malarial fever that appeared annually and seemed, according to Francois, to be more prevalent along the Mississippi than on the western part of the Missouri River.

Several weeks elapsed before Francois sent the following letter by courier.

River of Kansas   November 25, 1834 [10]

Cher oncle,

I am writing to you by way of Mr. Hughes, our trader among the Wea and Peoria who is going to Jefferson Barracks for court-martial. Right now, the Indians for the most part are hunting. I presume they will do a lot of pelts from now into the spring. We made 6000 in annuities. We had a lot of competition. Four stores at all the places where payments were made, that gave the merchandise at so low a price that it is impossible to make the least profit. As for us, we didn't want to give away the goods but we sold them at a lower profit. This year we did not share the annuities of the Kickapoo. Pinsonneau received from them 4000. The Kansa have not been paid, not having assembled at their village. Then the Indians do not exchange all their money for merchandise. They have other needs, such as horses, animals, food, and whiskey.

They always keep a good amount for those articles. Then, I am told, there is one salesman of whiskey who made from four to five hundred dollars in the final payments and right now the whole eastern side is filled with whiskey salesmen. We have six bundles of fine beaver, 200 of otter, 15 packs of raccoon, and 50-60 of deerskins and a little of muskrats. I believe that with the Kansa a good quantity of skins will be exchanged and that we will get about all their annuities or the greater part.

I gave to Pinsonneau the bill for the Indian to whom you had advanced credit for a horse. He promised me that he would make him pay. Marie paid ten dollars that she owed you. The Indians still have money from their annuities as

---

10. *PMC*, Letter 608. Envelope: [To] Monsieur Pierre Menard Sr., Kaskaskia, Illinois; [filing note] Francois Chouteau, 25 November 1834, Received December 17, 1834, answered the [....].

we are trading a little every day. Frederick and Cyprien have arrived from the Marais de Cygne. They went to hunt there. They killed 50 pieces of game and returned well pleased. I would have liked to have been a part of the crowd also but we couldn't all leave the post.

Berenice is in good health as well as the children. It appears that the sickness is going to pass us by.

We wish to you as well as to my aunt good health.

I am with respect,
Your nephew
Francois Chouteau

I beg of you when you will write us, to address the letter: West Port, Jackson County. The post office is near our home. I beg of you to forward the [enclosed] *letter to my children as soon as possible.*

The courier of for Francois's letter, Mr. Hughes, who was on his way to the Jefferson Barracks military installation, was the American Fur Company's trader among the Weas. Exactly one year before to the day, the Wea trader was reported to be a man named "Andre." Several factors combine to confuse the identity of this person (or these persons) at the Wea Post. No first name was given for the Mr. Hughes of the preceding letter. This was typical of Francois's style – he used first names for relatives, French friends, children, and Native Americans. Anglo-Americans were usually called "Mr." and then the surname. An Andrew Hughes served as an Indian agent during the time of these letters, but there is no evidence that he was the same person as either Andre or Mr. Hughes. It is remotely possible that these persons were one and the same, but not likely.

Mr. Hughes, as mysterious as many other persons mentioned in these letters, was obligated to report to Jefferson Barracks in St. Louis. Was Mr. Hughes himself being court-martialed? Possibly. During 1834-1835, a rash of court-martials occurred at Jefferson Barracks. The post was plagued with cholera and a twenty-two percent desertion rate.[11] A private named P. Hughes was court-martialed there in October 1835. Even allowing that the wheels of justice grind slowly, a year seems a long time for Hughes to await his trial (he was carrying Chouteau's letter to St. Louis in November 1834). Or perhaps Hughes was to be a witness, and if so, his name may be buried somewhere in government records.[12] Francois may have assumed Pierre Menard knew about Hughes and the court-martial, as he did not explain it.

The selling of whiskey to the Indians continued to be a problem. It was perhaps easier for the government to control the selling of whiskey in Indian Territory than it was within the state of Missouri. The "eastern side" mentioned by Chouteau referred to Jackson County, where many merchants sold liquor to anyone with the money for it.[13]

---

11. Letter from Louise Arnold-Friend, US Army Military History Institute, to Dorothy Marra, November 22, 1999.

12. Letter from David Wallace, Old Military and Civil Records, National Archives, to Dorothy Marra, December 6, 1999.

13. For additional information about the selling whiskey to the Indians, see Tanis C. Thorne's article "Liquor Has Been Their Undoing: Liquor Trafficking and Alcohol Abuse in the Lower Missouri Fur Trade." *Gateway Heritage* 13 (Fall 1992): 4-23, and William E. Unrau's *White Man's Wicked Water: The Alcohol Trade and Prohibition in Indian Country, 1802-1892*.

In August 1834, Kansa subagent Marston Clark was reassigned from the Kansa Agency to become subagent of the Shawnees, Ottawas, Weas, Piankeshaws, and Peorias. The Kansa Agency was abruptly closed with no explanation. A year earlier, in August 1833, Francois's old crony, Shawnee subagent John Campbell, had been discharged. Clark replaced Dr. F. W. Miller, Campbell's replacement. It was then Cyprien Chouteau, in his Shawnee Post at the Turner site, who had to deal with Marston Clark.

Clark packed up his grudge against the Chouteaus and carried it intact to his new assignment. His first action as Shawnee subagent was to license four competitors for the Cyprien Chouteau post: Flourney & Co., John O. Agnew, Henry McKee, and George B. Clark, Marston's son.[14] All were Americans, whereas in the old days, they would probably have all been French. Although the French often banded together and networked within their community, they were not the only ones who filled positions with family members. The Clarks were a case in point.

Francois's next letter was written to Cadet on a scrap of paper, probably in a hasty effort to get his message onto an outgoing steamboat. He was having second thoughts about entrusting four letters and various documents to a relative of the blacksmith of the Delaware-Loups.

Jackson County   December 4, 1834[15]

Cher frere,

I write you a little letter because I am in a place where there is no paper. I wish for you to let me know if you have received four letters and several receipts from the man of the Mountain with the receipt from Mr. Roux for 40 which I paid him. There was a letter for you, one for Mr. Menard, one for my children at the Barrens, and one for Mme G. Kennerly. Donlape the blacksmith of the Loups tells me that he knew a good opportunity that was going straight to St. Louis, one of his relatives, and that I could be assured that my letters would be delivered to you, so I confided my papers to him, etc. etc.

Nothing new. I wish you good health.

Your affectionate brother,
Fcois Chouteau

The Mr. "Donlape" whose relative was to carry the packet of papers to St. Louis was Robert Dunlap, the blacksmith for the Delaware-Loups.[16] One of the letters was for Mrs. George Kennerly, Berenice's sister Alzire. Probably Cadet was to see that the letters reached their proper destinations.

An interpretive dilemma arises from the reference to the receipts from the man of the mountain and the receipt from Mr. Roux. With the insertion of a comma after mountain, the receipt from Mr. Roux becomes a separate item. In that case, Mr. Roux was probably the Reverend Benedict Roux, the first resident Catholic priest of western Missouri, whom the Chouteaus were pledged to help. Perhaps they advanced forty dollars to him, for Father

---

14. *H. Doc. No. 97*, 23rd Cong. 2nd sess. (Serial 273).
15. Francois Chouteau to Pierre (Cadet) Chouteau Jr., December 4, 1834, *Chouteau Family Collections*, MHS. No envelope.
16. Barry, *Beginning of the West*, 211.

Roux was always short of money, as documented in his letters to Bishop Rosati in St. Louis. The time and the place were right for this to be a reference to the pastor of the French Catholics. There is, however, no record of any forty-dollar donation or loan to Father Roux.

On the other hand, it is possible that Francois was singling out a particular receipt from the "man of the Mountain," a Mr. Roux. Joaquin Antoine Le Roux was a St. Louis man who had taken to the Rockies in search of furs and went occasionally to the Southwest in quest of Spanish silver. Perhaps Francois bought furs from him.

This puzzle demonstrates the kind of problems caused by the lack of punctuation in these letters.

Five months elapsed between the December 1834 letter and the next one, also to Cadet, dated May 1, 1835. During that time, at least two other letters were written but did not survive. In Francois's following letter, and in letters to Pierre Menard dated May 5, 1835, and May 14, 1835, Chouteau stated that he had written to Mr. Menard at Ste. Genevieve. On the same day that he penned the following letter, he had already written Cadet another letter and sent it by post. Either these letters did not reach their destination or they were not filed for future reference. The following letter accompanied the fur shipment aboard Mr. Shallcross's steamboat. Notice the unusual dateline – "entrance to the river."

At the entrance to the river   May 1, 1835 [17]

Cher frere,

I write you by Captain Shalcross who leaves tomorrow morning. I wrote you today by the post. You will receive by this boat 190 packs. I counted them during the night with the captain. He found 190 and I 185. It is possible that I made a mistake, being very tired, having been on horseback all day. I cannot tell you at present the quantity of each kind of fur. You will know that at another opportunity because of having loaded quickly during the night but it is principally all the packs from our post down below, which are deerskins, raccoons, and [musk] rats. The otter and beaver are still at the post with other furs which I bought in Independence. I believe there will be 10 packs of beaver and much otter. The barge is nearly thirty miles from the post down below. The men are all sick with the fever because of loading and unloading in the water. Their feet and legs are useless. I have been obliged to send others to their aid. I presume that the barge will be here in six days, etc. About the skins from Jeffrey and William Owens, which I bought thirty miles from Liberty and which you will receive by this boat, I am going to tell you the quantity, etc.

Deerskins	*5,343 # at 27 ct.*	*Bear skins*	*46 at 1.50*
Raccoons	*535. at 25*	*Wax*	*30# at 15. ct*
Muskrats	*1000. at 20*	*One sac* [18]	*25*
Beaver	*.42# at 4*	*Three elk skins*	*at 1-each*
Otter	*28. at 4*	*70 packs of deerskins, weight as you see it above.*	

---

17. Francois Chouteau to Pierre (Cadet) Chouteau Jr., May 1, 1835, *Chouteau Family Collections*, MHS. No envelope.

18. Annotation on the letter made by historian John McDermott equates one sack to six bushels.

Robidoux passed here just a few days ago. I presume that he will have told you that he sent off a package [of merchandise] *to the Pawnees. You must know if that is according to your arrangements. I think of buying more furs. I have bought about 1500 in our neighborhood with the money that we got from the Kansa. I have drawn on you in favor of Samuel C. Owens for 2133. — I will try to have all the other packs ready for the first opportunity, although there remained 30 packs of raccoons at the post of the Kansa, etc. etc.*

I wish you good health.
Your affectionate brother,
Francois Chouteau

When Francois was at his Kansas City warehouse, the dateline of his letters read "River of Kansas." The preceding letter from "entrance to the river" identified a different point of origin: "the piece of land at the entrance of the Kansas River" that Francois had entered "for the company" and reported in his February 24, 1832, letter to Pierre Menard. In a letter to Cadet the previous October, Francois had written that Gilliss intended to enter the land in accordance with Pierre Menard's wishes, but this apparently did not happen.

The post "down below" that Chouteau mentioned was the Kansas City warehouse; however, the 190 packs that Shallcross was bringing down to Cadet were loaded at the steamboat landing at the entrance to the Kansas River. Why were the furs from the Kansas City warehouse being picked up at another site? A possible scenario is that the water in the Missouri River, like the Kansas, was very low. Perhaps the steamboat could not anchor close enough to Chouteau's Landing to load the furs. Therefore, the furs were carried by wagons to the pick-up site at the entrance to the river where, apparently, the water was deep enough.

Meanwhile, furs from the Kansa Post that should have also been on the way to St. Louis were still being loaded and unloaded from the barge stranded by low water in the Kansas River.

The letter that Francois wrote to Cadet earlier in the day may have described this arrangement. (This letter is not in any collection.) Francois's letter of May 14, 1835, to Pierre Menard supports this theory, as Francois referred to the shipment of furs he was then making as being "the remainder."

Captain John Shallcross, who carried Chouteau's letter along with the shipment of furs to Cadet Chouteau's American Fur Company warehouse, was, as explained in connection with Francois's letter of May 20, 1833, an experienced river pilot and would have been capable of making the difficult pick-up.

In addition to the pelts from the Kansas City warehouse, Chouteau had purchased furs from William Owens of Clay County and his partner Jeffries. The latter was possibly Thomas Jeffries, at one time a trader on the Upper Missouri. William Owens may have been the fellow who received a license for a ferry across the Platte River at Cow Ford in 1837.[19]

When voluble Joseph Robidoux came down from his trading post at Black Snake Creek, he dropped in at Chouteau's warehouse boasting of sending a package of merchandise to the Pawnees, for whom he was not licensed. Robidoux had no idea he was touching a sore point with Chouteau. Tales of Robidoux's antics abound in the legend and history of St. Joseph, Missouri, of which Robidoux was the founder. In 1826, Joseph Robidoux established

---

19. *Clay County Record Book* 3, 199 (October 2, 1837), Clay County Archives, Liberty, Missouri. Note that at the time Platte County was part of Clay County.

a post where Black Snake Creek empties into the Missouri River. He, too, worked for the American Fur Company and around his post a community of workers and Indians formed a permanent settlement. In 1843, Joseph Robidoux platted the city of St. Joseph, naming streets after some of his many children. After Robidoux's 1835 visit, Chouteau, always meticulous in business affairs, reported something he thought Cadet should know about – that is, Robidoux sending of merchandise to the Pawnees.

The listing of fur pelts included "muskrats"; historian John McDermott identified *rats de bois* (rats of the woods) as possums, although this letter used only the word for "rats," which usually meant "muskrats."

The following letter explained the reason that no letters were written to *"Cher Oncle"* from December 1834 to May 1835. Pierre Menard was in Washington City (D.C.), having traveled to the capital in an attempt to collect a debt owed by the federal government to Menard's former business partner, Barthelemi Tardiveau, for supplies and services rendered during the Revolutionary War. Tardiveau's estate was, in turn, in debt to Pierre Menard and the government notes were signed over to him. This was one of three trips Pierre Menard made to Washington City in an effort to collect this sum, but it was never paid to him or to his estate.[20]

River of Kansas   May 5, 1835 [21]

Cher oncle,

I'm taking advantage of Gilliss who leaves today to give to you news of us, because I suppose that you have returned from Washington and I hope you enjoy good health. I wrote a letter to you that I addressed Menard and Valle, Ste. Genevieve, where I answer you about the wagon and the money that you supposed that I will receive from [William? Marston?] Clark and Roland.

We have a lot of disappointment this year by the lack of water in the Kansas River. Our barge that set off to go down from the trading post of the Kansa has been gone since the beginning of March has not yet arrived. I expect it, however, within four or five days. All the men have fallen ill with the fever from loading and unloading in the water. I was obliged to send others to assist them. Right now the river is lower than it was in the month of January. We have around 450 bundles, 350 that we made at the trading post and 100 that I purchased from one place or another. Of that quantity, ten are of beaver, ten of otter, fifty to sixty of raccoons, rats and the remaining, deerskin.

We have caught some annuities from the Kansa, 2500. That money was only paid to me in the month of December. I put on board the steamboat St. Charles, three days ago, 250 packs. There remains to us 200 from the Kansa that haven't yet arrived, but which I await from one moment to another and that I will send on by the first occasion. I am going to see Major Cummins again about the money for Baptiste Pascal and Francoise. If [Marston] Clark has not handed over the money to Major Cummins, it is very doubtful [....] is more [....].

---

20. *Guide to the Microfilm Edition of the Pierre Menard Collection*, 5.
21. *PMC*, Letter 655. Envelope: [To] Monsieur Pierre Menard, Kaskaskia, Ill.; [filing note] May 5, 1835, Received the 10th.

I wrote to my boys at the Barrens every time the mail goes out since the month of February and the poor children tell me they haven't received a single one of my letters. I cannot conceive where they were sent. It is certain that business at the post office is not well managed.

Berenice joins herself to me to convey to you as well as to my aunt and to the whole family the expression of our sincere love. Our children have had a bout of the fever all this winter.

*I am respectfully your
affectionate nephew
Francois Chouteau*

*[....] the [....] of Berenice [....] a package of 15 [....] [....]
Francois and promised to come upon my return from college.
Read to Dowling on the 16th, Lorimer on the 11th and to Stephan on the 11th and to Langlois on the 11th and to send to John Latredo title, taxes on the 11th.*

The two notes written by Pierre Menard at the bottom of this letter are apparently unrelated. The meanings of both are unclear. In the first note, the "college" was almost certainly St. Mary's of the Barrens at Perryville. In the second note, perhaps the men whose names were listed had business or legal dealings with Pierre Menard. In that connection, some document was read to them, and they probably initialed the document, indicating that they were aware of its contents. (This procedure was used since making copies was so tedious.) A John Dowling of Galena, Illinois, wrote seven letters to Pierre Menard that are preserved in the *Pierre Menard Collection*.[22]

Lorimer could have been any member of that family, but was likely either trader Louis Lorimer Jr. or P. A. (Peter) Lorimer, from whom Pierre Menard received letters in the 1820s and 1830s.[23] Because the Lorimer family was prominent in the Indian trade along the south-central Missouri route of the Delaware Indians, Pierre Menard would have known and dealt with them.

John Langlois was employed by Pierre Menard in his various business enterprises and held Menard's power of attorney. The *Pierre Menard Collection* contains eight letters from Langlois informing Menard of business and family affairs that took place while Menard was absent from Kaskaskia.[24]

John Latredo and "Stephen" have not been identified. An A. J. Stephenson corresponded with Menard in the 1820s, but was probably not the person named here.[25] John Latredo may have been a lawyer or a county official, as he was linked with taxes and title.

It is also unclear what was read to these men. Francois's letter seemed to contain nothing of importance, unless it was the first paragraph, which documented that Chouteau had sent a letter to Menard and Valle during Menard's absence. Perhaps this earlier letter contained some action that did not meet a deadline because of Menard's absence. Less likely, but possible, is that what was read was unrelated to the letter, and that the notation was made on this letter simply because it was at hand.

---

22. *Guide to Menard Collection*, 93.
23. *Guide to Menard Collection*, 100.
24. *Guide to Menard Collection*, 99.
25. *Guide to Menard Collection*, 127.

Francois's information about the business that interested Pierre Menard was not extensive, considering that Menard had been out of touch for so long. The "Roland" mentioned was, as noted in connection with Francois's letter of August 4, 1834, John Ruland, Superintendent William Clark's special subagent. It is unclear whether the Clark referred to in connection with Ruland was Superintendent William Clark or Marston Clark, then Shawnee subagent.

The steamboat *St. Charles* that carried the fur packs to St. Louis was advertised for travel on the Missouri River from April to July 1834, and it was still operating in 1836. This must have been the vessel Captain Shallcross was commanding when the packs were loaded at night at the entrance to the Kansas River. Steamboats on the Missouri had an average life span of only three years, and when their scrapes and bruises made them unfit for the Mighty Mo, they were sold for use on more placid waters.

The following letter explained a little more about Baptiste Pascal and Francoise.

River of Kansas   May 14, 1835 [26]

Cher oncle,

I write to you upon very bad paper, not being able to find other at this moment. Our barge has at last arrived from among the Kansa with the remainder of the bundles of raccoons that Frederick left at the post, seeing that the water is so low. We await the first boat to send them. That barge took nearly six weeks to come down what one can do in four days when there is enough water not to get stranded. The agent Clark came here, and left just as quickly. I was away from the post when he came. Major Cummins tells me that he, Clark, had not handed over the money taken that belonged to Baptiste Pascal and Francoise. Baptiste Peoria tells me that [Marston] *Clark is to leave money in St. Louis with General* [William] *Clark to be turned over to Baptiste Pascal and Francoise. I really doubt very much that he will do that good deed – the only one he would have accomplished since he is agent. He says that he has resigned and that the governor reappointed him. Later on he was obliged to resign a second time.*

Major Cummins tells me he is very eager that Baptiste Pascal and Francoise come very quickly to receive the money from the annuities from last year and the annuities of this year at the same time; unless he does so, he will find himself in [....] *distribute that money among the nations. I have already written to you concerning this subject in a letter addressed to Menard-Valle, Ste. Genevieve. Therefore, I think they will do well to come to pick up the money and go back there if they do not want to stay. The competition for the next annuities will be stronger than ever. Of five stores that they have in Independence, five more are coming – that will make ten. I am told that there is a Mr. David from Kentucky, who has 400 sets of English dinner things. But we will always be a source of great pain for all of them, especially if we have nice merchandise. The total of our packs at the end of the month, I believe, will not be far from 500, everything having been counted.*

---

26. *PMC*, Letter 658. Envelope: Favor of Wm. Gilliss; [to} Monsieur Pierre Menard, Kaskaskia, Ill.; [filing note] May 5, 1835, Received the 10th.

I have often written to my sons and the poor children do not receive my letters. I cannot conceive where they are going.

Berenice joins me and [wishes] *all of you as well as my aunt, good health.*

I am, with respect your nephew,
Francois Chouteau

One persistent difficulty with the letters of this collection is that Francois, naturally, did not repeat facts that he knew Pierre Menard (or Cadet) already had at their command. Thus, Menard knew the background of the Pascal story, and consequently, the details of this business were never spelled out in the letters.

Pascal and Francoise were obviously Native Americans, as they were to receive annuities. Since Pierre Menard was acquainted with them, they were probably members of the Peoria Confederacy (Peorias, Piankeshaws, Weas, or Kaskaskias). Marston Clark was subagent for these peoples, and, in this connection, came in for a parting shot. Clark resigned from his position as Shawnee subagent early in 1835, and his resignation was accepted effective March 31, 1835.[27]

The competition for selling to the Indians at the annuity distribution had increased, Chouteau reported. The "Mr. David" from Kentucky was probably Cornelius Davy, an Independence resident and freighter on the Santa Fe Trail. A David Waldo was also a freighter on the Santa Fe Trail. He had received a medical degree in Louisville, Kentucky, but went into merchandising when he reached western Missouri.[28] Either of these men could have sold the "English dinner things" in Santa Fe, but certainly not to the Indians. (Francois must have been staggered by the figure of 400 pieces, and felt compelled to pass it along.)

Francois's next letter arrived at St. Louis through some means other than the postal service and was stamped and cancelled there, then sent to Kaskaskia.

River of Kansas   June 21, 1835[29]

Cher oncle,

I received your last two letters dated May 30 and 14 of June. I went to the Post Office last Saturday and I saw at the office two letters for Major Cummins, one from you, I presume, and the other from General Clark. I took the letters and was at his house. He was to be absent for several days, in such a way that I would not see him. I sent Baptiste [Peoria] *to the Weas to prepare them so as to try to have Marshall's debt paid. And I will do all I can with Major Cummins to engage him to be in favor of the payment by making him see that it was positively the wish of the Indians at the Treaty of Beaver Hill. And I will also see to be paid the money that you advanced to Baptiste Pascal.*

I will see the Major as soon as he arrives at home. I will discuss all that with him and I will write by the next mail and I will inform you of what the Weas will have said to Baptiste regarding the payment of their debt.

---

27. Barry, *Beginning of the West*, 284.
28. William Waldo, "Recollections of a septuagenarian," *Glimpses of the Past*, 5: 63, 68-78.
29. *PMC*, Letter 660. Envelope: [Stamped] St. Louis, June 20, Mo.; [postage] 10; [to] Monsieur Pierre Menard, Kaskaskia, State of Illinois; [filing note] June 21, 1835, Fs. Chouteau.

> *We are happy to know through one of your letters that our children were doing well at St. Mary's College and that there was no sickness then at that place. Gesseau wrote me that he was short of clothing but I see that you had some made for him and I am very relieved because we are remote from the poor children.*
>
> *Berenice joins me to wish you as well as my aunt, good health. I am respectfully,*
>
> *Your Nephew*
> *Francois Chouteau*

The Treaty of Beaver or *Castor* (French for beaver) Hill that Chouteau mentioned in the letter was signed in St. Louis in 1832. That treaty and the Council Camp Treaty of September 1829, among other issues, abolished Delaware and Shawnee land claims in Missouri in exchange for a cash payment.[30] Chouteau interpreted some part of that treaty as indicating that the Weas had agreed to pay Marshall what they owed him.[31] The question of this Wea debt dragged on for years. Beginning with Francois's letter of April 16, 1833, until 1838, this business was mentioned frequently.

At the time of the abovementioned treaties and the letters of this collection, the Secretary of War was still in charge of Indian Affairs. In 1832, a Commissioner of Indian Affairs was appointed, still operating within the War Department and called the Office of Indian Affairs, or OIA. In 1849, the OIA was reorganized under the Department of the Interior and became known as the Bureau of Indian Affairs or BIA, as it is to this day.

The following letter continued the saga of the Weas, Marshall, and Pierre Menard. Francois found himself, once more, the negotiator.

> *River of Kansas   July 6, 1835* [32]
>
> *Cher oncle,*
>
> *The first payment of the annuities begins today with the Shawnee, who receive 3000 and that this* [then?] *will be among the Weas, Piankeshaw, Peorias, Ottawas, and afterwards* [....] *the Kickapoo,* [....] *the Kansa. We have had our merchandise delivered to all our posts, and I believe that we will get our share. Major Cummins received your letter as well as one from the Secretary of War regarding the reclamation of William Marshall. He seems to be in good disposition, and I saw a few days ago the Chiefs who came here to see the Major and to speak regarding that affair, they did not all agree regarding the payment. Some wanted it, others wanted more. In the end, after much talking, they consented to pay* [....] *the year 1835.* [....] *as for the 500* [....] *for next year, their objection is that Marshall hired them to go in the swamps and that there they lost a fair amount of guns and of boilers for which Marshall had promised to pay them and if that is paid, they will pay the balance of the 500. They are to figure it out and give it to me.*

---

30. Charles J. Kappler, *Indian Affairs, Laws and Treaties*, 2: 370-372; *S. Doc. No. 512*, 23rd Cong., 1st Sess. (Serial 246): 408-409, 634-636.

31. For detailed explanation, see *PMC*, Letter 743 reproduced as appendix item 3g on page 212.

32. *PMC*, Letter 665. Envelope: [To] Monsieur Pierre Menard Sr., Kaskaskia, Ill.; [from] West Port, Mo., July 10, 1835; [postage] 22; [filing note] July 6, 1835, Fs. Chouteau.

As soon as they will remit it to me, I will write you and will inform you of everything. I am returning to you the receipts of Baptiste Pascal and Francoise that I showed to Major Cummins. I will make Baptiste Pascal pay the bill yet.

[....] [....] our barge is now at the Kansa with the merchandise for the annuities. I expect it from one day to another with the remainder of the packs. There will be about 50 to be sent by the first occasion.

We have a cold, damp spell that is bad for one's health. It causes sickness. Fires are burnt almost every day since the beginning of the month and we find it very agreeable. In spite of that weather, we are all fairly well. [....][....] to pass on to you as well as to my aunt, our sincere love.

I am with respect
Your Nephew
Francois Chouteau

[Pierre Menard's note on letter] Fs. Chouteau on the subject of annuities and money owed to Marshall. I informed him 16 August the present month to come and take care of his children that have [....] from the college [....] This letter did not leave the mail and tell [....] I did it on the 18th and tell him that he can be excused from coming, that his instructions will be sufficient. I tell [him] Menard has returned to college and that Gesseau is here. They will receive what I promised to inform him by the next mail.

Pierre Menard's notes on the bottom of the letter he had received from Francois announced that Gesseau and Menard had been expelled from school. At that point, however, Francois and Berenice were oblivious to the situation. Probably the school officials at St. Mary's had sent word to the boys' grandfather requesting that he fetch the miscreants, inasmuch as he was close at hand.

Gesseau was apparently deemed more at fault than Menard, for the latter had already been allowed to return. Cyprien Menard, then a student at the school, wrote to his mother about the turmoil: "It seems that the destiny that will be for Gesseau, our nephew, [is] not to stay here." Berenice's half-brother went on to say that he was tired of all the "embroilment" and wanted to leave – which he did.[33]

What exactly the boys had done was never made clear and can no longer be determined. Extensive investigation into the archives at St. Mary's turned up only the general information that there was a "revolt" that involved not only the Chouteau boys, but a large group of students who had been disobedient. In those days of strict discipline, this may have been nothing more sinister than standing on the teacher's desk. The president of the college, an Italian priest named Tornitore, spoke neither English nor French, the languages most used by the students. Undoubtedly his communication with the boys was hampered. (Although much of the faculty was foreign-born, almost all spoke either French or English and could have communicated with the students if the chain of command had permitted them to do so.) Pierre Menard's notes recording what he had said in letters to Francois were written on August 16th and August 18th, on the bottom of Francois's July 6, 1835 letter. The notes, therefore, are out of chronological sequence. The news of Gesseau and Menard's escapades reached Francois and Berenice the latter part of August. Francois's response was dated August 30th.

---

33. *PMC*, Letter 677.

The boilers mentioned in connection with the Marshall-Wea business were used in the preparation of animal skins. One method employed to remove hair from deerskins was to boil the skins in a lye solution made of water and ash from hardwood trees.

The following letter to Cadet contained much of the same information as in the preceding letter to Pierre Menard.

River of Kansas   July 6, 1835 [34]

Cher frere,

The first payment of the annuities begins today with the Shawnee. And then it will be at the Wea, Piankeshaw, Peoria and Ottawas, and then to the Loups, Kickapoos, and the Kansa. We have taken our merchandise everywhere and in good time, I hope that we shall recover our share, etc. I have done as you wished about the transport of the merchandise, iron and steel to the different Indians with whom you have contracted. I presume that the agents will have nothing to say, however, for the Shawnee two bars of iron and a bundle of steel is missing and for the Loups a bundle of steel. We were not able to count these well when the steamboat arrived. There was a great quantity and several marks had been defaced. I think that the best plan would be to tie each bundle with iron and to put on each one a little board with the name of each nation. Our barge reached the Kansa with the merchandise for the annuities. I expect it in two or three days with the rest of the packs. It will go up again about the 20th of August with the merchandise for the trade. That is about the time that the credits are made. In the letter I wrote you before this one I asked you for several articles which I want very much, which I hope you will not lose sight of and to which I have added – 50 traps, 40 rifles, 12 chiefs' outfits, 6 barrels of big biscuits for traveling. I want you to send this as soon as possible, even if only to Independence, if no boats were coming higher up. I have written you that we had enough traps. With what we got from Vanbebers, it was enough at that time, but since then a party has been formed of good Indians of the Loups, who are preparing to go hunt for beaver and they are very good at that hunt. We want to equip them and get them started as soon as the articles arrive. We will have approximately 50 packs to send at the first opportunity. As soon as the annuities are finished being paid I will write to you again, etc. The changes in the weather here have occasioned sickness. It is cold during 8 to 10 days and then intense heat. Since the beginning of the month we make a fire almost every day and it feels very agreeable.

Your affectionate brother
Fcois Chouteau

The Vanbebers who sold a few traps to Chouteau most likely was Alfonso (Alonzo) B. Van Bibber, who had been a partner with Albert Gallatin Boone in Westport prior to 1839 and who had an account with Ewing, Clymer & Company in 1839-1840 for Indian trade

---

34. Francois Chouteau to Pierre (Cadet) Chouteau Jr., July 6, 1835, *Chouteau Family Collections*, MHS. No envelope.

goods for which he paid in furs and peltries.[35] Other Van Bibber men in the fur trade of the late 1820s and 1830s included a trapper named Jesse Van Bibber, who in the 1820s worked at the mouth of the Verdigris River near present Muskogee, Oklahoma.[36] A Joseph Van Bibber was associated with the Iowa Agency from 1830 to 1833 as a blacksmith.[37]

The following letter was also written before the incident with Francois's sons had taken place.

River of Kansas   July 27, 1835[38]

Cher oncle,

I send to you enclosed here the sum total of the money that we got from the Indians for you, covering the 500 that remains to be paid to Marshall. I believe I wrote you that the Indians were causing difficulty because of the guns and boilers that were lost in the swamps. Apparently they want to subtract that amount and pay the balance. As yet I don't know the estimate of the loss. They promised to inform me of it, and as soon as I know it I will advise you. We did as usual: half the money that was paid to the Indians for the annuities. We had five merchants against us all the time of the transaction and they did not do the other half of the payment, because the Indians always retain some to purchase provisions for the horses, some whiskey and other things.

We only have the Kansa who have not been paid. They haven't as yet come out from their summer hunt. For those I believe we will have almost all their money. Of that they keep some also for things other than merchandise. But at least, we have the advantages in this post against all other traders. We have the remainder of our packs all here but I have not had the chance to send them on.

Berenice says that she will write you by the next mail. At this moment she is not so well. My two little ones get the fever from time to time, but that only makes them a little sick.

For a long time the Loups have been undecided whether they would accept the 3000 in merchandise that the government sent them. They say that the merchandise was purchased at too high a price – in a word, they were very near not accepting the stuff at all. Auguste remained several days with us and then he left for Arkansas with his daughter in good health. The heat is excessive here at home, but there is no sickness, for the present.

Berenice joins me to extend to you as well as to my good aunt the expression of our love. Give my compliments also to Charles and Peter also.

I am with respect your nephew
Francois Chouteau

---

35. "Ewing, Clymer & Company Account Book notes," Westport (Topical) Scrapbook [71.2], (KC395), WHMC-KC.

36. Harry R. Stevens, "Hugh Glenn," in *The Mountain Men and the Fur Trade of the Far West*, ed. Hafen, 2: 170.

37. "United States Indian Agencies Affecting Kansas," *Kansas Historical Collection* 16: 724-725.

38. *PMC*, Letter 670. Envelope: [To] Monsieur Pierre Menard Sr., Kaskaskia, Illinois; [filing note] July 27, 1835, Francois Chouteau, About the money collected from the Indians for Marshall.

Visitors to the Chouteau household in 1835 would have enjoyed the comforts of the large dwelling Francois had built on his farm in what later became known as the Guinotte Addition and then as the East Bottoms. The guests mentioned in this letter were Auguste, or A. P. Chouteau, and one of his daughters. As her name was not given, it could have been any of the five: Augustine, Emilie, Susanne, Marie Antoinette, or Aimee.

The weather of the summer of 1835 was so strange that Francois felt compelled to describe it, but he did not necessarily link it to the sicknesses suffered by his two sons, seven-year-old Benjamin and four-year-old Frederic Donatien. Every summer, strange weather or not, was to be feared for the regular outbreaks of malarial fevers, sometimes cholera, and the danger of smallpox.

The greetings Francois and Berenice sent were to Francois's brother Charles living in Kaskaskia, as arranged by Berenice and described in her letter to Angelique Menard on August 18, 1827. In 1835, Charles Chouteau was apparently still working in the Menard store. Peter, that is Pierre Menard Jr., was making a visit that apparently lasted all summer, since no letters were written from Peoria during that time. Perhaps Peter took advantage of the occasion to bring his new bride, Caroline Stillman Menard, to Kaskaskia. (They had been married in September 1834.) After his career as an Indian agent, Peter became a merchant in Peoria, and by 1839 had taken up farming near Tremont, Illinois. Peter Menard lived until 1871, reaching the age of seventy-four.[39]

At last the news of Gesseau and Menard's troubles at school reached Francois and Berenice. About two weeks had elapsed since it had happened.

River of Kansas   August 30, 1835[40]

Cher oncle,

I have received your two letters dated August 16 and 18 and it pained me and afflicted me much because of the conduct of my two sons at college. Certainly, I did not expect that they would behave in such a way. At least I anticipated that they would have conducted themselves as nice boys until next vacation and then I would have taken appropriate measures on their behalf if it were necessary. I beg of you to keep Gesseau in your house and not to allow him to go to St. Louis. As for Menard, I am going to wait in order to see if they have taken him back at college and then I will write to you what I have found out. I am obliged to undergo this mortification as indeed, I gave to my parents cause for sorrow. And upon reflection, I admit that I well deserve this. They are extremely happy, those who do not experience sorrow on account of their children.

I am in a moment of tribulation. My whole family has been ill. I almost lost Ben a few days ago from an inflammation with bilious fever. Right now he is a bit better and I hope to get him well. Berenice can't wait to have her baby. At our place there is much sickness, especially in Clay County. The fevers are very bad. Therese is often sick. Berenice tells me that she thinks it is liver trouble, the illness of her father.

---

39. *Guide to Menard Collection*, 42.
40. PMC, Letter 683. Envelope: [To] Monsieur Pierre Menard Sr., Kaskaskia, Illinois; [filing note] 30 August 1835, F. Chouteau.

As for me, I suffer a little from time to time with chest pains but I am more weak than suffering. If I could treat myself for that, I think I could get myself on my feet again. Mr. Sanford has just arrived here at present at ten o'clock at night. He is coming down in a mackinaw boat. By him, I sent a part of the money from the annuities. But I have not received those of the Kansa which were only paid a few days ago. I will forward it by the steamboat Diana, which will pass by here in eight or ten days, as well as sixty packs of different kinds of furs.

I wish to you good health as well as to my aunt and Berenice extends the same to all the family.

I am with respect
your nephew
Francois Chouteau

"Mortification" was the word chosen by Francois to describe his feelings about his sons being expelled from St. Mary's. His pride as a father was injured, and his status in the eyes of Pierre Menard was, he must have thought, damaged by the behavior of Gesseau and Menard. The comment that he had hoped they would be able to make it until vacation indicated that he had sensed trouble on the horizon. Perhaps that was the reason he was so upset that his letters did not reach his sons.

The "cause for sorrow" that Francois gave to his parents may have been a sort of generic guilt for misdeeds of the past. Or he may have been referring to a specific event, such as his youthful liaison with Marie of the Osages that resulted in the birth of James Chouteau. However, as such casual relationships between the French and the Native Americans were common, these affairs were generally not a cause of great distress. Francois's pensive mood led him down reflective paths not often explored in these letters.

Menard Chouteau, as his grandfather Pierre Menard had indicated in his note, had been allowed to return to school. Gesseau, then fourteen, was still in Kaskaskia. The school did not want him to return, and he probably did not want to.

Adding to Francois's misery, as expressed in the preceding letter, was the illness of his family and his own continued disability. He may have been conducting business from an armchair in a downstairs parlor. The "Therese" mentioned has not been identified with certainty. No Menard or Chouteau relative seems to be a likely candidate. Possibly Theresa was a child temporarily living with the Chouteaus, or perhaps Therese was the adult female slave, or the slave girl listed on the 1830 census.

Family difficulties almost eclipsed business affairs. Mr. John F. A. Sanford, agent since 1826 for the Mandan Subagency in the Upper Missouri, had ridden the current down the Missouri in a mackinaw boat, a flat-bottomed craft with a pointed prow and square stern, propelled by oars or sails. Sanford was married to Cadet Chouteau's daughter Emilie, and he presented the perfect opportunity for Francois to send a large sum of money to St. Louis.

The following letter showed Francois in a more cheerful frame of mind.

River of Kansas   September 18, 1835[41]

Cher oncle,

Finding myself in Independence at the time of the arrival of the last mail, I missed writing to you because I misjudged the hour of the departure of the mail. I wrote a few lines in haste to Cadet begging him to send my two boys to spend some time with me until I find a more advantageous place to put them. Menard still has need of a good school.

At four o'clock yesterday morning Berenice had a beautiful daughter that she proposes to show to you next spring. She is well enough in consideration of her situation. The children are well and no longer have temperatures. Ben is almost completely recovered. One cannot fill him up. He robs to eat. In a word, it remains for us to thank God to have been brought through many difficulties without any accidents. For I can assure you that in this country, when you have a lot of illness, it is very risky to be in the hands of the doctors who are here.

Our Indians have almost all left for the fall hunt. We have finished giving them on credit, with the exception of the Kansa. Frederick has left from here four days ago to go to give them credit. We have received 3000 of their money, the other 500 remaining has passed for debts and claims on the next annuities. From the Weas I will try to get the balance of what they owe you but I am sure that they will make difficulties because of the guns and boilers that they pretend to have lost. I will do a little discounting rather than have nothing at all.

Berenice joins me and wishes you, as well as my dear aunt, good health. Give my love to Peter, Charles, and to all the family. I am respectfully

Your affectionate nephew
Francois Chouteau

Francois and Berenice's first daughter, Mary Brigitte Chouteau, was born on September 17, 1835, at the Chouteau farm in Jackson County. Her baptism was delayed until the following May, when it took place in Kaskaskia. There was no longer a Catholic priest at Chouteau's Church, as Rev. Benedict Roux had given up on the Catholics of the western frontier and returned to St. Louis in April 1835.

Before he left, Father Roux made arrangements for the completion of the log church at a cost of $300, most of which was paid by Francois Chouteau. By the time Mary Brigitte Chouteau was born, "Chouteau's Church" was completed, but had no resident priest.[42]

At last the Chouteau family was healthy again, and seven-year-old Benjamin was well and ravenous. While Chouteau's opinion of the frontier doctors was poor, they doubtlessly did their best under adverse conditions. Although there may have been more physicians in the area, two names were prominent: Dr. Johnston Lykins was, for the most part, treating the Indian population, and Dr. David Waldo, as previously mentioned, was a licensed

---

41. *PMC*, Letter 687. Envelope: [To] Monsieur Pierre Menard Sr., Kaskaskia, Illinois; [from] West Port, Mo., September 18th; [postage] 18 3/4; [filing note] September 18, 1835, Fs. Chouteau.

42. Michael Coleman, Colette Doering, and Dorothy Marra, *This Far by Faith: A Popular History of the Catholic People of West and Northwest Missouri*, 2: viii.

physician, but spent his time in the more lucrative business of freighting on the Santa Fe Trail. Dr. Benoist Troost, often called Kansas City's first resident physician, was practicing in Independence in 1844, then settled in the Town of Kansas by 1848.

The date of the following brief note to Cadet appeared at the end of the message.

Entrance of the Kansas River[43]

Cher frere,

You will receive by the steamboat Hancock 29 rolls of skins of deer, 15 packs of raccoons and 10 chests of furs. Tell Sarpy that we paid the sum to Louis Rodgers. You will see that in a letter that I wrote you some time ago, I received the trunk of silver trinkets in good shape.

We're all pretty well.

Your affectionate brother,
Francois Chouteau

September 25, 1835

This note was evidently not the one in which Francois requested that Cadet arrange to send Gesseau and Menard home. Again Francois wrote only a short note to accompany furs being picked up at the "entrance to the river" landing.

The payment of a sum of money was to be recorded by Sarpy, who kept the books for Cadet Chouteau. This long-distance recordkeeping became standard practice as a greater portion of Francois's supplies came from Cadet rather than Menard and Valle. In this instance the payment went to Lewis Rogers, a Shawnee chief who led one of the three Shawnee bands that had signed the treaty of November 7, 1825. Rogers's band lived for some time on the Osage River in Missouri, but by 1838 had moved to the Shawnee reservation in Kansas.[44]

The steamboat *(John) Hancock,* mentioned in the note, had been operating on the Missouri River since 1834.

River of Kansas   October 22, 1835[45]

Cher oncle,

I received your last letter dated the first of October where I perceive with pain that you have left St. Louis sick to go back home. I am happy, however, that you are better from that indisposition. As for us, we are all well at this moment. The fever has entirely left the children who begin to regain their health and their strength. Berenice is well as well as her daughter. She will write to you as soon as our sons arrive who are not yet here. I expect them from one moment to another. My intention is not to withdraw them from school completely. I have their happiness at heart. If Mr. Odin returns, I will do all

---

43. Francois Chouteau to Pierre (Cadet) Chouteau Jr., September 25, 1835, *Chouteau Family Collections,* MHS. No envelope.

44. Barry, *Beginning of the West,* 376.

45. *PMC,* Letter 692. Envelope: [To] Monsieur Pierre Menard Sr., Kaskaskia, Illinois; [from] West Port, October 25; [postage] 18 3/4; [filing note] 1835 Oct. 22, Francois Chouteau.

in my power to return them to college. If not, I will try to put them elsewhere. But I am happy [confident] *that Mr. Odin will come to resume the presidency of the college.*

All our Indians are out hunting. I believe that we will again make a lot of packs this year. The Kansa left at the right time, well equipped. The Loups, also the Shawnee will do little or nothing and the Indians of the Marais des Cygne will do better. In the next payment of the annuities to the Weas, I will give them what you wrote up for me in one of your letters, and I will do all in my power to obtain the balance of the debt.

Berenice unites herself with me to wish you good health – as well as to my aunt.

I am with respect, your nephew,
Francois Chouteau

John Odin, the priest Francois hoped would become president of St. Mary's, assisted Father John Timon, the newly appointed president, in resolving some of the problems of the school. (Mr. Timon had been assisting former school president Father Tornitore when the "revolt" occurred.) The institution's dual purpose of training seminarians and teaching non-seminarians may have created part of the difficulty. Reverend Odin later became the bishop of New Orleans.

As the Indians of the Peoria Confederacy were settled on their land near the Marais des Cygne, Francois began to use the phrase, "Indians of the *Marais des Cygne*" to identify the Weas, Peorias, Piankeshaws, and Kaskaskias. They were sometimes called "Miami" Indians by others on the frontier.

By the time the following letter was written, Gesseau and Menard had returned to their parents' home.

River of Kansas   December 16, 1835 [46]

Cher oncle,

We have received your letter dated from November 28 where I see that you were a little sick, as well as my aunt. But I am happy [confident] *that you have recovered now. I received a letter from Michael Menard who asked me to try to purchase for him the claim of Francois Tremble in Canada and to offer him from 100 to 150 dollars for his right. According to the wish of Michael, I saw Tremble and made the above mentioned offer. He told me he could not sell his claims for less than 300 dollars. He told me that he left in the hands of Samson, Linitte or Rene Dupuis 100 in silver, and that he also has some more in property, but he doesn't know what, and for that he asks 300. Tell Michael that it is indeed the man of whom he speaks; the son of John Baptiste Tremble of the parish of St. Philip. Tell Michael that I would have written to him on this subject, but I see by your letter to Berenice that he is not in Kaskaskia.*

The Indians have not yet come out from their hunt. I will let you know when your treaty will be completed. We are all well enough with the exception of Gesseau who cut his toe in half a few days ago with a hatchet. But his foot is better and I believe he will be healed in two or three weeks. Menard is growing and doing well.

---

46. *PMC*, Letter 698. Envelope: [To] Monsieur Pierre Chouteau, St. Louis, Mo.; [from] West Port, Mo., December 18; [postage[18 3/4; [filing note] Frns. Chouteau.

Berenice says for me to tell you that for the time being she is in good health, and that she proposes to go show you her daughter next spring. She is small, but plump and healthy.

I have no other news to tell you. We have superb weather here. The Missouri is free [of ice] *and it is as nice as in October.*

Berenice joins me to give you as well as my aunt our love.

I am with respect
Your affectionate nephew
Francois Chouteau

Berenice and the boys will write you in the next mail.

The closing days of 1835 found Francois trying to broker a real estate transaction for Berenice's cousin Michel Menard, who lived in Texas and was the founder of Galveston. The Francis Tremble who owned the tract of Canadian land was listed on the 1830 Missouri census as a Jackson County resident. In 1840 his name appeared on *Plan de Westport*, a map drawn by the Catholic priest Father Nicolas Point. (More about this map later.)

"Samson, Linitte or Rene Dupuis," representing Tremble in the transaction, must have been Canadian lawyers. Probably Tremble had inherited the Canadian land from his father who lived in "the parish of Ste. Philip." In this case, a "parish" was not a unit of church members, but the French-Canadian designation for a district of government, originally identified by the parish church within its boundaries. Pierre Menard's father was married to his second wife at Ste. Philippe-de-Laprairie, Quebec.[47] The real estate Michael Menard wanted may have been known to Pierre Menard; possibly it was near the Canadian Menard land.

The latest of Gesseau Chouteau's exploits was described more completely in a letter the young man wrote to his Grandfather Menard on January 15, 1836 (See appendix item 5 page 215). Perhaps Gesseau Chouteau, after his two successful years as a student at St. Louis College, was restless and dissatisfied with life at St. Mary's and also at home, where he judged his family enslaved by the four-month-old Mary Brigitte, who, Gesseau complained, was "not bigger than my thumb and every person's mistress."[48] One misdirected swing of the axe and he had their attention.

Francois's next letter made no mention of Gesseau, and almost a year elapsed before his name appeared in a letter once more. At that time, Francois was able to point with pride to his first-born.

West of the Chouteau warehouse a new community was developing in what would later be called the West Bottoms. Kawsmouth, as the settlement at the mouth of the Kaw or Kansas River was called, probably began in the early 1830s, although there may have been French and French-Indian families farming on the river bottomland before that. Catholic missionary Charles Felix Van Quickenborn wrote that Flathead, Kutenai, and Iroquois Indians came down from the Upper Missouri, possibly with Fontenelle's outfit, as early as 1831 or 1832. They settled in the French community germinating in the West Bottoms, south of the mouth of the Kansas River. Father Van Quickenborn's records of the Catholic Kickapoo

---

47. *Guide to Menard Collection*, 27.
48. *PMC*, Letter 703.

Mission listed the names of children baptized and of marriages performed at Kawsmouth in the summer of 1836.[49]

Ignace Hatchiorauquasha, called John Grey by Anglo-Americans, was an Iroquois Indian who had worked in the fur trade for two decades. In 1836, Grey led twelve Iroquois families, mostly of French-Indian blood, to Kawsmouth.[50]

The population of Kawsmouth grew, developing as an agricultural rather than a commercial community. The French and French-Indian settlers farmed the rich floodplain, marked off into *arpents*. This French land measure was a long, narrow strip of land with a total area of about seven-eighths of an acre. These plots extended back from the houses built near the river. The sociable inhabitants could call to each other as they worked, and at midday, perhaps clustered under a tree for a bit of wine, cheese, and bread.

Five communities were then developing independently near the Missouri River on the Missouri side of the state line: Independence, Westport, Kawsmouth, Chouteau's Landing, and Kansas Landing (Town of Kansas). Of these, Independence and Chouteau's Landing were the most significant at the time these letters were written. The Kansas Landing at that time was scarcely more than a name and a big flat rock. John Calvin McCoy, tongue in cheek, bestowed the derogatory appellation "Westport Landing," indicating that the new steamboat dock and its environs were nothing more than a service area for his Westport.

In the mid-1830s, Chouteau's warehouse and landing were the center of activity in the area that became Kansas City. The warehouse, located near the foot of present Olive Avenue, stood on the riverbank near the landing, shielded by the point of an island in the river channel. This *lower* landing (where Francois's warehouses served as base for the American Fur Company, or Pierre Chouteau Jr. and Company operations) was the steamboat port most generally used for shipments bound for Westport or the Indian Territory beyond. The *upper,* or Kansas Landing, was as yet the lesser used.

Steamboats docking at Chouteau's Landing sidled near the bank, anchored in the channel that ran close to the shore, and bridged the water with a long gangplank to the riverbank. Down that gangplank came settlers, visitors, government officials, Indians, missionaries, and curious travelers, all eager to see what the westernmost frontier was like. Then the boatmen unloaded cases of goods for the Indian trade, merchandise to be sold to settlers, and staple food items: sugar, pepper, coffee, flour, milled grains. Up the ramp went the bundles of deerskins, fur packs containing hundreds of beaver, raccoon, bear, muskrat, wolf, and opossum pelts, and buffalo hides.

Only a half-mile west, and adjoining Chouteau's land, lay Gabriel Prudhomme's claim that was the site of the future Town of Kansas. The Chouteau family home and farm were east of the warehouse and landing. It probably resembled the Menard estate, currently preserved in Kaskaskia, Illinois, as it was in the early 1800s. The Chouteau family home was a frame structure, according to Frederick Chouteau's memory, two stories with a wide porch encircling the ground floor, as was the French style. Based on the Menard plan, the house would have been slightly removed from the necessary outbuildings: detached kitchen, smokehouse, cabins for slaves, privies, shelter for poultry and livestock, and a stable for horses. McCoy's remark that the Chouteau farm included "costly outbuildings" sparks the imagination but remains vague. Nearby were the indispensable herb garden and plots for

---

49. Gilbert J. Garraghan, S.J., *Catholic Beginnings in Kansas City, Missouri*, 93-94. See also *History of the Kickapoo mission and parish: the first Catholic Church in Kansas* by William W. Graves, compiler and co-authored by Gilbert J. Garraghan and George Towle.

50. Merle Wells, "Ignace Hatchiorauquasha (John Grey)," in *The Mountain Men and the Fur Trade of the Far West*, ed. Hafen 7: 169-170; Garraghan, *Jesuits of the Middle United States*, 1: 259.

vegetables and berries. Perhaps young fruit trees promised sweet harvests in years to come, next to where the vineyard was planted or planned.

Because the Chouteaus traveled back and forth to St. Louis and Kaskaskia so frequently, their letters lack details about daily living. These details were undoubtedly central to their conversations around the table at the Chouteau mansion in St. Louis and on the Menard estate in Kaskaskia.

Of all the steamboat passengers who disembarked at Chouteau's Landing – the travelers who bought supplies at Chouteau's warehouse, and the friends and family who visited the Chouteau home – no one thought to set pen to paper and leave a description of what it was really like.

Madame Berenice Chouteau, late in her life, was asked to identify the location of her husband's warehouse. She indicated that the foot of Troost Avenue was as close as she could come to a location – the river had eaten into the south bank, most if not all of the island that sheltered Chouteau's Landing was gone, a city had grown up, bluffs had been torn down, and many years had intervened, all sweeping away her landmarks.[51]

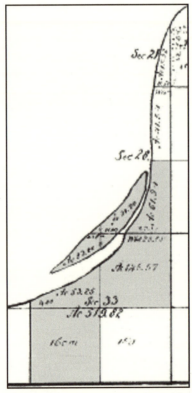

Francois Chouteau's land holdings in sections 33 and 28, Township 50 N, Range 33 W. The Chouteau home was probably located on the south bank near the east end of the island. Chouteau's Landing and warehouse were close by but may have been nearer to the center of the island. The channel, or slough between the island the mainland, between 100 and 300 feet wide, was heavily used by steamboats. The island extended to northeast for about one mile from just west of the Paseo Bridge.

---

51. "Site of Founding of Kansas City Passes to New Owner," *Kansas City Star*, 19 October 1930, 1(D).

"*Maison Emportee*" [House carried away]. *Père Nicolas Point, S.J., Collection,* Archives de la Compagnie de Jesus, province du Canada frantais.

7 End of the Pioneer Era

River of Kansas February 5, 1836[1]

Cher oncle,

I received your letter dated December 31, and I see with pleasure that you and your family were in good health. You note the arrival of Mr. Odin and that Mr. Timon is Superior of the College. I communicated this news to my sons who appear to be very pleased about this change and they tell me that they will be happy to return again to school. I will send them back by the first good occasion. Berenice wishes to go to see you. I believe it will be at the same time as the boys. Gesseau wishes to spend some time at school.

---

1. *PMC*, Letter 705. Envelope: [To] Monsieur Pierre Menard Sr., Kaskaskia, Illinois; [from] West Port, Mo., February [....]; [postage] 25; [filing note] Francois Chouteau, 6 February 1836.

Do me the pleasure to write if they will take them back at school. I want to know that before sending him back. You indicate to me that you received the letter that I had written to papa, but to your address. I wrote them at the same time and it is possible that I made a mistake in addressing the letters. You ask me to inform you whether it is the guns that you supplied that are lacking locks. I am unable to inform you for the time being. In his letter Frederick does not tell me where the guns come from. I will inform you in my next letter. I am unable to tell you anything positive with regard to the treaty. The Indians here have not all returned. However, they arrive daily and almost all who have returned have had a good hunt.

I have no news from among the Kansa, but I presume that the treaty is finished, at least until the Spring. I await your news from there from one moment to another. We have gone to get a load of pelts at the Marais des Cygne. The treaty was not finished at that place.

McCoy sold his store in Westport to Col. Chick, father-in-law of Johnson, the minister of the Shawnee. I presume that Johnson wants to speculate on the annuities of the Indians. He believes he has a strong religious advantage on his behalf. Without being sure, I give this as my opinion and I do not believe I'm much wrong. About the balance that the Weas owe to Marshall, they want to make a deduction for a certain number of guns and boilers that they say they have lost in the swamps. Baptiste [Peoria] tells me that they will not pay without that. If the number of guns and boilers is not considerable, it may be better to overlook it rather than to have nothing. Do me the pleasure to give me your advice about that subject.

I have no other news to give you. It is very cold here. The Missouri River is full of ice, and I think there is an ice jam higher up on the Kansas River. All my family is well. Berenice joins with me and wishes you health, as well as to my aunt, good health. Give our love to Charles, to Peter and to all the others – without forgetting Odile.

I am with respect, your nephew
Francois Chouteau

A glance back at the envelope of Francois's letter that preceded the one above confirms that he had, indeed, mistakenly sent the letter intended for Pierre Menard to his father Pierre Chouteau in St. Louis and vice-versa. A scan of the letters Francois wrote to his uncle shows that Chouteau almost consistently had Menard's letter before him as he replied, dealing with each point raised in Menard's letter.

The defective guns that Frederick had received for the Kansa Post, as Francois reported, were missing locks. In the flintlock gun, the lock was a part of the sparking device; it propelled the flint in an arc against a hard substance to create a spark to ignite the charge, and that in turn thrust the ball from the barrel of the gun.

Chouteau's letters from the mid-1800s described increased commercial activity in Westport. John Calvin McCoy had platted West Port (as it was then written) in 1834 on the prairie four to five miles south of Chouteau's warehouse. In 1836, McCoy sold his store to William Chick, who had recently come from Virginia. Chick's daughter Mary Jane married Methodist minister Rev. William Johnson in 1834. William was the brother and colleague of Rev. Thomas Johnson, founder of the Methodist Mission for the Shawnees. It was William Johnson's school that Menard Chouteau had attended in 1832-1833, as mentioned in

Francois's letter of May 20, 1833. Virginia, a younger daughter of William Chick, married John C. McCoy in 1836.

McCoy's Westport was a response to the rise of the Anglo-American population in western Missouri. As early as 1829, Francois was aware of the swelling population and wanted to open a store in Independence, an idea he presented to Pierre Menard in letters written in February and March of 1829. Deflated by the sinking of the keelboat *Beaver*, and perhaps by a lack of enthusiasm on Pierre Menard's part, Francois dropped the idea.

As the Anglo-Americans increased in number they formed their own network, made of business connections and intermarriage, just as the French had done in the previous century. (Notice the intermarriage of McCoys, Chicks, and Johnsons.) The predominant language was changing from French to English, and the manners and mores of the area changed with it.

The letter following brought Pierre Menard up to date on the activities of spring on the frontier.

River of Kansas   April 8, 1836[2]

Cher oncle,

I am displeased not to be able to send you two or three barrels of good tallow. Contrary to the usual, we were unable to obtain any from the Kansa this year. They find their provisions to be very scarce this year, and they ate the lard with their corn. The steamboat Diana arrived here the third of the present month. It brought us some sugar, salt, coffee, and some lead, but no merchandise. At this moment, the Missouri River is superb for navigation. It has risen about six feet since the ship went through.

We put our packs on board the steamboat St. Charles – 240 and in good order. I presume that they arrived in good condition. We still have our Spring treaty to complete and I presume that I will be able to buy some pelts in our area from the merchants and others.

Gilliss leaves in a few days to go down the Mississippi to explore some land that he purchased from Grand Louis who is a half-breed Sac. If he is in the region of the mines it is possible that he got a good deal especially if the half-breeds have a right to sell without the government setting up an obstacle.

Berenice proposes to go down in the St. Charles or the Diana. We are all pretty well and I hope that the present moment finds you likewise. Give our love to my aunt and believe me always,

With respect, your nephew
Francois Chouteau

"Grand Louis," the "half-breed" Sac, was Louis Bertholet, who was probably in western Missouri as early as 1818. He and several French laborers in 1822 built the first Chouteau post, in the area of present Kansas City at Randolph Bluffs. Chouteau surmised that there might be some special benefit to the *metis* who sold their lands. This advantage was not

---

2. *PMC*, Letter 718. Envelope: [To] Monsieur Pierre Menard Sr., Kaskaskia, Illinois; [from] West Port, Mo., 8 April 1836; [postage] 25; [filing note] West Port, Mo., 8 April 1836.

spelled out, but William Gilliss, who did buy the property mentioned in the letter, wrote to Pierre Menard in 1837 and in 1841 seeking Menard's help in securing proof of Grand Louis's tribal status.[3]

The practice of favoring the *metis* was fostered by the government in the hope that these part-Indian people would merge into the general population. According to agreements made in the Treaty of 1825 with the Kansa Indians, the Kansa mixed-bloods, among them several members of Chief White Plume's family, would receive twenty-three lots near present Topeka. Chouteau would certainly have been familiar with this, as, according to Frederick Chouteau,[4] Francois and Berenice raised Josette, the daughter of Louis Gonville, who was married to White Plume's daughter (niece?). Gonville's mixed-blood children received four lots and the name Gonville has since been associated with these "half-breed tracts."

The spring opening of the navigation season was eagerly anticipated by the settlers of western Missouri, and when the first steamboat of the year threw out its anchor beside Chouteau's Landing, a festive crowd awaited it. The cargo was heaved onto the landing platform – merchandise for the Indian trade and supplies to replenish bare pantry shelves. For isolated pioneers, the steamboat was a link to civilization, and eastbound passengers were ready when the ship was. Some wanted to visit families, and others wanted to "go home" – permanently.

In Francois's next letter, he acknowledged the progress of Berenice's current journey.

River of the Kansas   May 12, 1836[5]

Cher oncle,

The steamboat St. Charles has just arrived with our merchandise and I learned by it the arrival of my Berenice in St. Louis with her children in fine shape and of her departure for Kaskaskia. Apparently we are going to wage war here very soon with the Mormons. They have a force of 2000 men in Clay County who are organizing and making the arrangements necessary to attack us in Jackson County and we have to take measures in order to make serious resistance.

It appears that they are disposed to retake possession of their land by force. We want to make the most advantageous propositions to them before taking up arms. And if they are unwilling to make any arrangements, it is certain that we will have to fight them. This situation is alarming and upsetting in our area. But, generally, we are determined to fight to the end rather than consent that the Mormons remain here, and really, if it were the case, they would chase us from the country as they themselves were chased the first time. Consequently, I desire that Berenice not return here until the trouble be passed in one way or another.

Recently, by all the boats that come up the Missouri, the Mormons are coming from their satellites and all are well armed. Jackson County is the Promised Land where the New Jerusalem must be built.

---

3. *PMC*, Letters 788 and 1129.
4. Frederick Chouteau Letters May 6 and May 10, 1880, *Indians History Collection*, (MC590), KSHS.
5. *PMC*, Letter 721. Envelope: [To] Monsieur Pierre Menard Sr., Kaskaskia, State of Illinois; [filing note] 12 May 1836, Fs. Chouteau.

> *We learned with sorrow the loss that our poor brother Cadet endured of his youngest daughter Emilie. Doubtlessly, it is a great affliction for him and for his family. I have just learned through Cabanne who comes back from Fort Gibson the return to his post of Ligueste who had been gone a few months on a trip around the area inhabited by the Comanches. I do not know what he brings back from these places. I presume that this year the competition for the annuities of the Indians will be more considerable than ever. There are four new stores since Spring in Independence, in addition to six that were already there, and one more in West Port, Auguste Labaume and his brother-in-law.*
>
> *I finish by wishing you, as well as my good aunt, good health until the pleasure of seeing you again,*
>
> *I am with respect,*
> *Your nephew*
> *Francois Chouteau*

The Mormon crisis that Chouteau described involved members of the Church of Jesus Christ of Latter Day Saints (Mormons) and the residents of Jackson County. Joseph Smith founded the Latter Day Saints church in New York State in 1820. A large group of church members moved to Independence, Missouri, in 1832.

Initially, Jackson County folks welcomed the immigrants. But as the mostly rural and southern population realized that the newcomers were city-building, anti-slavery easterners, the locals became wary, then hostile. Although few Jackson Countians owned slaves, they were avid in their belief that it was their right to do so. Likewise, they did not want their farms carved into city blocks.

In early November 1833, a mob of Jackson Countians drove the Mormons out of their dwellings in Independence and across the Missouri River into Clay County. The homes of Latter Day Saints members were burned and their property confiscated. After some time in exile, the Mormons were, as Francois reported, preparing to return, claim their land, and assert their right to live in Jackson County. (Coming from their "satellites" meant coming from their outlying communities to regroup for this action.)

Generally, however, life went on in the usual fashion. People bought and sold land. Stores opened in Westport and Independence. Auguste Labaume was one of the new merchants in Westport. His name reappeared regularly in Chouteau's subsequent letters. This man may have been the Augustus Labaume listed on the 1830 census as living in St. Louis County. The ten stores in Independence bespoke a thriving community. Sam Owens operated one store, and others included Flourney & Co. and John O. Agnew, three of the four to whom Marston Clark had given licenses to trade with the Shawnees in 1834.[6] Even if Francois was not pleased to have new businesses competing for the Indian customer's money, the settlers of Jackson County and the trail travelers must have relished the array of merchandise!

On other topics, Francois commented on Berenice's excursion to St. Louis with eight-year-old Benjamin, five-year-old Frederic Donatien, and eight-month-old Mary Brigitte. While not mentioned, the older boys, Gesseau and Menard, must have been with their mother traveling to St. Louis, then immediately on to Kaskaskia. From there it was a short ferry trip to Perryville.

---

6. *H. Doc. No. 97*, 23rd Cong. 2nd sess. (Serial 273).

Cadet's daughter Emilie, who had recently died, was twenty-two. She had been married to John Sanford, who, as mentioned in Francois's letter dated August 30, 1835, had come from the Upper Missouri in a mackinaw boat.

John Pierre Cabanne, who brought the news of Liguest's return from the Comanche country, was originally from St. Louis. At the time of this letter, he was operating a fur trading post near Bellevue, Nebraska, where he traded with the Pawnees. What reason Cabanne had for being at Fort Gibson (present Oklahoma) was not explained. However, in 1825, Cabanne was trading in the Southwest, and the trip mentioned in the preceding letter could have been a return to a familiar area.[7]

Berenice did not take seriously the threat of war near her home, as Francois's next letter reported that she had returned.

River of Kansas   June 6, 1836[8]

Cher oncle,

Berenice arrived here May 31 with the children in good health after a passage of eight days – very happy and very agreeable from what she tells me. I also received your letter concerning the debt of the Weas that is for $500. I am going to try to make them well understand through Baptiste [Peoria] the meaning of your letter and tell them everything by word and try to get the payment. I paid Baptiste for this affair 25 dollars last year. By the steamboat St. Charles I sent 30 packs of which there are ten of good mountain beaver and the others otters, raccoons, and deerskins. We still have pelts at the Kansa, Wea, and I believe I can buy a few of them here. I will send this by the first good occasion as soon as I have some ready. Berenice informs me that Menard was to return to college with Amadee. I flatter myself that he will behave like a nice young man. He sent me a lovely present of a small box that contained a compass. I am going to write him quickly.

Morgan made up a pack and a half of beaver with the Loups because our merchandise hadn't yet arrived, without which he would not have had that – although he gave an extravagant price.

I have no other news to give to you presently. No one speaks of the war with the Mormons anymore, at least for the present. I am closing by wishing you as well as to my aunt wishes for good health until the pleasure of seeing you again. Give my love to Charles as well as to the whole family.

*I am with respect your nephew
Francois Chouteau*

Joseph Amadee Menard, who went to St. Mary's with Menard Chouteau, was Berenice's youngest half-brother. At sixteen years of age, he must have been more like a cousin than an

---

7. Ray H. Mattison, "John Pierre Cabanne," in *The Mountain Men and the Fur Trade of the Far West*, ed. Hafen 2: 72.

8. *PMC*, Letter 725. Letter in poor condition. Envelope: [Stamped] St. Louis [....], 3, Mo.; [postage] 10; [to] Monsieur Pierre Menard Sr., Kaskaskia, Illinois; [filing note] 6 June 1836, Frs. Chouteau.

uncle to fourteen-year-old Menard. In Francois's letter, Gesseau was conspicuous by his absence.

Meanwhile, back in western Missouri, the younger Chouteau children gave the household a lively character: Mary Brigitte, at nine months, still required much attention; Frederic Donatien, at five years, was probably straying from the hearth but still under his mother's eye; Benjamin, then eight-years old, began to move into his father's circle and would soon require some schooling.

Concerning the business, Chouteau pointed out that though Morgan had collected some furs, he would not make a profit because he paid too much for them. This man was probably Alexander Morgan, postmaster at Fort Leavenworth in 1836, supplementing his government income with a little trading on the side.

The following brief letter to Cadet referred to J. O. Agneux (John O. Agnew), the Independence merchant issued a license to trade with the Kickapoos in 1833 and another license to trade with the Shawnees, Ottawas, Weas, Piankeshaws, and Peorias in 1834.[9] Mr. S. C. Owens was the much-mentioned and ubiquitous Samuel C. Owens of Independence.

Used in the preceding letter and the following note to Cadet, the French expression "I flatter myself" meant "I am confident that."

July 10, 1836[10]

Cher frere,

I am sending you by the Diana 15 packs, in which there are four of beaver, etc. I am writing you a little letter because the boat has put to land only to take the packs. I have not yet had news of the money for the annuities but I presume that it will not be long in arriving. I have given a draft on you to Mr. J. O. Agneux for 1500. I flatter myself that you will have paid it and an order in favor of Mr. S. C. Owens for 200.

I wish you good health and your family as well, etc.

Your affectionate brother,
F. Chouteau

Missouri   July 18, 1836[11]

Cher oncle,

I went to see Major Cummins a few days ago to speak to him concerning the debt of the Weas on behalf of William Marshall. I asked him if he had a letter from Major Brent concerning that affair. He tells me he didn't and admits that the claim is just and that the Indians should pay it. The major [Cummins] *is a very good man, but very timid and*

---

9. *H. Doc. No. 97*, 23rd Cong. 2nd sess. (Serial 273).

10. Francois Chouteau to Pierre (Cadet) Chouteau Jr., 10 July 1836, *Chouteau Family Collections*, MHS. No envelope; note sent with fur shipment.

11. PMC, Letter 737. Envelope: [Stamped] St. Louis, July 30, Mo.; [postage] 10; [to] Monsieur Pierre Menard Sr., Kaskaskia, Illinois; [filing note] 18 July 1836, Frs. Chouteau, received 11 August and answered the 12th of the same.

fearful, and I believe he will say nothing, neither for nor against. In any case, he is unable to be of much help to us. We will try to convince the Indians to pay the debt to us. I believe I told you that I had paid Baptist Peoria twenty-five [dollars] for the affair. He tells me that indeed, he will speak again to the Indians this time.

The steamboat St. Charles just arrived here. It brought us some articles that were lacking to our inventory. I sent by the Diana moreover, four packs of beaver, some otter and deerskins. We made a good part of the beaver at our post this year. We have no word yet of our annuities. The Indians are eager to receive their money but I believe they will be paid late this year.

Here, from time to time, war with the Mormons is spoken of but I don't believe that will happen. They are not yet strong enough to take the Promised Land by force. Two Americans were killed on the Grand River, one supposes by the Iowas.

All my family is well. The children all had measles but presently they are cured. Berenice joins me to wish you the best of health and our love to all the family.

I am respectfully your affectionate nephew,
Francois Chouteau

The two Americans who were killed, as Chouteau reported, probably lost their lives as a result of the turmoil connected with the Platte Purchase. The United States Congress in 1836 approved a bill allowing the state of Missouri to annex a triangular-shaped wedge of land in the northwestern part of the present state boundaries. Known as the Platte Purchase, the region included the present counties of Platte, Atchison, Nodaway, Holt, Andrew, and Buchanan, where St. Joseph is located.

The land had been set aside for the Fox, Sac, and Iowa nations by a treaty signed in 1830. However, neighboring white settlers pressed in at the borders of the Indian land and found the soil rich and the hunting superb. The government made sporadic attempts to prevent these inroads: in 1835, Robert Cain, Joseph Todd, John B. Wells, and others moved onto the Indian land to farm. Cain built a house and tilled the land. For his effort, he received a military escort to Clay County and his house on the Indian land was burned, while the others suffered a similar fate.[12]

Nevertheless, white neighbors continued to infiltrate the area and pressured Missouri congressmen to remove the Indians and add the land to the state of Missouri. United States Senator Thomas Hart Benton introduced the Platte Purchase bill in Congress, where it was passed on June 7, 1836.

All three nations – the Sac, Fox, and Iowa – had been in the Platte region for many years and felt entitled to the land, both by prior claim and by government treaty. Confusion and dissatisfaction about the new treaty terms and boundaries caused unrest in northwestern Missouri. The Iowas, Chouteau supposed, expressed their anger through direct action, killing two men on the Grand River that lies east of the contested land.

The Major Brent mentioned in connection with the Wea debt may have been Thomas Brent, who in the late 1840s was stationed at Fort Leavenworth to escort caravans on the Santa Fe Trail.[13] Perhaps at the time of the preceding letter, this Major Brent had some position of authority regarding Indian affairs.

---

12. Howard Conard, ed. *Encyclopedia of the History of Missouri*, s.v. "Platte Purchase" 5: 151-155.
13. Louise Barry, *Beginning of the West*, 803.

As the 1830s progressed, Francois's letters continued to deal with familiar topics: family concerns, anxiety about the competition for Indian annuity money, gathering furs, collecting debts, and forwarding to St. Louis and Kaskaskia a variety of signed documents.

Trading Post   September 15, 1836 [14]

Cher oncle,

I would have written you before this letter, but I put it off until the payment of the annuities which at the present are almost finished. Major Cummins left last Monday to go pay the Kansa who are the last. You must suppose we had strong competition but in the end we have made half the money that was paid to our Indians – 10,000 dollars for our share. Aquins of the Weas did not want to pay the [$]500 that they owed to Marshall. They wanted to make a deduction against the amount for the guns and boilers and containers. Also [they said] *that Marshall has promised to pay them for these articles. Baptiste tells me that it is true that Marshall promised them something if they paid the debt. But he didn't say how much, so that they did not pay. But for all that, I don't believe the debt is lost. I was unable to go to the Weas. When they were paid I was busy elsewhere. I believe that if I had been there, I would have made them pay me by making a little sacrifice.*

But it is certain that they have to pay the debt in the end.

We have had a lot of aggravation in the payments of the last annuities. The competition was very strong and they were selling all at their prices. We were forced to sell very cheap also and so the Indians must all be very well equipped as far as merchandise goes.

This year we will make 20 bundles of beaver here, the greatest part already in St. Louis, and I believe that we still have three bundles here, and a few packs of deerskins. If I do not find a good occasion, I will myself take the money and the balance of the pelts in a pirogue as I have done before and I am sure that is more safe than in the steamboat. They tell me that the Commissioners have started the Great Council at Fort Leavenworth yesterday and that there are more than 1,000 Indians gathered together. I am told also that the Indians are proposing to ask for a good price for their claims.

All my family is well. Berenice joins herself to me to wish you, as well as my aunt, the best of health. Give our love to the whole family.

I am respectfully your loving nephew
Francois Chouteau

This letter introduced a new place of origin – Trading Post. The town of Trading Post, Kansas, cannot be considered here because it was not founded until the early 1840s. Moreover, the content of the letter indicates that Chouteau was at his usual place of business, the Kansas City warehouse. There is no way of knowing with certainty why he used the

---

14. *PMC*, Letter 749. Envelope: [To] Monsieur Pierre Menard Sr., Kaskaskia, State of Illinois; [from] West Port, Mo., September 16; [postage] 18 3/4; [filing note] Sept. 15, 1836, Frs. Chouteau.

designation of "Trading Post" or "House of Trade." Perhaps, however, he was establishing the identity of what was essentially the "home office." He was at that time responsible for four outlying trading posts, one each for the Weas, the Kansas, the Shawnees, and the Kickapoos. All of these branch operations reported to the fifth post that was the center of the operation, the Trading Post at present Kansas City.[15]

Francois wrote the preceding letter before the rash of steamboat accidents on the Missouri River that made 1836 one of the worst navigational seasons on record. According to the *Missouri Republican*, five steamboats sank in the Missouri that year. One was the *Diana*, though she was still afloat when the letter was written. The *Diana* perished near Rocheport, Missouri, 127 miles west of St. Louis, on October 10, 1836, with a valuable cargo of furs.[16] This cargo probably did not include Francois Chouteau's fur packs, as he did not lament the loss. Furthermore, the *Diana* went all the way up to the Yellowstone River and most likely was bringing down furs from the Upper Missouri. On November 26, 1836, heavily laden with furs, the *John Hancock* hit a snag and sank near Bellefontaine, presently a suburb of St. Louis. Inasmuch as these were American Fur Company vessels, Chouteau had previously used both ships to get his cargo to St. Louis. Strangely enough, Francois's distrust of steamboats, as expressed in the preceding letter, came before these disasters occurred. He would himself take the furs down to St. Louis in a pirogue!

The council at Fort Leavenworth mentioned in Francois's preceding letter was the meeting of Superintendent of Indian Affairs William Clark, other officials, and most of the Native Americans who would be removed from the Platte Purchase land – the Iowas, Sacs, and Foxes. For giving up their land, the Indians received a "present" of $7,500 and a reservation in present northeast Kansas. In addition, they were awarded a variety of payments, assistance, and improvements on their new land.[17]

In the letter that follows, new names appear with new obligations for Francois in his role as financial middleman. Meanwhile, he found himself buying furs to supplement the harvest of his hunters and trappers. After decades of over-harvesting, the supply of fur-bearing animals on nearby Missouri and Kansas prairies and streams was in decline. Both Indian and white hunters and trappers were forced to trek to the Rocky Mountains in search of furs.

River of Kansas   March 24, 1837[18]

Cher oncle,

I take advantage of the occasion of Frederick who is going to St. Louis to give you news of us. We are all well enough and hope the same with respect to you. I have done all in my power to buy up the land of Helen Decoigne but she declined. I offered to her what you had authorized me in the affair, and even more but nothing succeeded. And at this moment, I am going to tell you the cause. The pastors, the ministers, the agents, the interpreters – each have given her their advice. In such a way she did not know what to do and she finished by telling me that she [....] [is going to?] Kaskaskia and that there

---

15. For further information about the location of these various post, see appendix item 1 on page 191.

16. *Missouri Republican* [St. Louis], 30 November 1836.

17. Charles J. Kappler, *Indian Affairs, Laws and Treaties*, 2: 468-470.

18. PMC, Letter 771. Envelope: [To] Monsieur Pierre Menard, Kaskaskia, Illinois; [filing note] March 24, 1837, Fr. Chouteau.

she would sell you her land. I presume that you alone can make her understand reason. As yet I have not collected the debt of Poole. Mr. Owens who was to receive the money, is at Philadelphia. And Wilson who was to pay, is not here either. Be assured that as soon as I can do that, I will advise you immediately. Helen Decoigne owes us 145 dollars. If you make arrangements with her, I desire that you retain that amount for us. We await the steamboat Boonville from one moment to another, that goes as far as Robidoux's at the Black Snake, to take these packs as well as those of Pinsonneau and ours that number 200, deerskins and other fur pelts. As yet we do not have the return of the Indians which we equipped for the mountains last year. We made 24 packs of beaver. About half of what their expedition gave them from the mountains. But for this year I am not sure whether we have the same luck. At least, I hope so.

I have little news to tell you other than that half of Jackson County abandons the place to go to the bit of land added to the State of Missouri that the Americans call Platte Country. Baptiste and Helen are coming down with Frederick. I ask you to remind Baptiste of the claim of Marshall over the Weas. I am going to look into that affair especially in the upcoming annuities.

I wish you the best of health, as well as for you, Aunt. My love to Charles and all the family. I am with respect,

Your nephew,
Francois Chouteau

N.B.: I beg you to have the kindness to try to send me the little Negress of Mr. Valle, Nancy, if I am able to have her at a reasonable price. Berenice is eager for that for her own little girl. Then you can send her to me by Baptiste.

Berenice hoped that Nancy, a little slave girl, was to travel from Ste. Genevieve to the Chouteau farm so that Mary Brigitte, nearly two years old, would have a companion and caretaker. Apparently some inquiry about this had already been made, since Francois wanted Baptiste Peoria to bring the girl when he returned. The postscript was marked N.B. The abbreviation for the Latin *nota bene* are used to flag the reader's attention: "note well," that is, "take note!" This was a new development in Francois's letters.

Apparently, a Mr. Wilson was to give money to Mr. (Samuel) Owens for a debt owed to Mr. Poole. Mr. Owens being absent, Francois Chouteau was to collect the money. Was Wilson unable to contact Poole directly? Or did Poole owe money to the fur company, so that Francois was to leave Poole out of the loop and send the money directly to Sarpy? (Could this be the same debt owed by Poole in 1830?[19])

Two men named Pool were in the region in the early 1830s: James Pool worked at the Delaware-Shawnee Agency from 1828 to 1832[20]; a G. W. Pool led 334 Shawnees and 73 Ottawas from Ohio to the Shawnee reserve in Indian Territory in 1833.[21] While the date of the following letter mentioning Poole was 1837, it is probable that either or both of these men were still in the area, and it is unclear which one Francois meant.

---

19. See Pierre Menard to Francois Chouteau, February 4, 1830, in appendix item 3b on page 208.
20. *H. Doc. No. 137*, 22nd Cong., 2nd sess. (Serial 235): 69.
21. *S. Doc. No. 512*, 23rd Cong., 1st sess. (Serial 247): 4-10.

In 1838, Moses Wilson was one the fourteen men forming the original Town of Kansas Company. That group purchased the Prudhomme land that became the original site of the Town of Kansas.[22] He was probably the Wilson involved in this transaction. (Another man, Daniel Wilson, came through the area as a laborer on the steamboat *Yellow Stone*, but he would be a less likely candidate.[23])

Helen Decoigne, to review briefly, was probably a Native American of the Peoria or Kaskaskia tribe, as discussed in connection with Francois's letter written January 15, 1834. She owned land in Kaskaskia, near property owned by Pierre Menard. Menard wanted to buy Helen's land, but Helen was undecided about the sale. This business had dragged on for three years. Meanwhile, Helen had accumulated small debts that needed to be deducted from the sale money when or if that materialized. As Helen lived nearer to Francois than to Pierre Menard, Francois was to negotiate the transaction. (See appendix item 3g, page 212.)

Regarding the fur trade, Chouteau was awaiting the American Fur Company steamboat *Boonville* so that he could send a cargo of furs to St. Louis. Since the steamboat would be turning around at Joseph Robidoux's post at Black Snake Creek (present St. Joseph, Missouri), the cargo would be loaded on the return trip.

The dateline of the next letter shows the point of origin as not the customary *Riviere des Kans*, but "Missouri"!

Missouri   May 12, 1837[24]

Cher oncle,

I received your last letter, dated from April 18, by the steamboat St. Peters and I received also the little mulattress whom you sent to me. For that I am very grateful. Recently we are having a lot of worries with the expeditions that the Company is sending into the mountains. They arrive here badly disorganized and they need a lot of food and other arrangements are necessary before they can continue their trip. However, we are almost finished with our business with them for this time. And at the present, we will be able to look after our own affairs.

I saw Helen Decoigne who disembarked here from the steamboat Boonville. This boat brought her back a desk that she had on board. She also tells me she had made no definite arrangements with regards to her land. I believe it would be good for you to write a letter to the Chiefs or heads of the Weas concerning the debt that they still owe to Marshall. You could address the letter to me and I or Cyprien would read it to them at an appropriate time, that is to say, a little before they receive the annuities. I believe that will have a good effect. And we will support your letter with all our efforts. Perhaps we might have to give something. It would be better to do that than to lose everything.

I collected the debt of Poole that Wilson owed him in Independence, 286 dollars. I wrote to Sarpy to record the credit for that. The debt of Auguste Labaume will be due in June. As soon as I will have received it, I will write to Sarpy to record the credit.

---

22. *Kansas Town Company Records* (KC352), WHMC-KC.
23. Donald Jackson, *Voyages of the Steamboat Yellow Stone*, 169.
24. *PMC*, Letter 787. Envelope: [To] Monsieur Pierre Menard Sr., Kaskaskia, Illinois; [filing note] May 12, 1837, F. Chouteau.

I still have the note of Lebaume for 125 that you gave me in St. Louis, but I didn't have the opportunity to see Labaume. We have all sent our packs on the steamboat Boonville on its first voyage here and in which the poor Captain Bates lost his life the same day it departed from here. He is really a man to be missed. I wrote many letters to Menard but I do not believe he has received them all. I am also writing to him by this occasion. I am sending to him a little package that I am addressing to his brother [Gesseau] in St. Louis and I am recommending that he send it on at the first sure occasion. They are some very nice shoes that I send for him, and for Amedee a couple of small decorated purses.

I advise him in all my letters to be a nice boy and to apply himself well to his studies. I tell him that if I go to St. Louis in the month of August that it is possible that I will take him to see his mother during vacation.

As for Gesseau, he always writes to me by all the steamboats of which he has perfect knowledge. Sarpy gives me praise of him in all his letters. We are all pretty well. Little Bridget was a bit sick, but she is better. Ben is going to school in West Port. Do give my love to all the family. Charles has yet to write a small note.

Berenice joins me to wish you good health as well as to my aunt.

Believe me, with respect, your affectionate nephew,
Francois Chouteau

The caravan that had arrived at Francois's warehouse "badly disorganized" was surely forced into a disciplined supply train under Chouteau's organizational skills. But when the caravan arrived at its destination, all discipline ended. The precious bales of merchandise were split open with hunting knives, and their contents spilled onto the ground at the rendezvous in a valley of the Rocky Mountains.

The mountain rendezvous was an annual event during the 1830s and early 1840s; it was a festival, a gathering of trappers, traders, Indians, and fur company officials who came together to sell and to buy furs and merchandise. More than that, it was a wild carnival where everyone forgot their competition for furs and their tribal hostilities, and, aided by free-flowing whiskey, created the rendezvous spirit – spontaneous dancing and singing, contests of brute strength, competitive shooting with bow and rifle, horse racing, and jocular vying for the favors of young Indian beauties.

When the caravan of merchandise arrived, trappers and Indians traded with prodigal abandon – a red shawl for this woman, a hunting knife for that brave in payment of a lost wager, a string of bells for a handsome gray stallion, a new set of clothing, sugar, coffee, rifles, lead, gunpowder – on and on until at last the merchandise was gone. There were no more pelts to trade, and buying on credit had reached the limit. The caravan wagons, loaded with mountain beaver and other pelts, headed eastward, bound for St. Louis where the furs would be sorted and shipped. The trappers, hunters, and Indians, their heads aching from whiskey, their furs gone, gathered their supplies and their courage and once more struck out for the wilderness. Next year, they would be back to do it all over again.[25]

The Chouteau warehouse at Kansas City did not process the Rocky Mountain rendezvous furs. The packs gathered at Chouteau's Landing were the product of the Chouteau Kansa, Shawnee, Wea, and Kickapoo posts. The American Fur Company steamboat

---

25. Hiram M. Chittenden, *The American Fur Trade of the Far West*, 1: 43-44.

St. Peters had delivered Pierre Menard's letter and brought supplies for the thirteenth annual rendezvous.[26]

The first fur shipment of the year was on the *Boonville* that, like the *St. Peters,* was an American Fur Company steamboat. This vessel's captain, as Francois regretted, was that poor Captain Bates who "lost his life" shortly after the ship left Chouteau's Landing. The unfortunate Captain was drowned, "in the act of casting out an anchor, in the rope of which he was tangled, and dragged instantly to the bottom." The Jefferson City news account also echoed Francois's opinion of the man: "In the loss of Capt. Bates, the community have sustained a great loss; for he was an honest, a useful, and a good man."[27]

Steamboating on the Missouri River was a dangerous enterprise with deaths often resulting from exploding boiler, caused either by structural failure or excessive steam pressure. It was even more common for a boat to catch a "snag," a submerged tree that could tear the ship's bottom open. The *Boonville,* a single-engine side-wheel, sank in the bend above the mouth of the Kansas River in 1838, the year after Francois sent his furs downriver. The steamer was bound for Ft. Leavenworth, loaded with corn for the U.S. Government. It was a total loss.[28] Although sunken vessels threatened to clog the Missouri River channel, steamboats had become indispensable, and every year there were more of them puffing up the Missouri.

The school in Westport that Ben was attending was probably the one that pioneer Westport resident W. H. Chick recalled from when his family moved there in 1836. They "found a small school house, one room, built of logs out in the woods about half a mile from town."[29] His brother Joseph S. Chick located the school at "Archibald and Central."[30]

As for Gesseau, schooling was a thing of the past. After an almost brilliant start at St. Louis College, his academic prowess had, at St. Mary's of the Barrens, changed into rebellion. After being expelled from school and brought home in disgrace, Gesseau was, at the time of the preceding letter, at last back in his father's good graces. The young man was in the process of being accepted as an adult, a trusted person of business, and a source of pride and bragging rights for Francois.

Missouri   July 14, 1837[31]

Cher oncle,

I received by Pinsonneau your letter dated June 14 with the papers that were enclosed. I haven't yet seen Helen Decoigne concerning this business, that is to say, her land. But I will see her soon and I will try to terminate with her if that is possible. I will send to you the sale transacted in order. I will also pay you the 50 dollars for Baptiste Peoria. I collected your debt with Auguste Labaume, 550 dollars, and I wrote to Sarpy to record the credit. Again I had from you a bill on him [Labaume] *for 125 that I will*

---

26. Barry, *Beginning of the West,* 323.
27. *Jefferson Republic,* 8 April 1837, 2.
28. Folder 96, *E. B. Trail (1884-1965) Collection* (C2071), WHMC-C.
29. Washington Henry Chick, "A Journey to Missouri in 1822," *Missouri Valley Historical Society Annals of Kansas City* 1: 103.
30. Joseph S. Chick, "Methodism in Early Kansas City," *Missouri Valley Historical Society Annals of Kansas City* 3: 309.
31. *PMC,* Letter 803. Envelope: [Stamped] St. Louis [...] 27; [postage] 10; [to] Monsieur Pierre Menard, Kaskaskia, Illinois; [filing note] July 11, 1837, Fs. Chouteau, [....][....] of the annuities.

endeavor to have him pay if I have the chance. Since last Fall, in the month of October, I did not see Labaume. If I can see him, I have no doubt that I can be paid.

I also received your last letter and one for Shouanack of which we read the contents to him. I assure you he was very pleased and satisfied with everything that you wrote. That letter gave him considerable joy and he knows that you are really their friend. He assured us that he would take no merchandise for his annuities even if he had to wait ten years to get them; that the treaty that they transacted with the government promised them money. That is to say, that this is left to their own will to accept merchandise or money and that doubtlessly, he prefers money. With that they are able to buy their merchandise themselves, pay their debts, and finally, take care of their business much better than the government could do. And lastly, apparently the Indians are dissatisfied with the proposition to pay their annuities in merchandise. The Kansa are divided into two villages. Since they are very poor and miserable, perhaps one of the villages will continue to take the merchandise, but the other doesn't want to hear of it.

The Company has had a lot of trouble to retain their possession [of] the return of Fontenelle's 500 packs at the mouth of the river. Sublette wanted to take possession of the packs by force but the men held firm and stopped him from taking them. Then an express letter was forwarded to me immediately to inform me. Right away I sent out a man to go ahead of the barge with the order to land at Pinsonneau's and to unload all the packs into his shed in the hope that the steamboat St. Peters would not be later than five or six days. The things happened as I had figured and the boat took the packs. The Sheriff was in the neighborhood and at the mouth of the Kansas River to seize the barge. I am sending you a fine bag for lead that I addressed to Gesseau. It is the most beautiful handicraft of an Indian that I have yet seen. I entrusted it to my friend Cerre who was going down in the steamboat Howard.

Pinsonneau is to come back up here with his wife the first of next month. I beg of you to have the kindness to send me Menard on this occasion so that he may spend the vacation with us. His mother is eager to see him and that is very natural. And I hope to go to take him back myself and to have the pleasure of going to see you in Kaskaskia.

Berenice joins me and wishes you as well as my aunt good health.

Believe me always, with affection and respect,
Your nephew,
Francois Chouteau

The Delaware chief Shouanack was the son of Chief William Anderson, who, in October 1830, at an advanced age, brought approximately 100 of his people from their village on the James Fork in the Missouri Ozarks to their reservation in Kansas.[32] Menard's letter must have been written in French and converted by an interpreter into the Delaware language.

Five hundred fur packs were worth a small fortune, and Francois chose quick action rather than years in court, for he held onto the fur packs that the American Fur Company's Lucien Fontenelle had put on the company barge. Chouteau outmaneuvered the opposition

---

32. Barry, *Beginning of the West*, 178.

by having the packs taken to the riverfront Kickapoo post of Laurence Pensinneau, four miles north of Fort Leavenworth.

Four Sublette brothers were working on the Santa Fe Trail and in the Rocky Mountains during the mid-1830s. While William was the best known, the man referred to here was probably Milton Sublette. In 1835, the company of Fontenelle & Drips merged with Thomas Fitzpatrick, Milton Sublette, and Jim Bridger. If Sublette was entitled to some of these furs (as the sheriff may have thought), Chouteau forced him to make his claim in St. Louis.

The American Fur Company steamboat *Howard* that traveled on the Missouri River in 1836 was to bring Pierre Menard a gift of a "fine bag for lead." No specific description of this item was found, but it must have been a leather pouch used for carrying lead shot. Once more, the beauty of the Indian craftsmanship was pointed out. Perhaps Mrs. Prudhomme was, once again, the skilled artisan.

The "Friend Cerre" who carried the gift was the pal of Francois's youth, his cousin Gabriel Sylvestre Chouteau, nicknamed "Seres" (Americanized spelling) or "Cerre," the maiden name of his mother, Marie Therese Cerre, wife of Auguste Chouteau. As young men, Seres and Francois, then called Gesseau, had been partners licensed to trade with the Kansa, Osage, and Pawnee Indians; together, the cousins had built the Four Houses trading post in 1819.

The letter that follows detailed the continued dispute between the traders (although mostly Frederick Chouteau) and the government officials.

Missouri   October 17, 1837[33]

Cher oncle,

I received your last letter by my son Menard who arrived here in good health, with the nephew of Gilliss. I was very happy, as well as his mother, to see him. Because of his good behavior in school, I had promised him that at vacation he would be allowed to visit us. I will behave in such a way that he finds himself [....] [....] at the latest the 10th of next month. About the son of Lorimier, Maquaia, I will take care of it. I will see Francoise and I will try to have her agree to send him back to his father, telling her that it is in order to put him in school. I've been told that she is very unhappy with Lorimier.

All our Indians have refused the payment of their annuities in merchandise, even though the Loups and the Kansa took them. This was brought about through intrigue of the officers of the government. Among the Loups they carried on an election. The majority of the Chiefs were against. They [the government officials] *made the women vote and they say that there were five or six voices in majority obtained by the women in favor of taking merchandise. About the Kansa, the agent announced that he had heard that Frederick was the cause of the Indians refusing the merchandise, and consequently that his license was repealed and that he could no longer trade with the Kansa so, rather than lose the treaty of this year and the credits, he saw himself forced to advise the Chiefs to take the merchandise, which is what they did. And that avoided all difficulty*

---

33. *PMC*, Letter 822. Envelope: *St. Peters*; [stamped] St. Louis, Oct. 24, Mo.; [postage] 10; [to] Monsieur Pierre Menard, Kaskaskia, Illinois; [filing note] Oct. 17, 1827, Fs. Chouteau; [to] M. F. Chouteau, Kansas River.

against Frederick. The Indians said a lot of insults to the officers who endured it all quietly.

Without failure Berenice really had to come down on the St. Peters. Her suitcases were all packed. But two of our children have fallen very sick. Therefore, she was unable to go right now.

She joins me in wishing to you, as well as to my aunt, the best of health.

*I am respectfully,
Your affectionate nephew,
Francois Chouteau*

Kaskaskia   *November 22, 1837*

Cher Gesseau,

Yesterday on my arrival from St. Louis, your son Menard gave me the letter of the 2nd of the present month in which Helen Decoigne asked $1,000 for her land. Give it to her and conclude the business right away. Deduct what she owes me as well as Sarpy. Let's get back to our friend Labaume who says that Tisson should have had his bill endorsed for the $100 that he says he has paid. He never paid a penny. [....][....] on the second of May before it matures and until the moment when I'm giving it to you, it did not leave my hands. There is no endorsement.

The "dear Gesseau" note was penned on the bottom of Francois's letter dated October 17, 1837. The letter of November 2, referred to in Pierre Menard's note and carried by Francois's son Menard to Kaskaskia, is not in the *Pierre Menard Collection*. It may have been filed with either the Helen Decoigne papers or the August Lebaume bill.

Fifteen-year-old Pierre Menard Chouteau, second-born of Francois and Berenice, was trusted to travel by steamboat with a school chum, William Barkley, the nephew of Gilliss (no doubt under the watchful eye of the crew, given that most of the steamboats' captains were surely friends or acquaintances of the Chouteaus.) Menard's friend William Barkley attended St. Mary's College at the same time as the Chouteau and Menard boys. Pierre Menard was in some way Barkley's benefactor, perhaps paying for his schooling, as the young man wrote letters to Pierre Menard expressing gratitude. Five such letters appear in the *Pierre Menard Collection*.[34]

"Maquaia," son of one of the Lorimier men, had a Native American mother named Francoise. She may have been one of the Iroquois Indians who came from the Upper Missouri and settled in Kawsmouth, or perhaps she was the Francoise mentioned previously in Francois's letter dated May 5, 1835. That Francoise was linked with Baptiste Pascal. They were apparently Wea or Miami Indians. The Lorimier involved was also unidentified, but he was a member of the large Lorimier family that originated in Cape Girardeau. The Lorimiers, as pointed out, had special connections with the Indian tribes that crossed Missouri on the south-central land path through the Ozarks. This included the Weas, among whom

---

34. *Guide to the Microfilm Edition of the Pierre Menard Collection*, 84.

the Lorimier name appeared frequently. Louis Lorimier was married to a part-Shawnee woman, Marie Berthiaume.[35]

The letter that follows shows Francois once more in the role of financial go-between. The Bradshaw who was involved in the Lebaume-Tisson affair was probably related to Marie Louise Bradshaw, who married Francois's cousin, Joseph Papin. Joseph was the son of Marie Louise Chouteau Papin, sister to Francois's father, Pierre Chouteau.[36] A William Bradshaw signed a petition to the United States Congress in 1818, regarding the boundaries of the proposed state of Missouri.[37] A James Bradshaw was an early settler near Ste. Genevieve.[38] The "certificate" that Chouteau wanted from Bradshaw was something in the nature of an affidavit or statement.

Labaume of Westport, as mentioned previously, remains unidentified by any source other than Francois's letters and Pierre Menard's note. The other man involved, Tisson, probably came from one of the Tesson families living in St. Louis in the early to mid-1800s.[39] A Baptiste Tesson was doing some hunting in the Upper Missouri in 1843.[40]

Bitter cold gripped Chouteau's enclave and Kawsmouth as Francois reported happenings at the beginning of 1838. Postal service made winter correspondence possible, but the following letter was actually carried to St. Louis by someone who then posted it to Kaskaskia.

River of Kansas   January 28, 1838[41]

Cher oncle,

I received your last letter dated December 25 and I am happy to see that you, as well as all the family, were in good health, and I also see that you did not receive the letter that I wrote you of the same date as yours, December 25. I also had written another before that. Our Post Office department is not doing well. One can do no more. I also wrote to Sarpy and Gesseau at the same time and they have not received my letters. I received in your letter the certificate from Bradshaw. It arrived on time. Labaume has not yet arrived to claim his payment. He is to receive 800 dollars from Simpson & Owen from Westport. And if he comes himself – as I believe he will – he will no doubt have to pay. I have no word from him. I have terminated your business with Helen Decoigne. But she refused to sell to me except on the condition that I pay her the balance immediately. So, I preferred to do that so that it might be a closed matter. I drew an order from St. Louis for 500 dollars and I paid it. I will send you the exact bill in my next letter as I drew for a little more than was necessary. Enclosed you have here the bill of sale. I am happy [confident] *that you will find it in order.*

---

35. Louis Houck, *History of Missouri*, 2: 179.
36. William E. Foley and C. David Rice, *The First Chouteaus*, 211, 212.
37. Houck, *History of Missouri*, 3: 245.
38. Houck, *History of Missouri*, 1: 387.
39. Houck, *History of Missouri*, 1: 65.
40. S. Doc. No. 174, 28th Cong. 2nd sess. (Serial 416): 105, 162.
41. *PMC*, Letter 850. Envelope: [Stamped] St. Louis, Feb. 9, Mo.; [postage] 10; [to] Monsieur Pierre Menard, Kaskaskia, Illinois; [filing note] 28 January 1838, Rec'd 10th of Feb., Fs. Chouteau, The sale of Helen Decoigne.

> *As yet I cannot give you an idea of our treaty. The Kansa have not yet come out from the hunt. That is to say, at the present, I believe them to have arrived at their village. It's more than two weeks since I have no news of Frederick.*
>
> *I believe that we will have all our pelts here by March 15. The warriors who went in the flolide [?] will short us at least 100 packs. I have the pleasure to announce to you that Berenice has given me another daughter, the 16th of this month. Here I am at present with two daughters. And we are all in good enough health. And I hope it is the same for you.*
>
> *Berenice joins me to wish you a good year, as well as to my aunt. With respect, believe me always*
>
> *Your affectionate nephew,*
> *Francois Chouteau*
>
> *It is very cold here. The Missouri is solid like a bridge and we have hardly any snow.*

Catching the elusive Labaume was still on Chouteau's agenda as the year 1838 began. Simpson & Owen, who were to pay Labaume, owned lots 41 and 46 in Westport in 1837. The Owens was probably Samuel Owens, and Simpson could have been any one of several Simpsons in the area at the time. A James Simpson was blacksmith for the Shawnees at the Fort Leavenworth Agency from 1838 to 1844, and by various accounts may have also been involved in trade.[42] The more likely choice, however, is Richard "Duke" Simpson, who had been actively involved in the anti-Mormon movement in early 1833-1834,[43] and who along with James M. Hunter, was among the first merchants to accept John Calvin McCoy's offer of a free lot if they would build in the new community of Westport.[44] The Hunter and Simpson establishment was located on the southwest corner of Westport and Pennsylvania "where the Indian agents often left money to be distributed to the Indians."[45]

The event that Francois thought caused the shortage of 100 packs was apparently the Second Seminole War, 1835-1842. *Flolide*, in that case, was Francois's phonetic version of Florida. The Seminole Indians of that region were resisting removal from the area of present Florida.

The French word *fleole* denotes a kind of grass, and could have been used to designate a place where that grass grew. However, as Chouteau pointed out that his hunters had become "warriors," the Seminole War explanation seems to fit.

"The warriors who went in the *flolide*" were, then, Shawnees led by Captain Joseph Parks, "a distinguished man of mixed white and Indian blood, [who] organized a company of Shawnees and led them in the Seminole Wars."[46] Parks was an educated quarter-blood Shawnee who spoke several languages. He was an active supporter of the Indian Removal Act, and in 1833, himself led sixty-seven Shawnees from Ohio to Indian Territory. He was employed by the Office of Indian Affairs as an interpreter for the Shawnee Agency and was

---

42. Barry, *Beginning of the West*, 362, 533.
43. *History of Jackson County* (1881), 254-255
44. John C. McCoy Scrapbook, 93, (KC296), WHMC-KC. Nellie McCoy Harris, "Memories of Old Westport," in Missouri Valley Historical Society *Annals of Kansas City* 4: 466.
45. Westport Scrapbook, 45-46, *James Anderson Scrapbooks* (KC396), WHMC-KC.
46. Perl Wilbur Morgan, *History of Wyandotte County, Kansas and its People*, 36; see also Zelia Bishop, "Kansas City Traders and Merchants," *Kansas Magazine* (1951), 55.

often involved in negotiating treaties. Joseph Parks was a substantial landowner and a highly respected, prominent figure along the Missouri-Kansas state line.

Taking all this into consideration, it seems remarkable that Parks's enthusiasm for the removal program extended to going to Florida to fight the Seminoles who were resisting removal. And how did he convince the Shawnee warriors that these Seminoles were their enemies, when the memory of their own removal was so fresh in their minds?[47]

In family matters, Francois and Berenice Chouteau had become the parents of a second daughter, born the sixteenth of that cold January of 1838. She was named Therese Odile – given her mother's first name and the second name of her mother's sister, Marie Odile Menard Maxwell. So it was probably with special warmth that Francois and Berenice wished the Menards a Happy New Year as the year 1838 began.

On March 3, 1838, Francois wrote the following letter and sent it to Pierre Menard, using Andrew Drips as a courier:

River of Kansas   March 3, 1838[48]

Cher oncle,

I write this letter by way of Mr. Dripps who is leaving tomorrow morning for St. Louis. I presume that you have received my last letter, that is to say, the one I sent to you by Joseph Papin and that I addressed to Sarpy, wherein you should have found the [bill of] *sale of Helen Decoigne. I am also bringing to your attention that I drew on the house* [i.e., the business] *an order of 500 dollars in order to be able to give her the balance of the payment. She did not want to sell to me on any other condition. And I considered it better to finish with her right away. I think I have brought to your attention that I had received Bradshaw's certificate that you had sent to me. Our friend Labaume has not yet appeared. That will serve me well when he does come. I do not know exactly where he is. But I believe he is south of us trading with a few Indians.*

Helen Decoigne owed us altogether		440
I had her pay your bill		140
on the order of 500. I paid her		420
		(1000)
A balance remained for you	80	
I ask you to pay Bouvette	20	
and that adds up to	100	

that I collected for Jabor. And the entire balance that he asked me to collect for him. So you see I am indebted to you for 100 dollars. As yet I am unable to tell you the result of our treaty. Our pelts have not yet arrived from our other post.

It has been horribly cold here almost the entire month of February. The ice was more than two feet thick and the ground was frozen nearly 3 feet.

---

47. Barry, *Beginning of the West*, 243.
48. *PMC*, Letter 857. Envelope: [To] Monsieur Pierre Menard, Kaskaskia, Illinois; [filing note] March 3, 1838, Fr. Chouteau.

Berenice is purposing to go down in the month of April. And I think I'll have the pleasure of going to see you also. We are all well enough and I wish you good health as well as to my aunt and the family.

*And believe me with respect,
your affectionate nephew,
Francois Chouteau*

"Mountain man" Andrew Drips appeared on the fur trade scene as early as 1821, when he was a part of Manuel Lisa's Missouri Fur Company. At the time the letter was written, Drips was in charge of the American Fur Company caravan to the spring rendezvous in the Rocky Mountains.[49] From the late 1820s until 1840, Drips journeyed back and forth to the Rocky Mountains as hunter and trapper, guide, and organizer. In 1840, he and his Otoe Indian wife and their daughter settled in Kawsmouth. In 1842, Drips became a government Indian agent of the Upper Missouri Agency.[50]

The distribution of the money from Helen Decoigne's land sale assigned $20 to be paid to "Bouvette." A Jean Baptiste Bouvet (Bouvette, Bouvais) was listed as a property owner in Carondelet, Missouri, in the early 1800s.[51] "Jabor," for whom Francois collected $100, was probably a phonetic spelling of the name Jarboe, well known in Kansas City.

Joseph Jarboe and his family came to the Kansas City area from Kentucky in 1834. Jarboe was a merchant, and apparently Francois Chouteau collected $100 in debts that Jarboe himself was unable to collect – perhaps from local persons or perhaps from Indians – either group more willing, perhaps, to pay Chouteau than Jarboe, for whatever reason.

A letter written between those of January 28 and of March 3 is not in the *Pierre Menard Collection*. Chouteau had sent it to Sarpy and hoped that it had reached Pierre Menard. The Papin who had carried that letter to St. Louis was probably Joseph Papin, who later that year married Mary Josephine (Josette) Gonville. Considering Josette's close ties with the Chouteaus, Francois and Berenice were probably well acquainted with the Papins. The Papins and Chouteaus were also connected by the marriage of Francois's aunt Marie Louise Chouteau to Joseph Papin, probably the uncle of the Papin who married Josette Gonville.

The final paragraph of Francois's letter indicated that he was having no particular health problems. And yet, this was Francois's final surviving letter to Pierre Menard. Francois Chouteau died on April 18, 1838, at the age of forty-one. The cause of his death was probably a massive heart attack, as his 1833-1834 letters reported typical symptoms of heart trouble – chest pains and weakness.

Francois left six children: Gesseau, seventeen, working as a clerk in the American Fur Company store in St. Louis; Menard, sixteen, a student at St. Mary's of the Barrens in Perryville; Benjamin, ten, at home on the Jackson County Chouteau farm, attending school in Westport; and Frederic Donatien, seven, still at home with his mother and two little sisters, Mary Brigitte, three, and Odile, three months. Raising his family, like most of Chouteau's life work, was left incomplete. In Francois's short life he never sat for a portrait,

---

49. "Andrew Drips notes," Chouteau's (Biographical) Scrapbook [17.2], (KC395), WHMC-KC; Barry, *Beginning of the West*, 344.

50. Edward E. Hill, *The Office of Indian Affairs, 1824-1880*, 186; William A. Goff, "Andrew Drips at Kawsmouth and Kansas City," *The Westport Historical Quarterly* 6 (December 1970): 3-16. Also see *Andrew Drips (1790-1860) Collection* (KC335), WHMC-KC, for family Bibles and an obituary ([Kansas City?], September 2, 1860).

51. Houck, *History of Missouri*, 2: 65.

and so there is no picture of him. Although visually a phantom figure, Francois Chouteau's impact on the heartland was solid and real. He erected buildings, established businesses, pioneered financial networking, employed men, transported goods, and raised his family on the site that became Kansas City. He did not lay out streets nor envision a grand metropolis bearing a name he had given it, yet, if Francois Chouteau is not the founder of Kansas City, who is?

Berenice took her beloved Gesseau back to St. Louis for funeral rites and burial. This was extraordinary in those days when – because there was no embalming – funerals were customarily held the day after death. But Berenice, with her four young children, took Francois Chouteau back down the river that he had traveled so often. Ironically, in Francois's last letter to Pierre Menard, he had written that he hoped to come to St. Louis in April. And so he did.

The most immediate account of Francois's death came from Joseph Chick, son of pioneer Kansas Citian William Chick. "He [Francois] died suddenly while down on the river bank watching some cattle swim across the slew [slough]."[52]

The time directly before Francois's death may have been particularly stressful. Only four days after Francois collapsed and died, Andrew Drips, having returned quickly from St. Louis, led an American Fur Company expedition out of western Missouri on a journey to the Rockies. It was a large caravan consisting of seventeen carts and approximately 200 horses and mules, as well as Captain William Drummond Stewart and his party.[53] The yard at Chouteau's warehouse must have been a scene of turmoil – mules braying, horses stamping and snorting, men heaving cargo into wagons – and all the while, Francois, and probably Cyprien, counting the merchandise as it left the shelves. And everyone stepping around and over the touring dandies from the east. It was no wonder that Francois complained in his letter of May 12, 1837, that these expeditions were a "lot of worries."

The Missouri Saturday Evening News of April 28, 1838, reported as follows:

> DIED: Suddenly, on the _____ inst. at the mouth of Kansas river, Mr. FRANCIS CHOUTEAU, son of Pierre Chouteau, Sen., Esq., of this city. His remains were brought to this city on Tuesday last, and interred in the Catholic burying ground.[54]

A record of the funeral was written in the funeral book of the Old Cathedral in St. Louis: "On the twenty-fifth of April 1838, the rites of church burial were performed on the corpse of Mr. Francis G. Chouteau, forty-eight years of age, or thereabouts."[55] The notation was signed by J. A. Lutz, the same Catholic priest who, ten years earlier, had come to the Missouri frontier and attempted to evangelize the Kansa Indians.

Francois Chouteau was buried in the "Old Catholic Cemetery" on St. Charles Road, perhaps next to his "dear little Morgan." That burial ground at Franklin and Seventeenth had opened in 1828 after closure of the original Catholic cemetery on the bank of the Mississippi near the old Cathedral. The St. Charles Road cemetery closed in 1849 and the burials were later removed to Calvary Cemetery after it opened in 1857. At that time, Francois's remains were reburied in the Chouteau plot of Calvary Cemetery, where his

---

52. "Joseph S. Chick interview," October 19, 1908, General (series A), Kansa (subgroup 9), *Indians History Collection*, (MC590), KSHS.

53. Barry, *Beginning of the West*, 344-345.

54. *Missouri Saturday Evening News* [St. Louis], 28 April 1838.

55. *Funeral Book*, Archives of the Basilica of St. Louis the King (The Old Cathedral), St. Louis, Missouri.

name is listed on the family monument.[56] (A map of historic graves and monuments is available at Calvary Cemetery; the Chouteau plot is designated "A." – first, even in the cemetery.[57])

For years a legend has persisted that Francois Chouteau died on the plains of central Kansas, killed by a stampede of wild horses that he was attempting to bring back to his establishment for sale. According to this story, his teenage sons Gesseau and Menard were with him.[58] Support for this romantic Wild West tale has never surfaced. When Francois wrote to Pierre Menard on October 17, 1837, Francois's son Menard was in school at the Barrens. In that same October letter, Francois mentioned that Gesseau was working in the Sarpy store in St. Louis. There is no reason to think that either of the boys would have made the dangerous winter trip on horseback from St. Louis during the bitter winter of 1837-1838 when, as Francois described it, the Missouri was "solid like a bridge." In addition, notations in the *Funeral Book* of the Old Cathedral often specified an unusual cause of death – such as, "from cholera," or, merely, "accidental." No special notation was inserted in the funeral record of Francois Chouteau, nor did any letters surface in the Chouteau or Menard collections to support the story that Francois died under the hooves of wild horses.

Further substantiation of death from heart attack comes from Chick's vivid and detailed account of Francois watching cattle swim across a slough. While Chick erred as to the year (he gave it as 1840), the remainder of the account has the ring of truth. Most probably Francois collapsed within sight of his home. An island (later called Mensing Island) near Chouteau's Landing was likely used to graze cattle, and the slough was the channel of the Missouri River that separated the island from the south bank.

The death of Francois put his brother Cyprien Chouteau, then thirty-six, in charge of the American Fur Company's fur businesses in western Missouri and on the Kansas River. Cyprien may have kept both the Kansas City warehouse and his own Shawnee Post running for a period of time. Exactly who handled the day-to-day operation of the Chouteau warehouse from 1838 to 1844 is not known. Cyprien and Frederick Chouteau took responsibility for the business generally, assisted in later years by Francois's second son, Menard.

Cyprien's life, however, was centered at his post for the Shawnee Indians near present Turner, Kansas. He operated this post from 1828 to 1857, with considerable help from Francois during the early years.[59] After Francois's death, the importance of Chouteau's Landing and of the Kansas City warehouse declined. The staging area for the American Fur Company caravans to the Rocky Mountains was transferred to Cyprien's Post.

The flood of 1844 that destroyed Francois's Kansas City warehouse left Cyprien's Post untouched. Francois had described the Shawnee post in his letter to Pierre Menard dated December 2, 1828, as "a very elevated point. Water has to rise more than 40 feet to endanger us." Cyprien Chouteau's marriage to Nancy Francis in 1855 is well documented, but researcher Clyde Porter recorded that Cyprien had entered into an earlier marriage with a Shawnee woman named Maria Tucker. (Porter does not cite his source.) Cyprien's wife,

---

56. John Rothensteiner, *History of the Archdiocese of St. Louis*, 2: 157; Letter from Judith Peluso, Archives, Calvary Cemetery, St. Louis, to Dorothy Marra, August 9, 1999.

57. *Historic Tour Outline of Calvary Cemetery*, 5239 Florissant Avenue at Union Avenue, St. Louis, Missouri.

58. Charles E. Hoffhaus, *Chez les Canses: Three Centuries at Kawsmouth*, 174.

59. The 1828 date for inception of Shawnee (Cyprien's) Post based on Francois Chouteau's letter to Pierre Menard, December 2, 1828; an 1827 date was used by Daniel Boone, son of Daniel Morgan Boone, in an 1879 letter (*Kansas Historical Collection* 8: 433.)

Nancy Francis, was the daughter of a hereditary Shawnee chief. Nancy was orphaned when she was seven years old and then lived and was educated at the Quaker Mission in present Merriam, Kansas. Cyprien and Nancy Chouteau had three children. Cyprien retired from the Indian trade around 1857 and moved to Kansas City in 1862.[60] He died in Kansas City in 1879 at the age of seventy-nine, and was buried in Mount St. Mary's Catholic Cemetery, Kansas City.

Francois's youngest brother Frederick was twenty-nine years old at the time of Francois's death. Since the onset of Francois's poor health in 1831, Frederick had increasingly assumed responsibility for operating of the Kansa Post. After Francois died, Frederick, well-schooled in the business, continued to run the post for the Kansa Indians on the Kansas River near Mission Creek, where he had been since 1831 or 1832. It was thereafter known as Frederick's Post. Frederick had become comfortable living among the Native Americans, many of whom were his close friends. In 1830, Frederick had married a Shawnee woman whose name was variously given as Nancy Logan, Nancy Tooley, or Elizabeth Tooley.[61] She bore him four children. After her death, Frederick married Mathilda White, with whom he had three children. After her death, around 1855, Frederick married Elizabeth Carpenter, another Shawnee woman. She bore him three children. After the death of his third wife, Frederick married Elizabeth Ware.

Several of Frederick's children went to Oklahoma with their Shawnee relatives in the latter half of the nineteenth century.

Through the years, Frederick Chouteau bought and sold land in the Shawnee, Kansas, area in addition to operating businesses that included a ferry across the Kansas River. He built houses and saw them destroyed – one swept away by the flood of 1844, another burned by Quantrill's raiders during the Missouri-Kansas border conflict leading to the Civil War. In 1877, Frederick sold his Shawnee land and moved to Westport where, attended by his wife, Elizabeth, he died in 1891 at the age of eighty-two. He was also buried in Mount St. Mary's Catholic Cemetery, Kansas City.

The commerce that brought the French, and the Chouteaus in particular, to western Missouri was fading fast when Francois died. Writers on the subject mark the demise of the fur trade with dates ranging from 1838 to 1845.

Francois Chouteau had long since invested in other enterprises, for he must have foreseen the end of the fur trade. Although at his death he owned twelve hundred acres of what is now the heart of Kansas City, Chouteau would never have claimed to be a city builder. He was interested in making a business thrive, and where that business was, with its workers and transportation needs, a city grew. Chouteau was concerned not with cities, but with "the business," running his large farm, and raising his family. Perhaps he would have added a retail store in Westport or opened a bank if he had lived past the pioneer era. Francois left Berenice and their children well endowed with property, but unfortunately, not with the know-how to manage it.

While Berenice and her family were in St. Louis following Francois's death, the infant Odile was baptized on May 21, 1838. Berenice remained in St. Louis and Kaskaskia during the spring and summer of 1838. Then she and the younger children, Benjamin, Frederic Donatien, Mary Bridget, and baby Odile, returned to Kansas City. Sixteen-year-old Menard Chouteau probably returned in September 1838, at the same time as his mother. Gesseau

---

60. "Cyprien Chouteau and family notes," Chouteau's (Biographical) Scrapbook [17.3], (KC395), WHMC-KC; "Chouteau Family in Kansas City notes," Clyde Porter Scrapbook [56.1], (KC395), WHMC-KC.

may have returned to work in his father's warehouse, or he may have continued to work for Sarpy in St. Louis for a time.

Pierre Menard Chouteau's letter to his Grandfather Menard dated October 28, 1838, documented that he had been at "Westport" for a month. He went on to say, "I will spend the winter here with *Mamma* as she cannot resolve herself to spend the winter here alone."[62] He also told his grandfather that in the spring he would take a position in "Uncle Sarpy's store," though that apparently did not happen.

J. B. Sarpy visited Berenice and family in the fall of 1838, perhaps to take inventory of merchandise in the Chouteau warehouse as well as to see the family. After he returned to St. Louis, he wrote to Pierre Menard in a letter dated November 4, 1838, reporting, "I left the family of your daughter in good health. Berenice is quite decided to abandon [....] next spring and I approve that very much as she is not able to stay on her habitation without having someone to take charge of it."[63]

Why did Berenice not return to that place where her husband's family lived and some of her own siblings had established themselves? The fact that she took her husband's body to St. Louis for burial suggests that she intended to return there to live. Perhaps, however, her two oldest sons urged her to remain in western Missouri and make their father's legacy profitable for all of them. There is no way of knowing. In any case, Berenice did not move to St. Louis or Kaskaskia but remained in western Missouri, and in 1840 wrote the following three letters:

River of Kansas   May 9, 1840[64]

Cher papa,

Here is the second letter that I write to you in reply — no other news from any of the family. I also wrote to Sophie who does not keep her promise, for she promised to give me the news often of Ben from whom I have not received a word yet. I learned with sorrow that poor Alzire is still ill. It seems that we are a family for troubles in this world. But God be praised! And write me whether Edmond received the money through Mr. Henri and if he paid for what I owed him at the store. I beg you, dear papa, to ask Cousin Sarpy for the money to pay the school for my Ben. I am thinking about sending my Frederic next spring if we will not have a school here. Brigitte talks often of the fish from Grandfather's house and especially the good Aunt Sophie who is to send her a cake all the [....] and give news of my dear Theresa and my aunt. Say "hello" to all my brothers and sisters and tell them to come see me this summer. As for you, I do not believe that you would ever give me that pleasure. Give me news of the health of my beloved Cyprien and whether he has returned from his trip. I believe that a trip to the mountains would cure this good brother because several in his condition returned in good condition doing very well. Mr. Dripps and many others who have made that trip have returned in tip-top

---

61. Oliver H. Gregg, *History of Johnson County, Kansas*, 45; Foley and Rice, *The First Chouteaus*, 211.
62. *PMC*, Letter 913.
63. *PMC*, Letter 916, J. B. Sarpy to Pierre Menard, November 4, 1838.
64. *PMC*, Letter 1065. Envelope: [To] M. Pierre Menard, Kaskaskia, Illinois; [from] Westport, Mo., May 19, 1840; [postage] 25; [filing note] May 9, 1840, Berenice Chouteau, [....] [....] whether Edmond [....] [....] credit.

shape. Mr. Dripps and several others who have traveled there say that all diseases can be cured by going to the mountains.

Goodbye, dear papa, I am respectfully your very affectionate daughter,
Berenice Chouteau

> *N.B. Alexi was looking for a master before my arrival from down there* [St. Louis], *not wanting to ask anything further from Mr. Gilliss – I wish very much to have this black man because he is very good and I do not have enough men for my farm to make any progress. He greatly desires to come and stay with me for four or five years – that he will serve faithfully. But that he needs to leave from where he is living. I beg of you to see Polite on that subject and to write to me what he* [Polite] *would ask me. He* [Alexi? Gilliss?] *had told me to ask* [the price] *for that time that he* [Alexi] *would agree to serve.*

Once again, there emerged the familiar pattern in Berenice's correspondence: concern with family affairs and personal relationships. Berenice's son, Benjamin, then twelve, was following the family tradition of attending school at St. Mary's of the Barrens, where Berenice was thinking of sending her son Frederic Donatien, or Fred, then nine years old. The request that Cousin Sarpy give Pierre Menard the money for Ben's tuition suggests that, as François's estate was settled, Sarpy (i.e., the American Fur Company) owed Berenice money – probably payment for pelts delivered to St. Louis, and also the return of excess inventory from the Chouteau warehouse.

Berenice's oldest daughter, Brigitte, then five, was apparently a favorite of her Aunt Sophie, who could not do enough for the little girl, even as Berenice had pampered "little Sophie," sending her gifts, hugs, and kisses (as evidenced in Berenice's letters of January, April, and May of 1827).

Berenice's sister Alzire and all of Berenice's Menard siblings and half-siblings became increasingly important in the lives of Berenice and her children, as her letters demonstrate. From these letters and the ones written in her later life, it seems that as time passed, Berenice had little contact with the Chouteaus of St. Louis, though this was not necessarily true of her children.

In 1840, Edmond Menard, Berenice's twenty-seven-year-old half-brother, was assisting his father, gradually assuming responsibility for the Menard businesses. Edmond had ended his education in Emmitsburg, Maryland, in 1836, and after a few years in Vandalia and Springfield, Illinois, returned to Kaskaskia in 1840. The store Berenice referred to was the Menard and Valle store in Kaskaskia. A Mr. Guillaume (William) Henrie wrote letters to Pierre Menard from 1834 to 1846 from Prairie du Rocher, Illinois.[65] Apparently, in this instance, Mr. Henrie carried a sum of money for Berenice.

The Theresa mentioned in the preceding letter was probably Berenice's cousin, Therese Noemi Menard, daughter of Pierre Menard's brother Hippolyte (Polite). The aunt, being linked to Theresa, was her mother Rosalie Seguin, Hippolyte's second wife. Although a citation in the *Guide to the Microfilm Edition of the Pierre Menard Collection* is given further genealogical material on Theresa is missing.[66]

---

65. *Guide to Menard Collection*, 96.
66. *Guide to Menard Collection*, 31-32, I-5-11.

Like his brother Pierre, Hippolyte Menard had settled in Kaskaskia, raised two families, died, and was buried there. Berenice must have known these relatives quite well, as demonstrated by her reliance for assistance from "Polite" in the matter of Alexi. This "Polite" was probably Berenice's cousin Hippolyte rather than her uncle, as she would almost certainly have used "uncle" and more respectful phrasing if he had been her father's brother. (Berenice also had a brother named Hippolyte who died as a child.[67])

Cyprien Menard, Berenice's half-brother about whom she inquired in the preceding letter, had spent the previous winter in the mild climate of Cuba, probably in an effort to cure his chest ailment. Berenice, however, was recommending another solution.

The business about Alexi presents an interesting insight into the way slaves were managed by the French. That Alexi was a slave was demonstrated by the fact that he was looking for a new "master," and that he was being leased for a sum of money. Apparently, as he did not want to stay with Gilliss, he was able to express a preference. "He needs to leave from where he is living," Berenice wrote. It seems that Polite (Hippolyte) owned Alexi, but had leased him to William Gilliss. Alexi, however, did not want to stay with Gilliss, and Berenice did not want "to ask anything further from Mr. Gilliss," so she was trying to make the arrangement through Polite. The postscript also documents that Berenice was attempting to run the large Chouteau farm, but having difficulties.

The following letter, written in the same tone, recalled happenings during a visit by members of the Menard family in the summer of 1840.

River of Kansas   August 23, 1840[68]

Cher papa,

I was unable to write to you through Cyprien and Sophie because of the illness of Frederic, as I did not have the free time. He was very ill. But he is better now and he begins to take drives in the buggy every morning. I have worried a great deal over my Cyprien and my little sister Sophie is very upset in seeing Cyprien vomit blood as much as he vomited here. I believe, dear papa, that it would be prudent to send him back to a warm country this winter again, because he is of a weak health. This dear little boy. We are all well. And I hope that Spring [autumn?] *finds you likewise. Alexi has left from Mr. Gilliss the 13th of the present month. About Alexi – I will not go out of my way for him any more. I desire that Polite tells me what he is asking. If the price is agreeable to me, I will keep him. I think Mr. Gilliss has given him a time, that he should serve but two years. He is doing that only out of jealousy or malice as he ordinarily does.*

Goodbye dear papa. Believe me your obedient daughter
Berenice Chouteau

Berenice's lifelong concern for family was well demonstrated in this letter. Her son Fred was then nine years old. The reference to the morning buggy ride points once more to the belief that "good" fresh air had curative powers. (See Francois's letter to Pierre Menard of November 3, 1829, in which he judged that the Vasquez house "is unhealthy," presumably

---

67. *Guide to Menard Collection*, 28.
68. *PMC*, Letter 1099. Envelope: [To] M. P. Menard, Kaskaskia, Ill.; [filing note] Aug. 23, 1840, Berenice Chouteau.

because it was in a low, damp location.) Berenice's "little sister Sophie" was then eighteen, and Cyprien, Berenice's half-brother, was twenty-one. The phrases "little sister" and "dear little boy" were terms of endearment.

Cyprien Menard may have suffered from a lung illness similar to the one that claimed the life of his brother Francois Menard in 1831. Cyprien managed to overcome his malady, however, and lived to the age of fifty-one; he died in 1870 at Ste. Genevieve, where he had lived since 1846.[69]

The following and last letter of this compilation was also the last preserved of those Berenice wrote to her father. He died in 1844, and most of her subsequent letters were written to her half-brother Edmond:

River of Kansas   December 29 [1840] [70]

Cher papa,

You must have thought that I was very negligent but I assure you that it was not by total indifference but the grief that had taken away all possible courage and made me almost always sick, but thank God, since we have a good old Jesuit priest in our parish and that I never miss Sunday mass nor during the week when I have time. It seems to me that I can bear my pain with more strength. I have the little girl of Mr. Dripps that he left me to take to the convent when I will go down. I beg you to ask the nuns if I can have a place for her and send me two or three prospectus. There are many who wish to see the conditions and maybe I will bring several with me. We are all well enough at the present.

Your submissive daughter,
Berenice Chouteau

Andrew Drips, as noted, settled in Kawsmouth in 1840, but his constant journeying to the mountains made it difficult for him to care for his daughter. As the letter mentioned, the girl, Catherine, was staying with Berenice. She was the daughter of Drips and his wife, Maoumntameo, an Otoe Indian woman whom he had met in Oregon. The couple, with their child, returned to Missouri in the late 1830s. Catherine had been born in present Yellowstone Park around 1831. Her mother was not on the scene at the time of this 1840 date. Berenice arranged for Catherine Drips, then about eleven or twelve years old, to be educated at a convent school in Kaskaskia (it moved to St. Louis after the 1844 flood). When as a young woman Catherine returned to Kansas City, she married William Mulkey, early resident of the growing community.

The grief reflected in Berenice's letter was not specifically explained, as apparently her father already knew the cause. It seems certain that Berenice agonized over the death of her youngest and last child, Therese Odile. In comparison with the two previous matter-of-fact letters, this one shows a much-altered state of mind. Something tragic had happened, such as the death of a beloved child, and with it came the knowledge that there would never be another to replace her.

---

69. *Guide to Menard Collection,* 106.

70. *PMC,* Letter 1128. Envelope: [To] M. P. Menard, Kaskaskia, Illinois; [from] West Port, Mo.; [postage] 25; [filing note] Berenice Chouteau, December 19, 1840.

No death date for Odile has been established, but the internal evidence of the preceding letter, as well as J. S. Chick's affidavit that Odile died "in infancy,"[71] supports the conclusion that she died after August 23rd (the date of Berenice's preceding letter) and before early November, when Rev. Nicolas Point, the "old Jesuit," arrived. Odile would have been two, almost three, years old. (That she died before 1850 is documented by the U.S. Census for that year.) There was no Catholic priest in the area when Odile died, so there was no church funeral or record of burial. If any kind of record was made, it did not survive. Supposedly, church records were then kept at the Chouteau warehouse, since Chouteau's Church was not a secure building. Any documents in the warehouse were lost in the flood of 1844. When the old cemetery behind "Chouteau's Church" was closed in 1881, Odile was reburied in Mount St. Mary's Catholic Cemetery.[72]

Reverend Nicolas Point, S.J., came from St. Louis to Kansas Landing (he called it "Westport") in early November 1840. He served as pastor while he waited to join the missionary expedition of Father Pierre Jean De Smet, S.J. Although Berenice referred to him as an "old Jesuit," he was only forty-one, two years older than Berenice. Father Point served the community until Father De Smet and group arrived from St. Louis. Father Point set out with them on May 10, 1841, for the Oregon Territory. Father Point's map of his parish, *Plan de Westport,* along with its list of twenty-six names, has become a staple of the history of Kansas City's pioneer period. While the *Plan de Westport* shape resembles a piece of cherry pie, Father Point was actually a gifted artist. He painted a picture of his parish, St. Francis Regis, before he undertook the journey that inspired his dramatic interpretations of Indian life in the Northwest.[73]

Flooding was a perennial problem to those living on the riverbank. Berenice's half-brother Cyprien Menard, writing from Kawsmouth in May 1843, told his father that "Father De Smet and his missionaries are staying at the little church on the bluff, with sister Berenice"[74] who had "moved up on the hill and is there yet as the ground is yet too wet and muddy to allow her to retake possession of her lands. The boys are keeping bachelor's hall [at the landing]."[75] When there was no longer a threat of flooding, Berenice and family returned to their home at the landing "though she is afraid that the June freshet may make her move again."[76] – an ominous premonition for the following year.

On June 16, 1844, a mere three days after the death of her father (of which she may have been mercifully unaware), Berenice lost almost all of her material possessions in the flood of 1844. The water swept away the warehouse, rushed into her home, over the outbuildings, and across the fields and pastures of her farm. John C. McCoy came down to her house with

---

71. J. S. Chick in an affidavit filed with the transfer of title, July 15, 1853, when Chouteau lands were sold to Joseph Guinotte. "Francois Chouteau and family notes," Chouteau's (Biographical) Scrapbook [17.3], (KC395), WHMC-KC.

72. *Register of Interments,* 1: 34-35, Mount St. Mary's Catholic Cemetery, Kansas City, Missouri.

73. Michael Coleman, Colette Doering, and Dorothy Marra, *This Far by Faith: A Popular History of the Catholic People of West and Northwest Missouri,* 2: xix-xxii. See also, *Wilderness Kingdom, Indian Life in the Rocky Mountains, 1840-1847: the Journals & Paintings of Nicolas Point,* translated and introduced by Joseph P. Donnelly; and *Sacred Encounters: Father De Smet and the Indians of the Rocky Mountain West* by Jacqueline Peterson with Laura Peers.

74. Cyprien Menard to Pierre Menard, May 24, 1843, *PMC,* Letter 1410. Although Father Donnelly stated that the rectory cabin near Chouteau's Church at present 11th and Broadway was too small and dilapidated to be occupied, it apparently was used on occasion. (William J. Dalton, *The Life of Father Bernard Donnelly; with Historical Sketches of Kansas City, St. Louis and Independence, Missouri,* 155.)

75. Cyprien Menard to Pierre Menard, May 12, 1843, *PMC,* Letter 1407.

76. Cyprien Menard to Pierre Menard, May 24, 1843, *PMC,* Letter 1410.

an "old horse boat...and brought up Mrs. Chouteau and her household goods from her homestead below East Kansas, to high ground above."[77]

While the floodwaters still covered the low land where the Chouteaus had lived, the steamboat *Missouri Mail* arrived and anchored next to the flooded Chouteau residence. The ship's crew ran the gangplank into a second-story window of the house and may have salvaged a few items. When the floodwaters receded, the French-style wooden *maision* and all the farm buildings were gone. A new river channel cut over Chouteau's Landing where thousands of furs and skins had been loaded onto boats.

Berenice was left with no home, no business, and no agricultural land. Part of the Chouteau farm was under the Missouri River, and the rich alluvial soil of the remainder was covered with from two to six feet of river sand. There was no hope of tilling it again in the foreseeable future.

The flood of 1844 marked the end of the era dominated by the fur trade and the French pioneers. When rebuilding began, Americans who came mostly from Kentucky or Tennessee did it, along with Irish immigrants from the east coast who shouldered the hardest work. Chouteau's Landing was only a memory. Steamboats docked at Kansas Landing bringing goods, not to trade for Indian money or furs, but for the overland trade to the Southwest, and to stock retail stores patronized by the swelling population of what would soon be known as the "Town of Kansas."

Few of the French families resumed farming their flood-damaged *arpents* in the West Bottoms. Some took the Santa Fe Trail to New Mexico and Texas; others followed paths over the mountains to California and Oregon. Some may have returned to Ste. Genevieve, St. Charles, or St. Louis, and a handful remained, among them Berenice Chouteau and her family. Berenice now entered the period of her life in which she was known as the *Grand dame* of Kansas City.

---

77. *History of Jackson County* (1881), 405.

Plan de Westport (Missouri)

Drawn by Nicolas Point in 1840, the map is in fact a representation of the fledgling Town of Kansas community rather than the larger town four miles to the south. Also Father Point's interests only extended to his parishioners so only they are listed in his legend and placed on the map. Still, this is the earliest detailed map of the community and Father Point's sketches are the earliest pictures of Kansas City buildings and places.

The map, positioned so that west is to the top, has two important geographical features to note: the creek at the top of the map is Turkey Creek, not the Kansas River as some might suppose. Prior to the 1844 flood Turkey Creek emptied into the Missouri River at about Broadway. Francois Chouteau owned much of the section of land west of the creek to the mouth of the Kansas (State Line). The second important landmark is the large island that extends from the bottom of the picture. Though not shaped exactly as Father Point drew it, the nearly mile long island extended to the northeast from several block west of the Paseo Bridge to several blocks north of where North Olive would intersect the river. Nearly the entire island is now part of the south bank in the East Bottoms.

The Chouteau home (number 14) is depicted on the map as the easternmost residence away from the church – the figurative center of the community (number 1 on the map). There was roughly three miles between those two sites over rugged ground.

Translations of the twenty-six points on the legend are:
1. Church-Mission
2. Bellemare [Moyse Bellemaire]
   Clement [Lessert]
3. Gerber
4. Carboneau
5. Delaurier [Antoine Delorier]
6. Tremble [Francis Tremble]
7. Vertefeuille [Joseph Vertefeuille]
8. Laliberte [Pierre LaLiberte]
9. Rivard [Joseph Revard Jr.]
10. Petit Louis [Louis Prieu]
11. Campville [A. B. Canville]
12. Cadoret
13. Widow Rivard [Francoise Roy Rivard (Mrs. Joseph)]
14. Widow Chouteau
15. Grand Louis [Bertholet]
16. Philibert [Gabriel Philibert]
17. Peria [Pierre Perialt?]
18. Benjamin [Lagautherie?]
19. Gray [John Grey]
20 Prudhomme, Mercier
21. Edouard [Chosses]
22 Bowird
23 Ben.
24. Drips [Andrew Drips]
25 Smart [Thomas Smart?]
26. Meguille [James McGill?]

182   *Cher Oncle, Cher Papa: The Letters of Francois and Berenice Chouteau*

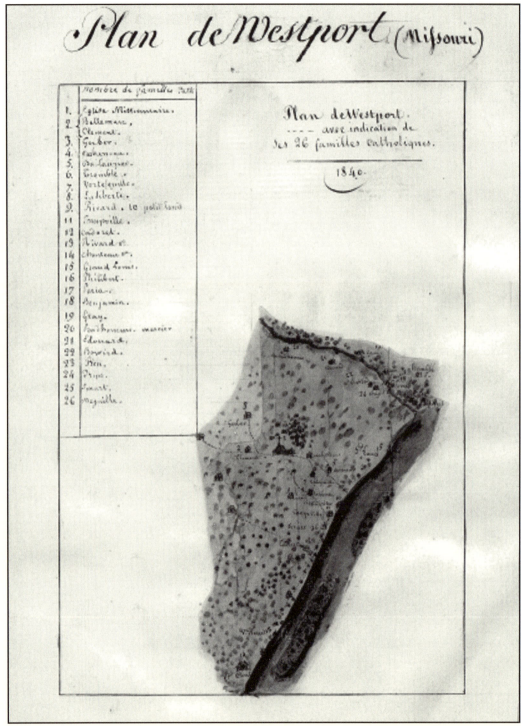

Nicolas Point's *"Plan de Westport (Missouri)"*. *Père Nicolas Point, S.J., Collection*, Archives de la Compagnie de Jesus, province du Canada frantais.

A portion of "*Kansas City, 1855*," drawn by F. Buckeridge. Note in the foreground the steamer Kate Sweeney owned by P. M. Chouteau. The Chouteau home is not visible in this view – it was located just behind the hill in the upper left. Main Street cuts south through the bluff. Missouri Historical Society, St. Louis.

8 Berenice's Later Life

Although the flood had robbed Berenice of much of the wealth her husband had left her, she built a new house on Pearl (First) and Market (Grand) streets. The large two-story Colonial frame house had "wide center halls...and long verandas and French windows."[1] It faced east with a large ell running back from the main building. This dwelling stood on raised ground and though not atop the bluff, it was well out of the reach of the river. The Santa Fe Trail coursed along in front of the house, which was set back in a large yard filled with flowers and shrubbery and kept in perfect condition. In the words of John McCoy, it was "a place where hospitality was dealt with a lavish hand. Inherent French politeness and wealth characterized the entertainment."[2]

---

1. "The Hill the City Left Behind" (*Kansas City Star*, 17 September 1922), quoting Mrs. Nellie McCoy Harris, in Kansas City Scrapbook, 117-123, *James Anderson Scrapbooks* (KC396), WHMC-KC.
2. "Incidents of the 'Knob Hill' or Aristocratic Residence Quarter of Kansas City of Early Days", typescript manuscript by William L. Campbell in "Recollections of Pioneers," Kansas City Before the Civil War Scrapbook [35], (KC395), WHMC-KC.; "The Faded Glimpses of Pearl Street," *Kansas City Star*, 29 October 1916, 10(C).

In 1853 Berenice sold the Chouteau farmlands, then consisting of 373 acres "lying north and east of Troost and Independence Avenue and 131 acres on the river at the state line."[3] Belgian immigration agent Joseph Guinotte paid "$8,000 or $10,000," according to the previous source. There is some discrepancy in the sale price, as a Cadet Chouteau memorandum listed parcels of land sold to Guinotte for $12.50 per acre, totaling $63,000.[4]

Berenice's post-flood home, "the Chouteau mansion," as it was called locally, was on the west side of Grand avenue just north of Second street,[5] on the "First Quality Hill" of Kansas City. It was there that Madame Chouteau began to live the good life. Her five children no longer required constant supervision. Gesseau was coming and going and Mack entered his father's old business, the Indian trade. Ben was nearly twenty; Fred was seventeen. Both boys received some schooling at St. Mary's in Perryville. Mary Brigitte was a young woman of fourteen. With her family and a complete domestic staff, Berenice settled into her comfortable routine. She entertained, played hostess to musical events and balls, contributed to charity, and drove about town in a fine carriage pulled by a pair of matched gray horses whose equipage was made of good leather, oiled and supple, and polished brass fittings.

Late in 1855 Berenice advertised her home for sale in the *Kansas City Enterprise*:

VALUABLE REAL ESTATE FOR SALE. A desirable place for Boarding House or residence, consisting of a house having seven rooms, a good kitchen, with rooms adjoining for servants, two good cellars, a spacious stable, crib and carriage house, smoke house, and other outhouses, with the grounds, consisting of five lots, well enclosed. The above property will be sold on very reasonable terms. For further particulars apply to Mrs. B. F. Chouteau at her residence, or this office.[6]

Madame Chouteau's household staff consisted of servants for routine duties, as well as persons with specialized skills: cooks, gardeners, and a full-time seamstress. Sewing for a large domestic establishment was a full-time occupation and allowed for no artistic flourishes with needle and thread. While Cecilia Grey was a young single woman, she worked for Berenice as a "fine needlewoman." Celia was the youngest daughter of John Grey, an early resident of Kawsmouth.

The U.S. Census of 1850 for Jackson County listed Berenice, her children Edmond (Gesseau), Pierre Menard, Frederic, Mary Brigitte, and six slaves. Benjamin was not present. The Chouteaus, however, were not recorded in the census of 1860 for Kansas City, because Berenice had moved to Ste. Genevieve by that time. It is likely that she was fleeing from the Missouri-Kansas border conflict that preceded the Civil War.

According to a Ste. Genevieve newspaper, Berenice moved to that community in 1860 and purchased a piece of property called "Little Rock."[7] Berenice's daughter Mary Brigitte had married steamboat captain Ashley Hopkins in 1853[8] and moved to Ste. Genevieve,

---

3. "Extensive Lands Now Part of Kansas City," *Kansas City Star,* 14 February 1926, 1(D).

4. "Francois Chouteau and family notes," Chouteau's (Biographical) Scrapbook [17.3], KC395, WHMC-KC.

5. The location is also often given as Market and Pearl Streets, using their pre-1875 names.

6. "Valuable Real Estate for Sale," *Kansas City Enterprise*, 10 November 1855.

7. "From Our Early Files," n.d., *St. Genevieve Fair Play,* clipping in "Chouteau Family in Kansas City notes," Clyde Porter Scrapbook [56.1], (KC395), WHMC-KC. This is also confirmed by the 1860 census that places her is Ste. Genevieve county that year.

8. "When Mrs. Chouteau's only daughter ran away and married Aston [sic] Hopkins, a steamboat captain, the mother forgave her and celebrated the marriage with a large reception." ("The Hill the City left behind," in Kansas City Scrapbook, 117-123, (KC396), WHMC-KC.

then to St. Louis. Mary Brigitte was in St. Louis when her first child was born in 1861.[9] When Berenice, sons Ben and Fred, and Mary Brigitte were all in Ste. Genevieve, they apparently shared a home.[10]

The Chouteau mansion in Kansas City was leased to John G. Adkins in 1860; G. W. Toler lived there during the Civil War. (Ben Chouteau married Ann Toler, daughter of G. W., in Jackson County in 1856.) In 1869, P. G. Wilhite bought the house, then left behind as the city expanded west and south away from that "First Quality Hill." The once grand Chouteau mansion was razed in the 1880s.

Although Mary Brigitte had moved to St. Louis by 1861 and died of cholera there in 1864, Berenice was still living in Ste. Genevieve in 1865, as documented by a letter she wrote from her "Little Rock" property.[11] Berenice's half-brother Cyprien Menard was also living in Ste. Genevieve during the years that Berenice was there.

Beginning with the "Little Rock" letter, Berenice's correspondence was written in English. Berenice apparently remained in Ste. Genevieve until the death of Cyprien Menard in 1870. By 1871, she was writing to her half-brother Edmond Menard from Kansas City, where her son Pierre Menard Chouteau and his family lived.

Pierre Menard Chouteau clearly was the son to inherit his father's business and social standing in the frontier community. In 1849, he had married Mary Ann Polk, whose father Robert Polke, brother-in-law of Isaac McCoy, was a trader with the Potawatomi Indians in present Linn County, Kansas. Polke traded there from the late 1830s until his death in 1843. The year Pierre Menard Chouteau married, at age twenty-seven years, he entered the Indian trade. Early that year, he was issued a license to trade with the Miami, Wea, and Piankeshaw Indians.[12] In December 1849, he was issued another license for the same tribes.[13] He operated a warehouse, reportedly one of the first to be erected after the 1844 flood.[14] There is some indication that he continued to be associated with one of the houses at the Town of Kansas levee as late as the early 1860s. Father De Smet, whose duties in St. Louis included purchasing supplies for the St. Mary's and Osage Missions, in 1849 had his goods shipped by steamer to the care of Menard Chouteau in Kansas, to await overland transport by ox or mule team to the missions.[15]

Sometime during the early 1850s, P. M. Chouteau, then known as "Mack," phased out of the Indian trade. He was a member of the original committee that, in February 1850, drew up a charter for the Town of Kansas. In December 1852, Mack Chouteau attended a meeting considering the merits of various railroad proposals to run a line into the city. He was elected secretary of the group.[16]

A career in steamboating developed after Chouteau's Indian trade venture. On May 8, 1854, he contracted with the U.S. Army to carry officers and troops to Fort Leavenworth. As captain of the steamboat *Isabel*, he picked up eight officers and 117 men at Alton, Illinois, and transported them to the Kansas fort.[17] By 1855, Mack bought his own boat, the *Kate Swinney* (sometimes written as *Sweeny*), a side-wheeler of 328 tons named for the daughter

---

9. *Guide to the Microfilm Edition of the Pierre Menard Collection*, 34.
10. "The Hill the City Left Behind," in Kansas City Scrapbook, 117-123, (KC396), WHMC-KC.
11. Berenice Chouteau to Edmond Menard, October 17, 1865, *William V. Morrison Collection*, (ISHL).
12. Louise Barry, *Beginnings of the West*, 793.
13. Barry, *Beginnings of the West*, 879.
14. Theodore Case, *History of Kansas City, Missouri; with Illustrations and Biographical Sketches of Some of Its Prominent Men and Pioneers*, 30.
15. Gilbert J. Garraghan, S.J., *Jesuits of the Middle United States*, 2: 650-651.
16. "Railroad Convention at Kansas, Mo.," *Jefferson Enquirer*, 18 December 1852, 4.
17. Barry, *Beginning of the West*, 1204.

of Captain W. D. Swinney of Glasgow, Missouri, and later Kansas City.[18] While returning loaded with furs to St. Louis from Fort Union, she hit a snag on August 1, 1855, at what is now known as "Kate Sweeny Bend," where the line dividing Union and Clay counties, South Dakota, meets the river. Two of her crew set out to walk to Sioux City but were never seen again and were supposed killed by the Sioux. Before leaving the wreck Chouteau sold the salvage to "some nearby settlers for $300."[19]

Within a few months he purchased a replacement in partnership with his brother-in-law Ashley Hopkins, who had previously owned the steamer *Australia*. The sale was made in mid-March and the "price paid was $36,000, one half in cash, the rest in the usual time."[20] The *Westport Border Times* of April 12, 1856, carried this item: "The elegant [....] steamer *Amazon* has been [....] [purchased by P. M. Chouteau?]. Captain Chouteau is well known in this community, as an experienced officer, and accomplished gentleman, and the *Amazon* will soon become a general favorite."[21] Among the "elegant" features was one of the first calliopes installed on a Missouri River boat. But fate struck again when "this fine steamboat – Calliope and all – got sunk about 11 o'clock [February 15, 1857]…a short distance up the Missouri River [near St. Louis at Rattlesnake Springs, three miles above the mouth, and now called Amazon Bend].[22] Mack's brother Ben was clerk on the boat and came down to the St. Louis landing in a rowboat to seek aid.

In 1872, a "Democrat" offered the name of Captain P. M. Chouteau as a candidate for mayor: "a prominent actor of the early foundation of our city; the first wholesale and commission merchant on our levee, and a most influential steamboatman during the era which gave to us the Santa Fe trade and inaugurated the status of our commercial prosperity. Then Captain Chouteau, no one in our midst is more extensively known to Western men, and none more favorably for honor or integrity."[23]

Except for the few years they spent in Indian Territory (Kansas), Mack Chouteau and his wife Mary lived in Kansas City all of their lives.[24] They had eight children. Pierre Menard Chouteau died in 1885 at the age of sixty-three from an accident in which he was struck by a train resulting in "injuries to the head."[25] He was buried in Mount St. Mary's Catholic Cemetery in Kansas City. His wife Mary survived him.

While Mack Chouteau never strayed far from Kansas City, his older brother Gesseau had the wanderlust and a thirst for adventure. He never married and was almost constantly

---

18. A later boat by the same name operated out of Kansas City in the late 1850s, and was one of the first steamboats to navigate up the Kansas River. (Charles P. Deatherage, *Early History of Greater Kansas City, Missouri and Kansas*, 661.)

19. Hiram M. Chittenden, *List of Steamboat Wrecks on the Missouri River: From the Beginning to the Present*, 82; "Steamboat Wrecks in South Dakota," *South Dakota Historical Collections* 9 (1918): 393; Frederick Way Jr. comp., *Way's packet directory, 1848-1994*, 267.

20. "Sale of the Steamer Amazon," *Liberty Tribune*, March 14, 1856, 4.

21. "Steamboats." *Westport Border Times*, 12 April 1856, 2; Chittenden, *List of Steamboat Wrecks*, 2.

22. "Amazon Sunk," *Liberty Tribune*, 10 April 1857, 1; Folder 96 and Volume 15: 11, *E. B. Trail* (1884-1965) *Collection* (C2071), WHMC-C.

23. "In Kansas City Forty Years Ago," *Kansas City Times*, 14 February 1912.

24. There is, however, a question about P. M. Chouteau's whereabouts during the decade of the 1860s. His mother was in Ste. Genevieve, as was his son Frank, who was attending the Ste. Genevieve Academy in 1860-1862. P. M. Chouteau does not appear in the 1860 census for either the Jackson County or Ste. Genevieve or in the few published Kansas City city directories between 1860 and 1869. His wife's obituary ("Mary A. Chouteau," *Kansas City Star*, 13 March 1899) suggested that the family lived in Westport during these years. Regardless, Mack was definitely in Kansas City in 1870 holding the office of city collector and living on Laurel Street between 11th and 12th.

25. *Register of Interments*, 1: 61, Mount St. Mary's Catholic Cemetery, Kansas City, Missouri.

on the move. In the spring of 1843, Gesseau and Cyprien Menard (uncle) and two Kennerly cousins were members of a group of young men from the St. Louis area who joined an international pleasure, exploring, and hunting party to the Wind River (Wyoming) led by Sir William Drummond Stewart. Cyprien Menard wrote in May 1843 to his father, Pierre Menard, describing some elements of the preparations for Lt. John Charles Fremont's expedition that was to accompany Stewart part way on its route to Oregon and northwest California: the gathering of excited young men, including Edmond Chouteau and his cousin Lucien Maxwell, the choosing of suitable animals (a horse named Jackson would not pull a cart or take a rider, so was to be left behind), and the breaking of camp.[26] They had spent ten days in the Town of Kansas and departed on May 28, 1843. By October, Gesseau, his cousins, and other young men headed home ahead of the main group.[27]

The War with Mexico, declared in May 1846, brought Gesseau, now assuming his given name, Edmond F. Chouteau, and a Kennerly cousin to the roster of the Missouri Volunteers in a unit of Stephen Kearny's Army of the West. Edmond was wounded in one arm.[28] After the war, in 1851, he joined a group traveling the California-Oregon Trail. While en route the party, which included Father De Smet and Paul Wilhelm, Duke of Wuerttemberg, was present at Fort Laramie when Edmond signed as a witness to the treaty with the Sioux, Cheyennes, Arapahoes, Crows, Assinaboines, Gros-Ventre Mandans, and Arrickaras on September 17th.[29]

Edmond Francois Chouteau died February 7, 1853. The cause of his death was not recorded.[30] William L. Campbell remembered Edmond as a "man of intensely kind disposition and a Chesterfield in manner."[31] Edmond's brother Mack was appointed administrator of his estate. Edmond was buried in the pioneer Catholic cemetery behind St. Francis Regis Church that in his childhood he had known as Chouteau's Church. In 1881, when that cemetery was dismantled, Edmond's body was moved to Mount St. Mary's Catholic Cemetery and reburied with the remains of his sister Odile.[32]

Berenice came again to live in Kansas City in 1870 or 1871, settling in with her son Mack, his wife Mary, and their children. The English-language letters Berenice wrote from Kansas City in the 1870s and 1880s were filled with accounts of the activities of her son and his family. In November 1874, they were living at 1111 Oak Street. By December 1879, they had moved to 910 Walnut.[33]

---

26. Cyprien Menard to Pierre Menard, May 12, 1843, *PMC*, Letter 1407, and Cyprien Menard to Pierre Menard, May 24, 1843, *PMC*, Letter 1410.

27. William Clark Kennerly (as told to Elizabeth Russell), *Persimmon Hill: A Narrative of Old St. Louis and the Far West*, 144, 164; Mae Reed Porter and Odessa Davenport, *Scotsman in Buckskin: Sir William Drummond Stewart and the Rocky Mountain Fur Trade*, 219, 237, 238, 244.

28. "Remarks of Clyde H. Porter, July 18, 1948, at the grave of Gesso Chouteau, St. Mary's Cemetery, Kansas City, Missouri," in "Francois Chouteau and family notes," Chouteau's (Biographical) Scrapbook [17.3], KC395, WHMC-KC.; Kennerly, 185, 196.

29. Charles J. Kappler, *Indian Affairs, Laws and Treaties*, 2: 594-596.

30. The next day William Walker recorded in his journal, "Heard that Edmund F. Chouteau died on Monday at 2 a.m.," which may suggest that Edmond died from illness rather than accident. (William E. Connelley, ed., "The Provisional Government of Nebraska Territory and The Journals of William Walker, Provisional Governor of Nebraska Territory." *Proceedings & Collections of the Nebraska State Historical Society* 7 (1899): 373.)

31. "Incidents of the 'Knob Hill' or aristocratic residence quarter of Kansas City of early days" typescript manuscript by William L. Campbell in "Recollections of pioneers," Kansas City Before the Civil War Scrapbook [35], KC395, WHMC-KC. The allusion is to the 4th Earl of Chesterfield, who was considered elegant, urbane, and suave – an ideal gentleman.

32. *Register of Interments*, 1: 34-35, Mount St. Mary's Catholic Cemetery, Kansas City, Missouri.

33. *PMC*, Letters 1825 and 2019.

When Berenice returned to Kansas City, she was in fairly good health. Her tall frame had taken on considerable weight, but contemporaries still considered her an impressive woman. By the late 1870s, however, Berenice's letters show that she had begun to decline.

Supporting her two youngest sons, Ben and Fred, who were plagued with ill health and unable to hold jobs, Berenice sank into poverty. She was able to survive largely through the generosity of her half-brother Edmond Menard, who sent her money when she asked for it. These sums, Berenice always promised, were to be deducted from the sale of various lands she had inherited from her father. Edmond's inability to close his father's estate enabled Berenice to borrow on the strength of expectations, probably well over the value of the lands. The estate was finally settled in Probate Court in 1881, thirty-seven years after Pierre Menard's death.[34]

The eight surviving letters Berenice wrote after she returned to Kansas City were all in good English, and written to Edmond Menard.[35] The last letter was dated October 6, 1880. Edmond Menard died in 1884. These Berenice letters portray her as religious and loyal to her church and to her children. She never wavered in her devotion to "Mack," Ben, and Fred; nor did she criticize or complain of them, though she had ample reason to do so.

Ben Chouteau married Ann Toler in 1856 in Jackson County and they had four children. His various attempts to establish a career were unsuccessful. He tried his luck in New Mexico where his Maxwell cousin had done so well, but nothing came of it. He died a pauper in Kaskaskia in late December 1876.[36] During his final illness, Ben was dependent on his Uncle Edmond for living expenses, medicine, and medical attention.

Fred Chouteau, Berenice's youngest son, like his brother Ben led an aimless life. He was unable to hold a job of any kind. Fred married Julia Gregoire in Ste. Genevieve in 1862, and they had two children, Claire and Frederick (who changed his surname from Chouteau to Laclede in 1894.)[37] Fred lived apart from his wife and children most of his married life. Berenice's letter of December 22, 1879, reported that "Fred is real sick." He died on September 2, 1881, and was buried in Mount St. Mary's Catholic Cemetery.[38]

A Bible that Berenice gave to her granddaughter Delia Chouteau, daughter of Mack Chouteau, contains a partial listing of births and deaths of Francois and Berenice and their children. The handwriting is probably not Berenice's, as it does not match her later letters. Several death dates that Berenice would have known are missing, numbers are smudged and have been misread, and the edges of the page are damaged and illegible. For a time this Bible was in the Boatman's Bank in St. Louis, but its current whereabouts is unknown.[39]

Until the end of her life, Berenice exhibited the strong will that characterized her from the earliest days. Francois had written that Berenice had "determined herself," and left little doubt that she could be dissuaded from her goal. Berenice was no timid, frightened young woman. She had snatched a loaded rife from her furious father-in-law, thus saving a boatman's life, and perhaps also those of herself, Edmond, Menard, and old Pierre Chouteau,

---

34. *Guide to Menard Collection*, 17.

35. Berenice Chouteau to Edmond Menard, *PMC*, Letters 1784, 1825, 1925, 1945, 1970, 2019, 2028, 2043.

36. The *Guide to Menard Collection* on page 30, listed the year of his death as 1870, but Edmond Menard letter to Berenice Chouteau, December 28, 1876, William Morrison Collection, ISHL, documents the 1876 date.

37. *Guide to Menard Collection*, 33.

38. *Register of Interments*, 1: 39, Mount St. Mary's Catholic Cemetery, Kansas City, Missouri.

39. A facsimile is in "Chouteau Family in Kansas City notes," Clyde Porter Scrapbook [56.1], (KC395), WHMC-KC.

as they might have all drowned had their uncontrolled boat overturned in the Missouri River. She had ridden on horseback into the forest near her home in an effort to save the lives of dying Indian babies.

In Berenice's final days, she still exhibited that strong will, reportedly refusing to wear her dentures, while protecting her dignity by neither granting interviews nor having her photograph taken, despite the urging of her family. It is said that she did not desire to have her picture survive because it could not be paired with an image of Francois.

Berenice outlived all of her nine children. She spent her last years with her daughter-in-law, Pierre Menard Chouteau's wife Mary. Therese Berenice Menard Chouteau died on November 19, 1888, at the age of eighty-seven. Berenice's body was taken to St. Louis, where she was buried in Calvary Cemetery alongside her beloved husband Francois Gesseau Chouteau, from whom she had been separated for fifty years.

Through the kaleidoscope of Francois and Berenice's letters emerges the ever-changing panorama of the French pioneer era in western Missouri. This picture in motion vibrates with images – the Chouteaus sailing up and down the Missouri River; fur company employees hauling goods up the Kansas River and furs back down; babies being born and dying; and the Native American tribes, both resident and immigrant, milling restlessly from village to hunting ground to new village, driven by forces they could not control. That world of commerce, as stressful and unforgiving as any in the twentieth century, operated for a century within the far-flung French network. But in the end the overwhelming onrush of the American population all but obliterated the world that revolved through Francois's and Berenice's letters to *Cher Oncle* and *Cher Papa*.

Appendix 1

Confluence of People and Place:
The Chouteau Posts on the Missouri and Kansas Rivers
by David Boutros

When the researchers working to translate and edit the Chouteau letters for *Cher Oncle, Cher Papa* began their task, they were confronted by a wealth of legend wrapped around a few truths. Much of the effort of this project has been to peel back the myth and test each seed of fact against the information within the letters and other contemporary documents and oral traditions. In this process some cherished tales have not withstood examination while other stories have been revealed.

Critical to most of the tradition of the Chouteaus coming to the western frontier was the nineteenth-century historians' desire to find a history for Kansas City. Many of those historians sought to prove that the founding and growth of the city was predetermined by its location, and secondarily by the vision and energy of its founders. "Where the rocky bluffs meet" at the great river's bend was destined to be a great metropolis, and one bit of proof of that fact was that a son of Missouri's renowned city-founding family, the Chouteaus, was the first to choose the south bank of the Missouri River at the confluence of the Kansas as the place for a center of a mighty commercial enterprise.

Embedded in this statement are some accurate assumptions, but it is useless to engage in a parochial debate about "firsts" or the linage of change – did Independence or Westport predate Kansas City – was the commerce of the frontier focused in Jackson County or were there other equally active, and perhaps more active centers. The reality was that the early inhabitants of the area were not concerned with questions of boundaries and borders, but rather sought routes and paths that linked people, regardless of place. They secured land to hunt or farm, convenient locations for commerce and exchange, and always chose to be close to neighbors for security and camaraderie.

A careful review of all the traditional knowledge of Francois and Berenice Chouteau reveals that most has its roots in John Calvin McCoy's "Tales of an Old Timer." A talented storyteller with a deep interest in the history of the region – to which he personally contributed in significant ways – McCoy arrived in western Missouri in 1830 to assist his father Isaac's missionary work and the removal of Indian tribes east of the Mississippi to the territory west of the state of Missouri. Calvin, as he was known to his friends, was also eager to make a success of his life, and he engaged in a variety of ventures that earned him both money and status. He is credited with being the founder of Westport, and the first to offload goods onto a natural rock landing that would become the heart of the Town of

Kansas. Many of Calvin's stories may have come from his firsthand knowledge and observation, and they are heavily sprinkled with his interpretation and assumptions. Writing for a variety of local newspapers and magazines from as early as the late 1860s, he entertained and educated his readers with colorful memories of old times. His tales are peopled with coarse and refined characters alike, graphic images of frontier hardships, and primitive places and practices. He was a skilled writer who used Biblical and Classical allusions with ease.

It is hard to tell exactly where McCoy collected his information beyond what he knew from personal involvement. Regarding the Chouteaus, he would have known Francois, and claimed to be friends with Frederick, Cyprien, and Berenice – in fact, he lived across the road from Berenice on Pearl Street for about fifteen years. That Calvin 'interviewed' old settlers, gathering their memories for his own, seems plausible. The question is the accuracy of the data he collected and the skill he used to integrate divergent facts into a single narrative – a question that must be asked about any researcher/historian.

Chronicled into numerous articles, McCoy's account of Francois and Berenice Chouteau is full of contradictions but has a general common thread – the couple was the first to realize the importance of this place. And it is this thread and its attending "facts" that were accepted and included in later histories. Several passages are quoted here to provide a taste of Calvin's style and an outline of his Chouteau story:

> *I said there were a few relics of the genesis still with us; aye, the first white woman that ever had a home west of Fort Osage lives here in her venerable old age of 85 years, still blessed with uncommon vigor of mind and body. She first saw the place in 1819, when on her way from St. Louis to the frontier trading post of the Black Snake hills (St. Joseph). It was her bridal tour with her husband on a keel boat, requiring about six weeks to make the trip. She is the daughter of the first territorial governor of Illinois – Colonel Peter Menard, of Kaskaskia. In 1821 she came again with her husband, Colonel Chouteau, when he established a trading post on the south bank of the river, opposite Randolph Point, which was at the time a noted crossing place for the Sauks [Sacs], Iowa and Kickapoo tribes, inhabiting the north, and the Osage and Kansas, of the south side, in their interchange of courtesies, whether friendly or otherwise. Six buildings and other valuable improvement was made, and this was her home until 1826, when the great flood in the Missouri of that year compelled a hasty retreat to the hills of Clay county, and every vestige of the improvement and post were swept away. Again, in the flood of 1844, a similar calamity befell her valuable and costly homestead, warehouse and large farm, being utterly obliterated and ruined by the deposit of from 2 to 6 feet of sand left over a large portion of the land. Having in the early years of the settlement and city abundant means, she was noted for her good works and generous charity to the poor and her church. I doubt not our city has many noble, self-sacrificing, generous women, but without disparagement of their merits, I beg to say that this worthy old pioneer is the noblest Dorcas of them all, and will go up the Master with an offer of sheaves that will be as generous as any. A sketch of the first twenty years of her residence near the Kaw's mouth and her clear recollection of the events and persons of that earliest period would be not only interesting, but would be a valuable starting point in our city's history.*
>
> *The limits allowable in a newspaper article, however, will admit of only this brief mention, pleasant as the task would be to extend its interesting details.*
>
> *Late in the fall of 1820 five persons arrived at the point just mentioned, Randolph Point, in a pirogue, (an extra large canoe or double dugout) from St. Louis. The leader of the party was Louis Bertholet, a large swarthy looking French and Iroquois half-bred, his wife and step-son (Louis Preu); a youth and two French employees constituted the others.*

They were sent up by the American Fur company to make preliminary cabins and arrangements for the establishment of a trading post at that point in the following spring.

They had built one log cabin and commenced another when a party of migratory Sauk Indians came along and tore them down and with hostile treats and demonstrations ordered the party to leave instanter; this order was complied with, the party betook themselves again to their pirogue floated a mile or so down the river, and waiting until the Sauks had left, the plucky half-breed returned and landed on the Clay county side near the mouth of the creek at the upper Randolph landing. Selecting a favorable site for defense, in a secluded bend of the creek he there constructed a small temporary shelter and fort wherein to pass the winter while waiting the promised arrival in the following spring of Colonel Chouteau with his large outfit of men and supplies.

These consisted of two keel boats loaded with goods suited for the Indian trade and general use and thirty-five men nearly all of them French of Canada or St. Louis. Indeed this class were almost exclusively employed by the early Indian and rocky mountain fur traders of the upper Missouri.

Mrs. Chouteau accompanied the expedition with her two children, Gesso and Menard. [A break in the article jumps the story to events after the 1826 flood.] *She remained six weeks at the Randolph bluffs waiting for the flood to abate and then went with her children and two employees in a pirogue to Ste. Genevieve, Mo. I should have stated that fifteen of the men were sent back to St. Louis with the empty keel boats and twenty were retained; most of whom were at the date of the flood, (which occurred in April) out with trading parties. As soon as the stage of water would permit, Chouteau moved what goods and other valuables were saved from the flood up to about the north end of Harrison street, at the foot of the river hills, built several log houses and remained there two years, at that time three others were located at this point, viz., Daniel Morgan Boone, a son of the famous pioneer, Gabriel Phillibert, and Beneito Vasquez – the latter was sub Indian agent for the Kansas Indians. Boone was farmer and Phillibert, blacksmith, by government appointment, for that tribe. These, however, the next year, (1827) went up westward and established the Kaw agency on the Kansas river, eight miles above Lawrence, but quite a little village grew up at the new Chouteau location, at Harrison street, and up the river Louis Roy had a cabin and clearing at Oak and Second street, Louis Uneau at Main and First, where he ferried people across the river on a frail contrivance made of two canoes with a platform deck thereon, and Calise Mantardine had his cabin near the railroad bridge and a few acres cleared on the hill between Main and Wyandotte streets. West Kansas bottoms was then a trackless uninhabited forest until 1831 when eight families of Frenchmen with Indian wives and half-breed children came down the Missouri from its upper sources and the rock mountains and lands at this frontier outskirt of civilization. Their names were Gabriel Prudhomme, Becket, Perriault, Jondra John Gray, and his son-in-law Ben Lagotrie and Crevieur and his son. These all either entered or bought small tracts of land in the bottoms, and commenced preparations for a permanent settlement. Prudhomme bought the claim of Chouteau at the foot of Harrison street, and entered the old town tract of 257 acres. Chouteau then moved up to his trading post on the south bank of the Kansa river, two miles above Argentine, then in charge of his brother Cyprien. Grey was a half-breed Scotch and Iroquois, and was, a year or two later, killed by the wife of Perriault, who was a native of the Snake tribe, and the only Indian I ever know to have red hair.*[1]

---

1. John C. McCoy Scrapbook, 31, (KC296), WHMC-KC.

Another article repeats some information, adds some, and also contradicts keys dates and places.

> There was no other military or trading post above Fort Osage in 1819. Some years after, (in 1825), a trading post was established by Col. Francis Chouteau, father of our present worthy City Collector, on the South bank of the river, about four miles below the city, opposite the Clay county bluffs. But the great flood in the Missouri in April, 1826, made a clean sweep of all his building and he never rebuilt them at that point, but removed to the South bank of the Kaw river, about six miles above its mouth. He afterwards (about 1830) opened a large farm with costly buildings, about one mile below the lower limits of the city, upon what is now know as the Guinotte tract. He owned about 1200 acres, and the only warehouse and steamboat landing up to 1839 between Wayne City and Fort Leavenworth. Every vestige of improvement on this last place was again swept away by the flood of 1844, leaving a deposit of sand from two to five feet deep over the whole farm....[2]

Yet a third article again adds new and sometimes contradictory information.

> About two years before this (1820) a trading post was established on the north bank of the Kansas river, about twenty-five miles up that stream which was named "The Four Houses" being four log houses so built as to answer the purpose of a fort and security from possible attacks of savages. That post was occupied only two years and then abandoned.[3]

The workable narrative collected from all of McCoy's writings contains a wealth of information that rings true when compared to other independent sources, but also many bits that fail when put to the same test. Of particular interest is the location of the Chouteau posts and the time frame of the events. What follows is not intended to debate Calvin McCoy on the truth of his story, but to lay out the plausible history of the Chouteaus as the researchers have pieced it together.

Nearly 400 miles from St. Louis by the serpentine Missouri River, a traveler in the first quarter of the nineteenth century would arrive at the mouth of the Kansas River. There at the convergence of the two rivers, the Missouri turns to the north toward its upper reaches, and the Kansas extends to the west into the plains to be fed by many streams and creeks. It was in the region of the confluence that the Native American inhabitants found crossroads and junctures of trade and war. And when the first explorers and settlers from the east came, it was there that they established forts and trading posts. By the time Francois Chouteau came to the Kawsmouth with his cousin Gabriel Sylvestre (Seres) Chouteau in 1816, there was already a network of independent traders and trappers occupying the land along with wandering bands of Indians hunting the forests and engaged in exchange with these traders.

The Kansas River was, and is, a major tributary. Its first surveyor Angus Langham in 1826 observed that its mouth was almost 600 feet wide and its channel often 900 feet wide in its shallow, sandy bed. The turbulence at the juncture of the two rivers created a small lake and determined that settlement be away from its immediate vicinity, removed at least a half-mile up or down stream.

Francois Chouteau and his cousin Seres Chouteau established the Four-Houses post as McCoy suggested, "on the north bank of the [Kansas] river one mile above the mouth of Cedar creek, near the P.R.R. station of Lenape. It was called "Four Houses," being four log

---

2. John C. McCoy Scrapbook, 3, (KC296), WHMC-KC.
3. John C. McCoy Scrapbook, 27, (KC296), WHMC-KC.

houses arranged in a square, answering the purpose of a fort."[4] However, it was in place probably as early as the summer of 1819. In October of that year, Major Thomas Biddle noted that the Chouteau cousins "have a trading-house not far from the mouth of the river Kanzas, and their capital is about $4,000."[5]

Competition for trade in the area was fierce, coming primarily from the posts of Andrew Woods, and Cyrus Curtis and Michael Eley locating on the right (west) bank[6] of the Missouri, a half-mile to a mile above the Kawsmouth. McCoy erroneously asserted that these were short-lived and unsuccessful ventures that survive only a year or so.[7] In fact they were vigorous operations that eventually forced Seres Chouteau to seek his fortunes elsewhere. As early as April 1820, Pierre (Cadet) Chouteau Jr. and J. B. Sarpy in the Berthold, Chouteau, and Pratte Fur Company's St. Louis office were writing to Seres that the Woods-Curtis-Eley threat was "doing all that is in their power to crush you."[8] Two years later the situation had not improved, and had become more complicated because Francois Chouteau was asserting his independence from his older partner/cousin Seres: "Gesseau [Francois Chouteau] wanted to take the merchandise for his own account, because he alleges, with reason, that the profits are so limited that it is not worth the trouble to increase the number of partners in a small operation."[9] Cadet offered Seres the option to move elsewhere and turn his Four Houses operation over to Cyprien (Chouteau?) – which he apparently did.[10]

What is unclear is where Francois was at that time. Tradition (e.g., McCoy) stated that by mid-1822, Francois had his Randolph Bluffs post. But a troubling fact is that a year later in July 1823, Prince Paul Wilhelm of Wuerttemberg did not find him there.

Prince Paul's journal recounted the toil and difficulties of pushing and pulling keelboats and barges against the Missouri's current, the challenges of snag filled channels that needed to be hacked clear before the boat could progress, and the problems of storms and floods, and of ravenous insects. He gave details of where he went, what he saw, and to whom he spoke. He stayed several days at the home of Grand Louis Bertholet, situated exactly where McCoy placed it on the small creek at the Randolph Bluff landing on the Clay County side of the river. The Prince hunted on the south bank, met with a band of Kansas Indians there, and visited at a temporary camp of *voyageurs* who came to talk with him. But nowhere in his writings does he mention Francois Chouteau, his home, or post.[11]

However, Berenice clearly remembered and stated that she came to Jackson County in 1822.[12] – not 1821 as McCoy wrote. One can wonder if she was correct about the year or that she was somewhere other than Randolph Bluffs in Jackson County – it should be noted that

---

4. John C. McCoy Scrapbook, 45, (KC296), WHMC-KC.

5. *American State Papers: Indian Affairs*, 2: 202.

6. Louise Barry, *Beginning of the West*, 99-100; "Fur posts at Kawsmouth," Chouteau's (Topical) Scrapbook [17.1], (KC395), WHMC-KC. The right and left bank is determined while facing downstream.

7. John C. McCoy Scrapbook, 42, (KC296), WHMC-KC.

8. John B. Sarpy to G. S. Chouteau, November 6, 1820, *Chouteau Family Collection*, MHS.; Pierre Chouteau Jr. to C. G. Chouteau, April 30, 1820, *Chouteau Family Collection*, MHS.

9. Pierre Chouteau Jr. to G. S. Chouteau, July 19, 1822, *Chouteau Family Collection*, MHS. This letter is transcribed in Appendix 2.

10. Again contradicting McCoy, the Chouteau letters suggests that Four Houses continued to be used until the new Kansa and Shawnee posts were built in 1827-1828.

11. Paul Wilhelm, Duke of Wurttemberg. "First Journey to North America in the years 1822 to 1823," *South Dakota Historical Collections* 19 (1938): 299-318.

12. Sworn affidavit by Berenice F. Chouteau dated October 26, 1887, recorded May 28, 1890, Book B423, page 404 (150360), Jackson County, Missouri. Issue related to the church land acquired by Rev. Benedict Roux.

Bates County, the location of an Osage trading post at which Francois held a license to trade in November 1825,[13] was technically part of Jackson County at that time. Or, as the researchers for *Cher Oncle, Cher Papa* believe, that Jackson County should be interpreted more broadly to mean the western frontier.

The year 1822 was significant for other reasons. As mentioned, Seres Chouteau departed the Kawsmouth region that year, leaving Francois and his younger brother Cyprien as the reigning Chouteaus in the area. Fort Osage, the westernmost station of the failed United State government factory system, closed and left the trade in the west essentially unregulated except for the licenses granted by Superintendent of Indian Affairs William Clark and his underlings. Lastly, serious interest was rising in the overland trade with Santa Fe and new faces and opportunities were beginning to appear.

The nature of the fur business was such that two or more independent agents could and did operate out of the same facility. The researchers, lacking evidence one way or the other, have retained the traditional establishment date of 1822 for Chouteau's Randolph Bluffs post. However, another reasonable theory is that Francois brought Berenice and their children to Four Houses in 1822, and did not build the Randolph Bluffs warehouse until the following year. This would explain why Prince Paul did not mention the Chouteaus and conforms with a point that will be made later about retailer's licenses Chouteau purchased in Clay County.

Regardless, it is known that Francois Chouteau did have a post at Randolph Bluffs whether it was in place as early as 1822 or not. Frederick Chouteau, who unlike McCoy, was on the scene before the 1826 flood washed the post away, clearly remembered it being there on the north bank of the river,[14] not on the south bank in Jackson County as McCoy believed. One of the results of the publishing of the Chouteau letters in *Cher Oncle, Cher Papa*, is that Frederick's memory can be tested. A comparison of Francois's and Frederick's accounts of the sinking of the keelboat *Beaver*, reveals that Frederick was generally accurate in his reminiscences.[15] Moreover, evidence and interpretation support Frederick.

- The south bank, as McCoy intimated in the preceding quote, was off limits to white settlement prior to the Treaty of 1825. Francois Chouteau, as revealed in his letters, was a stickler for following the rules, and though he could have gotten permission for building on Indian lands, there was no particularly good reason for him to do so.
- The south bank was lowland, unprotected, and opposite the main channel of the river. It would have been more difficult to land and unload goods and would have presented problems of exposure and flooding.
- There is a curious incongruity in McCoy's tale: comparing the floods of 1826 and 1844, he commented that "the first was caused by a great accumulation of snow on the western plains, which was suddenly melted by a sudden change

---

13. *St. Louis Superintendency, 1827-1828*, OIA, RG234, Microfilm roll 747, Frames 439-441, NARA. Dated November 20, 1825 the license reads "At the or near the old Fort on the Marais des Cygne with the Osages. The old post was a short-lived extension of Ft. Osage.

14. "Reminiscences of Fredrick Chouteau," *Kansas Historical Collection* 8: 423. "I came to Randolph, Clay County, Missouri, about two miles below Kansas City, on the opposite side of the Missouri river, in the fall of 1825, October or November." Some historians have suggested that Frederick was misquoted in the interview, but this ignores an additional statement later in the paragraph that Baronet Vasquez took "goods in my brother's boat across the Missouri river and up to the yellow banks, just above where Wyandotte is" as the first annuity payment for the Kansa.

15. See pages 54-56.

of temperature and assisted by heavy rains...."[16] This would suggest that warning of disaster was short. Moreover, McCoy also stated that when the flood came in 1826, Chouteau made "a hasty retreat to the hills of Clay county." While reasonable to assume that Clay County may have been closer than high ground on the south side of the river, this still seems an odd response to the disaster. Short of hands and time why would Francois carry his goods across the rising river?

- Sometimes the evidence is what is not said: Major S. W. Kearny wrote in his diary for October 12, 1824,

   Started [from Liberty, Missouri] *at day break; morning cool, frosty and a heavy fog on the water. Made 3 1/2 miles to breakfast. Came up to Mr. Chouteaus Trading House to dinner, where we found the Kickapoos, and the Kansas were expected to-morrow made some purchases; In the afternoon passed the Kansas River and halted one mile above it, on the left Bank, opposite to Curtis and Ely's Trading House, having made 16 miles.*[17]

   Did Kearny cross the Missouri River to reach Chouteau's post? If so, why did he not mention it, particularly since he would need to cross it again to be on the left bank opposite from Curtis and Eley's house? The more reasonable assumption is that Kearny was touring Clay County. As will be discussed shortly, Chouteau had built his post at the crossing (ford and later ferry) of a major north-south trail used by the Indians to conduct commerce across the Missouri River. Kearny was following established roads improved from the Indians' paths.[18] Support for this theory also comes from tracing a journey from Liberty to the Chouteau Bridge, then along the river to the north end of the Downtown Airport – a distance very close to the sixteen miles Kearny reported.

- Lastly, a very telling fact was that Francois Chouteau paid $22.50 to the Clay County Collector for a retailer's license on November 10, 1823 and $23.61 for another license on February 15, 1825.[19] There would have been no reason for the financially careful Chouteau to purchase such licenses unless his business resided in Clay County.

To state it bluntly, regardless of all the many Kansas City histories previously written, Francois Chouteau's 1822-1826 post on the Missouri River was not in Jackson County but rather in Clay County.

But where then was the post located? In the 1950s, historian James Anderson, along with descendants of the Chouteaus and other French families of Kansas City, argued successfully that the newly city-acquired Milwaukee Bridge should be renamed the Chouteau Bridge in honor of the early trading post having been nearby. They were in fact correct, but instead of being close to the south end of the bridge it was located about a half-mile to the west of the north end. The key to determining this location is the site of the settlement of Randolph in the early part of the nineteenth century.

---

16. John C. McCoy Scrapbook, 45, (KC296), WHMC-KC.
17. Barry, *Beginning of the West*, 103.
18. This same route was followed by Prince Paul Wilhelm of Wuerttemberg in 1823 from Liberty to the cabin of Grand Louis. (Paul Wilhelm, Duke of Wurttemberg, "First Journey to North America in the years 1822 to 1823," *South Dakota Historical Collections* 19 (1938): 299-300, 311-312.)
19. *Clay County Record Book 1*, 21 & 42, Clay County Archives, Liberty, Missouri.

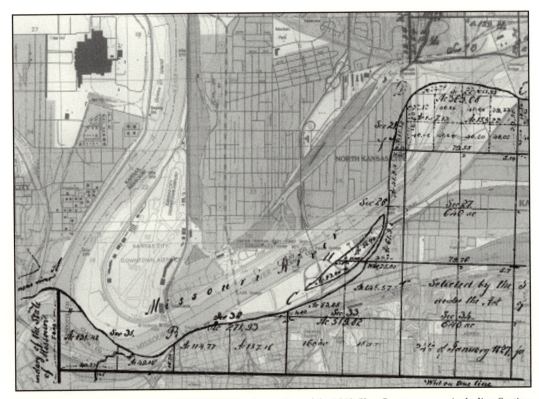

The 1827 Jackson County survey of T50N R33W and a portion of the 1819 Clay County survey including Section 18 of T50N R32W are overlaid on a current U.S. Geological Survey map to show the location of the Missouri River relative to today's channel.

As suggested earlier, and to again quote McCoy, "Randolph Point was, previous to the advent of the white man, a famous crossing place for the Indian tribes of the north and south sides of the Missouri river in the interchange of visits, peaceable and otherwise, and that fact was the inducement with Francis Chouteau, in 1820, for selecting that point for a trading post of the American Fur Company."[20]

Landscapes change – towns and rivers move. But ravines and bluffs were more resistant to change until big earthmoving equipment became common. To find nineteenth-century Randolph required locating old landmarks, one of which was cited by McCoy: "on the Clay county side near the mouth of the creek at the upper Randolph landing." Grand Louis becomes the key to finding this creek. The *History of Clay and Platte Counties* placed Grand Louis cabin in Section 18, Township 50 north, Range 32 west.[21] Prince Paul stated that Louis's cabin was near the river on the west face of a chain of bluffs and on the road south from Liberty.[22] Only three cuts through the bluffs in Section 18 have a west face, and only two of those are natural: the first at a small unnamed creek about a half-mile west of the the Chouteau Bridge and the second at Rock Creek about a half-mile farther west. Newspaper

---

20. John C. McCoy Scrapbook, 5-6, (KC296), WHMC-KC.
21. *History of Clay and Platte Counties, Missouri*, 113.
22. Paul Wilhelm, Duke of Wurttemberg, "First Journey to North America in the years 1822 to 1823," *South Dakota Historical Collections* 19 (1938): 311.

articles from the Liberty Tribune support this location.[23] Randolph was not so much a town as a settlement of between six and twelve families. Calise Montardeau purchased a ferry across the Missouri River from Richard Linville in 1826, which was reportedly also located where Grand Louis Bertholet lived at Randolph Bluff.[24] In 1838, Calise received a certificate of patent for the point of land on the south bank across from Randolph.[25]

The flood of April 1826 washed away Chouteau's trading post which was surely close to the river bank to facilitate the loading and unloading of goods. McCoy's statement that

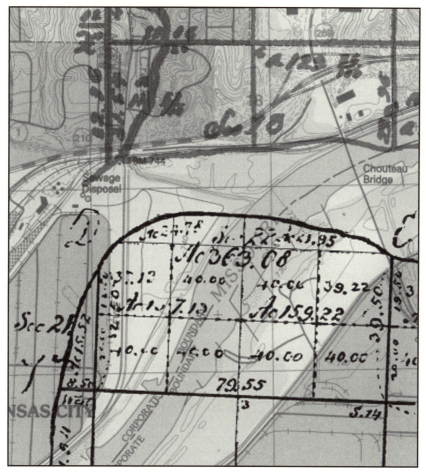

A portion of the 1827 Jackson County survey and the 1819 Clay County survey overlaid on a current U.S. Geological Survey map. WHMC-KC.

---

23. *Liberty Tribune*, 21 April 1899, 22 June 1906, 22 May 1908. A very interesting article appeared in the *Liberty Tribune* 12 June 1885, telling the tale of D. B. Moreland unearthing in the vicinity of Old Randolph an "old-fashioned frying pan, a peculiar tin can, and a lot of shreds of decaying wearing apparel and papers, none of which was legible.

24. Barry, *Beginning of the West*, 148-149.

25. The Certificate of Patent 9031 was issued from Washington, D.C. on September 7, 1838 to Callice Montardeau [sic] for the southwest fractional quarter of section 22, Township 50 north, Range 33 west. The discrepancy in dates between occupancy and filing likely meant little. Possession was ownership until someone challenged the claim. As new people came to the frontier, the older settlers would often file to legitimize their holdings.

Berenice resided in the Clay County hills until the waters receded and then went downriver to St. Louis and Ste. Genevieve seems reasonable,[26] since her third son died and was buried in St. Louis on October 25, 1826,[27] and her fourth son was born there in March of 1827.

Francois quickly recovered from the catastrophe of the flood and by October of 1826 had settled on the south bank near the present juncture of Harrison or Gillis and the Missouri River, as noted by John Glover who wrote in his diary, "Traveled on and came to Shotoes [i.e., Chouteau's] Trading house 1 mile below the Kaw river on the Missouria."[28] It is here too that Baronet Vasquez established the Kansa Agency, though McCoy also disagrees with Frederick Chouteau as to whether the agency was there prior to the flood. Frederick stated that Vasquez was at Randolph at his brothers' post.[29]

The letters in *Cher Oncle, Cher Papa* indicated that the Chouteaus resided there until 1829, and perhaps also at the new post for the Shawnee and Delaware on the Kansas River. It is this trading house that is described in Francois letter of December 2, 1828 (see *PMC*, Letter 273 on page 38).

The location of the Shawnee post can be determined by the various references and the channel of the Kansas River. Francois, true to form and experience, positioned the trading house near the established Indian trails, which would be improved for the military and the new settlers. Again, McCoy reliably reports from a surveyor's firsthand knowledge that there were two ancient, well-beaten Indian trails through the Kawsmouth area. The first route as already discussed "continued south [crossing Brush Creek near Troost Avenue] toward the Osage, and north from the river to the country occupied by the Ioways, Sauks and Kickapoos in Northern Missouri and Iowa."[30] The second trail came from Fort Osage westward through Independence, crossing the north-south trail near Prospect and Linwood, then to the state line near Westport, "and continuing westward up the Kaw valley *ad infinitum*."[31] It was at the site of his post that Francois understood the new military road south from Ft. Leavenworth would ford the Kansas. He and Cyprien built their Shawnee post on the right (south) bank on Shawnee land, across from the abandoned "half-breed establishment on the Kanzas, about 12 miles from the mouth" on the left (north) bank of the river.[32] The Kansas River surveyor Angus Langham identified this village at between the eleventh and twelfth mile from the mouth.[33] His map, which corresponds closely to the current river channel, noted a rise on the south bank in that vicinity – the likely spot for what would be called Cyprien's Post.[34]

---

26. Others suggested that the family moved to Four Houses after the flood. (*History of Jackson County (1881)*, 378.)

27. *Guide to Menard Collection*, 30.

28. Marie George Windell, "Westward Along the Boone's Lick Trail in 1826, The Diary of Colonel John Glover," *Missouri Historical Review* 39: 195.

29. "Reminiscences of Fredrick Chouteau," *Kansas Historical Collection* 8: 423.

30. John C. McCoy Scrapbook, 25, (KC296), WHMC-KC.

31. John C. McCoy Scrapbook, 11, (KC296), WHMC-KC.

32. *OIA, St. Louis Superintendency*, 1829-1831, M234, Microfilm roll 749, Frame 1285, NARA.

33. The mouth of the Kansas River in 1964 (year of the Kansas City quadrangle) was about 900 feet west and 1,100 feet south of its location in 1826. This reflects significant changes that have occurred including the 1844 which caused Turkey Creek to flow into the Kansas rather than the Missouri. The current channel is substantially as it was in 1826 until about twenty-five miles from the mouth.

34. One writer recently suggested the post was located about a mile south near Morris School. There is no serious evidence to support this theory which called for the river channel to have moved in 1836. Such a calamitous event was not mentioned in Francois's letters or any other sources consulted. Moreover, Cyprian's Post continued to operate until the late 1850s, seemingly without disruption.

A quote from Father Benedict Roux, the first Catholic pastor of the Kawsmouth French community, causes confusion about the Chouteau's home:

> *I am at present at the trading house of Messrs. Chouteau.... I cannot...speak too highly in praise of Mr. Gesseau and of his wife and brother...but I do not expect to remain long with them, as they are right in the Indian county and too far away from the Catholics for me to carry on my ministry with convenience.*[35]

This statement has been interpreted to suggest that the Chouteau family resided at their Shawnee post in November 1833 when Rev. Roux wrote to Bishop Joseph Rosati. Perhaps this is so, but a more likely scenario was that they were at the Chouteau's Landing – the headquarters post. Father Roux was a scholarly man, slight of build, who was not suited to mission work on the frontier. The main body of his Catholic parishioners were located well away from the trading house – in fact when the "Chouteau's Church" was constructed in 1834 on top of the bluffs near what would become 11th and Pennsylvania, it was very nearly three miles over rugged terrain from the landing. Moreover, the post, surrounded by visiting Indians, would have seemed to be "right in the Indian county." Lastly, Francois's letters of the period do not suggest an extended stay at the Shawnee post.

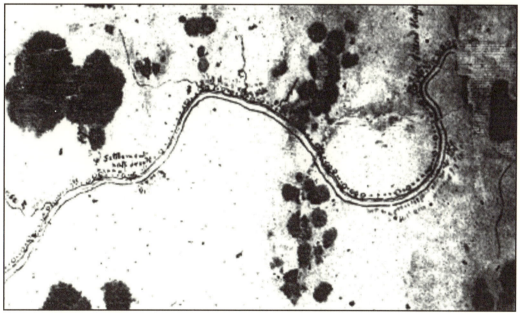

A portion of Angus Langham's 1826 survey map of the Kansas River from its mouth to about fifteen miles out. The map is damaged in the area that would show the mouth of the river. Each small circle represents a survey point in his log. The "Half-breed settlement" was located at the 11th to 12th mile from the mouth. The oblong shape depicted on the south bank represents a rise of land on which the Shawnee post was most likely located. KSHS.

---

35. Gilbert J. Garraghan, S.J., *Catholic Beginnings in Kansas City, Missouri*, 46-48.

The location of Francois Chouteau's main trading house developed in the late 1820s on the Missouri River was roughly a half-mile east of the Paseo Bridge. Its main landmark was a mile-long island, once called Chouteau's Island, but more commonly known as Mensing Island after a farmer who built his home there in the late 1850s. The island is now completely attached to the mainland, but in the early 1830s when Chouteau built his steamboat landing, it was a fifty-five acre scrub covered grazing pasture. The main channel of the Missouri passed between the island and the south shore – a 100 to 300 foot wide "slough".[36] It was at this place that Francois Chouteau "died suddenly while down on the river bank watching some cattle swim across the slew [slough]."[37]

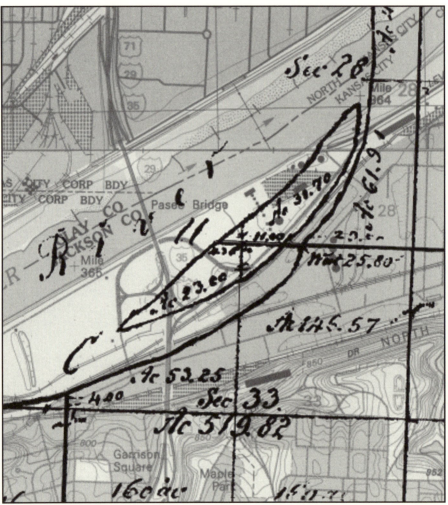

A portion of the 1827 Jackson County survey of T50N R33W overlaid on a current U.S. Geological Survey map. WHMC-KC.

---

36. J. S. Chick, "Kaw River, Recession of at Kansas City," in *Encyclopedia of the History of Missouri: A Compendium of History and Biography for Ready Reference*, ed., Conard, Howard, 3: 510.

37. "Joseph S. Chick interview," October 19, 1908, General (series A), Kansa (subgroup 9), *Indians History Collection*, (MC590), KSHS.

Descriptions of the place suggest that it was a well-developed farm, warehouse operation, and a steamboat landing which Francois built in the early 1830s as the steamers became more common. The Chouteau farm was large, perhaps patterned after Berenice's father's plantation that fronted the Kaskaskia River to the east of the town of the same name. Unfortunately no photographs or drawings of the establishment and farm have been located. The best image of the plantation comes from an 1872 interview with Pierre Menard Chouteau about the devastation of the 1844 flood.

> *The flood of 1827 [sic] ... was quite moderate in dimension as compared with the one that followed it seventeen years later. The Harlem bottoms were totally submerged, and all of the bottoms immediately below this city, with the exception of the Guinotte bottoms farm. This mere fact that these Guinotte bottoms were above high water-mark in 1827 caused it to be purchased by the Chouteau family, and in due time the rich, loamy bottom lands, now an almost barren sand-bar, became a fine, large plantation, with hundreds of acres of fertile fields surrounding the fine old homestead of the Chouteaus.*
>
> *The residence of Mr. P.M. Chouteau (now City Collector) was a spacious double log house with two wings, all covered with weatherboarding. The house had three heavy chimneys built at the ends and one in the center. There were numerous barns, ware houses, hemp the tobacco houses, besides the Negro quarters, clustered around the large house, hundreds of head of stock, horses, cattle and hogs, roamed at will in the quiet bottoms, and all seemed as peaceful and prosperous as could be.*
>
> *The winter of 1844 was somewhat like the present one, deep snows fell in the mountains and very little in this valley. The "June Rise" of 1844 came booming down the river, the channel of which ran down just west of the north end of the railroad bridge and struck fair against the rocky bluff at the foot of Broadway, and then ran along the south shore of the river bank down to Randolph bluffs, where it crossed over and washed the base of the Clay county bluffs. A large island covered with heavy timber existed where now only a low sand bar is seen opposite the gas works.*
>
> *The plantation of P. M. Chouteau, below the city, was gradually submerged. Inch by inch the angry, muddy stream crawled upon the fertile face of the fields: the slough soon became filled with water, but the wealthy planter remained with his family, expecting every day that the water would go down. One morning the family awoke to find themselves surrounded by four feet of water. Cattle, horses, and hogs were wading and swimming about in the stream; a hundred acres of fine hemp standing in shoals in the field was nearly covered. Upon nearly every every [sic] shock were perched chickens, turkeys, or little pigs. The family had barely time to escape to the main shore when the current became quite rapid, and raised to the second story of the house. While a party of young men were endeavoring to save some of the furniture from the upper story, the steamer* **Missouri Mail** *hove in sight up the river. The boys, eager for a joke, dressed up in female apparel, and got upon the roof of the house and hoisted a signal of distress. The steamer rounded to and came to the house. The boys went on board, took a drink, and were taken by the boat to the bluffs, where Chouteau shipped a few tons of water-rotted hemp to the St. Louis market.*
>
> *The flood was about two weeks going down but when it left it had changed the face of the low lands. In many places the sand had been piled up ten feet deep, in others it had taken off the rich top soil and left only the sandy subsoil. The Choteau [sic] plantation was worthless. What had been rich land was now poor. No one would buy it at five dollars per acre. It was nearly twelve years before the bottom land would sell at any price.*

It finally sold at $ 12 [?] per acre. The old house stood against the flood until the chimneys were fairly battered down by the huge trees that were hurled against them. When the chimneys went down away went the house. The stream was dotted with floating houses and barns, some surmounted with chickens, dogs and pigs, all alive and taking an involuntary ride.[38]

At the height of his career, Francois Chouteau supervised five trading houses: the Kansa post operated by his brother Frederick, the Shawnee post run by Cyprien, and posts for the Weas and for the Kickapoos. The fifth was the large Kansas City warehouse and steamboat landing. Additionally he established a landing at the point of land on the right bank of the Kansas where it joined the Missouri – literally on the state line. Other places were associated with, and abandoned by the Chouteaus as circumstances demanded, such as the Randolph Bluffs post, the Harrison Street home, Four Houses, and various Kansa post locations.

An amazing fact of the frontier was the ability for people, and through them information, to travel long and rugged distances though the wilderness. Primitive roads and paths connected places, and the rivers and streams joined most destinations. As suggested, the French and later settlers who arrived in the Kawsmouth region built the first community upon a network of family and friendship, linking people in a barter of services and goods and relationships. The scattering of homes and pastures and trade buildings were transitory landmarks. But the people, regardless of their place or role, created the geography of the community.

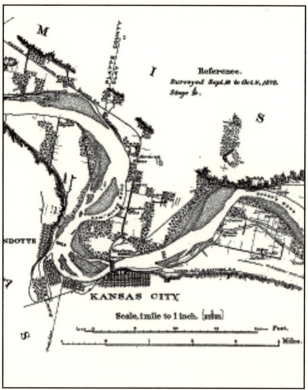

A portion of Plat XIV of the 1878 survey of the Missouri River. WHMC-KC.

---

38. "High Water." *Kansas City Times*, 7 January 1872, 4.

Appendix 2

Pierre (Cadet) Chouteau Jr. to Gabriel (Seres) Chouteau, July 19, 1822

(Subject: Where Gabriel (Seres) Chouteau will operate a post.)

This letter from Pierre (Cadet) Chouteau Jr. to Gabriel Sylvestre (Seres, Cerre) Chouteau is included to demonstrate how the family-business interaction worked among the French fur traders. Written in French, Cadet's letter supports the concept that from 1820 to 1826, Francois Chouteau was operating two posts: Four Houses and Randolph Bluffs.

Berthold, Chouteau, and Pratte[1]
St. Louis
July 19, 1822

To: G. S. Chouteau
  River of Kansas

Dear cousin

We would have liked very much to have seen you before the departure of all the expeditions left for the Missouri, to confer about the business that concerns you personally, but as we were deprived of this pleasure, I thought I should inform you by this letter of what has happened. Geusseau [Francois Chouteau] wanted to take the merchandise for his own account, because he alleges, with reason, that the profits are so limited that it is not worth the trouble to increase the number of partners in a small operation; we are leaving it to you and to him to settle it, if it is possible for you, and if it is mutually agreeable to you; but if this arrangement does not take place, since we are convinced that the services you could render at all the other posts will always be advantageous to us, we make you an offer to come up in one of our barges to spend the winter with the Otos or the Mahas, or in whatever place you think the most advantageous for our interests, and for your services we offer to allow you five hundred piastres; and if you accept this proposition will you please be so kind as to inform us at once, and, if so, we rely on your usual zeal for putting in the necessary order our business at the post you are occupying at present, and turning it all over to Cyprien [Chouteau?].

But if the propositions we are making you do not suit you, we are ever ready to give you an outfit for your own account, for whatever post suits you.

We salute you very cordially,
Berthold, Chouteau, and Pratte

---

1. *Pierre (Cadet) Chouteau Jr. to G. S. Chouteau, July 19, 1822,* Chouteau Family Collections, MHS.

N.B. In spite of the high prices we gave for the furs Beaver 300 – Otter 300 – Raccoon 37 1/2 = deerskins 37 1/2 a pound – all under cordage – the outfit to the Kans lost nevertheless 1585.24 which remains to our account as we had agreed – you have a credit of 1091.98. The amount of the bill we received from [Cotte? Cotle?] *– so you see that it is hardly to be expected that anything can be made in such a small post where there is competition. I did my best with Francois to get you to continue this year together, but he remained always of the opposite opinion, that the post did not justify a partnership, so I hope the offer that we made will seem acceptable, and that you will not hesitate to come up in our barge – This (or these) post (or posts) offer much more in the way of resources, and our object is to push the business as much as possible on the upper Missouri – If, contrary to my expectations, you do not want to go up (which would inconvenience us, as we have counted on you), we have merchandise to furnish you as usual, but where to go with it? To be a fourth at the Kans? All other places are outfitted in almost the same way – the merchandise was delivered to Ceprien* [illegible word] *I beg you to leave an inventory* [illegible word] *of everything and send it to us, including the horses, saddles, etc.*

Adieu keep well and believe me
your affectionate cousin,
Pr. C. Jr.

All the family are well and my uncle has been in the country for some time.

Appendixes

Appendix 3

Pierre Menard to Francois Chouteau, 1829-1836

In an effort to offset the one-sidedness of the correspondence in this book, one letterbook summary and six letters from Pierre Menard to Francois Chouteau are offered. Pierre Menard's letters often dealt with topics and questions broached by Francois. All the Menard letters are copies of letters from either *Letterbook J* (IHS) or the *Pierre Menard Collection* (ISHL), because the originals that Francois received from Menard and others were probably kept in the Chouteau warehouse or home, and were therefore swept away in the flood of 1844.

3 a.

Pierre Menard considered the following letter, a reply to Francois Chouteau's letter of February 15, 1829 (page 50), significant enough to justify having a clerk copy it into a letterbook before sending it. The letter sheds light on Pierre Menard's style of conducting business: he told Francois plainly what to do, then offered some generic advice. One important fact is revealed in the letter below – the Shawnee Indians negotiated a signed hunting treaty, not merely a verbal one.

September 30, 1829 [1]

Cher Gesseau,

William Meyers is the person that I appoint to trade with the Piankesaws, Weas, and Peorias. I directed him to go take his equipment from you at your place. Give him what you judge necessary for the post that he will operate. I gave him some prices that he must sell to the Indians. I don't believe that you should ask above 5 over per blanket of 3 points and I fear that if you will ask more, he [i.e., they, the Indians] *could take their furs and trade in Independence.*

If you sell [to] *them at a lower price by his hand,* [2] [you] *would take away* [i.e., get] *half of the skins. Try to appease the Shawnee and not to let them sign a treaty elsewhere. If you think that you will have appropriate merchandise before that time for their $1000 that they have deposited in the hands of Captain Vashon.*

---

1. Pierre Menard to Francois Chouteau, September 30, 1829, Letterbook J, *Pierre Menard Collection*, IHS.

2. "By his hand" meant through William Meyers; that is, Pierre Menard was telling Francois "if you have Meyers sell things at a lower price, you will collect more furs."

I'm afraid to go see you in the course of the winter. Francois[3] *is proposing to go soon with his father. My love to Berenice and your dear Children as well as Frederick and receive for yourself my sincere esteem.*

Pierre Menard

3 b.

Pierre Menard's letter of February 4, 1830, was partially answered in Francois Chouteau's letter dated April 22, 1830; however, at that time, Chouteau was so involved in the conflict with Kansa Agent Marston Clark that he, Francois, did not reply to all of Menard's concerns. Chouteau to Menard, June 6, 1830 (page 83) and July 15, 1830 (page 86), also responded to some of the issues raised in Menard's letter.

Kaskaskia   February 4, 1830[4]

Mr. Frs. Chouteau
Kansas River

Dear Gesseau,

I'm sending you James Conner's note – as a favor to Marshall - to the bearer for the amount of $133. (it should be 33% more) and on the back, the order of the said Conner to Mr. Vashon to pay the said note. Mr. Vashon could perhaps have some difficulty because Connor did not send his vouchers in duplicate before 4 May of his specific salary in the order of the said Connor. I have James Connor's power of attorney since he will be like an interpreter which is recorded at the Superintendent in St. Louis and I always received his salary and given a receipt to the agent as his attorney in fact. I am therefore sending you enclosed, the bill for James Connor's salary from August 31 until December 31, 1829 that you will not show to Mr. Vashon only in case it becomes necessary to receive this payment. If Mr. Vashon wants to pay he can send me an order on General Clark. If he has no money available to give you I had paid on the order of the same Connor the amount of his salary from June until August 31, 1829 and I had written to Mr. Vashon when he was on the White River to keep the money in his hands for me. He did not. I believe that he had paid Connor and Pool before receiving my letter and on account of that I lost the money that I paid on Connor's order and waited six months longer for the one that I had lent to Pool. Marshall gave me this note of Connor's to place toward the credit of his account as soon as I will receive it.

We heard our Cyprien was sick at the seminary. I returned from there three days ago. I left him fairly well.

---

3. Apparently this was Francois Menard, who, having developed a serious illness (tuberculosis?) had left college in Bloomingdale, New York, and was living at home in Kaskaskia. Did Pierre Menard mean to convey that his son Francois would like for his father (meaning Pierre Menard) to come with him soon to see Francois and Berenice, but that he (Menard) was afraid to come in the winter?

4. Pierre Menard to Francois Chouteau, February 4, 1830, Letterbook J, *Pierre Menard Collection*, IHS.

Appendixes

We learned with sadness that your dear Gesseau had fallen in the fire and burnt one hand a lot and his face a little. We're happy that this will not have serious consequences.

We are all well enough except Francois, however François is always convalescing a little. Embrace Berenice and your dear children for us all and receive the assurance of our sincere esteem.

P M

Remember us to Cyprien and Frederick to whom we send our best wishes.

I have not received any news from you for a very long time. Cadet told me that you were hoping that the Indians would have a good hunt. Give him our regards from all of us. I learned that Liguest was trading at the old factory [Ft. Osage at Sibley?] *and that he had traded the furs of the Weas, Peorias, and Loup and that is not our agreement with the company. Write to me and tell me what the prospects are for the collection of this treaty and the one in the spring.*

Your friend
P M

3 c.

The following summary of a letter written by Pierre Menard to Francois Chouteau demonstrates the caution of a successful businessman. Pierre Menard wanted to document that he had sent the letters mentioned, and that he was not keeping a copy of his "family" letter to Francois. Menard's careful methods are showcased in the letters of *Cher Oncle, Cher Papa* with the sending back and forth of receipts, certificates, and other papers (with an eye to possible legal action, no doubt). Francois replied to Pierre Menard in a letter of March 20, 1831 (page 90).

Kaskaskia   February 22, 1831[5]

Wrote this day to Francois Chouteau a family letter, etc., not business, mentioned to him the loss of my dear son, Francois, and so on. I'm asking him to give me his opinion about the place bought by the company from Madame Widow Baronet [Vasquez] *and if he does not have himself the right of improvement that is to say, the right of preemption. I am including for him two letters for the Peorias, one from me and one from the chiefs of the Kaskaskia nation and one for Bt* [Baptiste] *Peoria. I am not keeping a copy of my letter to Gesseau. The letters left by post the 23rd all alone [...] the envelope for F. Chou. etc. [...] paid 56/4.*

---

5. Letter summary, Pierre Menard to Francois Chouteau, February 22, 1831, Letterbook J, *Pierre Menard Collection*, IHS.

3 d.

Pierre Menard's letter of February 13, 1833, was probably a rough draft that was never sent; the entire letter was marked through with a large X, and various lines were scratched out and rewritten as shown. The rewritten version of this letter seems to be the one dated February 20, 1833 (Item 3e).

Kaskaskia   February 13, 1833 [6]

Mr. François Chouteau
Kansas River

My dear Gesseau

No point with

I am writing to Gilliss by this post so that he can arrange the business of the debts of the Loup Indians for what they must pay to Menard and Valle for the amount that they owe to Gilliss and Marshall. According to the third article of the treaty with the Kickapoos these last ones are to pay Menard and Valle five thousand. Five hundred dollars for the larger amount that they owe Gilliss, Menard, and Valle. ~~Wm. Marshall, John Campbell, and P. Menard for a [...] on this amount. Menard and Valle are to pay.~~ *On that amount Menard and Valle must pay William Marshall, John Campbell, etc., etc. The same Kickapoos are to pay Pierre Chouteau Junior $6500 that they owe Ogle upon which Pierre Chouteau is to pay Pierre Menard Junior, and to diverse people in case there are [any] and to Pinsonneau, etc., etc. The remainder must be put for the availability of Mr. Ogle by Pierre Chouteau Junior but it is necessary that the four Indians mentioned in the treaty approve the bill claimed against their respective nations. You know that there are always some flatterers among the Indians such as a certain Canadian that hangs around with the band of the project and serves as their interpreter. You will see by the agreements made for us and the Indians of which the originals are in the hands of the Chiefs that it is necessary that my obligations be retired. The copy is in Gilliss's hand. According to the copy you'll easily figure out what must be done. Use some of your influence with the Kickapoos so that they may recognize what they have owed the traders for a long time and I believe very sadly.*

3 e.

Pierre Menard's letter of February 20, 1833, is probably the corrected version of the previous letter. Francois replied in letters dated April 16, 1833 (page 112), and May 20, 1833 (page 114).

---

6. Pierre Menard to Francois Chouteau, February 13, 1833, Letterbook J, *Pierre Menard Collection*, IHS.

Kaskaskia   February 20, 1833 [7]

Mon cher Gesseau,

I am writing to Gilliss and am sending a copy of the agreement that I made with Menard and Valle and another one like it that I made with the Kickapoo for M & V [Menard and Valle] and also for your brother Pierre Chouteau. Upon seeing these copies, either yourself or Cyprien, you will see right away what must be done. You [must watch?] Gilliss and use some of the influence that you have with the Kickapoo so that the bills they owe to the traders mentioned be acknowledged by the four chiefs mentioned in the said agreement and that this be written and signed by the said chiefs on the original agreement which is in possession of the said four chiefs. And that this be similar to the form of the one I am sending to Gilliss.

I also ask you to ask our mutual friend, the Major Cummins, if he has received instructions to pay William Marshall payable $1225.00 on [from] the annuities of the Weas payable $725 on those of annuities of 1833 and $500 on those of 1834. I am the bearer since last November about the orders of Marshall's on Major Cummins and if he has received any instructions from the commissioner on this subject, I will send them to you so that he may accept them. Write to me and mark for me how the treaty is this year, etc., etc.

PM

Compliments from the family.

3 f.

The letter below combined Pierre Menard's family sentiments and his very direct method of operating a business. Nothing was to be hidden in the Meyers-Chouteau disagreement, as Menard passed along what each had said about the other. The letter was copied into Menard's letterbook to provide a record of exactly what he had said about the situation. For Francois's remarks on this topic, see his letter dated February 25, 1833 (page 111).

March 19, 1833 [8]

Mon cher Francois,

I received [your letter] *yesterday with pleasure upon my arrival from St. Louis dated Feb. 25. I learned with pleasure that you are a father of one more big boy* [9] *and that my Berenice is well. I think [understand] that you were obliged to send Frederic to Meyers post and I observe all that you tell me on that subject. I will see Meyers*

---

7. Pierre Menard to Francois Chouteau, February 20, 1833, Letterbook J, *Pierre Menard Collection*, IHS.

8. Pierre Menard to Francois Chouteau, March 19, 1833, Letterbook J, *Pierre Menard Collection*, IHS.

9. This boy was Benedict Pharamond, born February 22, 1833, Francois and Berenice's second child born in Jackson County. He died August 6, 1834.

tomorrow at Ste. Genevieve and will communicate to him your letter and will have him understand that he was wrong in leaving his post so quickly. He told me upon arrival yesterday that the treaty was finished for this season. I received today a letter from Edmond.[10] *He is asking me for Indian shoes. I would like for you to have 3 or 4 pairs made for me the same as those that Berenice sent to my wife last fall, made by Mrs. Prudhomme.*[11] *I wish that they be like the larger ones that she sent, etc. etc. We still do not have any news that the treaty was ratified. So* [when?] *they tell me that Kane*[12] *arrived. I will see him and if I learn through him that the treaties were ratified, I will write you by the next mail as well as Gilliss, etc., etc., etc.*

Accept the Assurances of my affection, etc.
Pierre Menard

3 g.

Pierre Menard's following letter recounts the history of the Wea debt to Marshall, mentioned so often in the Chouteau letters, and relating in particular to Francois's letters dated July 18, 1836, and September 15, 1836 (*PMC*, Letters 737 and 771). The copy of this letter made and kept at the Menard office recorded not only the Wea debt history, but also what he had said about Helen Decoigne's land.

Kaskaskia   August 12, 1836[13]

Mon cher Gesseau,

Your letter of July 18th and Berenice's were awaiting [me and] *duly received yesterday. You tell me that Major Cummins told you that the Weas should pay if he has not received a letter from Major Brent that is due to his hastened departure from St. Louis as the same that he promised* [me] *he would write. He received orders to leave for Alabama from where he has not yet returned. I am confident, however, that through your influence and the help of Baptiste* [Peoria] *you will get the Weas to agree without difficulty to pay me this debt that I paid to Marshall myself for them. The black agent Le Signe*[14] *and the other chiefs came to Kaskaskia to ask me to pay $1750 for them that*

---

10. Edmond was probably Pierre Menard's son Edmond, then attending Georgetown College (Georgetown University) in Washington, D.C.; Edmond Chouteau did not go away to school until November 1833.

11. Mrs. Prudhomme was Susan (she may also be known as Margaret D. Durand), widow of Gabriel Prudhomme, interpreter and mountain man whose property was the site of the original Town of Kansas. According to Father Bernard Donnelly, Susan was a Canadian *metis*. ("Historical Death," *Kansas City Times*, 30 January 1877, 4). See also "Gabriel Prudhomme and family notes," Fur Trade Biographies, Chouteau's (Biographical) Scrapbook [17.2], (KC395), WHMC-KC.

12. Elias K. Kane wrote letters to Pierre Menard in 1828 and 1834 concerning Indian treaties and other Indian business. Perhaps he was a government official of the War Department, which at that time handled matters relating to Native Americans. (*PMC*, Letters 275 and 622.)

13. *PMC*, Letter 743.

14. Apparently this was not a federal agent for the Indians, but an Indian leader or chief.

they told me they owed Marshall. I refused to do it but after they asked the commissioner [Superintendent of Indian Affairs, William Clark] *for it and that Marshall, out of pity for them, lowered it by $525.00, I did not hesitate to pay Marshall. It never occurred to me that they could or would want to cause the least difficulty and I am confident that they will pay honestly this year and not subject me to other difficulties. Your aunt, Edmond*[15] *and Sophie arrived the day before yesterday from the Barrens where they paid a visit to Masters Amadee and Menard whom they found in good health and very satisfied. I am confident that they will continue like that. Berenice wrote to my wife that you are to come down. I am confident that it will be early enough to come with me to the college for the distribution of prizes. We are getting news from Cyprien* [Menard]. *He is very satisfied at Emmettsburg College. I am enclosing a sale* [receipt?] *for Helen Decoigne's land that I own. I left the price blank but it will give her from $_____ to $_____.*[16] *It's a lot more than the land would sell at the present and not only that, it inconveniences my two farms. It will be necessary for it to go up in value before too many years. If Elsigne*[17] *sells it that will need to be recognized.*

You must act in this respect with much discretion. It must not be made known. You will need signatures from two respectable witnesses. Major Cummins if he was present with you would even suffice. You can pay her with the money that you will receive from the annuities of various Indians. Except that she wants to take part of it in merchandise.

[....] [....] would prefer to leave that in your hands and I will have it counted from the same amount at the [....] Madame Edmond[18] *and Sophie are leaving tomorrow for a visit to St. Louis. Hug Berenice, the boys*[19] *and the girl*[20] *for us. Our regards to your brothers.*

Your very sincere friend,
Pierre Menard

---

15. Probably Edmond Menard, as the name is linked with Angelique's and Sophie's; Edmond Menard wrote a letter from Philadelphia in July 1836 and may have been en route to Kaskaskia, given that his next letter was written from there.

16. Perhaps Chouteau and Menard had not previously agreed upon the price, as Menard wrote a dollar sign, then the word "white," which the translator interpreted as a blank space.

17. Elsigne has not yet been identified; possibly this was the same person as "LeSigne," the black agent mentioned in Menard's letter of August 17, 1836 (PMC, Letter 743).

18. Probably this was the wife of Edmond Menard; it is possible that Edmond came home in August 1836 to be married.

19. These boys were Francois and Berenice's sons that were at home at this time, Benjamin and Frederic.

20. Mary Brigitte Chouteau.

Appendix

4

Pierre Menard Chouteau to Pierre Menard, June 24, 1835

(Subject: Pierre Menard Chouteau greets his grandfather, Pierre Menard.)

The following short letter from Pierre Menard Chouteau, thirteen-year-old son of Francois and Berenice, to his grandfather Pierre Menard sketches a charming vignette of their relationship. The letter contains several errors, since it was written in English by a boy whose first language was French. That Pierre Menard was an involved grandparent is evident from this letter and also from those of Francois Chouteau, especially the June 21, 1835, letter (*PMC*, Letter 661), and others written throughout 1836-1837.

St. Mary's College   June 24, 1835[1]

Dear Grand Father,

This is the first time that I take the permission to write you a letter even though the letter that you had written to me by my uncle[2] *[....][....] possibly my letter will be long for the first time since I am at college. The teachers did not have anything to tell me against me about my studies or for the rules of the college and I will try to continue the same thing. Goodbye, dear Grandpa.*

Your very affectionate nephew [sic],[3]
Pierre Menard Chouteau

---

1. *PMC*, Letter 661.
2. This "uncle" was Pierre Menard's son Amadee Menard, who was in school at St. Mary's of the Barrens at this time. The letter "Menard" (Pierre Menard Chouteau) received was probably included in an envelope that his Uncle Amadee received. (Amadee was two years older than Menard Chouteau.)
3. Pierre Menard Chouteau, although he spoke English, was probably just learning to write it; he said his letter would be "long" when he probably meant "short" and he used the word "nephew" when he meant "grandson."

Appendix 5

Edmond Francois (Gesseau) Chouteau to Pierre Menard, Jan. 15, 1836

(Subject: Gesseau's apology to his Grandfather Menard after being expelled from school.)

The following letter was written in French by Edmond Francois (Gesseau, Gesso) Chouteau, Francois and Berenice's fifteen-year-old son. The lad had been expelled from school, and lived under his grandfather's watchful eye in Kaskaskia for several weeks before returning to his home in western Missouri. Gesseau's letter followed the French tradition of requesting his elder's blessing at the beginning of a new year, but, in addition, presents an interesting picture of the family dynamics. Refer back to Francois Chouteau's letters of August 30, 1835, and December 16, 1835 (*PMC*, Letter 683 and 698), for a review of the situation.

Kansas River   January 15, 1836[1]

Chere [sic] *Grandpapa,*

[....][....] a narration of many events which occurred to me since my departure from St. Louis on Easter [?] *as* [when] *I had the satisfaction of seeing you, is my letter. The fever which I then experienced left me and I set out from St. Louis and safely arrived home from where I anticipated writing you immediately. I got an unlucky crushing of my finger and afterwards a misapplied blow from an axe which severed one of my toes and materially injured my foot. I hope* [these events] *will be a sufficient excuse in the eyes of a loving grandfather. A new year beginning its revolution gives me an earnest and ardent desire to obtain that benediction from a loving grandfather which alas, I know I have forfeited by my neglects of myself and thoughtlessness but far from being through malice as has often been hinted, I myself was lured into evil instead of luring others, but I hope the only favor which I ask – your good graces –* [you] *will allow me, when I inform you that I have undertaken a total changement of my self.*

Adieu – my health is perfectly in accord with my wishes and I would hope you to be the same. The family generally are well except Mary Brigitte[2] *who's not bigger than my thumb and every person's mistress.*

Your loving and obedient grandson,
Edmond Chouteau

---

1. *PMC*, Letter 703.
2. Edmond's little sister, Mary Brigitte, was then four months old.

Appendix

Francois Chouteau's Scribe

A sample of Francois Chouteau's scribe, probably executed with a quill pen, appears below in a reproduction of one of his letters to Pierre Menard.[1] The letter also provides an example of the kind of manuscript damage that complicated the work of translators. In addition to being torn, this particular letter was apparently exposed to water.

Berenice Chouteau's Handwriting

The handwriting of Berenice Chouteau is shown below in a reproduction of an 1827 letter,[2] one of the oldest in the body of *Cher Oncle, Cher Papa*. Berenice wrote many additional letters to her father that he did not keep, for they were personal rather than business letters. She also wrote letters to her stepmother and other family members. The Berenice letters of this collection are chiefly personal, but contained some business references that Pierre Menard desired to keep on file.

---

1. Francois Chouteau to Pierre Menard, December 2, 1828, (*PMC, Letter* 273). See page 38 for translation.
2. Berenice Chouteau to Pierre Menard Jr., May 19, 1827, (*PMC, Letter* 214). See page 31 for translation.

No 2 1828

De la Maison de Mr. Chaine 2 8bre 1828.

Chère oncle

Je suis sur ma route pour aller a la maison de traite de Kans porter une charge de marchandise, je voulais vous écrire par le Major Graham mais il a parti sans que je le sache, Clark et Dorty deux sauvages qui doivent passer chez vous vous remettrons celle ici, Mr. Chaine me dit qu'il croit que les sauvages me payeront le crédit que je leur est faite, je croiyait qu'il avait la partie de leur argent, a Independance où il y a un magazin petit vilage qui est a dix a douze mile d'ici, mais Mr. Chaine me dit que non, qu'ils ont payé les dettes qu'il avaient contracté ici, et je sais qu'il ont encore de cette argent, la bande de John n'est pas encore de retourne de la chasse, je pense qu'il feront quelque chose, je vois de m'aranger mieux avec cette bande q'avec les autres, les Kans sont disperse en beaucoup de bande, il y a un bon partie d'aller dans le large il ne sont pas encore sortie il y a aussi une bande sur la rivière _____ qui toute avec osege, je tacherai de les attendre ici autant que possible, les Chawanon trouve que nous vendon un peu chèr et qu'ils peuvent avoire a meilleur marché a Independance mais il ne considere pas, ou pretande ne le pas considere que nos marchandise sont infiniment superieure a ce qu'il trouve alleure, pour les anuites, il les ont ut a bon marché, et vous verai a la fin qu'on ne leur a point survendu, il connait sans doute la bonne marchandise mais ils ont trop de _____ tion, de Conaitre tous les prix, j'ai lu aux Chiefs la lettre de Michel Menard, et Mr. Chaine leur a interpreté j'ai aussi dit a Mr. Chaine que si il avait besoin d'une maison vous me marque de lui faire faire, et que je prendirai les mesure necessaire pour cela, il me dit qu'il etait assez bien logé pour cette hiver, et qu'il n'en auria pas besoin Gilespe vient d'arive, et ces sauvage sont de l'autre coté d'Independance, il est aller voire le Major Cambell, chez madame vasquis

Saint Louis 19 mai ――― 1827.

Chér frère, ――

J'ai appris avec paine que tu étoit toujours malade je désire savoir de tes nouvelles par la prochaine ocasion, et je te Conseil de venir a Saint Louis Consulter un Medecin français qui est ici gesseau est arivé, et nous attandons Cyprien qui sera ici Dans peu de jours, pour aller nous promener au feu j'ai reçu des nouvelles d'alzire par Madame Kenerly elle n'a pas ecrit parceque elle pense etre ici dans deux ou trois semaine. fait bien des Compliment a grand mama, a audile

Crois moi pour la vie ton affectionné
Soeur Bérénice Chouteau

The Pieces of the Puzzle:
A Glossary of People, Places, and Things

About the Glossary: This section is an alphabetical listing of selected persons, places, and things, accompanied by a brief identification or definition. The persons are either mentioned in the Chouteau letters or are of interest because of their relationship to the central figures of this book. Names of unidentified individuals in the letters are not included in the Glossary. A picture of the subject is presented when available and appropriate. There are no pictures of Francois and Berenice Chouteau. However, an impression of their appearance may be gained from photographs of their children included here, particularly Benjamin and Mary Brigitte.

Complete citations for the pictures used may be found in the *Illustrations and Maps List* on page vi.

The glossary information was taken chiefly from the Chouteau letters (*PMC*) and *Guide to the Microfilm Edition of the Pierre Menard Collection*; *The Beginning of the West* by Louise Barry; *Fur Trade of the Far West* by Hiram Chittenden; *The Mountain Men and the Fur Trade of the Far West* by LeRoy Hafen; *Dictionary of Missouri Biography* (*DMB*) edited by Lawrence O. Christensen, William E. Foley, Gary R. Kremer, and Kenneth H. Winn; and *This Far by Faith* by Michael Coleman, Collette Doering, and Dorothy Marra. Also useful were the research notes on the French and on the fur trade in the Kansas City area compiled by James Anderson, Mildred Cox, and others, and now found in the *Native Sons of Kansas City Scrapbooks* in the Western Historical Manuscript Collection-Kansas City.

For further information about the Indian agencies, including specific names and dates of agencies and personnel, see *The Office of Indian Affairs, 1824-1860, Historical Sketches* by Edward Hill. For information about Indians who lived in Indian Territory (Kansas), see *The End Of Indian Kansas: A Study of Cultural Revolution, 1854-1871* by H. Craig Miner and William E. Unrau; for maps of reservations and selected treaties, see *Historical Atlas of Kansas* by Homer E. Socolofsky and Huber Self. Additional sources are cited as appropriate, and supplementary material is suggested.

⚜⚜⚜⚜⚜⚜

Agency (Indian) – A government establishment consisting of a cluster of buildings from which regulations, assistance, and annuities were distributed to a tribe or tribes. A subagent, assisted by an interpreter, a blacksmith, and an agriculturalist, usually manned the agency, supervised by an agent who usually did not live there. The agency system began in 1824 while the War Department handled Indian concerns.

Agnew, John O. – An early settler in Independence with a general store on the north side of the square that dealt mainly with goods for the Mexican trade. He is missing from both the

1830 and the 1840 Jackson County census, so apparently was in this area for only a brief time. When Marston Clark moved from being the Kansas subagent to being the Shawnee subagent, his first action was to license four competitors for the Cyprien Chouteau post: Flourney & Co., John O. Agnew, Henry McKee, and George B. Clark, Marston's son. He also issued them a license to trade with the Kickapoos in 1833 and another license to trade with the Shawnees, Ottawas, Weas, Piankeshaws, and Peorias in 1834. John O. Agnew should not be confused with John C. Agnew, who came to Independence in 1847.

American Fur Company Warehouse, 1835. North side of Walnut Street between Main and Levee Streets, St. Louis, Missouri. MHS.

American Fur Company – John Jacob Astor created the American Fur Company in 1826, partly by gaining control of the St. Louis company of Berthold, Chouteau, and Pratte (also called the French Fur Company). From that company Astor formed the Western Department of the American Fur Company, with Pierre (Cadet) Chouteau Jr. in charge of the St. Louis regional headquarters. Astor's business technique was to eliminate competition by buying and dismantling the threatening company. In addition to trading for furs offered by Indians, the company also hired the cream of personnel from defunct businesses, adding these men to the roster of American Fur Company trappers and hunters. Francois Chouteau's establishment at present Kansas City was a part of the American Fur Company.

When Astor retired in 1834, the American Fur Company split: Astor's business associate Ramsey Crooks purchased the Northern Department, and Pierre (Cadet) Chouteau Jr., with a partner, took over the Western Department and it was renamed the Pratte, Chouteau and Company (but was often still called the American Fur Company). Crooks's Northern Department was officially named the American Fur Company. (See also Hiram Chittenden's *Fur Trade of the Far West*; for further references and historic overview, see William Swagerty and Janet Lecompte's *Introduction to the Papers of the St. Louis Fur Trade*.)

Anderson, William (d. 1831) – A principal chief of the Delaware Nation, Anderson, though partly white, was staunch in his devotion to the ways of his nation. In 1830, he led the first of the emigrant Delawares into Indian Territory (Kansas), wintering along the north bank of the Kansas River, about seven miles west of the Missouri state line.† Before he died in September 1831, possibly of smallpox, Chief Anderson wrote a letter in which he recorded the names of his four sons: Shouanack, Pushkies, Secondyan, and Sacacoxy (Sarcoxie).‡

† Richard Cummins to William Clark, November 4, 1830, *OIA, Fort Leavenworth Agency, 1824-1836*, M234, Microfilm roll 300, Frame 188-189.
‡ Louise Barry, *Beginning of the West*, 208.

Annuities – In this context, an annuity, as negotiated in treaties, was the periodic payment in merchandise or money made by the United States government to Indian tribes. These treaties for lands and rights removed the Indians from areas desired by white settlers, particularly east of the Mississippi River and in the state of Missouri.

Arpent – A French land measure unit that is long and narrow and equal to .85 of an acre; it is still used in Quebec and some parts of Louisiana.

Astor, John Jacob (1763-1848) – A native of New York, Astor made his fortune in real estate and in the fur trade. In the early 1800s, he founded the Pacific Fur Company, sometimes called Astoria, headquartered at the mouth of the Columbia River in present Oregon. It failed in 1813 and was sold to the British. In 1826, Astor bought the French Fur Company of St. Louis, owned by Berthold, Chouteau, and Pratte, to create the American Fur Company. The Western Department of the American Fur Company was supervised by Pierre (Cadet) Chouteau Jr. This was the company with which Francois Chouteau was associated. In 1834, Astor sold the American Fur Company and retired from the fur business. (See **American Fur Company**.)

Astoria – See **Astor, John Jacob**.

Barclay, William – A nephew of William Gilliss who attended St. Mary's of the Barrens with Pierre Menard Chouteau. Barclay was apparently sponsored by Pierre Menard, as the young man wrote Pierre Menard several letters from the early 1830s to 1840 expressing respect and gratitude. (See also *Guide to the Microfilm Edition of the Pierre Menard Collection*.)

"The Barrens" – St. Mary's of the Barrens, in Perryville, Missouri. DePU. The Seminary building is in the distance behind the church.

Barrens, The – Officially named St. Mary's of the Barrens, a Catholic school for boys in Perryville, Missouri, but often called simply "The Barrens." Founded in 1818 by the Vincentian order of Catholic priests as a seminary, St. Mary's of the Barrens was later expanded to include non-seminarians. While the institution was referred to as a "college," it corresponded more closely to a present-day high school. One writer explained the significance of the term "Barrens": "The country bordering on the Mississippi river…has three natural divisions. There are forest lands, barrens,…and prairies. 'Barren' is a provincial term, denoting an intermediate condition between forest and prairie. In early settlements of Kentucky, large tracts of country were…covered with scattered stunted forest trees, intermixed with hazel and other shrubs, and producing a luxuriant growth of prairie grass. From its appearance the explorers supposed the soil to be unsuitable for cultivation, and called these tracts 'barren,' a term now applied extensively in the west to similar tracts."†

† R. Clark, "The Prairie," in *The United States Illustrated: The West*, 27-28.

Bates, Captain (d. 1837) – Captain of the steamboat *Boonville* who drowned after becoming entangled in a anchor rope and was "dragged instantly to the bottom."† Francois Chouteau in his letter dated May 12, 1837, noted, "He is really a man to be missed," which is echoed by the newspaper account of the death, "In the loss of Capt. Bates, the community have [*sic*] sustained a great loss; for he was an honest, a useful, and a good man."

† *Jefferson Republic*, 8 April 1837, 2.

Beckwourth (Beckwith), **James** (1798-1866) – Born in Virginia of an African slave woman and her owner Jennings Beckwith. Jim Beckwourth, as he was known, was provided an education by his father and eventually freed from slavery. He joined various expeditions, traveled extensively in the West, and became a skilled guide and trapper. Beckwourth wrote that he spent the winter of 1825-1826 packing furs for Francois Chouteau at his Randolph Bluffs warehouse below the mouth of the Kansas River. Beckwourth's autobiography, *The Life and Adventures of James P. Beckwourth: Mountaineer, Scout, and Pioneer and Chief of the Crow Nation of Indians*, published in 1856, brought him wide recognition. (See also *DMB*.)

Bertholet, Louis (178?-1844) – Called "Grand Louis," Bertholet was the son of French Canadian Louis Bertholet (d. ca.1800) and Marie, a Sac Indian. Grand Louis reportedly was born in Cahokia, Illinois, but lived in St. Charles, Missouri, and was an early trapper and trader near the mouth of the Kansas River. His mother lived in the house of the Saucier family in Cahokia (Francois Chouteau's grandparents' home), probably as a domestic servant. In 1812, Grand Louis married Margaret Gauthier of St. Charles in a civil ceremony. They were remarried in the Catholic Church in St. Charles in 1818. Madame Grand Louis stated in 1860 that she and her husband came to the mouth of the Kansas shortly after they married, presumably in 1819.† Grand Louis is generally credited with leading an advance team of workers to build the first fur trade depot for Francois Chouteau in 1822, on the north side of the Missouri River (Clay County) about three miles below the mouth of the Kansas River. Bertholet lived in one of the cabins at or near Chouteau's fur trade depot. He stayed and farmed for a number of years in Clay County after the Missouri River flood of 1826 washed away the entire Chouteau establishment, Grand Louis farmed in Clay County for a number of years. About 1830, he settled in Kansas City's West Bottoms and died there in 1844.

† "The Last Witness, or Reminiscences of Kansas City Fifty Years Ago," *Westport Border Star*, 28 July 1860.

Bertholet, Madame Grand Louis (1793-1863?) – A French woman, Margaret Gauthier was born in St. Charles. After marrying Grand Louis, she came to western Missouri with her husband (and reportedly also brought along her mother Elizabeth Becquet.) Margaret was almost certainly the first white woman to live in what is presently Kansas City.† This claim is often made for Berenice Chouteau, but she apparently did not precede Madame Grand Louis. Madame Bertholet died in Independence in about 1863.

† "The Female Voyageur: First White Woman to Ascend the Missouri," *Kansas City Times*, 6 December 1872.

Blondeau (Blando), **Maurice** – A trader first noticed in the Michigan fur trade, Blondeau was hired by Zebulon Pike to accompany a lost soldier down the Mississippi. By 1824, Maurice Blondeau was running a tavern in Keokuk, Iowa, next to an American Fur Company trading post. Probably this was the man to whom Chouteau referred in his November 5, 1828, letter (*PMC*), saying that "Blando is negotiating among the Kansa."

Bodmer, Charles Karl (1809-1893) – A Swiss artist who traveled up the Missouri on the steamboat *Yellow Stone* with Prince Maximilian in April 1833, passing Chouteau's warehouse on his way to the Upper Missouri where he was to paint Native Americans and scenes of the region. Maximilian's *Travels in the Interior of North America, 1832-1834* was illustrated with eighty-one engravings made from Bodmer's drawings. (See also *DMB*.)

Boggs – A trader who, Francois Chouteau had heard, was to bring two wagons of merchandise into the Shawnee Village that was designated as Chouteau's trading grounds (June 6, 1830, *PMC*). During that year, a number of men named Boggs were in the area: Lilburn W. Boggs (1792-1860) came from Kentucky, operated a store in Franklin, Missouri, and was assistant factor at Fort Osage from 1820 to 1822, supplying Indian trade goods at the fort. L. Boggs's second wife was Panthea Boone, granddaughter of Daniel Boone. Boggs opened a store in Independence in 1826 and was engaged in the Santa Fe trade in 1832-1833. At about this time, he began his political career. In 1836, Lilburn Boggs became governor of the state of Missouri. A man named Angus G. Boggs signed as a witness to a treaty with the Shawnee and Delaware Indians in 1836. Three Joseph Boggs were also here: Lieutenant Joseph Boggs, veteran of the Revolutionary War and uncle of Lilburn, may have come to Jackson County as early as the late 1820s; he died in Westport in 1843. His son, also Joseph, ran an early ferry across the Missouri near the mouth of the Kansas from Clay County in 1825, and moved to Jackson County by 1828. Dr. Joseph O. Boggs, Lilburn's brother, ran a drugstore in Independence and Westport from the 1830s to the 1850s. Lastly, Thomas Boggs (son of Lilburn?) was a freighter on the Santa Fe Trail during the late 1820s and early 1830s and married Charles Bent's stepdaughter Rumelda. Either he or Lilburn Boggs was probably the man to whom Chouteau referred, inasmuch as both had merchandise and wagons.

Bonneville, Benjamin (1796-1878) – An explorer and military man who came from France to the United States in 1803, attended West Point military school, and was assigned to Fort Smith in the Arkansas Territory in 1821. Bonneville took a leave of absence to become a "mountain man," and in May 1832, left Fort Osage with 110 men, twenty wagons and a variety of livestock and equipment, funded in part by John Jacob Astor. The expedition to collect furs went poorly but it did explore new territory.

Boone, Daniel Morgan (1769-1839) – A son of Daniel Boone and one of the earliest white residents in Indian Territory (Kansas). By 1827, Daniel Morgan Boone was living at the **Kansa Agency** near the mouth of the Big Blue River (Kansas) serving as agriculturist for the Kansa tribe. Boone eventually settled in Kansas City and died there of cholera in July 1839. Daniel Morgan Boone is probably buried in an unkempt cemetery north of 63rd Street, east of The Paseo, Kansas City, Missouri.

Bourgmont, Etienne de Veniard, Sieur de (1679-1734) – A French explorer who, as far as is known, was the first white man to explore the lower and middle Missouri River. De Bourgmont established Fort Orleans, a small military post on the Missouri River near the mouth of the Grand River in present Carroll County, Missouri. From the base of Fort Orleans, he launched his expedition to the Padoucas. De Bourgmont returned to France in 1725, and Fort Orleans was abandoned. (See also Frank Norall, *Bourgmont: Explorer of the Missouri, 1698-1725,* and *DMB*.)

Bridger, Jim (1804-1881) – A trapper, fur trader, guide, and trailblazer in the Rocky Mountains. After his mountain days, Bridger opened a store in a building in Westport that still stands on the northwest corner of present Westport Road and Pennsylvania in Kansas City. Bridger died in Kansas City and is now buried in Mount Washington Cemetery, Independence. (See also *DMB*.)

Bureau of Indian Affairs (BIA) – A United States government agency established in 1824 to administer matters related to Native Americans. The agency was then called the Office of Indian Affairs (OIA) and was under the authority of the War Department. (It was also sometimes informally called the Indian Department.) Thomas McKenney was its first Director, serving from 1824 to 1830. In 1849, the Office of Indian Affairs was transferred from the War Department to the newly created Department of the Interior, and was then renamed the Bureau of Indian Affairs, as it is still known today.

Cadet – See **Chouteau, Pierre Jr.**

Campbell, John (d. 1836) – Usually called "Major Campbell," John Campbell was subagent at the Shawnee Agency from 1825 until 1833, when he was notified of his removal from office. Campbell had been with the Shawnees when they lived temporarily in south-central Missouri, and he assisted them in their journey to their reservation in Indian Territory. He filed a plan for a town near Westport in which John Calvin McCoy had bought three lots. Campbell, however, went east to fight the charges that had caused his dismissal as subagent, and died on the trip. Later, Campbell's plan became an addition to McCoy's West Port. John Campbell had a reputation as a jovial, hospitable presence on the frontier.

Castor – A French word meaning "beaver."

Cerre (Seres) – See **Chouteau, Gabriel Sylvestre**.

Cerre, Marie Therese (1769-1842) – Born in Kaskaskia, Illinois, she was the wife of Auguste Chouteau, co-founder of St. Louis. Their children were: Marie Therese, Catherine Emilie, Auguste Aristide, Gabriel Sylvestre, Marie Therese Eulalie, Marie Louise, Emilie Antoinette, Henry Pierre, and Edward Rene.

Chaine – See **Shane, Anthony**.

Chalifoux, Eleonora – The wife of Pierre La Liberte. (See **La Liberte**.)

Chick, Joseph S. (1828-1908) – A son of William Chick, J. S. was an early Kansas City businessman. After a few years in New York, he returned to Kansas City after the Civil War and became prominent in the banking business. Chick contributed his recollections about early days in Kansas City in various articles he wrote and in a 1906 interview for the *Kansas City Star*.

Chick, William (1794-1847) – An early settler in Westport who had opened a store there by 1836. He later moved to Kansas City where he built a warehouse on the levee, about one mile west of the Chouteau warehouse. While the Chouteau establishment was washed away in the flood of 1844, Chick's survived and became a nucleus for post-flood development. William Chick's daughter, Virginia, became the wife of John Calvin McCoy in 1837; another daughter, Mary Jane, married Methodist Missionary William Johnson; yet another daughter, Sarah Ann, married John Polk, brother of Mary Polk, who married Pierre Menard Chouteau.

Chouteau, Auguste (1749-1829) – A son of Marie Therese Bourgeois and Rene Chouteau, Auguste at the age of fourteen founded the city of St. Louis at the direction of the absent Pierre de Laclede Liguest. Under Laclede's guidance, Chouteau developed skills as a fur trader and was especially successful among the Osages. His influence among that tribe, along with that of his brother Pierre Chouteau, brought both Spanish and French government officials to the Chouteaus' doorstep when it was necessary to deal with the Osage Indians. After the Louisiana Purchase, Chouteau adapted to the new United States government and soon made himself indispensable to it, also.

Auguste Chouteau was wealthy, influential, and socially prominent; his businesses included, in addition to the fur trade, a retail store, a gristmill, a distillery, and a bank. His marriage to Marie Therese Cerre produced nine children, among them Gabriel (Seres) Chouteau, cousin, partner, and friend of Francois Chouteau. But it was Auguste's nephew Cadet Chouteau who became the kingpin of the fur trade in the next generation. (See also Foley and Rice, *The First Chouteaus*, and *DMB*.)

Chouteau, Auguste Pierre (1786-1838) – The firstborn son of Pierre Chouteau Sr. and his first wife Pelagie Kiersereau, who was also known as A. P. Chouteau. The Pierre Chouteau Sr. used his influence to secure a West Point appointment for his son who graduated from the academy in 1806, but pursued a military career for only one year before resigning to become a fur trader. A. P. had a reputation as an affable person, well liked and kindly. As a trader he operated in Arkansas for a time, and then settled in Oklahoma. His business enterprises never thrived and he died mired in debt.

Lt. Auguste Pierre Chouteau. MHS.

Chouteau, Benedict Pharamond (1833-1834) – The second of Francois and Berenice's children born in Jackson County (February 23, 1833) and the first baptized there. The first pastor of the Catholic congregation of present Kansas City, Father Benedict Roux, baptized Benedict Pharamond Chouteau on February 27, 1834. The child's first name, Benedict, undoubtedly honored the celebrating priest, and the second name, Pharamond, honored Francois's brother Pharamond, who had died in 1831. Baby Benedict died in St. Louis on August 6, 1834, and was buried in the Old Catholic Cemetery in which his father would be interred four years later. (*Guide to the Microfilm Edition of the Pierre Menard Collection* confuses Benjamin and Benedict; the list of Francois and Berenice's children on page 30 indicates that Benedict Pharamond was married. The next reference, on page 33, is identified as I-3-5-7, Benedict Pharamond, and assigns to him the wife of Benjamin, that is, Ann Toler. Benjamin's reference, which should be I-3-5-4, is missing.)

Chouteau, Benjamin (1828-1876) – A son of Francois and Berenice Chouteau, Ben Chouteau was born on Christmas Day in St. Louis and baptized in that city the following July. He went to school in Jackson County and attended St. Mary's of the Barrens in Perryville, Missouri. Benjamin Chouteau and Ann Toler were married in Jackson County in 1856, and they had four children. Ben never developed a career or had a permanent job. After a life full of illness and disappointment, he died destitute in Kaskaskia. A corrected death date of 1876 was established by Edmond Menard's letter to his sister Berenice, dated December 28, 1876 (*William Morrison Collection*, ISHL).

Benjamin Chouteau. WHMC-KC. This picture of his son may give an impression of Francois Chouteau's appearance.

Chouteau, Berenice (1801-1888) – The daughter of Pierre Menard and his first wife, Marie Therese Michelle Godin, was born Therese Berenice Menard on August 13, 1801, in Kaskaskia, Illinois. She was called "Berenice." (Confusion has arisen as T. B. Chouteau – that is, Therese Berenice Chouteau – has sometimes been mistaken as F. B. Chouteau.) Berenice was the fifth of the six children born before her mother's death in 1804. In 1806, Berenice's father took his second wife, Angelique Saucier. Berenice grew up in an affluent home. (See **Menard, Pierre**.) She was probably tutored in Kaskaskia, and perhaps briefly attended a school for girls during the winter of 1809-1810 that she spent in St. Louis. Berenice could read and write French, and, in later life, English.

In 1819, Berenice married Francois Gesseau Chouteau. His mother, Brigitte Saucier, was half-sister to Berenice's stepmother Angelique Saucier. Francois and Berenice were cousins by marriage only and shared no common bloodline. Berenice had no Saucier blood, for her mother had been a Godin. (Angelique Saucier, Berenice's stepmother, was Francois's aunt.) In the letters collected in *Cher Oncle, Cher Papa*, Francois, when writing to Pierre Menard, addressed him as "*oncle*," because Menard was married to Francois's mother's half-sister. Pierre Menard was also Francois's father-in-law, but this apparently was a less important relationship. Berenice, also, when writing from the Chouteau home in St. Louis to her father in Kaskaskia, sent compliments from "my aunt and uncle" (Pierre and Brigitte Chouteau.)

Berenice and Francois were the parents of nine children. The first seven were boys: Edmond Francois (1821) and Pierre Menard (1822) were born in St. Louis and brought to western Missouri when Berenice and Francois settled there, probably in 1822. The next two sons were also born in St. Louis, both in February: Louis Amadee (1825) and Louis Sylvestre (1827). For these births, Berenice traveled back to St. Louis in the autumn, before the Missouri River froze. Both Amadee and Sylvestre died in infancy. The next child, Benjamin, was born in St. Louis on Christmas Day, 1828. In 1831, while Berenice was expecting another child, Francois became ill. Not wishing to leave him, she remained in western Missouri. Frederic Donatien was born August 24, 1831, the first Chouteau child born in Jackson County. Benedict Pharamond (1833), Mary Brigitte (1835), and Therese Odile (1838) were all born in Jackson County.

After her husband died in 1838, Berenice attempted to run the large Chouteau farm in the East Bottoms. The flood of 1844 destroyed what Francois had left – the fur trading warehouse, the farm buildings, and the Chouteau home. Some acreage was lost to the river, and what remained was made unfit for agriculture by being buried under sand from two to six feet deep. Berenice promptly built her new home on a hill out of the river's reach, and in the 1850s sold her lands in the East Bottoms to Joseph Guinotte. After living in that home nearly fifteen years, Berenice moved to Ste. Genevieve during the Civil War. She returned to Kansas City in 1870 or 1871, and lived the rest of her life in the home of her son Pierre Menard (Mack) Chouteau. Berenice survived her husband by fifty years and outlived all of her nine children. Therese Berenice Menard Chouteau died November 19, 1888, in Kansas City. She was taken to St. Louis to be buried beside her husband in Calvary Cemetery.

Early historians often claimed that Berenice Chouteau was the first white woman to live in western Missouri. While that distinction almost certainly belongs to Madame Grand Louis Bertholet, Berenice's move to western Missouri is significant in that she was one of the first white women to make a real commitment by bringing her "life" here – babies, slaves, furniture – in short, the equipage for permanent residence.

Chouteau, Charles B. (1808-1884) – A son of Pierre Chouteau Sr. and his second wife, Brigitte Saucier Chouteau, Charles was born in St. Louis. He was one of Francois Chouteau's four younger brothers. In 1827, Berenice Menard Chouteau, Francois's wife and Charles's sister-in-law, made arrangements for Charles to move to Kaskaskia and work in the store of her father Pierre Menard. (Berenice's letter to Angelique Menard, dated April 18, 1827, and included in this collection, described the situation that led to this arrangement.) By 1843, Charles Chouteau was working in the fur trade at Frederick's Post on the Kansas River. As late as 1848, Charles was issued a trading license, along with Frederick, to do business with the Kansa Indians. (Note: Charles B. Chouteau should not be confused with the more prominent Charles Pierre Chouteau (1819-1901), the son of Pierre (Cadet) Chouteau Jr., who eventually assumed responsibility for his father's far-flung business empire.)

Chouteau, Cyprien (1802-1879) – A son of Pierre Chouteau Sr. and his second wife, Brigitte Saucier Chouteau, Cyprien was born in St. Louis five years after his brother Francois. Cyprien, like Francois, probably received a patchwork education in St. Louis. He could read, write, and speak both French and English, and probably some Indian languages. In 1822 or 1823, Cyprien came to western Missouri to join Francois in the fur trade business at the Randolph Bluffs trading post, on the north bank of the Missouri River. By 1828, Cyprien was operating a trading post for the Delaware and Shawnee Indians on the south bank of the Kansas River (near present Turner). At some point Cyprien supposedly married an Indian woman, but little is known of this union. In 1855, he married Nancy Francis, the daughter of a Shawnee chief. They had three sons who settled in Oklahoma, and a daughter Mamie, who married Joseph Karl Guinotte of Kansas City. Cyprien was no longer in

Cyprien Chouteau. WHMC-KC.

the fur trade when he sold his land in the Shawnee area, and in 1859, bought a farm between the present Kansas City streets of 24th and 27th, near Kensington. As the area was then rural and isolated, bushwhacker raids were common and soon forced Cyprien and his family into the city proper. They purchased a house at 412 Charlotte, where Cyprien lived until his death in 1879. He is buried in Mount St. Mary's Cemetery.

Chouteau, Edmond Francois (Gesseau, Gesso) (1821-1853) – The eldest son of Francois and Berenice Chouteau, Edmond was usually called "Gesseau," his father's middle name. Edmond Chouteau was born in St. Louis and brought to western Missouri probably in 1822, when he was a little over a year old. He attended a "Mr. Dogles's school" in Independence in 1829. By 1833, Edmond, then twelve, was enrolled at St. Louis College (that is, high school). Later he attended St. Mary's of the Barrens, Perryville, Missouri, where his brother Menard was enrolled. Expelled from the Barrens in 1835, by 1837 Edmond had become a clerk at the American Fur Company store operated by J. B. Sarpy in St. Louis. After the death of his father in 1838, Edmond Chouteau accompanied several fur hunting expeditions to the Rocky Mountains and fought in the war with Mexico in 1846. He died in Kansas City in 1853 and was buried in the Catholic cemetery behind St. Francis Regis Church. His body was moved to Mount St. Mary's Cemetery in 1881, at which time his sister Odile, who died as an infant, was buried with him.

Chouteau, Francois Gesseau (1797-1838) – A son of Pierre Chouteau Sr. and his second wife Brigitte Saucier Chouteau, Francois was born in St. Louis on February 7, 1797, the first of Brigitte's five sons. Francois spent his early childhood among the Osages while his father was commandant of Fort Carondelet during the time of the Chouteau brothers' exclusive trade privilege with the Osages. When that ended in 1802, the family returned to St. Louis where Francois apparently received a day-school education that prepared him for business. He was able to read, write, and keep accounts. (Extensive inquiry turned up no evidence that his schooling extended beyond about the age of fourteen.) He spoke French and English, Osage, and perhaps other Indian languages.

At around the age of fourteen, Francois went back to the Osage country, and under the tutelage of his half-brother, Paul Liguest Chouteau who was trader with the Osage, began his life in the fur trade. Francois and his cousin Gabriel (Seres) Chouteau linked fortunes when Francois was ready to leave the Osage country. Together, Seres and Francois applied for licenses to trade with various tribes west of Missouri, built the Four Houses trading post, and began to do business.

In 1819, Francois married Therese Berenice Menard, a daughter of Pierre Menard of Kaskaskia. According to legend, the young couple sailed in a pirogue up the Missouri River in search of a site for a trading post and their new home. In fact, Pierre Chouteau, Francois's father, was familiar with the area of the Missouri and Kansas rivers. He had spent a winter with the Kansa Indians as a younger man. Probably he suggested that Francois locate near the mouth of the Kansas River, as it was a popular gathering place for Indians. Francois and Berenice came permanently to western Missouri probably in 1822.

Francois's life as a fur trader was a mobile one; he was either on horseback or in a boat taking merchandise up the Kansas River, bringing fur pelts down to the warehouse on the Missouri River (the Kansas City warehouse), taking his family to St. Louis, or engaged in countless other travels. Chouteau's first post, the one at Randolph Bluffs in Clay County, was destroyed by the flood of 1826. Almost immediately he set up a new business on the south bank of the river, near the foot of present Olive. It was to this warehouse that the thousands of furs harvested by the Indians and French hunters and trappers were brought in preparation for the transfer to St. Louis, where they were sent on to either New Orleans or to a destination to the North, en route to their final destination in Europe – probably London or Paris. Eventually Francois Chouteau was the manager of five fur trading establishments: the Kansa Post, the Shawnee Post, the Wea Post, the Kickapoo Post, and the large Kansas City warehouse. But Chouteau recognized a decline in the fur business, partly as a result of over-harvesting of fur-bearing animals. In an effort to diversify, he began to invest a great deal of time and energy in his farm in what is now called the East Bottoms. Chouteau also bought and sold real estate, and served as a one-man banking system on the frontier, as there were no banks. He was highly respected in the area, and considered the leader of the community. Family and close friends called him "Gesseau," while, the American settlers on the frontier, referred to him as "Colonel" Chouteau, a salute to his brief military service and his status among them.

Francois Chouteau took seriously his responsibilities as a family man, and in his letters expressed regret at having to be away from home. He and Berenice had nine children. Francois Chouteau's life was cut short before he saw his many labors come to fruition. He died, probably of a massive heart attack, on April 18, 1838. Berenice took him back to St. Louis, where he was buried in a pioneer Catholic cemetery. His remains were afterward removed to Calvary Cemetery.

Although Francois Chouteau neither envisioned a city nor platted a town, he bids fair to be called the "father of Kansas City," the place where he put down roots and made the location a landmark. In old St. Louis, merchandise sent up the river was marked "Chouteau's Town," steamboat captains told their crews to dock at Chouteau's Landing, the log church atop the rugged hill behind Chouteau's warehouse was called "Chouteau's Church," and the street running on the south side of the church lot (present 12th Street) was known as

"Chouteau Street." Members of the original company forming the Town of Kansas had known Chouteau; the fact that, in the end, the name they chose honored the Kansa, predecessors of them all, in no way diminishes the stature of Francois Chouteau.

Chouteau, Frederic Donatien (1831-1881) – The sixth son of Francois and Berenice Chouteau, born April 14, 1831, at the Chouteau family home in Jackson County. He was the first of Francois and Berenice's children born on the western frontier. Fred attended school in Westport and then had a brief stint at St. Mary's of the Barrens in Perryville. As a young man, he made sporadic attempts to find work in New Mexico and Kansas with little success, as he was plagued with poor health and bad luck. In 1862, Fred married Julia (Adele) Gregoire in Ste. Genevieve. They had two children, Clara and Frederick; the latter, as an adult, legally changed his name from Chouteau to Laclede. Frederic Donatien Chouteau died September 2, 1881, probably in Kansas City. He is buried in Mount St. Mary's Cemetery in Kansas City. (Frederic Donatien should not be confused with his uncle, the pioneer fur trader Frederick Chouteau, who was Francois's brother.)

Chouteau, Frederick (1809-1891) – The youngest son of Pierre Chouteau Sr. and his second wife Brigitte Saucier Chouteau, Frederick was born in St. Louis in 1809. In the fall of 1825, Frederick joined his brothers Francois and Cyprien on the north bank of the Missouri River at Randolph Bluffs to learn the fur trade under the supervision of his brother Francois. By 1829, Frederick was trading among the Kansa Indians at Horseshoe Lake. He moved his post for the Kansa Indians to Mission Creek in 1831-1832. In 1830, Frederick married a Shawnee woman, Nancy Logan (also called Nancy or Elizabeth Tooley). They had three children. He and his family lived on Mill Creek in west Shawnee until the flood of 1844 destroyed their home and farm, after which Frederick built a house on higher ground. According to Frederick's "Reminisces," he closed his Kansa Post on Mission Creek in 1845 and went with the Kansa Indians to their new reservation at Council Grove, Kansas. He remained there until 1852, when he returned to eastern Kansas. Following the death of his first wife, Frederick married Mathilda White. After she died, he married Elizabeth Carpenter, and after her death, he married Elizabeth Ware. Frederick had eleven children by his first three wives.

Frederick Chouteau. KSHS.

During his working years, Frederick also operated a ferry across the Kansas River at Edwardsville and dealt in real estate. Frederick was an adopted son of the Kansa Nation, and, as he was fluent in Shawnee, Kansa, French, and English, represented these tribes in various negotiations. Frederick moved to Westport in 1874 and by 1877 had sold all his land in the Shawnee area. Many of his children moved to Oklahoma with their Native American relatives. Frederick lived the rest of his life in Westport and before his death had become one of the wealthiest men in the area. Frederick Chouteau died in 1891 and is buried in Mount St. Mary's Cemetery.

Chouteau, Frederick Edward – See **Laclede, Frederick**.

Chouteau, Gabriel Sylvestre (Seres, Cerre, "Sara") (1794-1887) – A son of Auguste Chouteau and Marie Therese Cerre, Gabriel, Francois Chouteau's cousin, was called "Seres," a nickname and Americanized spelling of "Cerre," the maiden name of his mother. Seres was Francois Chouteau's first partner in the fur trade, trading with the Kansa and the Osage nations as early as 1816. In 1819, Factor George Sibley at Fort Osage observed a train of packhorses loaded with Indian merchandise owned by "Sara" Chouteau. During the winter of 1819, Seres and Francois built the "Four Houses" trading post. (See **Four Houses**.) By 1822, the Seres-Francois partnership had dissolved, and Seres moved to the Upper Missouri where he operated a trading post. Francois's letter of July 14, 1837, reported that his friend Cerre was delivering a gift of Indian craftsmanship to Pierre Menard.

Chouteau, James G. (b. 1815) – The natural son of Francois Chouteau and Marie of the Osages, born January 12, 1815, and baptized May 12, 1822, by Rev. Charles de la Croix at the Osage Village. Godparents for James were Pierre Papin(?) and Madame Williams. A James Chouteau, age ten, was admitted to the Harmony Mission School (Bates County, Missouri) on October 10, 1823. He also received an allotment of land in the 1825 Osage Treaty. It can be assumed that he moved with the tribe to Oklahoma. The name of James Chouteau continued to appear in the Osage register of baptisms until 1870, though this likely was not always the same person. A curious and inconsistent entry exists in the Necrology Scrapbook at the Missouri Historical Society in St. Louis, which states that a James Chouteau, "son of Pierre Chouteau," died in 1883 at the St. Vincent's Institution for the Insane. He reportedly had been an inmate for twenty-two years and was ninety-six years old. This may have been Francois's son and the newspaper reporter seriously confused the family relationship and dates.

Chouteau, Jean Pierre – See **Chouteau, Pierre Sr.**

Chouteau, Louis Amadee (1825-1826) – The fourth child of Francois and Berenice Chouteau was born in St. Louis on Feburary 16, 1825, and died there in October 1826, after a brief interlude on the western frontier. The cause of death was not recorded, but it was the time of "summer fever." Louis Amadee was buried in the pioneer cemetery of St. Louis, on the Mississippi riverbank, next to the Old Cathedral.

Chouteau, Louis Sylvestre (1827-1829) – The fourth child of Francois and Berenice Chouteau. Born in St. Louis, he was nicknamed "Morgan," perhaps in honor of the Chouteaus' friend, Daniel Morgan Boone. The child was a toddler in the Chouteau home in western Missouri, but died of a summer illness on July 13, 1829, in St. Louis, and was buried in the Old Cathedral cemetery.

Chouteau, Marie Therese (1733-1814) – The grandmother of Francois Chouteau, Marie Therese Bourgeois was born in New Orleans. She married a French baker named Rene Auguste Chouteau, and they became the parents of at least one child, Auguste Chouteau. (Some genealogies list an elder son, Rene, of whom nothing is known.) Rene Chouteau deserted his family and apparently went back to France. Marie Therese cast her fate with Pierre de Laclede Liguest and in 1764 moved up the Mississippi to Laclede's new trading center, St. Louis. The couple had four children: Jean Pierre (Pierre Chouteau Sr., the father of Francois Chouteau), Marie Pelagie, Marie Louise, and Victoire. Marie Therese lived with Laclede for fifty years, but their children bore the name "Chouteau" since she never divorced her husband, Rene. Despite the irregularity of her marital status, Madame Chouteau was the *Grande Dame* of St. Louis.

Marie Therese Chouteau. WHMC-KC.

Chouteau, Mary Brigitte (1835-1864) – A daughter of Francois and Berenice Chouteau, Mary Brigitte was born on the Chouteau farm in Jackson County. She eloped with steamboat captain Ashley Hopkins in 1853 and moved to Ste. Genevieve. Mary Brigitte later moved to St. Louis where she died of cholera and was buried in Calvary Cemetery. Her only child died in infancy.

Mary Brigitte Chouteau. WHMC-KC. This picture of her daughter may suggest how Berenice Chouteau appeared when she came to western Missouri.

Chouteau, Paul Liguest (1792-1851) – The son of Pierre Chouteau Sr. and Pelagie Kiersereau Chouteau, Paul Liguest spent his childhood among the Osages while his father commanded Fort Carondelet. Usually called "Liguest," he was five years older than his half-brother Francois. Liguest was trading with the Osage Indians by 1816, and coached young Francois in the procedures of the fur business. While he was still listed as an Osage trader, Paul Liguest was appointed subagent for the Osages. This probably occurred in 1824 when an agency was established for the tribe. In May 1830, P. L. Chouteau was appointed agent for the Osage Agency. Later that position reverted to subagent. Liguest's first wife was Constance Dubreuil, and they had five children. After her death in 1824, he married Aurora Hay; they had a son. Liguest's half-brothers Francois, Cyprien, Frederick, and Charles had frequent contact with him, since his operation was only 100 miles south of them on the Marais des Cygne.

Chouteau, Pharamond (1806-1831) – The third son of Pierre Chouteau Sr. and Brigitte Saucier Chouteau, Pharamond was born in St. Louis in 1806. He worked briefly in the fur trade with Francois, but was never in good health and died at age twenty-five.

Chouteau, Pierre Jr. (Cadet) (1789-1865) – A half-brother to Francois Chouteau, Pierre was known as "Cadet," French for "younger brother." The father of both was Pierre Chouteau Sr., but Cadet's mother was Pelagie Kiersereau. When John Jacob Astor's American Fur Company began operations in St. Louis, Cadet Chouteau became the head of its Western Department. Francois Chouteau's letters to Pierre Menard frequently mentioned his brother Cadet. Francois's surviving letters to Cadet deal chiefly with business such as shipments of Indian trade goods Francois had ordered from the American Fur Company store in St. Louis that Cadet operated. Cadet Chouteau was a dominant figure in the fur trade from the late 1820s until the fur trade waned in the 1840s.

Cadet Chouteau was married to Emilie Gratiot, and they had five children. He was involved in many business ventures, among them lead mining and real estate. He

Pierre Chouteau, Jr. [Cadet]. MHS.

became quite wealthy, was politically active, and was an important presence in St. Louis society. (See also Foley and Rice, *The First Chouteaus*, and *DMB*.)

Chouteau, Pierre Sr. (1758-1849) – This prominent resident of St. Louis was the son of Marie Therese Bourgeois and Pierre de Laclede Liguest. Pierre Chouteau was born in New Orleans and brought to St. Louis by his mother and Laclede. Inasmuch as his mother never divorced her husband Rene Chouteau, Pierre Chouteau Sr., in accordance with French law, bore the name Chouteau rather than Laclede. Early in his career, Pierre Chouteau gained control of the lucrative Osage trade and set into motion the longstanding goodwill and friendship between many Indian tribes and the Chouteau family that resulted in the great successes of the Chouteaus in the fur trade. Chouteau's first wife, Pelagie Kiersereau, bore four children: Auguste Pierre (A. P.); Pierre Jr. (Cadet); Pelagie; and Paul Liguest. Pierre's first wife died in 1793, and he took as his second wife Brigitte Saucier. Their children were Francois, Cyprien, Pharamond, Charles, and Frederick. Pierre Chouteau Sr. died in St. Louis and is buried in Calvary Cemetery. (See also *DMB*, and Foley and Rice, *The First Chouteaus*.)

Pierre Chouteau Sr. WHMC-KC.

Chouteau, Pierre Menard (1822-1885) – The second son of Francois and Berenice, was born in St. Louis and came to western Missouri when he was about three or four months old. Called "Menard" as a child and young man, Pierre Menard Chouteau was later known as "Mack." Menard attended school locally until he was about eleven years old, when he was sent to St. Mary's of the Barrens, Perryville, Missouri. He studied there until his father died in 1838. As an adult, he was in the fur trade, steamboat business, and several other enterprises. In 1849, he married Mary Polk; they had six children. Pierre Menard Chouteau was elected treasurer of the Town of Kansas in 1853 and also served in that office in the 1870s. He lived most of his life in Kansas City and died there in 1885 as a result of injuries in a train accident. He is buried in Mount St. Mary's Cemetery.

Pierre Menard Chouteau. WHMC-KC.

Chouteau, Therese Odile (1838-1840) – The last of Francois and Berenice Chouteau's nine children, Odile was born in January, only three months before her father died. Odile's death date was not recorded, but the internal evidence of Berenice's letter of December 19, 1840 (*PMC*), suggests that she died in the autumn of that year. In addition, J. S. Chick, in his later life, made a sworn affidavit that Odile had died "in infancy." She was buried in the cemetery near St. Francis Regis Church (first called "Chouteau's Church"); after Mount St. Mary's Cemetery opened, her casket was moved there and buried in a grave with her brother Edmond Francois (Gesseau) Chouteau.

Chouteau's Church – The log church built for the Catholics of western Missouri, mostly by funds donated by Francois and Berenice Chouteau, and therefore called "Chouteau's Church." In 1839, Jesuit missionary priest Father Herman Aelen renamed the church St. Francis Regis. The church was located at 11th and Pennsylvania on a ten-acre plot then owned by the first pastor of the French Catholics, Father Benedict Roux. It stood until 1858 when it was torn down (the log rectory near it survived until the 1880s) and replaced by a brick structure. The present Cathedral of the Immaculate Conception at 11th and Broadway sits on what remains of the ten acres.

"*Westport*," drawn by Nicolas Point, S.J. ASJCF. St. Francis Regis Church (Chouteau's Church).

Chouteau's Landing – See **River of Kansas Post**.

Marston G. Clark. WHMC-KC.

Clark, Marston Greene (1769-1846) – Born in Lunenburg County, Virginia, Clark moved to Indiana in the early 1790s where he engaged in a variety of occupations, including farmer, tavern keeper, surveyor, ferry operator, and occasional member of the Indiana General Assembly and Senate. He had an illustrious military career during the Indian Wars, including service as aide-de-camp to General William Henry Harrison's army on its march to the Battle of Tippecanoe. Rising to the rank of Major General by 1825, he was sometimes called "General" Clark in local records. (He is not to be confused with his cousin William Clark of Lewis and Clark fame, who was Superintendent of Indian Affairs, St. Louis; William Clark was also known as "General Clark.") Marston G. Clark was subagent for the Kansa Indians from February 1829 until August 1834, when the Kansa Agency was closed. Clark then accepted an appointment as subagent for the Shawnees, but left in 1835 to return to Indiana. He again served in the Indiana General Assembly (1835-1836) and in Whig politics, including as a presidential elector for Harrison during the 1840 election. Marston Clark died at his home in Salem, Washington County, Indiana, on July 25, 1846. His son George Clark appeared in the Kansas River area briefly in 1834. (For additional information on the Marston Clark–Chouteau brothers feud, see William E. Unrau, *The Kansa Indians*.)

Clark, William (1770-1838) – Explorer of the Lewis and Clark expedition fame, William Clark was born in Virginia, and early in life set his sights on a military career. His elder brother, George Rogers Clark, had established himself as a national hero, and William aimed to follow in his footsteps. Although William Clark played a significant role in Missouri history, he is best known as the intrepid explorer of the trackless west, the skilled Indian diplomat, and tireless diarist of the Corps of Discovery.

William Clark.
WHMC-KC.

In the Chouteau letters, William Clark is known as "General Clark," Superintendent of Indian Affairs in St. Louis from 1807 until his death in 1838. He supervised the enforced migration of the eastern Indians tribes to Indian Territory (Kansas or Oklahoma), and attempted to carry out government policy in a humane way. The Chouteaus, including Francois, were generally on quite friendly terms with William Clark.

The position of Superintendent of Indian Affairs was awarded to Clark after he and Meriwether Lewis returned from their successful exploration of the Missouri River to its source, and then crossed the mountains to reach the Pacific Ocean. This journey provided President Jefferson the information that there was no continuous water route to the Pacific. Clark, an even-tempered, patient man, counterbalanced Lewis's fiery enthusiasm and lent stability to the expedition.

After his return from the journey to the Pacific, Clark married Julia Hancock, cousin to George Hancock Kennerly, who married Modeste Alzire Menard, Berenice Chouteau's sister. When his first wife died, Clark married Kennerly's widowed sister, Harriet Kennerly Radford. By the two marriages, Clark had seven children, two of whom died in infancy. William Clark died in St. Louis and was buried there. (See also *DMB*.)

Clermont (II) (d. 1828) – An Osage Indian chief who, in 1802-1803, was encouraged by Pierre Chouteau to move his band of people from the Osage River in Missouri to the Verdigris River in northern Oklahoma. The missionary William F. Vaill wrote that Clermont was, "a man of noble countenance and stately figure of robust constitution, and vigorous intellectual powers.... He was...[an] intriguing politician, and a most eloquent speaker."† Clermont died in May 1828. Descendants bearing his name were also distinguished leaders. The town of Claremore, Oklahoma, not far from the Osage village, was named in honor of the "chiefs Clermont." (See also *DMB*.)

† Grant Foreman, *Indians and Pioneers: The Story of the American Southwest before 1830*, 136.

Comanche Indians – A segment of the Shoshones, the Comanches were first heard of around the Green River in Wyoming, and when they acquired horses by the early eighteenth century, they migrated south following buffalo herds. By the nineteenth century they were in the southern plains, that is, southern Arkansas, Oklahoma, and northern Texas.

Connor, James (Ah-lah-a-chick) – A Delaware Indian of importance who, in 1832, worked as an interpreter at the Delaware-Shawnee Agency. Jim Connor (or Connors) was the Connor mentioned frequently in the Chouteau letters. Connor was involved in government-Indian negotiations for many years, and his signature is found on treaties and documents.

Cornstock, Peter – A principal chief of the Shawnee Nation, he signed the treaty of 1826, whereby the Shawnees gave up their land in the United States and agreed to move to Indian Territory (Kansas). Cornstock led bands of Shawnees from Ohio to Indian Territory in 1828 and 1832. In Chouteau's letter of November 3, 1829, his name was spelled "Cornstok."

Coureurs de bois – A French phrase meaning unlicensed fur trader and/or hunter, trapper. (Literal translation: a messenger or traveler of the woods.)

Credits – A term, in most cases, meaning debits; in these letters "credit" means the amount owed by the Indians to the trader. This amount was deducted from the Indians' annuities or payment for furs and *credited* to the Indians' account.

Cree Indians – Native Americans whose original home was eastern Canada. They gradually migrated to western Canada and into Montana to hunt buffalo. At present, 76,000 Cree Indians live in Canada and about 2,000 live on reservations in Montana.

Creole – In these letters, a person born in Louisiana of French or Spanish parents, or a person born in the Gulf states of part black and part French or Spanish parents.

Crooks, Ramsey (1787-1859) – Born in Scotland, Crooks came to Montreal in 1805. By 1807, he was in St. Louis, active in the fur trade. He became general manager of John Jacob Astor's American Fur Company, and when Astor sold the company in 1834, Crooks bought the Northern Department. (Cadet Chouteau and associates bought the Western Department.) Under Crooks's ownership, the company maintained the name American Fur Company.

Cummins, Richard – The Indian agent for the Shawnee Agency beginning in 1830, when he replaced George Vashon. In 1834, all of Indian Territory (Kansas) was divided into two subagencies: one for the Osages and one for all the rest. The Shawnee Agency at that time was responsible for the Shawnees, Delawares, Piankeshaws, Weas, Peorias, and Kaskaskias. Cummins remained agent until the Indian Department once more shuffled tribal responsibility in 1837 and created the Fort Leavenworth Agency with Cummins as its agent. In 1849, he was "removed." Francois Chouteau suggested that Cummins was a mild-mannered man who attempted to get along with everyone.

Curtis, Cyrus (1784-1844) – An Indian trader in partnership with Michael Eley, both of whom had come down from the Upper Missouri trade. (See also **Eley, Michael**.) Curtis received his first license to trade with Indians on the Missouri and its waters in September 1817. He may also have been associated with Andrew Woods in addition to his partnership with Eley; in an April 30, 1820, letter from Cadet Chouteau to Serre Chouteau, Cadet lamented the great competition at the mouth of the Kansas among the three traders (the Curtis-Eley structure was near the post of Woods). Later that year in November, J. B. Sarpy wrote to Sere that he "presume these two great men, Woods and Curtis, are doing all that is in their power to crush you."† Curtis and Eley received a one-year license in July 1822 to trade with the Osage, Kansa, Otoe, and Ponca Indians. Prince Paul, on his 1823 tour, referred to the two "large houses" of Curtis and Woods, apparently each operating separately. (See also **Woods, Andrew**, and **Wuerttemberg, Prince Paul Wilhelm of**.) According to Prince Paul, the Curtis-Eley post was in Indian Territory (Kansas), near the mouth of the Kansas River, on its right bank (present Kansas City, Kansas). Curtis and Eley were granted a two-year license in September 1823. Although this was their last recorded license, they apparently operated their post after the license expired. In the early days of Francois Chouteau's Randolph Bluffs post – that is, 1822-1826 – his chief competitors were Curtis and Eley. They were loosely associated with the American Fur Company, while Francois Chouteau's arrangement with that firm was apparently more binding and specific, probably because his brother Cadet headed the operation that included Chouteau's post.‡ What happened to the Curtis and Eley post is not known (it was no longer open in the 1830s). Its operators went their separate ways: Eley to Santa Fe and Curtis to Liberty, where he was doing business by 1825. Cyrus Curtis died in Liberty, Missouri, in 1844.

† Pierre Chouteau Jr. to C. G. [sic] Chouteau, April 30, 1820; John B. Sarpy to G. S. Chouteau, November 6, 1820, *Chouteau Family Collection*, MHS.

‡ Barry, *Beginning of the West*, 99-100; "Fur posts at Kawsmouth," Chouteau's (Topical) Scrapbook [17.1], (KC395), WHMC-KC.

Cyprien's Post – See **Shawnee Post** or **Chouteau, Cyprien**.

Dagenai – A name variously spelled "Dajane," (by Chouteau) and "Dashney," or "Dashnay," in letters by John Campbell and Richard Graham. The latter two, employed by the Office of Indian Affairs under the auspices of the War Department, revealed that a Noel Dashney was employed by the department as an interpreter, probably among the Weas.

Datchurut – A family name in Ste. Genevieve in 1769.† Frederick Chouteau reported that Baptiste Datchurut "had been living among the Kaw Indians for a good many years, and could speak their language well, and was the interpreter for the Kaws. He had a Kaw wife. He came from St. Louis a free Negro...."‡ "Big Baptiste" was a boatman sometimes employed by Francois Chouteau to steer a keelboat or pirogue to St. Louis on the Missouri River. Towards the end of his life when he became gravely ill, his brother Zabette brought Baptiste to Frederick Chouteau's house and asked him to care for Baptiste. Frederick agreed to do so, and Baptiste died there. Zabette followed the river keel-boating, sometimes for the American Fur Company, going way up on the Yellowstone. He was a rough fellow."‡

† Houck, *History of Missouri*, 2: 26.

‡ "Reminiscences of Frederick Chouteau," *Kansas Historical Collection* 8: 428.

Davy, Cornelius (d. 1853) – A prominent resident of Independence during the 1830s and 1840s, Davy was a leader of a group of Independence businessmen who raised money to help purchase a building to serve as a Catholic church. Davy was a freighter on the Santa Fe Trail and in 1853 was killed on that trail. In his will Davy left land for an Independence cemetery.

De La Croix, Charles (1792-1869) – A Catholic missionary priest who is supposed to have come to the mouth of the Kansas River in 1822; there is, however, no documentation to support this story. Father de La Croix did travel to the Osage Indian villages in 1821 and 1822. The record of his religious activities there is kept in the archives of the Diocese of Wichita, Kansas.

Delaware Indians – The most important tribe of the Algonquian Confederacy when Europeans came to North America, the Delawares lived in the Delaware River basin in New Jersey, Delaware, eastern Pennsylvania, and southeastern New York. They were hunters and also raised crops. The Delawares were pushed westward by other Indian tribes and white settlers, and by the 1820s, were near the White River in Missouri, where William Gilliss traded with them. By 1829, they had arrived in Indian Territory (Kansas) at the reservation assigned to them on the north bank of the Kansas River in present Wyandotte and Douglas counties. By the twentieth century, most of the Delawares had moved to Oklahoma and joined the Cherokee Nation.

Francois Chouteau and other French fur traders in Missouri referred to the Delawares as "Loups." While there is no clear explanation for this, several elements in the Delaware culture support the designation. These people referred to themselves as "Lenape," and one subtribe of that group was the "Minsi," who honored as their totemic animal the wolf, or, *loup* (French for wolf). (For more on this topic, see Chapter 3, note 28 on page 62, following letter of Chouteau to Menard dated August 20, 1829.)

De Smet, Pierre Jean (Peter), S.J. (1801-1873) – A Belgian Catholic priest of the Jesuit order who led missions to the Indians of the Northwest. De Smet devoted his life to the service of his church, his adopted country, and the Native Americans who called him "Blackrobe." It is estimated that he traveled 180,000 miles on horseback in his lifetime. De Smet's unique relationship with Native Americans was legendary. He learned their languages, respected their culture, and valued their friendship. Father De Smet was well known in western Missouri, as he traveled through Westport on his journeys to the Northwest. In May 1841, De Smet's missionary group was joined in Westport by Father Nicolas Point, who had temporarily served as pastor at St. Francis Regis Church (see **Point, Nicolas, S.J.**). Until the end of his life, Father De Smet worked for the causes in which he believed. (See also *DMB*.)

Donnelly, Bernard (1810-1880) – A Catholic priest, native of Ireland, ordained at St. Mary's of the Barrens, Perryville, Missouri, in 1845. Father Donnelly was appointed pastor of Independence, with missions at Town of Kansas, Westport, Liberty, Clay County, and "about a hundred other places," according to him. In 1858, he became pastor of Immaculate Conception Church, which had replaced the log church of St. Francis Regis in Kansas City. Father Donnelly was particularly fond of the French parishioners in his charge and recorded information and stories about them in his journal and in church records. During the Civil War Battle of Westport, Father Donnelly spent hours on the battlefield, ministering to and comforting the wounded and dying of both Confederate and Union armies. Father Donnelly was a great civic booster and personally solicited support for the railroad bridge to cross the Missouri River. Father Donnelly is buried in Mount St. Mary's Cemetery, Kansas City.

Dorion – A man of mixed blood with the name Dorion (first name unknown), he was a trader on the Upper Missouri in the early 1800s. The name Dorion also appeared on the roster of the Lewis and Clark expedition. Pierre Dorion, probably the son of the Lewis and Clark Dorion, was an interpreter in expeditions to the Upper Missouri. A grandson, Baptiste Dorion, was an interpreter on the steamboat *Yellow Stone* during the 1830s.

Dougherty, John A. (1791-1860) – An Indian agent and fur trader born near Bardstown, Kentucky, Dougherty came to St. Louis before he was twenty. He entered the fur trade as a trapper and trader in the Nebraska and Dakotas region, but returned to St. Louis, and in 1823 was married there. Dougherty was well known around Council Bluffs where he served as deputy Indian agent. When Agent O'Fallon retired in 1826, Dougherty became Indian agent of the Upper Missouri and remained in that position until 1839. After spending most of his life on the frontier, both in the fur trade and as a government worker in the Indian Department, Dougherty retired in 1855 to a costly home in Liberty, Missouri, where he died and was buried. Dougherty is mentioned several times in the Chouteau letters; he was one of the passengers on the ill-fated keelboat *Beaver*. He is not to be confused with the Native American whose last name was Dougherty, also mentioned in a Chouteau letter.

Maj. John Dougherty. MHS.

Draft – A check, also called an "order" or a notice that "we will draw on you" for money. This exchange of papers made possible the sale of merchandise and services on the frontier without the use of real money. Hard currency was difficult to obtain and a banking system had not yet been introduced. Financial transactions usually consisted of letters and notes notifying a person or company that some amount was being deducted from or added to their funds. At other times, a letter requested the recipient to pay some amount of money to the bearer of a signed note.

Drips, Andrew (1789-1860) – A "mountain man" associated with various fur companies, including the American Fur Company. In 1842, he was appointed Indian agent for the Upper Missouri Agency. When his term as agent was completed in 1846, he returned to the fur trade. His daughter Catherine, whose mother was an Otoe Indian, was educated in St. Louis and married William Mulkey of Kansas City.

Maj. Andrew Drips. MHS.

Eley, Michael (Ely, Elie) (d. 1832) – A trader born in Virginia, Eley came to Fort Osage in July 1815 to serve as assistant factor. He remained there until 1820 and then apparently joined Cyrus Curtis in a partnership to trade with the Indians. Their trading post was in Indian Territory near the mouth of the Kansas River. The Curtis-Eley post survived the 1826 flood, but the partnership dissolved around that time and Eley moved to Santa Fe in 1827, where he died in 1832. (See also **Curtis, Cyrus**.)

Ellsworth, Henry L. (1791-1858) – A government-appointed commissioner who came to Indian Territory (Kansas) in August 1833 to investigate the living conditions of the immigrant Native Americans, and to mediate a peace among several disputing tribes. Ellsworth and his party spent several months in Indian Territory in 1833-1834.

Engagee – A French word meaning a hired person. (See also *Voyageur*.)

Factory – In the context of the fur trade, a factory was a government-established fortified trading post operated by government employees (superintended by a "Factor") and military personnel. At these posts, the government set prices on trade goods and the value of furs. The purpose of the factory system was to regulate the fur trade and prevent inflated or depressed prices. Although the factory system operated from 1796 to 1822, it was never effective because the government did not prevent free-lance traders from bargaining with the Indians, undercutting the government price on trade goods, or paying more for furs than the government posts would pay. Enforcement of regulations was nearly impossible in the rugged territory west of the Mississippi, and the factory system was discontinued in 1822.

Fish – See **Jackson, William**.

Fontenelle, Lucien (1800?-1840) – A fur trader Fontenelle in 1825, had a one-year license to trade at the mouth of the Kansas River.† By 1830, he and Andrew Drips formed a partnership for a fur trade business and operated a trading post near present Bellevue, Nebraska. Fontenelle and Drips brought their furs through the region of present Kansas City, both by packhorse and boat. Fontenelle abandoned his mountain trade in 1839, and lived with his family near Bellevue until his death in the spring of 1840, caused by the excessive use of liquor.

† *H. Doc. No. 118*, 19th Cong., 1st sess. (Serial 136); S. Doc. No. 58, 19th Cong. 2nd sess. (Serial 146).

Fort Carondelet – A fortified trading post among the Osage Indians built by Auguste and Pierre Chouteau in 1794-1795 on Osage land in present Vernon County, Missouri. The fort was named after Spanish official Baron Francisco Luis Hector de Carondelet. (Spain then controlled Louisiana Territory, where the fort was located.) Pierre Chouteau Sr. and his family lived at Fort Carondelet until 1802, when the Chouteaus lost their monopoly of the Osage trade and abandoned the fort.

Fort Cavagnial – The first military post in Kansas, built by the French in 1744 on the Missouri River in present Leavenworth County, Kansas. The fort was named in honor of the then-governor of French Louisiana, Francois Pierre Rigaud, baron de Cavagnial. Its first commandant was Francois Coulon de Villiers. The fort was intended to regulate the fur trade and supervise the Kansa Indians, but it was never effective. It was abruptly abandoned in 1764. (See also "Fort de Cavagnial: Imperial France in Kansas, 1744-1764," by Charles E. Hoffhaus.)

Fort Gibson – A military post located in Oklahoma on the Grand River, in present Muskogee County. It was founded in 1824 to stabilize the area where the Osage Nation lived. The fort was abandoned and reopened several times, and it figured in the Civil War. In 1936, Fort Gibson was restored as an historic landmark.

Fort Leavenworth Agency – The agency created in 1837 by the Office of Indian Affairs and responsible for the Delaware, Kansa, Shawnee, and Kickapoo Indians. Richard Cummins was named agent. The Fort Leavenworth Agency was not located at the military installation of Fort Leavenworth, but occupied the buildings formerly used by the Shawnee Agency, "five or six miles nearly south of the mouth of the Kansas River, on the north east corner of the Shawnee land and between their principal settlements and the whites"† (i.e., just across the state line, south of Westport, in present Johnson County). Agencies that intermittently used facilities at the military establishment of Fort Leavenworth were the Council Bluffs Agency and the Upper Missouri Agency.

† Richard Cummins to William Clark, May 18, 1838, *OIA, Fort Leavenworth Agency, 1824-1851, 1836-38*, M234, Microfilm roll 751.

Fort Leavenworth, Kansas – See **Leavenworth, Henry**.

Fort Orleans – See **Bourgmont, Etienne de Veniard Sieur de**.

Fort Osage – A military and trading post on a site chosen by William Clark as he and Lewis returned from their journey to the Pacific, Fort Osage was originally called Fort Clark. It was built on a high bluff overlooking the Missouri River, forty river miles east of present Kansas City. Fort Osage was one of two government factories replacing Belle Fontaine, the first trading factory in the Louisiana Purchase. Fort Osage opened in 1808 with George Sibley as the first factor and was closed in 1822 when the factory system was dismantled. (See also *The Genesis of Missouri* by William Foley, and George Sibley in *DMB*.)

Reconstructed Fort Osage. WHMC-KC.

Four Houses – A trading post built in 1819 by Seres Chouteau and his cousin Francois Chouteau, it was located about twenty land miles above the mouth of the Kansas River, where Cedar Creek empties into the Kansas River. It was probably on the north bank. Its name is descriptive: four log houses built in a square with their corners touching, thus forming a fort-like structure with an open courtyard in the center. This post was abandoned in 1828 or 1829 when the new Chouteau Kansa Post was opened on Horseshoe Lake.

Fox Indians – See **Sac and Fox Indians**.

Frederick's Post – See **Kansa Post** and **Chouteau, Frederick**.

Fremont, John Charles (1813-1890) – A military officer and explorer born in Virginia of a French father and an American mother, Fremont surveyed the route of the Oregon Trail and promoted the advantages of Oregon and northern California. He led several expeditions to that area, and his glowing reports aroused widespread interest. Edmond F. Chouteau was sometimes a member of Fremont's party. In the Civil War, Fremont supported the Union. He was married to Jessie Benton, the daughter of United States Senator Thomas Hart Benton from Missouri. (See also *DMB*.)

French Fur Company – The Berthold, Chouteau, and Pratte operation that sponsored Francois Chouteau's first Missouri River trading post, established in the early 1820s. The firm was also known as the French Northwest Trading Company or the French Fur Company. In 1826, John Jacob Astor bought the company and made it the Western Department of the American Fur Company.

French Settlement – Another name for Kawsmouth, used especially by nineteenth-century historians. (See also **Kawsmouth**.)

Gauthier, Margaret – See **Bertholet, Madame Grand Louis**.

Gilliss, William (1788?-1869) – A fur trader and prominent Kansas Citian, Gilliss was born in Maryland of a French mother and a Scottish father. He ran away to sea at the age of fourteen and was still a young man when he abandoned his maritime career and came up the Mississippi from New Orleans. Eventually he moved with his mother and brother to Kaskaskia, Illinois. He was listed on the 1830 Missouri Census as residing in Ste. Genevieve. Gilliss became associated with Menard and Valle in the fur trade, doing business with the immigrant Indians living in camps in the central Missouri Ozarks. His trading post at the James River captured a great deal of the Indian trade. Gilliss lived with the Delaware Indians and was adopted into their tribe. Around 1830, Gilliss, following the Delaware Indians, moved to the valley of the Kansas and Missouri  William Gilliss. WHMC-KC. rivers. As the fur trade diminished, Gilliss became a merchant, land speculator, and civic promoter in Kansas City, where he lived until his death. (See also *DMB* and "Trader William Gilliss and Delaware Migration in Southern Missouri," by Lynn Morrow.)

Giraud, Michael – See **Trading Post**.

Glover, Colonel John – A potential western Missouri settler who left his home in Kentucky in October 1826 to explore the land both north and south of the Missouri River near the mouth of the Kansas River. Glover's diary of the trip described his progress, noted the topography of the land, and recorded his expenses. His diary, brief and to the point, provides an early record of a variety of sites in western Missouri. He quite clearly stated that he went past Chouteau's (Shotoe's) place on the south bank of the Missouri River, thus indicating that after the spring flood of 1826, Chouteau wasted no time in getting into business on the south bank, since Glover's observations were made in October or early November 1826. Apparently Glover never moved to Missouri.

Godin, Marie Therese Michelle (1773-1804) – The mother of Berenice Menard Chouteau, Marie Therese Godin was born in Kaskaskia to parents of French heritage. She married Pierre Menard at Immaculate Conception Church in Kaskaskia in 1792, and they had five children: Marie Odile, Marie Josephine (died at age two), Pierre Jr., Hippolyte (died at age seven), Therese Berenice, and Modeste Alzire. Marie Godin Menard died at age thirty-one.

Gonville, Mary Josephine (Josette) (1817?-1845) – A daughter of Louis Gonville and a Kansa woman who was either the niece or daughter of Kansa Chief White Plume. Josette was raised in the home of Francois and Berenice Chouteau, who served as her godparents when she was baptized in April 1835. She married Joseph Papin in October 1837 in Chouteau's Church. Josette is thought to be the first "white" child born in Kansas. By reason of her Kansa mother, Josette received one of the twenty-three "half-breed tracts" west of Topeka for which Chief White Plume had successfully negotiated in the Treaty of 1825. Louis Gonville, Josette's father, was issued a trading license in 1807, apparently to do business on the Kansas River. By 1819, Gonville was living in the Kansa village. In 1828, Isaac McCoy brought a group through the Kansa village where White Plume lived, and pressed Louis Gonville into service as an interpreter although he spoke almost no English.

Graham, Richard (1780-1857) – An Indian agent for the Osage, Delaware, and Kickapoo Indians, Graham was appointed April 2, 1821. He was then employed June 7, 1824, as agent for the Delaware and Shawnee Indians and from 1828 to 1829 served as agent for the Shawnees. He was "discharged" in 1829 and subsequently defended his financial records to his superiors. After he left the Indian Department, Graham tried his hand at the Rocky Mountain fur trade, then moved on to California during the Gold Rush. Instead of looking for gold, he set up a sawmill and made his fortune.

Richard Graham.
MHS.

Grand Louis – See **Bertholet, Louis**.

Grey, John (Gray, Gre, Ignace Hatchiorauquasha) (179?-1843?) – Grey was the English name of a French-Iroquois man who became an Iroquois leader and worked in the fur trade as a hunter, trapper, and guide in the northwest Rocky Mountains. He and his wife Mary Ann Charles, a French and one-quarter blood Mohawk (Iroquois Confederacy) were natives of western New York State. Their children were Thomas Grey, Mitchal(?) Grey, Charlotte Grey LaGruthe(?), Margaret Grey Johndraw, and Cecelia Grey Uneau McDaniel. In 1835 or 1836,

John Grey and his wife Mary Ann Charles (?) drawn by Nicolas Point, S.J. WSUL.

Grey and his family, as well as perhaps ten other French-Indian families, joined the small community of trappers and farmers in "French Settlement," or Kawsmouth (present West Bottoms). Grey served as guide for Father Peter De Smet's 1841 missionary expedition to Oregon Territory, of which Father Nicolas Point was a member.

Grinter, Moses (1810-1878) – The operator of the Kansas River ferry for the Delaware Indians, in 1836, Grinter married Anna Marshall, the half-Delaware daughter of trader William Marshall. The Grinters had ten children. In the late 1850s, the Grinters built a two-story brick house on the north bank of the Kansas River, west of the old military road that ran from Fort Leavenworth to Fort Scott. (The house has been preserved.) Across the river from Grinter's house was the "Shawnee establishment" (Cyprien's Post.) The Grinter Ferry (also called Delaware Ferry and Military Ferry) was much in demand by travelers on the Oregon and California trails. James Grinter, a younger brother of Moses, assisted in the operation of the ferry.

Guinotte, Joseph (d. 1867) – A Belgian immigration agent, Guinotte came to western Missouri by way of Mexico, where he had lived for a time. His function was to arrange passage, housing, and employment for Belgians who agreed to come to the United States, most of them as farm workers. In 1853, Guinotte purchased land left to Berenice Chouteau by her husband, Francois: 373 acres lying east of Troost and north of Independence Avenue in the "East Bottoms." It became known as the Guinotte Addition. Guinotte also acquired 131 acres of Chouteau land at the river and State Line. In the early 1850s, Guinotte brought a contingent of Belgians to the East Bottoms. Nearly two-thirds of the colony died of cholera, apparently contracted en route from New Orleans. The victims were buried in a mass grave on the bank of the Missouri River. Guinotte brought an educated young woman from France to be his frontier bride. Joseph and Aimee Guinotte's children were: Jules, Joseph Karl, Lydia, and Emma. Two historic families of Kansas City were united when Cyprien Chouteau's daughter, Mary Francis, married Karl Guinotte.

Half-breed – See *Metis*.

Hopkins, Ashley C. (d. 1867) – A steamboat captain who in 1853 married Mary Brigitte Chouteau, daughter of Francois and Berenice. Hopkins had owned the steamboat *Australia*, and in 1856 purchased the steamer *Amazon* in partnership with his brother-in-law Pierre Menard Chouteau. The boat sank February 15, 1857, near St. Louis.

Hughes, Andrew S. – An employee of the Indian Department, in 1837, Hughes was subagent for the Great Nemaha Subagency for the Iowas, Sacs and Foxes. The agency was located on the Missouri River, just above the mouth of Wolf Creek in present Doniphan County, Kansas.

Hunot (Uneau, Eanneau, Euneau, Uno) – The last name of several men living in the 1820s and 1830s in the area that became Kansas City. (Most modern histories use the spelling "Uneau.") Chouteau's letter to Menard dated March 20, 1831, reported that a man named Hunot(?) had purchased the land on which the Vasquez house stood. The Uneau family came from Detroit and settled in New Madrid around 1802.† They came to western Missouri with the Chouteaus in the early 1820s. At the time of the Vasquez sale, an Uneau family lived at the foot of Main Street in present Kansas City, and operated a ferry across the Missouri River (a thrill ride consisting of two canoes lashed together with a plank deck spanning the boats). Joseph Uneau married Cecilia Grey, daughter of John and Mary Grey. (See **Grey, John**.)

† "Hunot (Uneau) notes," Fur Trade Biographies, Chouteau's (Biographical) Scrapbook [17.2], (KC395), WHMC-KC.

Illinois Confederacy – See **Peoria Confederacy**.

Indian Removal Act – An 1830 Act of Congress requiring the removal of all Native Americans to lands west of the Mississippi River. Thomas Jefferson first suggested this plan, and it was enacted during the presidency of Andrew Jackson. The removal of the eastern Indians took place chiefly during the early 1830s.

Iowa Indians – A Native American tribe of the Siouan family and language, the Iowas were found in Minnesota on first contact with whites. The Iowa Indians were on the Platte River in Nebraska, Iowa, and Missouri around 1804 when Lewis and Clark encountered them. In 1836, they agreed to move to the Great Nemaha Reservation with the Sac and Fox Indians. Today the Iowas live in northeastern Kansas and in Oklahoma where they still have close ties to the Sac and Fox tribes.

Jackson, William (d. 1834) – A Shawnee chief sometimes called "Chief Fish," Jackson was a white man who had grown up with the Shawnees in Ohio and traveled with them to their new land in Indian Territory (Kansas). Jackson died in Wyandotte County in October 1834.

Jarboe, Joseph (1792-1867) – An early settler in the Kansas City area, Jarboe brought his family from Kentucky to western Missouri in 1834. Later, his son William J. Jarboe worked in the A. B. Canville store on the Missouri River levee and eventually owned and operated his own store. A younger son, David Mulholland Jarboe, also figured in Kansas City history.

Jesuits (S.J., Society of Jesus) – A Catholic religious society of men, both ordained priests and lay brothers, founded in France in 1534. Many Jesuits came as missionaries to the Indians in North America in the seventeenth, eighteenth, and nineteenth centuries. Father De Smet and Father Nicolas Point were members of this order. Jesuit missionaries who served along both sides of the Missouri-Kansas state line during the late 1830s were: Felix van Quickenborne, founder of Kickapoo Mission; Herman Aelen, who gave the name St. Francis Regis to the log structure originally called "Chouteau's Church"; John Verreydt, missionary to the Potawatomis at Sugar Creek Mission, Kansas; and Anthony Eysvogels, who worked briefly at both the Kickapoo and the Sugar Creek missions. In addition to serving the Native Americans, the latter group of men also ministered to the Catholics of Westport, Independence, Kansas Landing, and Kawsmouth after the first pastor of that area, Rev. Benedict Roux, left in 1835.

Johnson, Thomas (1802-1865) – A Methodist minister, Johnson came to eastern Indian Territory (Kansas) in 1830 and founded the first Shawnee Methodist Mission and School. It was located in Wyandotte County near present Turner. In 1838, Thomas Johnson and his wife Sara Davis Johnson, with support from the Methodist Church and the U.S. government, built the Shawnee Methodist Mission and Indian Manual Labor School at its present location on West 53rd Street in Johnson County, Kansas. (It is now a museum and historical site.)

Thomas Johnson. WHMC-KC.

Johnson, William (1805-1842) – A Methodist minister and brother of Thomas Johnson, William came with Thomas to Indian Territory (Kansas) in 1830 and opened a school for Delaware Indian children in 1832. Menard Chouteau attended the Johnson school for a few months.

Shawnee Methodist Mission and School located near present Turner (1830). WHMC-KC.

Kansa Agency – An establishment operated by the Indian Department to supervise and aid the Kansa Indians. Unlike other Indian agencies with their own agents, this agency had a subagent who answered directly to Superintendent William Clark in St. Louis. The first subagent of the Kansa Agency was Baronet Vasquez, appointed in 1825. He operated the agency from his home located on the riverbank at what is now Gillis Street in present Kansas City. In 1827, Kansa chiefs and government officials chose a new site for the Kansa Agency on the north bank of the Kansas River, between present Topeka and Lawrence. After the death of Vasquez, Marston G. Clark served as Kansa subagent from 1829 to 1834. In July 1834, the Kansa Agency was closed.

"First White settlement in Kansas, established 1827, by Col. Daniel Morgan Boone, 'Farmer' for the Kansas Indians. Site, seven miles northwest of Lawrence." Note White Plume's stone house pictured in the upper left corner. KSHS.

Kansa Indians (Kanza, Konza, Kansas, Cansa, Canses) – A Native American tribe of the Siouan language group that originated near the Great Lakes or in the southeast, perhaps in North Carolina. The Kansa migrated across the Mississippi River and had located on the

Missouri River by 1688. As the fur trade developed, the Kansas moved farther west to be nearer the sources of beaver and buffalo. After living in present Kansas for more than a century, the Kansa Nation was removed to Oklahoma. The name "Kansa" is often interpreted as "people of the south wind." (For further information, see William E. Unrau, *The Kansa Indians*.)

Kansa Post – The designation for several posts operated by Francois Chouteau to trade with the Kansa Indians. The first post was in partnership with his cousin Gabriel (Seres) Chouteau at the Four Houses, located at the mouth of Cedar Creek, about two and one-half miles east of present DeSoto, Kansas. In the autumn of 1829, Frederick Chouteau, under the supervision of his older brother Francois, opened a Kansa trading post at Horseshoe Lake, near the three villages of the Kansa Indians and the Kansa Agency. The location of the post was seven miles west of present Lawrence. In 1832, Frederick moved the post to the mouth of the American Chief (Mission) Creek. The post was operating at that location when, in 1843, Frederick's brother Charles joined him in the business. In 1845, Frederick Chouteau closed that post and went with the Kansa Indians to Council Grove, Kansas, where he operated until around 1853 when he sold out to Price Kelly and returned to Johnson County, Kansas.

Kansa Village – The designation for several villages occupied by the Kansa tribe. In 1785, the Kansa tribe was still on the Missouri River; in 1790-1791, they moved to a site on the Kansas River east of the mouth of the Big Blue River (two miles east of present Manhattan, Kansas). The Kansa Indians remained at that location in one large village of 125 lodges until 1829, when they divided into three groups and resettled as follows: Fool Chief's village, consisting of about fifty houses for 700 to 800 people, was located on the north bank of the Kansas River, six miles west of Soldier Creek; Hard Chief's village, with 500 to 600 people, was located on high ground south of the Kansas River in present Dover Township, Shawnee County; American Chief's village, with about 100 people, was in low land south of the Kansas River on the west side of Mission Creek (then called American Chief Creek). American Chief's village was two miles below Hard Chief's village. (For further information about the Kansa Indians, see *The Kansa Indians* by William E. Unrau.)

Kansas City Warehouse – See **River of Kansas Post**.

Kansas Landing – See **Town of Kansas**.

Kansas Outfit – The designation sometimes used by Francois Chouteau, Cadet Chouteau, and Pierre Menard to identify Francois's operations in western Missouri and eastern Kansas. It appeared on bills of freight beginning in 1825 but was not used consistently.

Kansas River – See **River of Kansas**.

Kaskaskia Indians – A Native American tribe of the Illinois Confederacy, that spoke an Algonquin language. In the seventeenth century, these Indians were located in southern Wisconsin and northern Illinois, but had moved to southern Illinois, around Cahokia by the eighteenth century. From early times, the Kaskaskia had a close and friendly relationship with the French. The Kaskaskias had by 1832 signed an agreement ceding their Illinois lands and moved to Indian Territory (Kansas) to join other Illinois Confederacy Indians, the Peorias, and other relatives, the Miami subtribes of Piankeshaws and Weas.

Kaskaskia, Illinois – The French settlement in Illinois where Berenice Menard was born, raised, and married to Francois Chouteau. Kaskaskia was founded in 1703 by French people, most of whom had come up the Mississippi from New Orleans. Kaskaskia was located

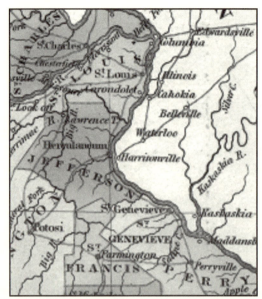

Portion of map, *"Missouri"*, published by A. Finley, Philadelphia, 1831. WHMC-KC. Kaskaskia is in the lower right corner.

between the Kaskaskia and Mississippi rivers directly across from where Ste. Genevieve would be built thirty years later, about sixty miles southeast of present St. Louis. After a checkered history during the Revolutionary War and afterwards, Kaskaskia came into its own in 1809, when it became the capital of the Illinois Territory. When Illinois became a state in 1818, Kaskaskia briefly served as the capital until that honor was bestowed first on Vandalia, then Springfield. Kaskaskia was nearly washed away in the flood of 1844 and when the Mississippi river channel moved in 1881, it left the remains of the old French village on an island. Subsequent floods took away the remnants of the town, and today Kaskaskia is an historical footnote. However, spared from the many floods of the Mississippi, and as a museum operated by the Illinois Historic Preservation Agency, Pierre Menard's mansion remains virtually unchanged since it was finished in 1802.

Kaw – An alternative reference or name for the Kansa Indians or the Kansas River, i.e., the Kaw tribe or the Kaw River.

Kawsmouth – The settlement extending from the mouth of the Kansas River to Chouteau's Landing. See **Town of Kansas**.

Kearney, Colonel Stephen W. (1794-1848) – The commander of "Army of the West" in the War with Mexico, 1846-1849. Edmond Francois Chouteau, eldest son of Francois and Berenice Chouteau, was a lieutenant in the light artillery under Kearney's command. (See also *DMB*.)

Keelboat – A roughly built freight boat (or "barge") sixty to eighty feet long, with a shallow draft and a keel enabling it to sail into the wind. When there was no wind, the boat was propelled with poles and/or ropes pulled by men or animals on the bank. Frederick Chouteau remembered, "Keel-boats were made in St. Louis. They were rib-made boats, shaped like the hull of a steamboat, and decked over. They were about eight or ten feet across the deck and five or six feet deep below deck. They were rigged with one mast, and had a rudder, though we generally took the rudder off and used a long oar for steering. There were four rowlocks on each side. Going up the Kaw river we pulled all the way; about fifteen miles a day. Going down it sometimes took a good many days, as it did going up, on account of low water."†

 † "Reminiscences of Frederick Chouteau," *Kansas Historical Collection* 8: 428.

Keelboat on the Missouri River. WHMC-KC.

Kennerly, George Hancock (1790-1867) – A military officer, Kennerly in 1825 married Modeste Alzire Menard, the sister of Berenice Menard Chouteau. Kennerly was born in Virginia, and served as a U.S. Army captain in the War of 1812. He moved to St. Louis where his cousin Julia Hancock, wife of Superintendent of Indian Affairs William Clark, was probably instrumental in finding a position for him. Kennerly was appointed to the Sioux subagency in June 1824. He subsequently resumed his army career with the rank of captain in the Quartermaster Corps. As sutler at Jefferson Barracks in St. Louis, Kennerly accompanied military expeditions in the west, often with his wife coming along. The Kennerlys lived at Jefferson Barracks for most of their married life. When William Clark's first wife, Julia, died, he married Kennerly's sister, Harriet Kennerly Radford. The Kennerly, Clark, Radford, and Chouteau cousins formed a boisterous clan at Jefferson Barracks.

George Hancock Kennerly. MHS.

Kennerly, Modeste Alzire Menard (1802-1886) – The last child of Pierre Menard and his first wife, Marie Therese Godin, Alzire was one year younger than her sister Berenice Menard Chouteau. In 1825, she married George Hancock Kennerly and lived most of her life in St. Louis, where her husband was sutler at Jefferson Barracks. Alzire and George Kennerly were the parents of nine children. Alzire was a widow for nineteen years and died two years before her sister Berenice.

Kickapoo Catholic Mission – See **Van Quickenborne, Charles**.

Kickapoo Indians – A Native American tribe, originally from Wisconsin, that moved to Illinois, where they displaced the Peorias who migrated across the Mississippi. While in Illinois, the Kickapoos traveled each year to the plains (i.e., present Kansas) to hunt. Eventually they ceded their Illinois lands to the United States. By the 1830s, a large village of Kickapoo Indians was located northeast of Fort Leavenworth, Kansas, where they still live.

Kiowa Indians – A Native American tribe originally located in Montana, the Kiowa split into groups and migrated south and east, arriving in the Arkansas River area by the early nineteenth century. The Kiowa Apaches, one of the many Kiowa bands, were great horsemen and roamed far and wide in war or hunting parties. By the late twentieth century, most of the Kiowa bands were living in Oklahoma.

Labaume, August – A Westport merchant around 1836-1838, Labaume was originally from St. Louis. He figured in a financial transaction in the Chouteau letters.

Laclede, Frederick (1865-1903) – The son of Frederic Donatien Chouteau (son of Francois and Berenice Chouteau) and Adele Gregoire of Ste. Genevieve, he was born Frederick Edward Chouteau and called "Freddie" by the Chouteaus. In 1893, Freddie had his surname changed to Laclede by court order in Minnesota, and his descendants have since used that name.

Laclede, Pierre de (1729-1778) – A New Orleans merchant who, with Auguste Chouteau, founded St. Louis in 1764. Laclede usually signed the name "Liguest" after Laclede, to distinguish himself from other Lacledes in the St. Louis area. He was the common-law husband of Marie Therese Chouteau. They had four children: Jean Pierre Chouteau (Pierre Chouteau Sr.), Marie Pelagie, Marie Louise, and Victoire Chouteau. All carried the surname "Chouteau" inasmuch as Marie Therese Chouteau had not divorced her husband, Rene Chouteau. (See also *DMB*.)

La Liberte, Pierre (1792-1853) – An early resident of "Chouteau's Town," La Liberte sold to Rev. Benedict Roux the forty acres on which the first Catholic church was built in Kansas City. He and his wife Eleonora Chalifoux received six dollars for their property.

La Liede – A man identified as the Shawnee blacksmith in Francois Chouteau's letter to Pierre Menard dated February 15, 1829 (*PMC*).

Lamont, Daniel (1798-1837) – A Canadian partner in the Columbia Fur Company, a competitor of the American Fur Company, during the 1830s.

Langlois, John Adrien – An associate of Pierre Menard who held Menard's power of attorney and handled financial transactions in his absence. John was probably the son of Jean Pierre Langlois, a native of France who lived in Kaskaskia and then New Madrid.

Leavenworth, Colonel Henry (1785-1834) – A member of the Third U.S. Infantry, Colonel Leavenworth founded Cantonment Leavenworth in 1827. All cantonments became forts in 1832. The fort was located twenty-nine miles northwest of present Kansas City on the Missouri River. It is the longest continually operated military establishment west of the Mississippi.

Henry Leavenworth. KSHS.

Lefevre, Francoise Nicolle (1761-1840) – This stepmother of Angelique Saucier Menard was a widow who became the third wife of Francois Saucier.

Lemme, J. (Lemai, Lemay, Leme, Lemi, Lemmau) – A merchant in Independence identified by Isaac McCoy in 1829 as J. Lemme. These letters confirm that Lemme owned a store there. In 1830, he may have joined a hunting expedition comprised of "Chemie, Picotte, Pascal, Lemi and P. D. Papin," who hoped they would "do better next season."†

† P. D. Papin to P. M. Papin, July 28, 1830, *Chouteau Family Collection*, MHS.

Lessert, Clement (1796-1854) – An interpreter for the Kansa Indians from 1825 to perhaps as late as 1847, Clement Lessert had been an early settler near the mouth of the Kansas River. He married Julia Roy (Roi) in Jackson County in 1829. When the Kansas Agency moved west in 1827, he moved to the new location on the Kansas River. By 1840, Lessert had purchased land in Kansas City and was a member of the Catholic parish of Father Nicolas Point

License – In the fur trade, a license was a permit from the government to trade with specific Indian tribes. (It was NOT a hunting or trapping license.)

Liguest, Pierre de Laclede – See **Laclede, Pierre de**.

Liguest – See **Chouteau, Paul Liguest**.

Lisa, Manuel (1772-1820) – A prominent St. Louis fur trader, born in New Orleans of Spanish parents. Lisa was a competitor and sometime partner of the Chouteaus and Menards. In 1809, Lisa, Pierre Chouteau Sr., and Pierre Menard took goods to the upper reaches of the Missouri River to trade with the tribes of that region. (See also *DMB*.)

Loisel, Regis (1773?-1804) – A Canadian in the Indian trade, Loisel was a clerk in the Chouteau businesses and also associated with Clamorgan in the Missouri Fur Company. In 1800, Loisel was given a license to build an establishment on the Upper Missouri. Loisel's Post was a few miles below Fort Pierre, and was the first post in Sioux County, South Dakota. The buildings burned before 1810. Members of the Loisel family lived in St. Louis and Cahokia in the early 1800s. (See also *DMB*.)

Lorimier – A name prominent in the late eighteenth and early nineteenth century in eastern Missouri and in the fur trade of southern and western Missouri. In 1805, Louis Lorimier served as a judge of the Court of Common Pleas and Quarter Sessions, although he could neither read nor write, except to pen his own lavish signature. Through his many business dealings, he was largely responsible for making Cape Girardeau the wealthiest settlement in Upper Louisiana before it was taken over by the United States in 1803. Shawnee, Delaware, and Wea Indians traded with and married members of the Lorimier family. Lorimiers continued to be important in the fur trade through the 1830s, ranging far up the Missouri River. (See also Louis Lorimier in *DMB*.)

Loups – See **Delaware Indians**.

Lutz, Joseph Anthony (1801-1858) – A Catholic priest who came from Germany to St. Louis intending to be a missionary to the Indians. He came with Baronet Vasquez in 1828 to evangelize the Kansa Indians. (See Coleman, *This Far by Faith*, and Garraghan, *Catholic Beginnings in Kansas City, Missouri*.)

Lykins, Dr. Johnston (1800-1876) – An early missionary, doctor, and town leader in the Kansas City area. Born in Virginia, Lykins studied medicine in Lexington, Kentucky. He worked in Indian missions in Indiana and Michigan before marrying Delilah McCoy, daughter of Isaac McCoy, in 1828. Lykins and his bride moved west and founded a Baptist mission for the Potawatomi and Shawnee Indians. He also gave medical assistance to the Indians. In 1843, Lykins moved to the Town of Kansas. After his first wife died, Lykins married Martha (Mattie) Livingston. Lykins served as mayor of the Town of Kansas in 1853, and was a charter member of the First Baptist Church of Kansas City. Johnston Lykins died in Kansas City in 1876.

Maquaia – One of the French-Indian sons of Louis Lorimier, whose name may mean "stranger" in the Iroquois language.

Marais des Cygne River – A French phrase meaning "swamp of the swans." Marais des Cygne River begins in Kansas, southwest of Topeka, where it provides water for the present Melvern Lake. It meanders northeast through Ottawa, Kansas, then turns southeast into Miami County and the town of Trading Post, near the state line. When it crosses into Missouri northwest of Rich Hill, it joins with the Marmaton and Little Osage to become the Osage River. The Marais Des Cygne region was the location of active trade by the Chouteaus with the Osage, and in later years, with the immigrant tribes of Weas and Piankeshaws.

Marshall, William – A fur trader listed in the 1830 Missouri Census as residing in Ste. Genevieve, Missouri, Marshall traded with the migrating eastern Indians when they lived in south-central Missouri, sometimes as a partner of William Gilliss and sometimes as his rival. Marshall followed the Weas and Delawares to their reservations in Indian Territory (Kansas), but later returned to the Ozarks of south-central Missouri.

Maximilian, Prince (1782-1867) – The Prince of Wied-Neuwied, a Germanic state, Prince Maximilian journeyed through the region of the Missouri and Kansas rivers on a scientific expedition in April 1833. His *Travels in the Interior of North America, 1832-1834*, illustrated with eighty-one engravings made from Charles Karl Bodmer's drawings, represents a major primary source of information on the region and its inhabitants.

Maxwell, Hugh Herbert (1791-1833) – Brother-in-law of Berenice Chouteau, Maxwell was married to her oldest sister, Marie Odile Menard. Maxwell worked in the Indian trade and died an early death at the age of forty-two. Herbert and Odile were the parents of twelve children. One of their sons, Lucien Maxwell, settled in New Mexico and received the largest land grant ever given in the United States, the Maxwell Land Grant.

Maxwell, Marie Odile Menard (1793-1862) – The eldest sister of Berenice Menard Chouteau, called Odile, was the firstborn of Pierre Menard and his first wife Marie Therese Godin. Odile married Hugh Herbert Maxwell in 1810, and they had twelve children. She apparently lived all her life in Kaskaskia, died, and was buried there.

McCoy, Isaac (1784-1846) – A Baptist missionary born in Pennsylvania, McCoy was a leading advocate for the resettlement of some eastern Indians to west of the Mississippi. (See **Indian Removal Act**.) He arrived in western Missouri in 1830 and began his task of surveying lands in Indian Territory (Kansas) that were being set aside as Indian reservations. (See also *DMB*.)

Isaac McCoy. KSHS.

McCoy, John Calvin (1811-1889) – The son of Isaac McCoy, John C. McCoy opened one of the first general stores in Westport and platted the town of Westport in 1833. His "memories of an old timer" relating to the early days – 1830s, '40s, and '50s – comprise much of the lore, legend, and history of pioneer Kansas City. (See also *DMB*.)

John Calvin McCoy. KSHS.

McKenney, Thomas (1785-1859) – From 1824 to 1830, McKenney served as head of the newly organized Indian Department or Office of Indian Affairs, a part of the War Department until 1849. (See also **Bureau of Indian Affairs**.)

McNair, Dunning (d. 1831) – A temporary subagent for the Kansa Indians, McNair was appointed in 1828 to take the place of Subagent Baronet Vasquez who died in August 1828. McNair served as Kansa subagent until Marston G. Clark replaced him in 1829. He was brother to Alexander McNair, Missouri's first governor.

Menard, Amadee (1820-1844) – The youngest son of Pierre Menard Sr. and his second wife Angelique Saucier Menard, Joseph Amadee was a half-brother to Berenice Menard Chouteau and uncle to her children. Edmond (Gesseau) and Menard were his classmates at St. Mary's of the Barrens and were close to his age. Amadee died at the age of twenty-four.

Menard, Edmond (1813-1884) – A son of Pierre Menard and Angelique Saucier Menard, Jean Baptiste Edmond Menard was a half-brother of Berenice Menard Chouteau. After the death of their father, Edmond managed the Menard estate and businesses. It was to Edmond that Berenice directed her letters after Pierre Menard's died in 1844.

Menard, Francois Xavier (1807-1831) – A son of Pierre Menard and Angelique Saucier Menard, Francois Menard attended college in Auburn, then Bloomingdale, New York. He died at the age of twenty-four, probably of tuberculosis. His death evoked an emotional letter from Berenice (February 3, 1831, *PMC*).

Menard, Francoise Virginie (b. 1810) – The daughter of Hippolyte Menard, Pierre Menard's brother, who lived in Kaskaskia with his family. In 1830, Francoise Virginie married Savinien St. Vrain in Kaskaskia. The couple had two sons, Francois Pierre and Jean Theodule.

Menard, Hippolyte – There were four persons named Hippolyte Menard at the time of the Chouteau letters. Berenice Menard Chouteau's uncle Hippolyte Menard was her father's brother, who emigrated from Canada to Kaskaskia, Illinois, where he became a farmer. Berenice had a brother named Hippolyte Menard (1799-1806) who died at the age of seven. And finally, she had two cousins named Hippolyte Menard: one, the son of her father's brother, Jean Marie Menard, lived only a few days in 1794; the other, the son of her father's brother, Hippolyte Menard, was born in 1804. He apparently remained in Kaskaskia, where he married Eloise Chenier in 1837. No death date is listed for this Hippolyte Menard. "Polite" was a nickname for Hippolyte.

Menard, Louis Cyprien (1819-1870) – A son of Pierre Menard Sr. and Angelique Saucier Menard, therefore Cyprien was a half-brother to Berenice Menard Chouteau. Cyprien Menard attended school at St. Mary's of the Barrens, then pursued his college studies in Emmitsburg, Maryland. After several years of poor health in the late 1830s and early 1840s, Cyprien lived in St. Louis for several years. He married Augustine St. Gemme in Ste. Genevieve in 1845, and they had nine children. In June 1846, he settled in Ste. Genevieve where he lived the rest of his life.

Menard, Marie Odile – See **Maxwell, Marie Odile Menard**.

Menard, Michel B. (1804-1856) – The son of Pierre Menard Sr.'s brother Michael, who lived in Canada. Michel Menard was the founder of the city of Galveston, Texas. In business as well as in family matters, Michel Menard and the Pierre Menard family maintained a close relationship. (See *Guide to Menard Collection*.)

Menard, Modeste Alzire – See **Kennerly, Modeste Alzire Menard**.

Menard, Pierre Jr. (1797-1871) – Usually known as "Peter," Pierre Menard Jr. was the son of Pierre Menard Sr. and his first wife, Marie Therese Godin, and thus a full brother to Berenice Menard Chouteau. In 1818 and 1819, Peter Menard studied at Georgetown College (Georgetown University) in Washington, D.C. In 1827, he was appointed subagent by the United States Indian Department and moved to Peoria, Illinois, to serve the Indians there. He enlisted in the Black Hawk War in 1832, and then returned to Peoria where he married Caroline Stillman that same year. Peter Menard became a merchant and a land speculator in Illinois, owning large tracts of land in the area that became Chicago and its environs. After the death of his first wife, he married Emily Briggs and they lived in Tremont, Illinois. Although he tried many ventures during his lifetime, Peter Menard never had his father's golden touch. Peter Menard died at the age of seventy-four.

Menard, Pierre Sr. (1766-1844) – A merchant, politician, Indian agent, and father of Berenice Menard Chouteau, Menard was born in Canada near Montreal. He left home at the age of fourteen after an abbreviated education, to enter the fur business in the Mississippi valley. By the time he was sixteen, Menard was in Illinois country, trading and accepting notes of credit from other traders. Menard settled in Kaskaskia, Illinois, around 1791 and began shipping merchandise westward to be traded with the Indians in exchange for fur pelts. Menard was associated with several fur enterprises: Manual Lisa's outfit; the American Fur Company; and Pratte, Chouteau & Company (essentially the company of "Cadet" Chouteau).

Pierre Menard Sr. CHS.

Menard was a partner with J. B. Valle in Ste. Genevieve in a mercantile operation supplying Indian goods to traders and selling retail to townsfolk. A second Menard and Valle store did business in Kaskaskia. In addition to these enterprises, Menard dealt in real estate, operated a ferry across the Kaskaskia River, and was engaged in shipping furs to New Orleans and to buyers in the North.

Pierre Menard also was active in Illinois politics. When the Territory of Illinois became a state, Menard was elected Lieutenant Governor. He was deeply involved in Indian affairs, especially the movement of the eastern tribes to the trans-Mississippi regions. Although Menard was field agent for the migrating Indians, his efforts on their behalf far exceeded the demands of office. He permitted the tribes to camp on his land during the winter months before they moved westward. He battled government bureaucracy for months to recover $1,000 in annuities that had been withheld or stolen from the Piankeshaws.

Pierre Menard's first marriage was to Marie Therese Godin, and they had six children, including Berenice Menard Chouteau. His second marriage was to Angelique Saucier, and they had eight children. Pierre Menard visited his daughter Berenice and her family at "Chouteau's Town" in 1831 and perhaps at other times. Pierre Menard died on June 13, 1844, leaving a large and complicated estate that was tied up in probate court for nearly forty years. (See *Guide to Menard Collection*.)

Menard, Therese Berenice – See **Chouteau, Berenice**.

Menard & Valle – A firm consisting of two stores owned in partnership by Pierre Menard of Kaskaskia, Illinois, and Jean Baptiste Valle of Ste. Genevieve, Missouri. The stores were located in Kaskaskia and Ste. Genevieve, and dealt largely in Indian trade goods. The home of Felix and Odile Pratte Valle, built in 1818, survives today in Ste. Genevieve as the Felix Valle State Historic Site owned by the State of Missouri. The Federal-style limestone building exhibits an authentically restocked recreation of the mercantile store of Menard & Valle.

Felix Valle Home (1814), Ste. Genevieve, Missouri. WHMC-KC.

Metis – A French word meaning a person of French, or Creole, and Indian parentage. The term commonly used during Chouteau's time was "half-breed."

Meyers, William (Myers, Mairs) – An employee of Francois Chouteau, who, on Pierre Menard's recommendation, hired Meyers to operate a trading post among the Wea Indians, as Meyers had previously been acquainted with that group in south-central Missouri. Meyers worked for Francois Chouteau from the fall of 1829 until the spring of 1833, when he joined his wife in Ste. Genevieve. Meyers was a great friend of Frederick Chouteau, who named his first son William Meyers Chouteau.

Miami Indians – A Native American tribe that originated around the Great Lakes, perhaps near the St. Joseph River, present St. Joseph, Michigan. They migrated south into Ohio. In 1790, the Miamis, Peorias, and other tribes in Ohio joined under the leadership of Chief Little Turtle in an unsuccessful war to prevent white settlement of Indian lands. Eventually, some of the Miami Indians moved to Indian Territory (Kansas) while others, after a period of wandering, settled in Indiana. The Piankeshaws and Weas are Miami subtribes. Indians of the Illinois Confederacy, such as Peorias and Kaskaskias, are closely related, speaking almost the same language as the Miamis, and are sometimes identified as Miamis.

Mongrain, Noel – An interpreter and guide among the Osage and Kansa Indians. The Baptismal Register of the Osage Nation records that in 1820, nine children of Noel Mongrain and M. Paku Shan (probably Osage) were baptized. Other persons with the surname Mongrain also worked among the Indian tribes.

Montardeau, Calise (Montardy, Montardine) (ca.1798-1847) – An early settler at Kawsmouth, he reportedly purchased from Richard Linville in 1826, a ferry across the Missouri River, which was located where Grand Louis Bertholet lived at Randolph Bluff.† After the 1826 flood he moved his operation closer to the mouth of the Kansas and continued to run his ferry until 1830. He was married to Marianne Valle, who supposedly was an educated woman who kept a diary that is not known to have survived.

† Barry, *Beginning of the West*, 148-149.

Morgan – In a letter to Menard January 15, 1834 (*PMC*, Letter 522), Chouteau complained of the competition from a trader named Morgan. Possibly this was Alexander Morgan, sutler (storekeeper) at Fort Leavenworth in 1834.

Mormons – Members of the Church of Jesus Christ of Latter Day Saints. They are followers of Joseph Smith, who founded the church in 1830. As a young man in upstate New York, Smith professed to have received angelic visits, in one of which he was given the Book of Mormon. Following the publication of that book in 1830, he gathered a number of believers and in 1831, sent a group to Jackson County to assess the possibility of moving there, with an eye to converting the nearby Indians. Jackson County residents were distrustful of these newcomers because of their beliefs, and the Mormons who had moved to Independence were evicted from their homes in 1833. In 1834, they attempted to return to reclaim their property. It was to this activity that Francois Chouteau referred in his letters. The Mormons never mounted a military assault on Jackson County and eventually moved to Utah. (See also Joseph Smith in *DMB*.)

Mount St. Mary's Cemetery – A Catholic cemetery opened in 1877, located at 22nd and Cleveland, Kansas City, Missouri. The French pioneer Catholics who were originally buried in the cemetery near St. Francis Regis Church at present 11th and Pennsylvania were moved to Mount St. Mary's after 1877.

Office of Indian Affairs (OIA) – See **Bureau of Indian Affairs**.

Ogle, John – A fur trader operating in the 1820s near William Gilliss at the James River Delaware camps. Like others who traded with the migrating eastern Indians, Ogle was supplied by Menard and Valle of Ste. Genevieve. By 1828, Ogle was in the area of the Missouri and Kansas rivers. He was in some way associated with Pierre Menard and then later, the American Fur Company when Francois Chouteau reported to Pierre Menard that Ogle was trying to trade with the Shawnee Indians.

Osage Indians – An important Native American tribe of the Siouan linguistic family, the Osages probably originated in the Northeast and migrated through the Ohio Valley. By 1673, they were in Missouri in two villages on the south fork of the Osage River. Their names, "Little Osage" and "Great Osage," referred to the size of the village, not the stature of the people. The Osages were hunters, gatherers, farmers, and craftsmen, especially noted for making fine bows from the Osage orange (hedge apple) tree. The Osages had no equals as hunters and trappers, and because they could produce a great number of high-quality fur pelts, the French and Spanish governments gave them special treatment. By 1808, migrating eastern tribes had forced the Osages to move to land on the Neosho River in Indian Territory (eastern Kansas). Eventually the Osages moved to Oklahoma. In the early twentieth century, oil was discovered on their lands, making them a wealthy people.

Otoe Indians – A Siouan tribe related to the Missouris and the Iowas, the Otoes were hunters and farmers. They probably came from the Great Lakes area and migrated south and west for reasons unknown. By the mid-1700s, they had arrived on the Platte River in Nebraska. Eventually they absorbed their relatives, the Missouris, and together they settled on the Big Blue River on the Kansas-Nebraska border.

Ottowa Indians – A Native American tribe originating around the Great Lakes in Michigan and Wisconsin. The French first met the Ottawas in 1615. These Indians were great traders, being the middlemen in the French fur trade in that area. The name "Ottawa" is an Indian word meaning trader. The Ottawas migrated south in Wisconsin, and finally into the Mississippi River country of the Midwest. In 1832, the Ottawas removed to Indian Territory (Kansas).

Owens, Samuel C. (d. 1847) – An Independence merchant and landowner during the 1820s through the 1840s, Owens operated a store in Independence and assisted in financial transactions of various kinds. Francois Chouteau used Owens's skills and services when needed. Samuel Owens was also in partnership with the Aull brothers of Lexington, Liberty, and Independence in a freighting operation on the Missouri River and the Santa Fe Trail. According to John C. McCoy, James Aull and Samuel Owens joined Doniphan's regiment in the War with Mexico. Owens became the leader of a volunteer group of traders and was killed in battle on the Plains of Sacramento, a short distance from Chihuahua, on February 28, 1847. A few months later in June, Aull was robbed and murdered in his store in Chihuahua.

Samuel Owens. WHMC-KC.

Pack – A standard measure for a bundle of furs that contained a specific number of a single kind of pelt: 10 buffalo robes; or 14 bear skins; or 60 otter pelts; or 80 beaver pelts; or 8 raccoons; or 120 foxes; or 600 muskrats.

Padouca Indians (Plains Apache) – A North American Indian tribe known to have been living in the area of present Scott County, Kansas, in the late 1600s and early 1700s. They were hunters and warriors and also grew some crops. In 1724, Etienne Veniard de Bourgmont, commandant of Fort Orleans, led a military unit to the grand village of the Padoucas in order to make peace between that tribe and the tribes of the Missouri and Kansas rivers. (See also *Bourgmont: Explorer of the Upper Missouri, 1698-1725*, by Frank Norall.)

Parks, Joseph (1794-1859) – A quarter-blood Shawnee man who was in western Missouri and eastern Kansas after 1833, when he led sixty-seven Shawnees from Ohio to their reservation in Indian Territory. Parks was an educated man who spoke several languages, and was a staunch supporter of the Indian Removal Act. With the military rank of captain, he organized a company of Shawnee warriors to fight the Seminoles who were resisting removal from Florida. (See Chouteau to Menard, March 18, 1838.) Parks was employed as an interpreter at the Shawnee Agency; he owned land, and was a prominent and respected figure along the Missouri-Kansas state line area.

Pawnee Indians – A Caddoan group of Native Americans that, by the late eighteenth century, had settled in the Platte Valley of Nebraska. The Council Bluffs Agency on the Missouri River distributed their annuities and negotiated with them. The Pawnee Loups were a band of Pawnees living on the Loup Fork of the Platte River.

Pensineau, Laurent (Pinsineau, Pensineaux) (d. 1848) – A fur trader who worked for the American Fur Company among the Kickapoo Indians in 1833 under Francois Chouteau's supervision, and continued with them until around 1840. Laurence Pensineau's Kickapoo Post was at Kickapoo Landing on the Missouri River, four miles north of Fort Leavenworth (about two miles south of Weston, on the Kansas side). The Pensineau family came from New Orleans to St. Louis in the early 1800s. Several other persons of this name were in the western Missouri-eastern Kansas area.

Peoria, Baptiste (1800-1874) – As a chief of the Confederated Kaskaskia and Peoria, Piankeshaw, and Wea Indians (Illinois Confederacy), as well as a guide, interpreter, and negotiator, Baptiste Peoria was well known in Indian Territory (Kansas), Missouri, and Illinois during the early 1800s. When the eastern Indians lived in the Ozarks in the 1820s, Baptiste Peoria was active in that region. As late as 1854, he signed a treaty involving the Miami (Piankeshaw and Wea) Indians. Francois Chouteau on many occasions employed Baptiste Peoria to carry money or messages to St. Louis or Kaskaskia.

Baptiste Peoria. KSHS.

Peoria Confederacy (Illinois Confederacy) – A political and social union of several Algonquian-speaking tribes, which included five subtribes: Cahokia, Kaskaskia, Michigamea, and Tamarosa. They lived in present Illinois, Indiana, and neighboring areas. As the number of Illinois Indians declined, those remaining moved to the region of Kaskaskia, Illinois, and became known by the name of that town. Other Illinois Indian groups eventually were resettled on common land in Indian Territory (Kansas) where they were known as the Peoria Confederacy. At the time of the Chouteau letters, this confederacy included the Weas and Piankeshaws (Miamis), Kaskaskias, and Peorias.

Peoria Indians An important tribe of the Illinois Confederacy, the Peorias spoke the Algonquian language, as did other Illinois Indians such as the Kaskaskias, Michigameas, and the Cahokias. In the 1700s, the Peorias were forced from their home in Wisconsin by the Kickapoo, Fox, and Sac Indians. For a time the Peorias were in Illinois, then they settled near Ste. Genevieve, Missouri. By 1832, the Peorias had given up their land in the United States and moved to the Marais des Cygne River in Indian Territory (Kansas), where they were joined by their close relatives, the Piankeshaws, Kaskaskias, and the Weas. Although the Miamis were separate, all of these last-mentioned tribes are sometimes called "Miami" Indians.

Philibert – Several Philibert men were in Missouri during the 1800s. Joseph Philibert was listed on the 1830 Missouri Census as residing in St. Louis. In the 1820s, he had been a gunsmith for the Delawares living at the James River. Philibert worked for and with William Gilliss and became his chief clerk and friend. Philibert moved with Gilliss to the Kansas River valley when the Delawares settled on their reservation there in 1829, but in 1833, Philibert went back to the James River area where he remained. Gabriel Philibert was blacksmith for the Kansa Indians from 1827 to 1831. In 1832, his sister Marie Philibert married Daniel Boone, grandson of the famous pioneer.

Piankeshaw Indians – Also called the "Miamis," the Piankeshaws are an Algonquian tribe that lived near Green Bay, Wisconsin, in the mid-seventeenth century. The Piankeshaws moved south of Lake Michigan, then were pushed through Ohio, Indiana, Illinois, and Missouri by other migrating Indians and by European immigrants. By 1827, the Piankeshaws had settled in Indian Territory (Kansas) with their close relatives, the Weas, along with the less closely related Peorias, and Kaskaskias. The Piankeshaws and the Weas are subtribes of the Miamis.

Pirogue – The French word for canoe. A pirogue, however, was much larger than an ordinary canoe. Frederick Chouteau described it as "a craft sixty or seventy feet long, made like a canoe, out of cottonwood trees of the largest size found in the Missouri bottoms, sometimes four feet through. Two of these were placed together side by side, tied solidly together. They would carry from ten to fifteen tons."†

† "Reminiscences of Frederick Chouteau," *Kansas Historical Collection* 8: 428.

Platte Purchase – The triangular-shaped wedge of land that was added to the State of Missouri in 1837 by purchase from the Fox, Sac, Potawatomi Indians, as well as from other

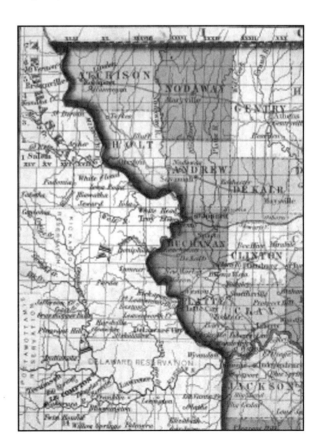

A portion of map, *Colton's Missouri*, published by Johnson and Browning, NY (1859). Showing the counties of the Platte Purchase and Indian lands in Kansas Territory. WHMC-KC.

tribes with smaller claims, who agreed to various compensations, including land in Indian Territory (Kansas). Senator Thomas Hart Benton of Missouri was largely responsible for pushing the approval bill through Congress. The Platte Purchase, which included Robidoux's Black Snake Hills Post (present city of St. Joseph), extended the western boundary of the state to the Missouri River. The newly added region was eventually divided into six counties: Platte, Buchanan, Andrew, Holt, Nodaway, and Atchison.

Point – A unit of measurement of card, paper, or cloth thickness that is equal to 0.001 inch.

Point, Nicolas, S.J. (1799-1868) – A Belgian Jesuit priest, Father Point served as pastor of St. Francis Regis Church at Kawsmouth from November 1840 to May 1841. The log church where he held services had previously been known as "Chouteau's Church," and was located at 11th and Pennsylvania on the grounds of the present Catholic Cathedral of the Immaculate Conception at 11th and Broadway. During his stay in western Missouri, Father Point sketched a map of his parish. This *Plan de Westport,* with its list of parishioners, has become a standard reference for matters related to the French pioneers of Kansas City. In May 1841, Father Point joined Father Pierre De Smet, who was traveling to the Oregon Territory to establish Catholic missions among the Indians. Father Point was a gifted watercolorist who painted scenes of Indian life in the Northwest.

Ponca Indians – A Siouan tribe of Native Americans that spoke a language similar to that of the Kansa Indians. The Poncas lived at one time in the Minnesota area, then migrated south and west, settling near the Nebraska-South Dakota state line, where they were at the time of the Chouteau letters. Eventually they were forced to move to Oklahoma.

Pool (Poole) – Two men named Pool were in the western Missouri area in the early 1830s. James Pool worked at the Delaware-Shawnee Agency from 1828 to 1832 (he was probably the Pool mentioned in Chouteau to Menard, March 24, 1837). A G. W. Pool led a group of Shawnees from Ohio to their reservation in Indian Territory in 1833.

Potawatomi Indians – A Native American tribe that originated on the East Coast and spoke an Algonquian language. According to their legends, a message from the Spirit World instructed them to move west. They migrated to Michigan and were living there as hunters-gathers when the Europeans arrived around 1640. The French introduced the horse into their culture and the Potawatomis became buffalo hunters and trappers of fur-bearing animals. The tribe subdivided and various groups lived in Michigan, Wisconsin, and Indiana. When Congress passed the Indian Removal Act in 1830, a large segment of Potawatomi people fled to Canada and remained there. In the early 1830s the Potawatomis were relocated to the area that would become the Platte Purchase, and after it became part of Missouri, to reservations north of the Missouri line near Council Bluffs and, in Kansas, on the Marais des Cygnes River near the Kickapoo and Miami tribes. In the late 1840s, the tribe again divided with part going to Oklahoma and the Prairie Potawatomi band resettled on a reservation near Mayetta, Kansas, where they still live.

Prices on the frontier in 1832 – A beaver pelt was worth $6.00; first quality gun powder was $1.50 per pound; lead was $1.00 per pound; shot was $1.25 per pound; three point blankets were $9.00 each; two and one-half point blankets were $7.00 each; scarlet cloth was $6.00 per yard; butcher knives were $.75 each; North West fuzils (flintlock muskets) were $24.00 each; tin kettles of various sizes were $2.00 per pound; sugar was $1.00 per pound; coffee was $1.25 per pound; raisins were $1.50 per pound; assorted beads were $2.50 per pound; buttons were $5.00 per gross; and mirrors were $.50 each.†

† Chittenden, *The American Fur Trade of the Far West,* 1: 9.

Prince Paul Wilhelm of Wuerttemberg – See **Wuerttemberg, Prince Paul Wilhelm**.

Prospectus – A guide to the curriculum, regulations, and fees of a school.

Prudhomme, Gabriel (d. 1829) – Owner of the land at the foot of present Main Street, which became the core of Kansas City. Prudhomme was killed in a tavern brawl in 1829. In 1838, his wife, Susan Prudhomme, sold the land to the town company that would plat the original Town of Kansas. There was no clear title, however, and the company was not able to sell lots until 1846. Susan Prudhomme was the Cree Indian artisan whose stitchery and beadwork were so admired by Francois Chouteau.

Quick, John – A Delaware chief who, in 1830, accompanied the Isaac McCoy surveying party that marked the lines of the new Delaware reservation in Indian Territory (Kansas). Quick participated in negotiations with the Pawnee regarding the north line of the reservation because it came near Pawnee land. In September 1830, Chief Quick approved the dimensions of the Delaware reservation.

Randolph Bluffs Post – Francois Chouteau's first fur trading post in the area of present Kansas City was located on the north bank of the Missouri River (Clay County), approximately one-half mile west of the north end of the Chouteau Bridge. This post or warehouse thrived with several log buildings: warehouse, Chouteau home, and other houses for workers. The Randolph Bluffs post was destroyed by the flood of 1826 and was not rebuilt. Chouteau's next post (River of Kansas Post) was erected on the south bank of the Missouri River.

River of Kansas – A significant waterway in Kansas that is formed by the Saline with its tributaries the Smoky, the Solomon, the Republican, and the Big Blue, after which the combined waterway is known as the Kansas (Kaw) River. Travelers named the river in the 1600s after a tribe of Native Americans who lived in the area. (See **Kansa**.) At Kansas City, the Kansas River empties into the Missouri River just before that waterway bends to the north.

River of Kansas Post (Kansas City warehouse) – Francois Chouteau's second post in the area of present Kansas City was on the south bank of the Missouri River at what is now Olive Avenue (just east of the south end of the Paseo Bridge). For the purpose of clarity, the River of Kansas Post is referred to as the Kansas City warehouse in this book. Like the Randolph Bluffs Post, this establishment consisted of several buildings. A landing was developed near the warehouse for the loading of furs and unloading of merchandise. Another landing was later developed on a point of land at the mouth of the Kansas River. Both landings were destroyed in the flood of 1844.

Robidoux, Joseph (III) (1783-1868) – A fur trader who was born in St. Louis, and spent most of his life in the fur trade. In 1803, Robidoux built a trading post at the mouth of Black Snake Creek, where it empties into the Missouri River. Robidoux created such havoc by his unorthodox business methods that a group of his competitors paid him to stay out of the Indian country for two years. By the early 1830s, Robidoux was again at Black Snake Creek. The settlement that grew around that trading post became St. Joseph, Missouri. In addition to two marriages to women in St. Louis, Robidoux had relationships with several Indian women. With all his numerous offspring, plus those of his brothers, the Robidoux name is well represented among Native Americans in the Midwest and Rocky Mountains. (See also *DMB*.)

Joseph Robidoux (III). KSHS.

Roux, Benedict – The first Catholic pastor of the Kawsmouth French community, Father Roux was an idealistic Frenchman who came to America in 1831 to evangelize the Native Americans. He was scholarly, slight of build, and spoke only French and Latin. The St. Louis bishop Joseph Rosati recognized that Father Roux was not suited to Indian mission work, but yielding to Father Roux's persistence agreed to send the priest to establish a parish for the French Catholics near the mouth of the Kansas River. In November 1833, Father Roux arrived at Chouteau's Landing, having traveled by horseback through Liberty and Independence. In April 1834, he purchased forty acres from Pierre LaLiberte and a log church – "Chouteau's Church" – was built in 1835. But differences with parishioners over dancing, which the conservative French priest considered immoral, caused Father Roux to given up on the Catholics of the western frontier and returned to St. Louis in April 1835.

Ruland, John (1789-1849) – A special assistant to Superintendent of Indian Affairs William Clark, John Ruland (Chouteau's "Roland") was an aide referenced in Clark's diary. Ruland distributed some Indian annuities, solved special problems, and conducted negotiations.

Sac and Fox Indians – Two closely related Native Americans tribes who spoke an Algonquian language, the Sac and Fox dwelt in Michigan, but in the early seventeenth century they were driven from the area by the Ottawa and other tribes. The Sac (also written Sauk) and the Fox fled into present Wisconsin where the French found them around Green Bay in 1667. The Sac were farmers but spent much time hunting and raiding. The Fox were fierce warriors constantly fighting with the Ojibwa, the Sioux, and the Illinois, as well as the French who waged a war of extermination against them. Reduced to a mere handful by 1730, the Fox incorporated into their long-standing allies, the Sac, and became known collectively as the Sac and Fox. The Sac and Fox moved into Illinois territory in the mid-1760s. In 1804, they were tricked into a treaty that required them to move west of the Mississippi. Many refused to go and tensions continued until 1832 and the start of the ill-fated Black Hawk War. After that war the Sac and Fax moved west, first to land that would become Missouri's Platte Purchase and eventually onto reservations in Iowa, Kansas, and Oklahoma.

Saint Francis Regis Church – The first Catholic church of present Kansas City. It was a log cabin structure built in 1835, largely with funds contributed by Francois and Berenice Chouteau. For that reason, it was called "Chouteau's Church" until 1839, when a missionary to the Potawatomis, Father Herman Aelen, S.J., who also ministered to Catholic settlers in western Missouri, named it St. Francis Regis. The church stood on what is now the corner of 11th and Pennsylvania streets. It was razed in 1857, and replaced with a brick church that was the predecessor of the present Cathedral of the Immaculate Conception. Its nearby rectory, often called Father Donnelly's cabin, was torn down in the early 1880s.

Saint Louis College (St. Louis University) – Founded in November 1818 by the Catholic Bishop of Louisiana, Reverend Louis William Du Bourg, the first location of the college was in a private residence on the Mississippi riverbank. In 1826, at the bishop's request, the Jesuits took over the operation of the college. They were already in the area, having established a religious house in Florissant, Missouri, in 1823. (Pierre DeSmet was part of the original group at Florissant.) By 1829 the college had moved to a site about one mile northwest of the city – "At the edge of the wilderness." It was in this single brick building at Ninth and Washington that Edmond Chouteau attended classes. In 1867, land at Grand and Lindell became the permanent site of St. Louis University. St. Louis University received a formal charter from the State of Missouri in 1832 making it the oldest university west of the Mississippi and the second oldest Jesuit-operated university in the country. (Georgetown University was the first).

Saint Louis College erected in 1828. SLU.

Saint Mary's – Local sites referred to as St. Mary's are St. Mary's Catholic Church in Independence or Mount St. Mary's Cemetery in Kansas City. (See **Mount St. Mary's Cemetery**.) In the Chouteau letters, St. Mary's always referred to St. Mary's of the Barrens at Perryville, Missouri. (See **Barrens**.)

Sainte Genevieve – An historic Missouri village located on the west bank of the Mississippi River, fifty-four miles southeast of St. Louis, Ste. Genevieve was settled by the French in 1732(?). It was the home of the Valle family, as well as many other persons associated with the Indian trade in Missouri. Ste. Genevieve was also noted for its lead mining that remains a significant industry into modern times.

Sarpy, Gregorie Berald (1764-1824) – A St. Louis businessman Gregorie Sarpy married into the Chouteau family by taking as his wife Marie Pelagie Labbadie, daughter of Pierre de Laclede Liguest's daughter Marie Pelagie Chouteau Labaddie. Gregorie Sarpy was one of fur trader Manuel Lisa's partners when Lisa took from Auguste and Pierre Chouteau the valuable Osage Indian trade that the Chouteaus had monopolized for years. Gregorie was the father of Jean Baptiste Sarpy.

Sarpy, Jean Baptiste (1799-1859) – The "cousin Sarpy" mentioned in the Francois Chouteau letters, J. B. Sarpy was a St. Louis businessman who began his career as a clerk in Cadet Chouteau's American Fur Company store in St. Louis and later became a partner as well as the manager of the store. J. B. Sarpy gave Francois Chouteau's eldest son Edmond a position in the store after Edmond ended his school days.

Saucier, Angelique (1783-1839) – Born in Cahokia, Illinois, the daughter of Francois Saucier and Angelique Roy (Roi) *dit* Lepensee, Angelique Saucier became the second wife of Pierre Menard in 1806 and thereby became stepmother to three-year-old Berenice Menard. Angelique lived the rest of her life in Kaskaskia, Illinois. She and Pierre Menard had eight children: Francois Xavier, Henri, Jean Baptiste Edmond, Emilie, Matthieu Saucier, Louis Cyprien, Joseph Amadee, and Sophie Angelique. As Berenice Menard Chouteau's stepmother, Angelique was mentioned often as "my aunt" in the letters written by Francois Chouteau and as "dear *mama*" in Berenice's letters.

Saucier, Brigitte (1778-1829) – The daughter of François Saucier and Marguerite Cadron, and thereby the elder half-sister of Angelique Saucier, in 1794, Brigitte became the second wife of Pierre Chouteau Sr. Their first child was Francois Gesseau Chouteau, and Brigitte subsequently gave birth to four more sons: Cyprien, Pharamond, Charles, and Frederick.

Brigitte Saucier (Chouteau). An 1870s(?) painting after an earlier work. WHMC-KC.

Saucier, Francois (1740-1821) – The Saucier name was well-known on the Missouri-Illinois state line. Francois Saucier came from a family that had been prominent in Cahokia, Illinois, before he and his brother Mathieu founded the town of Portage des Sioux, Missouri. Francois Saucier was married three or four times. Four of his daughters married men of significance in the mercantile development of western Illinois and eastern Missouri: Pierre Menard, Pierre Chouteau Sr., James Morrison, and Jesse Morrison. (See also *DMB*.)

Section – A portion of land comprised of 640 acres, or 1/36 of a township. A common section was usually divided and sold in four parts of 160 acres each ("quarter section").

Seminole Indians – A Native American tribe that originally lived in Alabama and Georgia, but by the early 1800s was in Florida. They fought against the United States in an effort to retain their Florida land. Eventually the Seminoles were removed to Indian Territory (Oklahoma). (See also **Parks, Joseph**.)

Seres – See **Chouteau, Gabriel Sylvestre**.

Shallcross, John – Reportedly a native of Louisville, Kentucky, Shallcross worked his way to become a Steamboat captain employed by the American Fur Company. He was one of a series of Shallcross captains operating on the Missouri River. Among the vessels he commanded on the Missouri River were *Diana* (1820s to her sinking in October 1834), and the *Grey Eagle* the *Black Locust*, and the *Peyona* (1840s).

Shane, Anthony (1762?-1834) – The "Chaine" of Francois Chouteau's letters, Anthony Shane, was interpreter at the Delaware-Shawnee Agency in 1832. He was also a partner in the Shane and Wells trading post that existed during the 1830s, located near Westport at the state line. Francois Chouteau identified Anthony Shane as an "underagent of the Kansa." Shane was also involved in treaty negotiations and performed other services related to Indian affairs. Born Antoine Chene to a French Canadian father and Ottawa Indian mother, he grew up among the Shawnee tribes on their lands in Ohio. He reportedly was the person who identified the mutilated body of Tecumseh after the Battle of Thames on October 5, 1813. The September 29, 1817, treaty with the Wyandots, Senecas, Delawares, Shawnees, Potawatomis, Ottawas, and Chippewas (Article 8) allotted to him one section of land on the east side of the St. Mary's River,† near Rockfort, Ohio, where the Shanes Crossing Historical

Society has restored a double-log (two-story) house they believe was his home. His wife Lamateshe was a Delaware Indian who was converted to the Baptist Church by Isaac McCoy. Although Catholic, Shane had a close association with McCoy. Shane came to Kansas with the Shawnees in 1828. Charles Shane, mentioned in Chouteau's letter dated February 15, 1830, was the son of Anthony Shane.

† Charles J. Kappler, *Indian Affairs, Laws and Treaties*, 2: 148.

Shawanock (Shouanock) – One of four sons of Delaware head chief William Anderson, Shawanock also became a Delaware chief and was a signatory of the peace treaty among several tribes brokered by the Ellsworth group in November 1833.

Shawnee Indians – An Algonquian tribe of Native Americans who in 1650 lived in Cumberland Valley, Tennessee, but probably originated farther north. Closely related to the Fox, Sac, and Kickapoo tribes, the Shawnees moved into the Ohio Valley where they resisted white expansion but were defeated in 1794. They again lost at the Battle of Tippecanoe in 1811 and were forced into Illinois, then across Missouri. By 1828-1829, most of them had moved into Indian Territory (Kansas). "Shawnee" means "southerner," perhaps a name given them by other Indians when the Shawnees lived in present Tennessee. (Francois Chouteau wrote their name as *chavenon* in his letters.) By the twentieth century, the Shawnees had moved to Oklahoma.

Shawnee Methodist Mission and Indian Manual Labor School – See **Johnson, Thomas**.

Shawnee Post – The trading post known as "Cyprien's Post" by the 1840s and referred to as the "Turner Site" by modern archeologists, the Shawnee Post was built in 1828, as described by Francois Chouteau in his letter to Pierre Menard dated December 2, 1828. Father Joseph Anthony Lutz wrote in a letter: "Messrs. Francis, Cyprien and Frederick Chouteau have begun to erect at the Kanzas River a large building which will soon be looked upon as a sort of emporium for the sale and exchange of goods among the Shawnee and Kanzas Indians."† The Shawnee Post was located on the south bank of the Kansas River about twelve miles above the mouth of the river. Grinter House stands today on the north bank and across the river from the old post, which disappeared years ago.

† Garraghan, *Catholic Beginnings in Kansas City, Missouri*, 32.

Shawnee Village – An Indian town established by Shawnee Indians who had come to Indian Territory (Kansas) from 1825 to 1829. The village was in present Johnson County, south of the Kansas River and five miles west of the state line, near the present intersection of Nieman Road and Johnson Drive.

Simpson, Richard "Duke" (1770-1853) – Of the several Simpson men who were in the Kansas City and Westport area during the late 1830s and 1840s, Duke Simpson was the most likely to have been related to these letters. He had been actively involved in the anti-Mormon movement in 1833-1834, and along with James M. Hunter was among the first to receive a free lot from John C. McCoy as an enticement to build in Westport. Located on the southwest corner of Westport and Pennsylvania in the heart of Old Westport, the Hunter and Simpson establishment was "where the Indian agents often left money to be distributed to the Indians."† Its principals were involved with both the local and the freighting businesses. Also, a James Simpson was employed as a blacksmith for the Shawnees at the Fort Leavenworth Agency in 1838-1844, and by various accounts may have also been involved in trade.

† Westport Scrapbook, 45-46, (KC396), WHMC-KC.

Sol – An old French monetary unit, equal to about one cent.

Sublette, Milton (1801-1837) – Of the five Sublette brothers (Andrew, Milton, Pinckney, Solomon, and William) engaged in the fur trade, Milton was the one mentioned in the Chouteau letters because he was involved in the contention over 500 fur packs at the mouth of the Kansas River (Letter, July 14, 1837 on page 164). In 1830, Milton joined with Jim Bridger, Thomas Fitzpatrick, Henry Fraeb, and Jean Gervais to form the Rocky Mountain Fur Company, but four years later the company was absorbed by the superior resources of the American Fur Company (Pratte, Chouteau & Company.) Milton died of an injury that required his legs to be amputated. Milton's older brother William Sublette (1799-1845), a mountain man, trapper, and fur trader during the 1830s and 1840s was the most well known Sublette. He appeared regularly in Westport and as a land speculator, was one of the original fourteen shareholders in the Town of Kansas Company. William Sublette eventually moved to St. Louis and died in Pittsburgh, Pennsylvania, en route to the East Coast.

Subscription school – A privately founded and operated school with tuition paid in money or goods by the parents or guardians of the students. This type of school was also often funded with subscriptions, that is, money collected from the community.

"Kanzas City," Ballou's Pictorial Drawing-room Companion, 4 August 1855. Perhaps drawn after an early daguerreotype, represents the Town of Kansas ca. 1850. WHMC-KC.

Town of Kansas – The settlement, early on called Kawsmouth, that dated from as early as 1818, and extended from the mouth of the Kansas River to Chouteau's Landing. The Town of Kansas was sometimes derisively called "Westport Landing" because of its use beginning in 1834 as an offloading site for goods destined for the stores in Westport, located about four miles to the south. Later, it was more properly referred to as "Kansas Landing" in recognition of the organization of the Town of Kansas in 1838 by fourteen investors from Kawsmouth, Westport, and Independence. The site was centered on a rock outcrop at the river's bank that formed a natural wharf, or landing, for the steamboats to load and unload goods. It was located on Gabriel Prudhomme's farm, roughly at the foot of present-day

Main Street. In 1850, the Town of Kansas was incorporated by Jackson County, and three years later by the state of Missouri, as the City of Kansas.

Trading Post (Kansas) – A trading post established in 1835 near the Marais des Cygne River, it was operated by Frenchmen for the American Fur Company. Possibly Paul Liguest Chouteau built the post, originally for the Osage Nation. In 1839, a license was issued to Pierre (Cadet) Chouteau to operate this post for the "newly arrived" Potawatomi Indians. The first operator for whom a name is known was Michael Giraud (Giareau) who was there by the early 1840s. The post was located in present Linn County, Kansas, about three miles west of the Missouri line, and near present Paola, Kansas. The present town of Trading Post, Kansas, grew up around the old establishment, and acquired its name.

Turner Site – See **Shawnee Post**.

Uneau – See **Hunot**.

Jean Baptiste Valle and Jeanne Barbeau Valle. MHS.

Valle, Jean Baptiste (1760-1849) – A Ste. Genevieve merchant who was Pierre Menard's partner in the Menard and Valle stores in Ste. Genevieve and Kaskaskia from 1820 until Pierre Menard's death in 1844. Valle was the leading citizen of Ste. Genevieve, and his influence reached into the many elements of town life. J. B. Valle's son Felix Valle managed the Ste. Genevieve store from its beginning and assumed total responsibility for the business as his father aged. Madame Valle, wife of Jean Baptiste Valle, was the former Jeanne Barbeau of Prairie du Rocher, Illinois. (See also *DMB*.)

Van Bibber, Alfonzo (Alonzo) B. (d. 1842?) – Several Van Bibber men figured in the fur trade of the late 1820s and 1830s, as well as the development of Westport. Jesse Van Bibber was a trapper who had worked at the mouth of the Verdigris River near present Muskogee, Oklahoma. A Joseph Van Bibber was associated with the Iowa Agency from 1830 to 1833 as a blacksmith. The man who sold traps to Francois Chouteau, as mentioned to Pierre (Cadet) Chouteau Jr., in his July 6, 1835, letter was most likely Alfonso Van Bibber, who had been a partner with Albert Gallatin Boone prior to 1839 and had an account with Ewing, Clymer & Company in 1839-1840 for Indian trade goods for which he paid in furs and peltries. The Boone and Van Bibber families were variously intertwined, with two of Daniel Boone's sons marrying Van Bibber daughters.

Van Quickenborne, Charles F., S.J. (1788-1837) – A Catholic missionary priest of the Jesuit religious order who worked along the Missouri-Kansas border during the 1830s, Father Van Quickenborne served Catholic Native Americans and the French Catholics at Kawsmouth and around Chouteau's establishment. He was the first minister to officiate at "Chouteau's Church" after it was completed in 1835. He also performed baptisms and marriages in the Osage Nation. Father Van Quickenborne visited the Kickapoo Nation in 1835, held religious services in Laurent Pensineau's trading post, and in June 1836, opened the Kickapoo Catholic Mission. It did not thrive, however, and was closed in 1840. Suffering from poor health, Father Van Quickenborne returned to St. Louis, where he died at the age of forty-nine.

Vashon, George – Often called "Captain," George Vashon was in June 1829 appointed agent of the Shawnee Agency for the Shawnees, Delawares, Piankeshaws, Peorias, Weas, and Kickapoos. Vashon left the Shawnee Agency in July 1830 to become agent of the Western Cherokee Agency in Oklahoma.

Vasquez, Antoine F., *dit* **Baronet** (1783-1828) – The son of a Spanish family prominent in the fur trade in the late 1700s, Baronet's father was Benito Vasquez and his mother Julia Papin *dit* Baronet. (The elder Vasquez was one of four fur traders awarded the Kansa Indian trade in 1794.) In 1806, Baronet was an interpreter with Zebulon Pike's expedition to Mexico where he was arrested and imprisoned. After returning to the United States, Vasquez joined the army and fought under William Henry Harrison at the Battle of Tippecanoe. On April 13, 1825, he was appointed subagent for the Kansas Agency, then located in his home on the river bank in present Kansas City, probably at what is now Gillis Street. The Kansa Agency was relocated farther west in 1827 for the convenience of the Indians. In August 1828, en route from St. Louis to the mouth of the Kansas River, Vasquez died of cholera. He had been traveling overland with Rev. Joseph Anthony Lutz, a German priest who hoped to establish a Catholic mission among the Kansa Indians.

After her husband's death, Madame Vasquez (Emilie Forastin Parent) sold their home to the American Fur Company and returned to St. Louis with her children. Her first attempt to voyage to eastern Missouri ended when the keelboat *Beaver*, on which she and her children were sailing, sank in the Missouri River near Independence. The Vasquez family survived the catastrophe and later completed their return to St. Louis. Francois Chouteau called her "Madame Baronet" as well as "Madame Vasquez."

Voyageur – A French word meaning a person who voyages or travels on waterways for a living. Operating his own small boat, a *voyageur* was often employed by a fur company to transport hunters, trappers, and their supplies to remote trapping and hunting grounds. The silence of the forests along the riverbanks was sometimes interrupted by the sound of these men singing French songs to establish rowing cadence. (*Voyageurs* were also referred to as *engagees*, meaning hired persons.)

Waldo, David (1802-1878) – Although best known for thirty years as a Santa Fe trade merchant and freighter, Waldo's first career was in medicine. He had received his medical degree in Lexington, Kentucky, before coming to Missouri in 1831. He may have practiced medicine briefly, but he soon entered into merchandising, freighting, and land speculation. Waldo lived and died in Independence. (See also *DMB*.)

War Department – The United States governmental unit that was in charge of the Office of Indian Affairs after it was established in 1824. Peter Porter was Secretary of War from 1828 to 1829. John Eaton held the office from 1829 to 1831.

Wea Indians – A band of the Piankeshaws/Miamis who lived in the area of present Chicago during the late seventeenth century. Pressure from the Potawatomis forced the Weas to move to Ohio, then to Indiana. By 1827, they had lost most of their land in the United States and settled in Indian Territory (Kansas) with their relatives, the Piankeshaws, Peorias, and Kaskaskias. The Weas are a Miami subtribe.

Wells – A Mr. Wells was in the Indian trade in the 1830s in partnership with Anthony Shane at their post north of Westport near the state line. (See **Shane, Anthony**.) This Wells may also have been the "little Wells" of Chouteau's letter dated February 15, 1829. In 1837, a J. B. Wells was growing timothy grain and fescue on contract for Fort Leavenworth. Other men named Wells appeared in the area at a much later date.

Westport Landing – See **Town of Kansas**.

White Hair, Chief – In the late eighteenth century and through much of the nineteenth century, several Osage chiefs were known as "White Hair." The first Chief White Hair was born in the early 1700s; he was related to Osage Chief Clermont. White Hair was friendly to the French fur traders, and allowed himself to be influenced by them, as well as by the U.S. government. White Hair I signed a treaty in 1808 ceding to the United States most of the Osage land in Missouri and Arkansas. White Hair II took over his father's role as friend to the fur traders and the United States. He released the government from obligations made in the 1808 treaty, but in doing so, lost the support of much of the Osage tribe. He died in the spring of 1832. The next Chief White Hair (Maiakita) was the son of White Hair II's sister. He was deposed in 1843. Other chiefs named White Hair continued to be prominent in Osage affairs until the 1870s. (See also *DMB*.)

White Plume, Chief (Manshenscaw) (d. 1838) – An influential chief of the Kansa Indians during the negotiations with the United States government over the compensation for Indian lands and the restriction of hunting grounds. Chief White Plume signed the Treaty of 1825 in which Kansa lands were ceded to the United States in exchange for a new reservation and other compensations, including "tracts"(allotments) for Kansa "half-breeds." A stone house was built for Chief White Plume near the Kansas Agency, and he lived in it for many years. By 1838, other Kansa leaders had risen to greater prominence than White Plume.

Widen (Wyden), **Raphael** – Pierre Menard's assistant, secretary, and accountant, Widen conducted business for his employer when Menard was absent from Kaskaskia. Widen was the "Raphael" mentioned in the letters of Francois and Berenice Chouteau.

Wilson, Moses Green – Born in West Virginia, Wilson came with his brother Thomas to Jackson County, Missouri in 1833. He operated a country store one mile west of the Blue River on the Independence-Kansas City road, near the Chouteau farm. It was near his store that a mob of about sixty men attacked the Mormons on October 31, 1833. Wilson was one of the original group forming the Town of Kansas Company in 1838, but sold his share to Robert Campbell and moved to California in 1845. (Mentioned in Chouteau to Menard, March 24, 1837.)

Woods, Andrew (ca. 1777-1832) – As a part of Manuel Lisa's Missouri Fur Company, Andrew Woods opened a post near the mouth of the Kansas River in 1820. He operated under licenses issued to the Missouri Fur Company. In addition to being mentioned by Prince Paul, the "Woods establishment" was referred to by Thomas Hempstead, a partner in the Missouri Fur Company.† Woods apparently discontinued his Kansas River post in 1824. He died in Jackson County in 1832.

† Barry, *Beginning of the West*, 99; "Fur posts at Kawsmouth," Chouteau's (Topical) Scrapbook [17.1], (KC395), WHMC-KC.

Wuerttemberg, Prince Paul Wilhelm of (1797-1860) – The duke of the small, independent Germanic state of Wuerttemberg (Germany had not yet been unified), Prince Paul visited America and toured in the West in 1823, hunting, observing plants and animals. He recorded facts and impressions in his *Diary*, which has become a valuable reference work that provides information not available elsewhere. Apparently Prince Paul did not meet the Chouteaus in June 1823 when he stopped near the mouth of the Kansas River, as he did not mention them.

Wyandot Indians – A Native American people of the Huron Confederacy who spoke a kind of Iroquoian language, their name means "dwellers of the islands." The Wyandots originated in Canada north of the Great Lakes. They did not hunt, but were great traders and ranged far on both land and water, trading whatever they had – mostly agricultural products grown by the women of the tribe. After their tribal lands were sold, the Wyandots migrated through Michigan, Ohio, Indiana, Illinois, and Missouri, arriving in eastern Indian Territory (Kansas) in 1842.

Yellow Stone (steamboat), *Yellow Stone Packet* (keelboat) – The American Fur Company owned two vessels named the *Yellow Stone*. The steamboat *Yellow Stone* made its appearance on the Missouri River in 1831. It was designed with a shallow draft so that it could navigate the Missouri all the way to the Yellowstone River. A keelboat named the *Yellow Stone Packet* preceded the steamboat, and this must have been the ship referred to in the note written by Pierre Menard on the envelope of Francois Chouteau's letter of March 3, 1829 (*PMC*, Letter 282). (See also *Voyages of the Yellow Stone* by Donald Jackson.)

Steamboat Yellow Stone, drawn by Karl Bodmer. WHMC-KC.

A Selected Bibligraphy

Archival Material

Andrew Drips (1790-1860) Collection, [NSA] (KC335), WHMC-KC.
"Andrew Drips notes," Chouteau's (Biographical) Scrapbook [17.2], *Native Sons of Kansas City Scrapbooks* [NSA] (KC395), WHMC-KC.
Archives of the Midwest Province of the Congregation of the Mission, St. Mary's of the Barrens, Perryville, Missouri.
Aull Family Business Records, 1830-1862 (C3038), WHMC-C.
"Calise Montordeau notes," Chouteau's (Biographical) Scrapbook [17.2], *Native Sons of Kansas City Scrapbooks* [NSA] (KC395), WHMC-KC.
Catalogue excerpts, University Archives, St. Louis University, St. Louis, Missouri.
"Clement Lessert notes," Fur Trade Biographies, Chouteau's (Biographical) Scrapbook [17.2], *Native Sons of Kansas City Scrapbooks* [NSA] (KC395), WHMC-KC.
Chouteau Family Collection, MHS.
"Chouteau Family in Kansas City notes," Clyde Porter Scrapbook [56.1], *Native Sons of Kansas City Scrapbooks* [NSA] (KC395), WHMC-KC.
Clay County Record Books, Clay County Archives, Liberty, Missouri.
"Cyprien Chouteau and family notes," Chouteau's (Biographical) Scrapbook [17.3], *Native Sons of Kansas City Scrapbooks* [NSA] (KC395), WHMC-KC.
Dougherty Family Papers, (MC331), KSHS.
E. B. Trail, (1884-1965), Collection (C2071), WHMC-C.
"Ewing, Clymer & Company Account Book notes," Westport (Topical) Scrapbook [71.2], *Native Sons of Kansas City Scrapbooks* [NSA] (KC395), WHMC-KC.
Fort Leavenworth Agency, 1824-1836, Letters received by the Office of Indian Affairs, 1824-1881 (OIA), Records Group 234, Microfilm roll 300, NARA.
Fort Leavenworth Agency, 1824-1851, 1836-1838, Letters received by the Office of Indian Affairs, 1824-1881 (OIA), Records Group 234, Microfilm roll 751, NARA.
Fort Leavenworth Agency, 1824-1851, 1843-1848, Letters received by the Office of Indian Affairs, 1824-1881 (OIA), Records Group 234, Microfilm roll 302, NARA.
Frederick Chouteau Letters, May 6, 1880, General (series B), Kansa (subgroup 9), *Indians History Collection*, (MC590), KSHS.
"Francois Chouteau and family notes," Chouteau's (Biographical) Scrapbook [17.3], *Native Sons of Kansas City Scrapbooks* [NSA] (KC395), WHMC-KC.
Funeral Book, Archives of the Basilica of St. Louis the King (The Old Cathedral), St. Louis, Missouri.
"Fur Posts at Kawsmouth," Chouteau's (Topical) Scrapbook [17.1], *Natives Sons of Kansas City Scrapbooks* [NSA] (KC395), WHMC-KC.

"Gabriel Prudhomme and family notes," Fur Trade Biographies, Chouteau's (Biographical) Scrapbook [17.2], *Native Sons of Kansas City Scrapbooks* [NSA] (KC395), WHMC-KC.

"Hunot (Uneau) notes," Fur Trade Biographies, Chouteau's (Biographical) Scrapbook [17.2], *Native Sons of Kansas City Scrapbooks* [NSA] (KC395), WHMC-KC.

"Incidents of the 'Knob Hill' or aristocratic residence quarter of Kansas City of early days" typescript manuscript by William L. Campbell in "Recollections of pioneers," Kansas City Before the Civil War Scrapbook [35], *Native Sons of Kansas City Scrapbooks* [NSA] (KC395), WHMC-KC.

"Interview with Nancy Chouteau, Wife of Cyprien Chouteau," October 1, 1908, *Byron Chouteau Miscellaneous Collection*, KSHS.

Isaac McCoy Papers, Microfilm roll 7, KSHS.

John A. Dougherty (1791-1860) Letter Book, 1826-1829 (C2292), WHMC-C.

John Calvin McCoy (1811-1889) Collection [NSA] (KC296), WHMC-KC.

"Joseph S. Chick interview," October 19, 1908, General (series A), Kansa (subgroup 9), *Indians History Collection*, (MC590), KSHS.

Kansas City Scrapbook, *James Anderson Scrapbooks* (KC396), WHMC-KC.

Kansas Town Company Records [NSA] (KC352), WHMC-KC.

Kaskaskia Papers, MHS.

"Land Data notes," Chouteau's (Topical) Scrapbook [17.1], *Native Sons of Kansas City Scrapbooks* [NSA] (KC395), WHMC-KC.

Letter. Judith Peluso, Archives, Calvary Cemetery, St. Louis, Missouri, to Dorothy Marra, August 9, 1999.

Letter. David Wallace, Old Military and Civil Records, National Archives, to Dorothy Marra, December 6, 1999.

Letterbook "J" [9/1829-2/1834], *Pierre Menard Collection,* IHS.

Louise Arnold-Friend, U.S. Army Military History Institute, to Dorothy Marra, November 22, 1999.

Menard Family Collection, Chicago Historical Society.

Menard and Valle Papers, Chicago Historical Society.

Necrology Scrapbooks, MHS.

Papers of the St. Louis Fur Trade, MHS.

Père Nicolas Point, S.J., Collection, Archives de la Compagnie de Jesus, province du Canada frantais, (ASJCF), Quebec, Canada.

Pierre Jean De Smet (1801-1873) Papers, Manuscripts, Archives, and Special Collections, Washington State University Libraries.

Pierre Menard Collection (PMC), ISHL.

Records of the Catholic Osage Mission on the Neosho River (St. Paul, Kansas), Diocese of Wichita, Wichita, Kansas.

Records of the Catholic Osage Mission on the Neosho River (St. Paul, Kansas), (Microfilm MS093), KSHS.

Register of Interments, Mount St. Mary's Catholic Cemetery, Kansas City, Missouri.

Rev. Benedict Roux folder, *Letters of Bishop Joseph Rosati,* Archives of the Archdiocese of St. Louis, St. Louis, Missouri.

Rev. Joseph Anthony Lutz folder, *Letters of Bishop Joseph Rosati,* Archives of the Archdiocese of St. Louis, St. Louis, Missouri.

Richard Graham Collection, MHS.

St. Louis Superintendency, 1827-1828, Letters received by the Office of Indian Affairs, 1824-1881 (OIA), Records Group 234, NARA.

St. Louis Superintendency, 1829-1831, Letters received by the Office of Indian Affairs, 1824-1881 (OIA), Records Group 234, NARA.
Ste. Genevieve Academy Record Book (C1234), WHMC-C.
Sworn affidavit by Berenice F. Chouteau dated October 26, 1887, recorded May 28, 1890, Book B423, page 404 (150360), Jackson County, Missouri.
U.S. Superintendency of Indian Affairs (SIA), St. Louis, 1813-1825 (MC741), KSHS.
Vasquez Family Collection, MHS.
Westport Scrapbook, *James Anderson Scrapbooks* (KC396), WHMC-KC.
William V. Morrison Collection, ISHL.

Government Documents

American State Papers: Indian Affairs. 2 vols. Washington, D.C.: Gales and Seaton, 1834.
Kappler, Charles J., comp. *Indian Affairs, Laws and Treaties.* 2 vols. Washington, D.C.: Government Printing Office, 1904.
Kurz, Rudolph Friederich. *Journal of Rudolph Friederich Kurz: an Account of His Experiences Among Fur Traders and American Indians on the Mississippi and the Upper Missouri Rivers During the Years 1846 to 1852.* Jarrell, Myrtis, and J. N. B. Hewitt, eds. Smithsonian Institution, *Bureau of American Ethnology Bulletin* 115, 234-237.
State of Illinois Census records. U.S. Bureau of the Census, 1820, 1830, 1840, 1850, 1870, 1880.
State of Missouri Census records. U.S. Bureau of the Census, 1830, 1840, 1850, 1860, 1870.
Territorial Papers of the United States. Washington, D.C.: Government Printing Office, 1934.
U.S. Congressional Serial Set
    H. Doc. No. 118, 19th Cong., 1st sess. (Serial 136).
    H. Doc. No. 104, 22nd Cong., 2nd sess. (Serial 234).
    H. Doc. No. 137, 22nd Cong., 2nd sess. (Serial 235).
    H. Doc. No. 45, 23rd Cong., 1st sess. (Serial 254).
    H. Doc. No. 490, 23rd Cong., 1st sess. (Serial 259).
    H. Doc. No. 97, 23rd Cong., 2nd sess. (Serial 273).
    S. Doc. No. 58, 19th Cong., 2nd sess. (Serial 146).
    S. Doc. No. 27, 20th Cong., 2nd sess. (Serial 181).
    S. Doc. No. 512, 23rd Cong., 1st sess. (Serial 246).
    S. Doc. No. 512, 23rd Cong., 1st sess. (Serial 247).
    S. Doc. No. 200, 25th Cong., 2nd sess. (Serial 316).
    S. Doc. No. 174, 28th Cong., 2nd sess. (Serial 416).
U.S. Department of the Interior, Bureau of Land Management (BLM), The Official Federal Land Patent Records Site." 13 July 2001. http://www.glorecords.blm.gov/ (18 July 2001).

Books and Articles

Abel, Anna Heloise. "Indian Reservations in Kansas and the Extinguishment of Their Title." *KHC* 8 (1904): 72-109.
Adams, Franklin G., ed. "Reminiscences of Frederick Chouteau." *KHC* 8 (1904): 423-434.
"Amazon Sunk." *Liberty Tribune,* 10 April 1857, 1.

Anderson, James. "The Roys and the Rivards at Chouteau's." *Missouri Historical Society Bulletin* 4 (July 1948): 257-260.
Bagen, John J. *St. Mary's of the Barrens Parish: The Early Days*. Perryville, MO: Association of the Miraculous Medal, 1987.
Bakeless, John, ed. *The Journals of Lewis and Clark: A New Selection*. New York: New American Library, 1964.
Baker, Harry S. "The First Lieutenant-Governor of Illinois." In *Chicago Historical Society Collections* 4 (1890): 149-161.
Barnes, Lela. "Journal of Isaac McCoy for the Exploring Expedition of 1828." *KHQ* 5 (August 1936): 227-277.
Barry, Louise. "William Clark's Diary, May 1826-February 1831." *KHQ* 16 (1948): 1-39, 136-174, 274-305, 384-410.
———. *Beginning of the West: Annals of the Kansas Gateway to the American West 1540-1854*. Topeka: Kansas State Historical Society, 1972.
Baughman, Robert W. *Kansas in Maps*. Topeka: Kansas State Historical Society, 1961.
Beckwith, Paul. *Creoles of St. Louis*. St. Louis: Nixon-Jones Printing, 1893.
Beckwourth, James P. *The Life and Adventures of James P. Beckwourth: Mountaineer, Scout, and Pioneer and Chief of the Crow Nation of Indians*. Edited by Thomas D. Bonner. New York: Arno Press, 1969.
Billon, Frederick. *Annals of St. Louis in its Territorial Days, from 1804 to 1821*. St. Louis: Nixon-Jones Printing, 1888.
Bishop, Zelia. "Kansas City Traders and Merchants." *Kansas Magazine* (1951), 51-56.
Blair, Ed. *History of Johnson County, Kansas*. Lawrence, KS: Standard Publishing, 1915.
Brackenridge, Henry M. *A Journal of a Voyage up the River Missouri, Performed in Eighteen Hundred and Eleven*. Baltimore: Pomeroy & Troy, 1816.
Bray, Edmund C., and Martha Coleman Bray, eds. *Joseph Nicollet on the Plains and Prairies: the Expeditions of 1838-1839 with Journals, Letters, and Notes on the Dakota Indians*. St. Paul: Minnesota Historical Society Press, 1993.
Brewer, Eileen. *Nuns and the Education of American Catholic Women, 1860-1920*. Chicago: Loyola University Press, 1987.
Brown, A. Theodore. *Frontier Community, Kansas City to 1870*. Columbia: University of Missouri Press, 1963.
"Burial notice – Francis Chouteau." *St. Louis Republican*, 25 April 1838.
Burns, Louis F. *Osage Mission Baptisms, Marriages, and Interments, 1820-1886*. Fallbrook, CA: Ciga Press, 1986.
Caldwell, Martha Belle, ed. *Annals of Shawnee Methodist Mission and Indian Manual Labor School*. Topeka: Kansas State Historical Society, 1939.
Callan, Louise. *The Society of the Sacred Heart in North America*. New York: Longmans, Green, 1937.
Case, Theodore Spencer. *History of Kansas City, Missouri; with Illustrations and Biographical Sketches of Some of Its Prominent Men and Pioneers*. Syracuse, NY: D. Mason, 1888.
"Catholic Church Annals of Kansas City (1800-1857)." Miscellany, *Catholic Historical Review* 3 (October 1917): 326-335.
Catholic Directory, 1836-1860. Wilmette, IL: P. J. Kenedy & Sons, published yearly.
Chapman, Carl H., and Eleanor Chapman. *Indians and Archaeology of Missouri*. Columbia: University of Missouri Press, 1983.
Chappell, Phil E. "A History of the Missouri River." *KHC* 9 (1906): 237-316.
Chick, Joseph S. "Methodism in Early Kansas City." *Missouri Valley Historical Society Annals of Kansas City* 3: 309-312.

———. "Kaw River, Recession of at Kansas City." In *Encyclopedia of the History of Missouri: A Compendium of History and Biography for Ready Reference*, edited by Howard Conard, 3: 510. St. Louis: Southern History Co., 1901.

Chick, Washington Henry. "A Journey to Missouri in 1822." *Missouri Valley Historical Society Annals of Kansas City* 1: 97-103.

Chittenden, Hiram M. *History of Early Steamboat Navigation on the Missouri River; Life and Adventures of Joseph La Barge*. 2 vols. New York: F. P. Harper, 1903.

———. *List of Steamboat Wrecks on the Missouri River: From the Beginning to the Present*. Washington D.C.: Government Printing Office, 1897.

———. *The American Fur Trade of the Far West: A History of Pioneer Trading Posts & Early Fur Companies of the Missouri Valley & Rocky Mountains & of the Overland Commerce with Santa Fe*. 2 vols. New York: Press of the Pioneers, 1935.

Christensen, Lawrence O., William E. Foley, Gary R. Kremer, and Kenneth H. Winn, eds. *Dictionary of Missouri Biography*. Columbia: University of Missouri Press, 1999.

Clark, R. "The Prairie." In *The United States Illustrated: The West*, edited by Charles A. Dana, 26-28. New York: Herrmann J. Meyer, [1853].

Coleman, Michael, Colette Doering, and Dorothy Marra. *This Far by Faith: A Popular History of the Catholic People of West and Northwest Missouri*. Kansas City: Diocese of Kansas City-St. Joseph, 1992.

Conard, Howard, ed. *Encyclopedia of the History of Missouri: A Compendium of History and Biography for Ready Reference*. St. Louis: Southern History Co., 1901.

Congregation of the Mission Vincent DePaul, Midwest Province. *Saint Mary's of the Barrens, Perryville, Missouri*. Perryville, MO: Association of the Miraculous Medal, 1993.

Connelley, William E., ed. "The Provisional Government of Nebraska Territory and The Journals of William Walker, Provisional Governor of Nebraska Territory." *Proceedings & Collections of the Nebraska State Historical Society* 7 (1899).

———. *History of Kansas*. Chicago: American Historical Society, 1928.

Cunningham, Mary B., and Jeanne C. Blythe. *The Founding Family of St. Louis*. St. Louis: Midwest Technical Publications, 1977.

Cutler, William G. *History of the State of Kansas*. Chicago: A. T. Andreas, 1883.

Dalton, William J. *The Life of Father Bernard Donnelly; with Historical Sketches of Kansas City, St. Louis and Independence, Missouri*. Kansas City: Grimes-Joyce Printing, 1921. Reprint, Kansas City: Cathedral of the Immaculate Conception, 1986.

Davis, Mary B., ed. *Native America in the Twentieth Century: An Encyclopedia*. New York: Garland Publishing, 1994.

Deatherage, Charles P. *Early History of Greater Kansas City, Missouri and Kansas: The Prophetic City at the Mouth of the Kaw, Early History from October 12, 1492 to 1870*. Kansas City: Interstate Publishing, 1927.

Denton, Doris. "*Harmony Mission, 1821-1837*." Master's thesis, University of Kansas, 1929.

Dictionary of Indian Tribes of the Americas. Newport Beach, CA: American Indian Publishers, 1995.

"Died ... Francis Chouteau." *Missouri Saturday Evening News*, 28 April 1838, 3.

Donnelly, Joseph P., ed. *Wilderness Kingdom, Indian Life in the Rocky Mountains, 1840-1847: The Journals & Paintings of Nicolas Point*. New York: Holt, Rinehart and Winston, 1967.

Doohan, John J. "River Front, Now Firmly Anchored, Was Subject of Long Fight for Possession." *Kansas City Times*, 4 May 1951.

Drumm, Stella M., ed. *Down the Santa Fe Trail and into Mexico: The Diary of Susan Shelby Magoffin, 1846-1847*. New Haven: Yale University Press, 1926.

Ekberg, Carl J. *Colonial Ste. Genevieve, An Adventure on the Mississippi Frontier*. Gerald, MO: Patrice Press, 1985.

———. *French Roots in the Illinois Country: The Mississippi Frontier in Colonial Times*. Urbana: University of Illinois Press, 2000.

Ellsworth, Henry Leavitt. *Washington Irving on the Prairie; or, A Narrative of a Tour of the Southwest in the Year 1832*. Edited by Stanley T. Williams and Barbara D. Simison. New York: American Book Co., 1937.

English, William Hayden. *Conquest of the Country Northwest of the River Ohio, 1778-1783; And Life of Gen. George Rogers Clark*. 2 vols. Indianapolis and Kansas City: Bowen-Merrill, 1896.

"Extensive Lands Now Part of Kansas City." *Kansas City Star*, 14 February 1926, 1(D).

"Faded Glimpses of Pearl Street." *Kansas City Star*, 29 October 1916, 10(C).

Faherty, William B., S.J. *Dream by the River, Two Centuries of Saint Louis Catholicism, 1766-1967*. St. Louis: Piraeus Publishers, 1973.

"Female Voyageur: First White Woman to Ascend the Missouri." *Kansas City Times*, 6 December 1872.

Foley, William E. *A History of Missouri, 1673-1820*. Columbia: University of Missouri Press, 2000.

———. *The Genesis of Missouri From Wilderness Outpost to Statehood*. Columbia: University of Missouri Press, 1989.

———, and C. David Rice. *The First Chouteaus, River Barons of Early St. Louis*. Urbana: University of Illinois Press, 1983.

Foreman, Grant. *Indians and Pioneers: The Story of the American Southwest before 1830*. Norman: University of Oklahoma Press, 1936.

Franzwa, Gregory M. *The Story of Old Ste. Genevieve*. St. Louis: Patrice Press, 1990.

Gardner, Mark L., ed. *Brothers on the Santa Fe and Chihuahua Trails: Edward James Glasgow and William Henry Glasgow, 1846-1848*. Niwot, CO: University Press of Colorado, 1993.

Garraghan, Gilbert J., S.J. *Catholic Beginnings in Kansas City, Missouri: An Historical Sketch*. Chicago: Loyola University Press, 1920.

———. *Jesuits of the Middle United States*. 3 vols. Chicago: Loyola University Press, 1983.

Goff, William A. "Andrew Drips at Kawsmouth and Kansas City." *The Westport Historical Quarterly* 6 (December 1970): 3-16.

Graves, William W., Gilbert J. Garraghan, and George Towle. *History of the Kickapoo Mission and Parish: the First Catholic Church in Kansas*. St. Paul, KS: Journal Press, 1938.

Gregg, Kate L. "The History of Fort Osage." *MHR* 34 (July 1940): 439-488.

Gregg, Oliver H. "History of Johnson County, Kansas." In *Atlas Map of Johnson County, Kansas*. Wyandott, KS: E. F. Heisler, 1874.

Guide to Calvary Cemetery. St. Louis: Calvary Cemetery.

Guide to the Microfilm Edition of the Pierre Menard Collection in the Illinois State Historical Library. Springfield: Illinois State Historical Society, 1972.

Hafen, LeRoy R., ed. *French Fur Traders and Voyageurs in the American West: Twenty-Five Sketches*. Lincoln: University of Nebraska Press, 1997.

———. *Fur Traders, Trappers, and Mountain Men of the Upper Missouri*. Lincoln: University of Nebraska Press, 1995.

———. *The Mountain Men and the Fur Trade of the Far West*. 10 vols. Glendale, CA: Arthur H. Clark, 1965-1972.

Harrington, Grant W. *Historic Spots, or Mile-stones in the Progress of Wyandotte County, Kansas*. Merriam, KS: Mission Press, 1935.

———. *The Shawnees in Kansas*. Kansas City, KS: Western Pioneer Press, 1937.

Harris, Nellie McCoy. "Memories of Old Westport." *Missouri Valley Historical Society Annals of Kansas City* 4: 465-475.

Heckman, William L. *Steamboating: Sixty-five Years on Missouri's Rivers, the Historical Story of Developing the Waterway Traffic on the Rivers of the Middlewest*. Kansas City: Burton Publishing, 1950.

Herring, Joseph. *The Enduring Indians of Kansas*. Lawrence: University of Kansas, 1990.

"High Water." *Kansas City Times*, 7 January 1872, 4.

Hill, Edward E. *The Office of Indian Affairs, 1824-1880: Historical Sketches*. New York: Clearwater Publishing, 1974.

Historic Tour Outline of Calvary Cemetery. St. Louis: Calvary Cemetery.

"Historical Death." *Kansas City Times*, 30 January 1877, 4

History of Clay and Platte Counties, Missouri. St. Louis: National Historical Company, 1885.

History of Jackson County. Kansas City: Union Historical Society, 1881.

Hoffhaus, Charles E. *Chez les Canses: Three Centuries at Kawsmouth: the French Foundations of Metropolitan Kansas City*. Kansas City: Lowell Press, 1984.

———. "Fort de Cavagnial: Imperial France in Kansas, 1744-1764." *KHQ* 30 no. 4: 425-454.

Houck, Louis. *The Spanish Regime in Missouri*. 2 vols. Chicago: R. R. Donnelly & Sons, 1909.

———. *A History of Missouri from the Earliest Explorations and Settlements until the Admission of the State into the Union*. 3 vols. Chicago: R. R. Donnelly & Sons, 1908.

Illustrated Historical Atlas Map of Randolph County, Illinois. Edwardsville, IL: W. R. Brink, 1875.

"In Kansas City Forty Years Ago." *Kansas City Times*, 14 February 1912.

Jackson, Donald, and Mary Lee Spence, eds. *The Expeditions of John Charles Fremont*. 3 vols. Urbana: University of Illinois Press, 1970.

———. *Voyages of the Steamboat Yellow Stone*. New York: Ticknor & Fields, 1985.

Jefferson Republic, 8 April 1837.

Johnson, Michael. *The Native Tribes of North America, A Concise Encyclopedia*. New York: Macmillan Publishing, 1994.

Jones, Dorothy. "John Dougherty and the Pawnee Rite of Human Sacrifice: April 1827." *MHR* 63 (April 1969): 293-316.

"Kansas City's Pioneer Mother Was Wife of First Settler on River Front." *Kansas City Times*, 2 October 1935.

Kennerly, William Clark (as told to Elizabeth Russell). *Persimmon Hill: A Narrative of Old St. Louis and the Far West*. Norman: University of Oklahoma Press, 1948.

"Last Witness, or Reminiscences of Kansas City Fifty Years Ago." *Westport Border Star*, 28 July 1860.

Lavender, David. *The Fist in the Wilderness*. Garden City, NY: Doubleday, 1964.

Leitch, Barbara A. *A Concise Dictionary of Indian Tribes of North America*. Algonac, MI: Reference Publications, 1979.

Liberty Tribune, 12 June 1885, 21 April 1899, 22 June 1906, 22 May 1908.

"Life of Pioneer Parish Priest Brings to Light Many Interesting Facts in Early History of K.C. and Environs." *Kansas City Journal*, 19 February 1922, 3(B).

"Life Tales of Early Days: Kansas City's First Baptismal and Marriage Records." *Kansas City Star*, 5 June 1898, 12.

Lutz, J. J. "Methodist Missions among the Indian Tribes in Kansas." *KHC* 9 (1906): 160-235.

Lytle, William M., and Forrest R. Holdcamper. *Merchant Steam Vessels Of The United States, 1790-1868: The Lytle-Holdcamper List*. Revised and edited by C. Bradford Mitchell. Staten Island, NY: Steamship Historical Society of America, 1975.

Marquis, Arnold. *A Guide to America's Indians: Ceremonials, Reservations, and Museums*. Norman: University of Oklahoma Press, 1974.

"Mary A. Chouteau." *Kansas City Star*, 13 March 1899.

Mathews, John Joseph. *The Osages: Children of the Middle Waters*. Norman: University of Oklahoma Press, 1961.

Mattison, Ray H. "John Pierre Cabanne." In *The Mountain Men and the Fur Trade of the Far West*, edited by Leroy R. Hafen, vol. 2: 72. Glendale, CA: Arthur H. Clark, 1965-1972.

———. "Kenneth McKenzie." In *The Mountain Men and the Fur Trade of the Far West*, edited by Leroy R. Hafen, vol. 2: 218. Glendale, CA: Arthur H. Clark, 1965-1972.

McCoy, John C. "Forty Years Ago." *Kansas Monthly* 2 (June 1879): 82-83.

McDermott, John Francis, ed. *Frenchmen and French Ways in the Mississippi Valley*. Urbana: University of Illinois Press, 1969.

———. *Old Cahokia, A Narrative and Documents Illustrating the First Century of its History*. St. Louis: St. Louis Historical Documents Foundation, 1949.

———. *The French in the Mississippi Valley*. Urbana: University of Illinois Press, 1965.

———. *The Western Journals of Washington Irving*. Norman: University of Oklahoma Press, 1944.

———. "Isaac McCoy's Second Exploratory Trip in 1828." *KHQ* 13 (August 1945): 400-462.

———. "The Exclusive Trade Privileges of Maxent, Laclede and Company." *MHR* 29 (July 1935): 272-278.

———. *A Glossary of Mississippi Valley French, 1673-1850*. St. Louis: Washington University, 1941.

McDonald, W. J. "The Missouri River and Its Victims – Vessels Wrecked from the Beginning of Navigation to 1925." *MHR* 21: 215-242, 455-480, 581-607.

"Metropolitan Catholic Almanac and Laity's Directory, for the Year of Our Lord, 1839." In *Sadliers' Catholic Directory, Almanac and Ordo*. Baltimore: Fielding Lucas, Jr., 1839.

Miller, William H. *The History of Kansas City: Together with a Sketch of the Commercial Resources of the Country with which it is Surrounded*. Kansas City: Birdsall and Miller, 1881.

Miner, H. Craig, and William E. Unrau. *The End of Indian Kansas: A Study of Cultural Revolution, 1854-1871*. Lawrence: Regents Press of Kansas, 1978.

Missouri Republican [St. Louis], 4 May 1828, 2 September 1828, 4 November 1828, 30 November 1836.

Missouri Saturday Evening News [St. Louis], 28 April 1838.

Montgomery, David R. *Indian Crafts and Skills*. Bountiful, UT: Horizon Publishers and Distributors, 1985.

Morgan, Perl Wilbur, ed. *History of Wyandotte County, Kansas, and Its People*. Chicago: Lewis Publishing, 1911.

Morrow, Lynn. "Trader William Gilliss and Delaware Migration in Southern Missouri." *MHR* 75 (January 1981): 147-167.

Nasatir, A. P. "The Formation of the Missouri Company." *MHR* 25 (1930): 10-22.

———. *Before Lewis and Clark: Documents Illustrating the History of the Missouri, 1785-1804*. 2 vols. Lincoln: University of Nebraska Press, 1990.
National Geographic Society (U.S.). *World of the American Indian*. Washington, D.C.: National Geographic Society, 1974.
Norall, Frank. *Bourgmont: Explorer of the Upper Missouri, 1698-1725*. Lincoln: University of Nebraska, 1988.
Oglesby, Richard E. *Manuel Lisa and the Opening of the Missouri Fur Trade*. Norman: University of Oklahoma Press, 1963.
———. "Pierre Menard." In *The Mountain Men and the Fur Trade of the Far West*, edited by Leroy R. Hafen, vol. 6: 307-318. Glendale, CA: Arthur H. Clark, 1965-1972.
Oswald, Delmont R., "James P. Beckwourth." In *The Mountain Men and the Fur Trade of the Far West*, edited by Leroy R. Hafen, vol. 6: 42. Glendale, CA: Arthur H. Clark, 1965-1972.
Patterson, Lotsee, and Mary E. Snodgrass. *Indian Terms of the Americas*. Englewood, CO: Libraries Unlimited, 1994.
Paul Wilhelm, Duke of Wurttemberg. "First Journey to North America in the years 1822 to 1823." Translated by William G. Bek. *South Dakota Historical Collections* 19 (1938): 7-474.
———. *Travels in the Interior of North America, 1822-1823*. Translated by Robert Nitske and edited by Savoie Lottinville. Norman: University of Oklahoma Press, 1973.
Pedersen, Lyman C., Jr., "Warren Angus Ferris." In *The Mountain Men and the Fur Trade of the Far West*, edited by Leroy R. Hafen, vol. 2: 144. Glendale, CA: Arthur H. Clark, 1965-1972.
Peterson, Jacqueline, and Jennifer S. H. Brown, eds. *The New Peoples: Being and Becoming Métis in North America*. Lincoln: University of Nebraska Press, 1985.
Peterson, Jacqueline, and Laura Peers. *Sacred Encounters: Father De Smet and the Indians of the Rocky Mountain West*. Norman: University of Oklahoma Press, 1993.
———. *People of the Troubled Waters: A Missouri River Journal*. Frederick, CO: Renaissance House Publishers, 1988.
"Pierre Menard Papers." In *Chicago Historical Society Collections* 4 (1890): 162-180.
"Pierre Menard." In *Chicago Historical Society Collections* 4 (1890): 142-148.
Porter, Mae Reed, and Odessa Davenport. *Scotsman in Buckskin; Sir William Drummond Stewart and the Rocky Mountain Fur Trade*. New York: Hastings House, 1963.
"Post of St. Louis Steam Boat Intelligence." *St. Louis Enquirer*, 15 June 1819, 3.
Rafferty, Milton D. *Historical Atlas of Missouri*. Norman: University of Oklahoma, 1982.
"Railroad Convention at Kansas, Mo." *Jefferson Enquirer*, 18 December 1852, 4.
Reavis, L. U. *Saint Louis, the Future Great City of the World and Its Impending Triumph*. St. Louis: G. A. Pierrot Printing, 1881.
"Reminisces of William M. Boggs, Son of Governor Lilburn W. Boggs." *MHR* 6: 86-90.
Root, George A. "Ferries in Kansas, Part I – Missouri River." *KHQ* 2 (1933): 3-28, 115-138.
Ross, Alexander. *The Fur Hunters of the Far West*. Edited by Kenneth A. Spaulding. Norman: University of Oklahoma Press, 1956.
Rothensteiner, John. *History of the Archdiocese of St. Louis in its Various Stages of Development from A.D. 1637 to A.D. 1928*. 2 vols. St. Louis: Blackwell Wielandy, 1928.
Roy, Jerry C. *Shawnee Indians in Johnson County, Kansas: Some Views from Contemporary Accounts*. Paper presented at Johnson County Community College, March 3, 1984.

"Sale of the Steamer Amazon." *Liberty Tribune*, 14 March 1856, 4.

Sandy, Wilda. *Here Lies Kansas City: A Collection of Our City's Notables and their Final Resting Places*. Kansas City: Bennett Schneider, 1984.

Saucier, Walter J. *Gabrielle's People*. Raleigh, NC: Walter Saucier, 1991.

Scharf, J. Thomas. *History of Saint Louis City and County*. 2 vols. Philadelphia: Louis Everts, 1883.

Schlafly, James. "Birth of Kansas City's Pioneer Church." *MHR* 44 (July 1950): 364-372.

_____. *New Light in the Early West: Berenice Chouteau*. New York: Benzinger Bros., 1959.

Schneider, Richard L. *Crafts of the North American Indian*. New York: Van Nostrand Reinhold, 1974.

Shea, John Gilmary. *Discovery and Exploration of the Mississippi Valley: with the Original Narratives of Marquette, Allouez, Membre, Hennepin, and Anastase Douay*. New York: Redfield, 1853.

_____. *History of the Catholic Missions among the Indian Tribes of the United States: 1524-1854*. New York: Edward Dunigan & Bro., 1855.

"Site of Founding of Kansas City Passes to New Owner." *Kansas City Star*, 19 October 1930, 1(D).

Socolofsky, Homer E., and Self, Huber. *Historical Atlas of Kansas*. Norman: University of Oklahoma Press, 1972.

Spencer, Thomas Edwin. *The Story of Old St. Louis*. St. Louis: Press of Con. P. Curran Printing, 1914.

Staab, Rodney. "Farmsteads of the Kansas Shawnee." *Kansas Anthropologist: Journal of the Kansas Anthropological Association* 14 (1993): 13-27.

_____. "The Kansa Indians of Wyandotte County." In *The Ethnic History of Wyandotte County*, edited by Loren L. Taylor, Vol. 2: 295-298. Kansas City, KS: Ethnic Council of Wyandotte County, 1992.

"Steamboat Wrecks in South Dakota." *South Dakota Historical Collections* 9 (1918): 393-402.

"Steamboats." *Westport Border Times*, 12 April 1856, 2.

Stevens, Harry R. "Hugh Glenn." In *The Mountain Men and the Fur Trade of the Far West*, edited by Leroy R. Hafen, vol. 2: 170. Glendale, CA: Arthur H. Clark, 1965-1972.

Sturtevant, William C., ed. *Handbook of North American Indians*. Washington, D.C.: Smithsonian Institute, 1986.

Swagerty, William R. "The Chouteaus and the St. Louis Fur Trade." In *A Guide to the Microfilm Edition of Papers of the St. Louis Fur Trade*, edited by Janet Lecompte. Bethesda, MD: University Publications of America, 1991.

Thorne, Tanis Chapman. "Liquor Has Been Their Undoing: Liquor Trafficking and Alcohol Abuse in the Lower Missouri Fur Trade." *Gateway Heritage*, 13 (Fall 1992): 4-23.

_____. *The Many Hands of My Relations: French and Indians on the Lower Missouri*. Columbia: University of Missouri Press, 1996.

Thrapp, Dan L. *Encyclopedia of Frontier Biography*. 3 vols. Glendale, CA: Arthur H. Clark, 1988.

Thwaites, Ruben Golden, ed. *Early Western Travels, 1748-1846*. 32 vols. Cleveland: A. H. Clark, 1904-1907.

Tracy, Joseph, ed. *History of American Missions to the Heathens, from Their Commencement to the Present Time*. Worcester, MA: Spooner & Howland, 1840.

Trexler, Harrison A. *Slavery in Missouri*. Baltimore: Johns Hopkins Press, 1914.

"United States Indian Agencies Affecting Kansas: Superintendents, Agents, Subagents, Millers, Blacksmiths, Interpreters, etc." *KHC* 16 (1925): 658-745.

Unrau, William E. *Indians of Kansas: the Euro-American Invasion and Conquest of Indian Kansas*. Topeka: Kansas State Historical Society, 1991.

———. *Kansa Indians: A History of the Wind People, 1673-1873*. Norman: University of Oklahoma Press, 1971.

———. *The Emigrant Indians of Kansas: A Critical Bibliography*. Bloomington: Indiana University Press, 1979.

———. *White Man's Wicked Water: The Alcohol Trade and Prohibition in Indian Country, 1802-1892*. Lawrence: University Press of Kansas, 1996.

"Valuable Real Estate for Sale," *Kansas City Enterprise*, 10 November 1855.

Waldman, Carl. *Who Was Who in Native American History: Indians and Non-Indians from Early Contacts through 1900*. New York: Facts on File, 1990.

Waldo, William. "Recollections of a Septuagenarian." *Glimpses of the Past* 5, no. 4-5: 59-94.

Way, Frederick, Jr., comp. *Way's Packet Directory, 1848-1994: Passenger Steamboats of the Mississippi River System since the Advent of Photography in Mid-continent America*. Athens: Ohio University, 1994.

Wells, Merle, "Ignace Hatchiorauquasha (John Grey)." In *The Mountain Men and the Fur Trade of the Far West*, edited by Leroy R. Hafen, vol. 7: 169-170. Glendale, CA: Arthur H. Clark, 1965-1972.

Westbrook, Harriet J. "The Chouteaus – Their Contribution to the West." *Chronicles of Oklahoma* 11 (June 1933): 786-797; 11 (September 1933): 942-966.

Wetmore, Alphonso. *Gazetteer of the State of Missouri. With a Map of the State...To which is added an Appendix, containing Frontier Sketches, and Illustrations of Indian Character*. St. Louis: C. Keemle, 1837.

"When the Indians Danced at Westport." *Kansas City Catholic Register*, 5 October 1916, 1.

Whitney, Carrie Westlake. *Kansas City, Missouri, Its History and Its People, 1800-1908*. 3 vols. Chicago: S. J. Clarke Publishing Company, 1908.

Wied, Maximilian, Prinz Von. *Maximilian, Prince of Wied's Travels in the Interior of North America, 1832-1834*. In *Early Western Travels, 1748-1846*, Vols. 22-25, edited by Ruben Golden Thwaites. Cleveland: A. H. Clark, 1906.

Williams, Samuel C., ed. *Adair's History of the American Indians*. Johnson City, TN: Watauga Press, 1930.

Windell, Marie George. "Westward Along the Boone's Lick Trail in 1826, The Diary of Colonel John Glover." *MHR* 39 (January 1945): 184-199.

Writers' Program of the Work Projects Administration in the State of Missouri. *Missouri: A Guide to the "Show Me" State*. New York: Duell, Sloan and Pearce, 1941.

Index

Locators in **bold** refer to illustrations; with "g" indicate items in Glossary

Acades, Mrs. (St. Louis milliner?), 29
accounting/banking services
   financial activities of Francois, 78ff., 126, 160, 167–168
   frontier style, 66, 70, 72, 111, 115, 116, 120–121, 146
   money viewed as superior to merchandise, 116, 162–163, 166–167
Adkins, John G., tenant of Chouteau Mansion, 185
Aelen, Herman (priest), 232–233g
Agency, Indian, 219g
Agnew, John O. (merchant), 132, 155, 157, 219g
Ah-lah-a-chick. *See* Connor, James
Alexi (slave), 177
American Chief (Kansa chief), 34, 54, 245g
American Fur Company, 220g
   post owned/operated by: Francois Chouteau, 81
   John Jacob Astor, ix, 15
   purchase of Vasquez house, 41
   warehouse, **20**
   Western Division (French Fur Company), 15, 37, 42, 51, 53, 58, 60, 62, 65–66, 149; charged as unfair competitor, 44; overseas customers, 111; Rocky Mountain rendezvous,
163, 171, 172; steamboats, 95, 123, 162, 164, 166; and Vasquez, 70, 91, 92
Anderson, William (Delaware chief), 111, 165, 220g
   father of Shawanock *(q.v.)*, 263g
annuities, 19, 50, 64, 65, 79. *See also under* letters of Francois; licenses
   defined, 40, 221g
arpent (French land measure), 149, 221g
Astor, John Jacob, ix, 15, 221g
Aull
   brothers (merchants), 70, 71
   James, death of, 70, 71

banking. *See* accounting/banking services
Barbeau, Jeanne. *See* Valle, Jeanne
Barclay, William, relationship to Chouteau family, 167, 221g
Barge from Fort Lewis, **23**
Baronet family. *See* Vasquez
The Barrens, 136, 221g. *See also under* educational facilities
Barry, Louise, ix
barter. *See* accounting/banking services; annuities
Bates, Captain, 164, 222g
Beckwourth/Beckwith, James, 20, 222g
Becquet, Elizabeth, mother of Madame Grand Louis Bertholet, 222g
Bent, Charles, 121

Benton
  Jessie (*See under* Fremont)
  Thomas Hart, and Platte Purchase Bill (1836), 158
Berthiaume, Marie, wife of Louis Lorimier, 168
Berthold
  Barthlomew, husband of Pelagie (the younger) Chouteau, ix, 17
  Chouteau, and Pratt (*See under* trading posts)
Bertholet
  Grand Louis, 24, 36, 153, 196, 222g; sale of land to Gillis, 154
  Louis, father of Grand Louis, 222g
  Madame Grand Louis (Margaret Gauthier), 222g
  Marie, mother of Grand Louis, 222g
Bible, of Berenice Chouteau, 188
Biddle, Thomas, 9
Black Hawk war, 128
Blondeau/Blando, Maurice (entrepreneur), 36, 37, 44, 222g
Blue Mills Landing (Missouri), 50
boats/boating. *See also* river travel
  average life of river boats, 137
  at Chouteau's Landing, 149
  keelboats, 246g; *Beaver,* wreck of, 54–56, 91, 266g
  mackinaw boat, 144
  pirogue, 159, 257g
  steamboating dangers on the Missouri, 164, 186
  steamboats: *Amazon,* 186, 242g; *Assiniboin,* 127–128; *Australia,* 186; *Boonville,* 162, 164; *Diana,* 115, 144, 153, 160; *Globe,* 80, 86; *Howard,* 166; *Independence,* 53; *Isabel,* 185; *John Hancock,* 146, 160; *John Nelson,* 71, 123; *Kate Swinney (Sweeny),* of P. M. Chouteau, 185; *Missouri Mail,* 95, 180; *Otto,* 88, 114, 121, 122; *St. Charles,* 137, 153, 156; *St. Peters,* 164, 167; *Western Engineer,* 53; *William D. Duncan,* wreck of, 75–76; *Yellow Stone,* 1–2, 53, 94, 101–103, 117–118, 223g, **268g**; *Yellow Stone Packet,* 53

Bodmer, Charles Karl, 223g
Boggs family (traders), Angus G., Joseph, Lilburn W., or Thomas, 85, 223g
Bonneville, Benjamin (1796-1878), 223
Boone family
  Albert Gallatin, 141, 265g
  Daniel (III), husband of Marie (Philibert), 257g
  Daniel Morgan, 49, 69, 223g, **244g**
  Elizabeth, grandchild of Daniel Morgan Boone, 69
  Eulalia, grandchild of Daniel Morgan Boone, 69
  Marie (Philibert), wife of Daniel Boone (III), 257g
  and Van Bibber family, 141, 265g
Bourgeois, Marie Therese. *See under* Chouteau
Bourgmont, Etienne de Veniard, Sieur de (1679-1734), 10, 223g
Boutros, David, 2, 3, 191–204
Bouvet (Bouvette, Bouvais), Jean Baptiste, 171
Bradshaw
  James, 168
  Marie Louise (*See under* Papin)
  William, 168
Brent, Thomas (major), 158
Bridger, Jim, 166, 223g–224g
Briggs, Emily. *See under* Menard
Buckeridge, F. (artist), 183
Bureau of Indian Affairs (BIA). *See under* United States government
business dealings
  between P. Menard and Francois, 16, 51, 62, 207–213 (*See also* letters of Francois Chouteau)
  sociocultural differences, 4, 16, 26, 33, 34, 49, 85

Cabanne, John Pierre (fur trader), 156
Cadron, Marguerite. *See under* Saucier
  first wife of Francois Saucier, 57, 262g
  mother of Brigitte (Saucier) Chouteau, 57, 262g
Cahokia (Illinois Territory), 11, 13
Cain, Robert (settler), 158

Campbell
    John (Indian agent), 41, 44, 48, 52, 61, 65, 67, 72, 73, 76, 97, 132, 224g
    William F., 187
Camp Missouri (Fort Atchinson, Neb.), 9, 9n16
Cape Girardeau, Missouri, 34–35
capitalism. *See* free enterprise
Carpenter, Elizabeth (Shawnee), third wife of Frederick Choteau, 174
Carroll County, Missouri, 10
Cedar Creek, 24
cemeteries
    Calvary Cemetery, Chouteau plot, 172–173, 189
    Mount St. Mary's Cemetery, Kansas City, 174, 179, 187, 254g
    Old Catholic Cemetery, St. Louis, 172
    St. Regis Church pioneer cemetery, 187
Chaine, Mr. *See* Shane, Anthony
Chalifoux
    Eleonora (*See* La Liberte, Eleonora)
    Marie Louise (*See under* Roy (Roi))
Charless, Joseph (ed. *Missouri Gazette*), 62, 64
Chartran[d]/Chardon, Joseph (boatman), 69, 70, 70n39
Chenier, Eloise. *See under* Menard
Chicago Historical Society, 2
Chick
    Joseph S., 59, 164, 224g; reported death of Francois Chouteau, 172; reported death of Odile, 179
    Mary Jane, daughter of William (*See under* Johnson)
    Virginia, daughter of William (*See under* McCoy)
    W. H., 164
    William, 152
Chihuahua, Mexico, 71
Chouteau
    Adele (Gregoire): mother of Frederick [Chouteau] Laclede, 248g; wife of Frederic Donatien Chouteau, 248g
    Aimee, daughter of Auguste (A.P.) Chouteau, 143
    Ann (Toler), wife of Benjamin Chouteau, 184, 188, 225g

Auguste (1749-1829), 224g–225g; cofounder of St. Louis, 8, 11; fur trader, 11–13; half-brother of Pierre, 12; husband of Marie Therese Cerre, 224g–225g; relationship with Indians, 8, 12; uncle of Francois Gesseau, 8
Auguste Pierre (A.P.) (1786-1838), 225g; brother of Pierre Jr., Pelagie, Paul Liguest, ix, 58; educated at West Point, 58; father of five daughters, 143; half-brother of Francois Gesseau, Cyprien, Pharamond, Charles B., 8, 129; husband of Sophie Labbadie, 118; son of Pierre Sr. and Pelagie (Kiersereau), ix
Augustine, daughter of Auguste (A.P.) Chouteau, 143
Aurora Hay, (second wife of Paul Liguest Chouteau), 103
Benedict Pharamond (Feb. 22, 1833–Aug. 6, 1834), son of Francois and Berenice, 112, 127, 211n9, 225; death, 130
Benjamin (1828-76): education, 164, 176; husband of Ann (Toler), 184, 188, 225g; later life, 188; son of Francois and Berenice, 7, 44, 80, 87, 127, 157, 225g; godparent of Eulalia Boone, 69
Berenice (Therese Berenice Menard; 1801-1888), 225g–226g; character of, 98, 188–189; and "Chouteau's Church," 123; correspondence, 2, 26; daughter of Pierre and Marie Therese (Godin) Menard, ix; death, 189; family, ix, 5, 7, 24, 25, 44, 92–93, 111–112, 127; frontier skills, 7, 24ff.; funeral of Francois, 172; godparent of Elizabeth Boone, 69; as *Grand Dame* of Kansas City, 179–180; handwriting of, 216; illness, 119, 121, 130, 131, 188; life after death of Francois, 174–180, 183–189; move to Missouri frontier (1822), 24, 24n5, 196; move to Ste. Genevieve, 184; name variants, 5n5;

Chouteau
- Berenice (*continued*)
    - physique, 7, 188–189; stepdaughter of Angelique (Saucier) Menard, 5–6; travels, 155; wife of Francois Gesseau (m. July 11, 1819), ix, 7
- Brigitte (*See under* Saucier)
- Cadet (*See* Chouteau, Pierre Jr.)
- Cerre (*See* Chouteau, Gabriel Sylvestre)
- Charles B. (1808-1884): brother of Francois, 143; son of Pierre Sr. and Brigitte (Saucier), ix, 29, 30, 59, 226g–227g, 245g
- Charles Pierre (1819-1901), son of Pierre Jr. (Cadet), 227g
- Constance (*See* Dubreuil, Constance)
- Cyprien (1802-1879), 62–63, 104, 227g; husband of Maria Tucker?, 173; husband of Nancy Francis, 173; later life and death, 173–174; trading post activities: after death of Francois, 173; before death of Francois, 19, 25, 26, 32, 48, 55, 59, 81, 109, 120, 132
- Delia, daughter of Pierre Menard (Mack) Chouteau, 188
- Edmond Francois (a/k/a Gesseau, Gesso), son of Francois and Berenice, 5, 7, 24, 26, 32, 69, 89, 90, 109, 227g; in "Army of the West," 246g; education, 67, 90, 100, 119, 120, 124, 126, 164; expulsion from school, 140, 144, 147; hatchet accident, 148; wanderlust and army volunteer, 186–187
- Elizabeth Carpenter, third wife of Frederick, 174
- Emilie: daughter of Auguste (A.P.) Chouteau, 143; daughter of Cadet (*See under* Sanford)
- Emily Anne (Gratiot), wife of Cadet, 58
- Francois Gesseau (1797-1838), 227g–229g; business acumen, 9, 62–63, 65, 66, 77–78, 82, 126–127; and "Chouteau's Church," 123, 145; early letters, 23–46; education and early life, 1–22; family, ix, 5, 7, 8, 24, 25, 127, 171–172; as founder of Kansas City, 171–172; funeral and burial, in St. Louis, 172; fur-trading posts, 15, 24, 26, 245g; husband of Berenice (m. 07-11-1819), ix, 6, 7; illness, 89, 90, 102, 103–104, 117, 122; later life and death of, 171–175; letter-writing habits, 152; military service, 27n15; name variants, 27; physique, 9; relationships with *Cher Oncle* and *Cher Frere*, 16, 51, 68, 81 (*See also under* letters of Francois); repaid by treaty, 34n30; scribe of, 216; son of Pierre and Brigitte (Saucier), ix; trading post activities, 54–56
- Frederic Donatien (1831-1881): husband of Adele (Gregoire), 109, 248g; illness, 177; later life, 188; son of Francois and Berenice, 92, 93, 127, 157, 175, 176, 229g
- Frederick (1809-1891), 59, 229g; conflict with Marston Clark, 104, 106, 114; dispute with U.S. government, 166–167; father of William Meyers Chouteau, 92, 104, 253g; husband of: first wife, Shawnee (Nancy Logan/Nancy Tooley/Elizabeth Tooley?), 92, 174; fourth wife, Elizabeth Ware, 174; second wife, Mathilda White, 174; third wife, Elizabeth Carpenter, 174; later life and death of, 174; OIA charges against, 98; reminiscences, 15n22, 24n3, 48m55–56, 68, 91, 92, 246g–247g; son of Pierre and Brigitte (Saucier), ix; trading post activities, 25, 26, 81–82, 109, 120, 174, 245g
- Frederick Edward (*See under* Laclede)
- Gabriel, father of Francois, 57
- Gabriel Sylvestre (Seres, Cerre, "Sara") (1794-1887), cousin of Francois Gesseau; son of Auguste and Marie Therese Cerre Chouteau, 9, 24, 25, 166, 229g–230g, 245g
- Gesseau (*See* Chouteau, Edmond Francois)
- James G. (b.1815), natural son of Francois and Marie (Osage), 8, 38n50, 144, 230g
- Jean Pierre (*See* Chouteau, Pierre Sr.)

Liguest (*See* Chouteau, Paul Liguest)
Louis Amadee (1825-1826), son of Francois and Berenice, 25, 26, 87, 230g
Louis Sylvestre (1827-1829), son of Francois and Berenice, 28, 32, 58–59, 68, 87, 230g
"Mack" (*See* Chouteau, Pierre Menard)
Marie Antoinette, daughter of Auguste (A.P.) Chouteau, 143
Marie Louise, daughter of Marie Therese Chouteau and Pierre de Laclede Liguest, 230g
Marie Pelagie, daughter of Marie Therese Chouteau and Pierre de Laclede Liguest, 230g
Marie Therese (Bourgeois): common-law wife of Pierre de Laclede, 224g, 248g; mother of, Auguste, ix, 224g; wife of Rene Chouteau, 224g
Marie Therese (Cerre) (1769-1842): mother of: Auguste Aristide, Catherine Emilie, Edward Rene, Emilie Antoinette, Gabriel Sylvestre, Henry Pierre, Marie Louise, Marie Therese Eulalie, 224g; Pierre, ix; wife of Auguste, 12, 224g
Mary Ann Polk, wife of Pierre Menard, 185, 232g
Mary Brigitte ("Brigitte"; 1835-1864) daughter of Francois and Berenice, wife of Ashley Hopkins, 145, 148, 157, 176, 184–185, 231g, **242g**; death from cholera, 185
Mary Francis, daughter of Cyprien (*See under* Guinotte)
Mary Louise, sister of Pierre Chouteau (*See under* Papin)
Mathilda White, second wife of Frederick, 174
Menard (*See* Chouteau, Pierre Menard)
Morgan/Little Morgan (Louis Sylvestre?), 5, 67, 68–69, 76 (*See also* Chouteau, Louis Sylvestre)
Nancy/Elizabeth Logan/Tooley, first wife of Frederick, 173–174
Nancy Francis, wife of Cyprien (m. 1855), 173

Odile (*See* Chouteau, Therese Odile)
Paul Liguest, 231g; half-brother of Francois Gesseau, Cyprien, Pharamond, Charles B., 8, 74; Indian agent, ix, 34–35, 43, 44, 81, 155, 156; Osage Agency, 97; robbery victim, 81; son of Pierre and Pelagie (Kiersereau), ix, 4–5, 58
Pelagie (the younger): daughter of Pierre and Pelagie (Kiersereau), ix; half-sister of Francois Gesseau, Cyprien, Pharamond, Charles B., 8; wife of Bartholomew Berthold, ix
Pelagie Kiersereau (d. 1793): first wife of Pierre Sr., ix, 13; mother of Auguste Pierre, Pierre Jr. (Cadet), Pelagie (the younger), Paul Liguest, ix, 58
Pharamond (1806-1831), son of Pierre and Brigitte (Saucier), ix, 29, 58, 59, 231g–232g
Pierre Jr. (b. 1789), 231g–232g; brother of, Auguste Pierre, Paul Liguest, Pelagie, ix; business relationship with Francois, 16, 52, 53, 60, 95, 110, 116, 132; half-brother of Francois Gesseau, Cyprien, Pharamond, Charles B., ix, 2, 8; leader of American Fur Co. Western Div., 15, 42, 58; son of Pierre and Pelagie (Kiersereau), ix
Pierre Menard (a/k/a Menard; Mack; b. April 28, 1822), son of Francois and Berenice, ix, 5, 7, 26, 28, 32, 87, 88, 109, 167, 232g; education, 99, 100, 102, 111, 114, 116, 119, 120, 126, 156; expulsion from school, 140, 144, 147; husband of Mary Ann Polk, 185; later life of, in Kansas City, 185–186; and Town of Kansas charter committee, 185
Pierre Sr. (Jean Pierre, 1758-1849), 230g; father of Auguste Pierre, Pierre Jr. (Cadet), Pelagie (the younger), Paul Liguest, Charles B, Frederick, Cyprien, Francois Gesseau, Pharamond, ix, 8, 58; fur trader, 11–13; half-brother of Auguste, 12; husband of: Brigitte (Saucier), ix, 13; Pelagie (Kiersereau), ix, 13;

Chouteau
- Pierre Sr. (*continued*)
  - natural son of Pierre de Laclede Liguest and Marie Therese Bourgeois Chouteau, 12; personality and talents of, 30; relationship with Indians, 8, 12; trip to Washington (D.C.), 6; relationship with second family, 58
- Rene: estranged husband of Marie Therese (Bourgeois), 12; father of Auguste, 12
- Seres (*See* Chouteau, Gabriel Sylvestre)
- Sophie Labbadie, wife of Auguste (A. P.) Chouteau, 118
- Susanne, daughter of Auguste (A.P.) Chouteau, 143
- Therese Berenice (*See* Chouteau, Berenice)
- Therese Odile (1838-1840): baptized in St. Louis, 174; daughter of Francois and Berenice, 170, 232g; death of, 178–179
- Victoire, daughter of Marie Therese Bourgeois Chouteau and Pierre de Laclede Liguest, 230g
- William Meyers, son of Frederick, 253g

Chouteau family
- 1830 U.S. Census, 79, 144
- 1850 U.S. Census, 184
- after death of Francois Gesseau Chouteau, 180–189
- home life on the farm, 109–124
- homes of: Chouteau farm, description, 203; "Chouteau Mansion," 183–185; on Guinotte Addition (East Bottoms), 143; on map, **108**
- landholding map, 150
- legends, myths, traditions: Berenice's love of music and dancing, 128; boat travel by pregnant Berenice, two children, and Pierre Sr., 30; bridal tour of Francois and Berenice, 9n15, 24, 192; circumstances of Francois Chouteau's death, 172; date and location of western Missouri trading post, 15n22, 16, 24; and documentary editing tasks, 191–204

relationship to and influence among Indians, 8, 12, 59, 81–82, 173, 174, 230g

Chouteau Family Collections, 2

Chouteau letters. *See also below* letters
- challenges of translation, 2–4

Chouteau's Landing, Missouri, 149–150, 173. *See also* trading posts

Chouteau Society of Kansas City, 2

churches. *See also* missionaries
- (Old) Cathedral, St. Louis, interment of Francois Chouteau, 172
- Catholic Diocese of Kansas City–St. Joseph, 2
- Cathedral of the Immaculate Conception, 105
- Chouteau's Church (St. Francis Regis), 105, 232g–233g, 260g; established, by Fr. Roux, 123, 145
- Immaculate Conception Catholic Church, Kaskaskia, 7
- Mormons (Church of Jesus Christ of Latter Day Saints), 155, 254g; anti-Mormon movement, 169
- St. Francis Regis Church, 105, 233g, 260g

Clark
- George B. (merchant), 132
- Harriett (Kennerly) Radford, second wife of William, 234g
- Julia (Hancock): cousin to George Hancock Kennerly, 234g, 247g; first wife of William Clark, 234g
- Marston Greene, 66, 70, 76, 79, 81, 132, 233g, 245g; conflict with Chouteaus, 80, 83, 86, 96, 98, 106, 112–113, 137
- William (Supt. of Indian Affairs), 13, 14, 33, 63, 65, 71–73, 76, 81, 87, 96, 116, 234g

Clay County, Missouri, 15, 24

Clermont (II) (Osage chief), 234g

Columbia Fur Company, 66

Connor, James (interpreter, Delaware Indian), 80–81, 234g

Cornstock, Peter (Shawnee chief), 71–72, 234g

correspondence. *See* letters

couriers/postal service, 40, 44, 49, 50, 75, 131, 134, 136

credit arrangements, between traders and Indians, 19, 47. *See also* Letters of Francois Chouteau
  Shawnee signed hunting treaty, 207
credit-debt cycle, 235g
  prices on the frontier, 258g
creole, 235g
Crooks, Ramsey, 235g
Crow, Dr. (physician), and smallpox vaccination program, 98
Cummins, Richard (Indian agent), 66, 88, 96, 98, 101–102, 104, 112, 235g
Curtis
  Cyrus, 235g
  Ellen, 195

Dagenai, Noel a/k/a Dajane/Dagney/ Dashney (interpreter), 51, 52, 236g
dancing, censured by priest, 5
Datchurut
  "Big Baptiste" (boat pilot), 54–56, 91, 236g
  Zabette (boat pilot), 56, 236g
Davy, Cornelius (merchant), 138, 236g
Decoigne, Helen, 126–127, 162, 163, 167, 169–171
De la Croix, Charles (priest), 236g
democracy, of Kansas Nation, 34
Depart de Westport (drawing), by Nicolas Point, S.J., 125
De Smet, Pierre Jean (Peter), S.J., 179, 185, 237g
  Village of the Kansas by Nicolas Point (drawing), **108**
DeSoto, Kansas, 24
Doniphan, Alexander, 71
Donnelly, Bernard (priest), 128, 237g, 260g
Dorion (Pierre or Baptiste?), 237g
Dougherty, John A. (Indian agent), 33, 41, 54, 56, 76, 237g
  stricken with cholera, 117, 118
Douglas (Dogles), Thomas (educator), 67, 69
Dowling, John, 136
draft, 237g
Drips
  Andrew ("mountain" man; fur trader), 92, 170, 172, 238g; husband of Maoumntameo, 171, 178

  Catherine, daughter of Andrew and Maoumntameo (*See under* Mulkey)
  Maoumntameo (Otoe from Oregon), wife of Andrew, 171, 178
drought, 94–95
Dubreuil, Constance, (first wife of Paul Liguest Chouteau), 103, 231g
Dunlap, Robert (blacksmith), 132
Dupuis, Paul, 105
Durand, Margaret D. *See* Prudhomme, Susan

earthquake, 6
Eaton, John (Secretary of War), 81, 87
economics, of the fur trade, 16–19. *See also* banking
education
  of Indians, 111, **244g**
  of males, 8, 30, 58, 59, 67, 69, 89–90, 252g
  of women, 6, 98, 120, 178, 226g
  alternatives, for Francois' sons, *67,* 90, 100, 111, 114, 119, 120, 124, 126, 140
  mentors and supporters, 98, 128
educational facilities
  The Asylum (boarding school), 30, 58
  Bloomingdale, N.Y. (for Francois Menard), 88
  convent school, in Kaskaskia, 178
  Georgetown University, 124, 252g
  Mr. Douglas's school, Independence, 67, 69, 120
  Quaker mission school, Merriam, Kansas, 173
  Shawnee Methodist Mission and School, **244g**
  Shawnee Mission Indian Manual Labor School (Mr. Johnson's school), 110, 111, 114, 116, 120, 152–153
  St. Louis College, 90, 100, 119, 124, 260g, **261g**; program of, 120
  St. Louis school for girls (est. by Mrs. Pinconeau), 120
  St. Mary's College, Auburn, N.Y., 89–90
  St. Mary's of the Barrens (boarding school), 100, 104–105, 119, 121, 124, 126, 176, 221g, 252g, 261g; Gesseau and Menard's expulsion from, 140, 143–145, 147; program of, 120

educational facilities (*continued*)
  subscription schools, 69, 264g
  Visitation Sisters convent and school, 128
  West Point, 59
  Westport schoolhouse, 164
Eley (Ely, Elie), Michael (trader), 238g
Ellsworth, Henry L., 124, 238g
Ellsworth County, Kansas, 10
entrepreneurship. *See* free enterprise

factory system (U.S. government trading houses), 14, 33–34, 238g
family relationships
  among siblings, 66
  basis of business, 4, 49, 58, 59
  concern over children's upbringing, 119, 120
  and education of sons, 120
  husband-wife, 4, 58
  reverence for, 4
financial matters. *See* accounting/banking
"First White Settlement… ," **244g**
Fish. *See* Jackson, William
Fitzpatrick, Thomas, 166
flintlock guns, 152
floods, 49, 68, 92, 173, 179
  of 1826, 199–200
  of 1844, that destroyed much Chouteau property, 179, 203–204
Florissant, Missouri, 57
Flourney & Co. (merchants), 132, 155
Foley, William F., ix–x
Fontenelle, Lucien, 91, 238g
Fontenelle & Drips Co., 166
Fool Chief (Kansa chief), 34, 54, 82, 245g
Fort Cavagnial, 10, 11, 239g
Fort Chartres (Illinois Territory), 11
Fort Leavenworth, 239g
  and Indian alcohol usage, 110–111
  Kansas, 10, 42
Fort Leavenworth Agency, 169
Fort Orleans (Carroll County), 10
Fort Osage, 14, 33, 196, 239g
Four Houses (1819-1828), 9, 24, 24n7, 26, 81, 194–195, 240g, 245g
Francis, Nancy. *See under* Chouteau
Francis (hereditary Shawnee chief), father-in-law of Cyprien Chouteau, 173–174

free enterprise
  and city building, by Francois Chouteau, 173–174
  of fur traders, 16, 34
  vs. patronage, 33
"Free Hunter" by Nicolas Point (drawing), **77**
Fremont
  Jessie (Benton), 240g
  John Charles (lieutenant), 186–187; husband of Jessie (Benton), 240g
French Fur Company, **240g**. *See also* American Fur Company
  (Berthold, Chouteau, and Pratte), sold to American Fur Company, 15, 25, 62
French heritage
  ethos of, 4, 5, 9, 26, 49
  of St. Louis, 11
  use of English language, 62–63
French Settlement, 240g
frontier life. *See also* accounting/banking
  after 1830s, 77–108
  difficult for women, 102, 111, 114, 116
  Rocky Mountain fur trade rendezvous, 163, 171, 172
  social aspect, 4, 5, 9, 11, 49, 54
  and violence, 115, 115n9
  for young Chouteaus, 1–22
fur trade. *See also* annuities; business dealings; credit arrangements; licenses; trading posts
  British and Spanish-French, 11
  business agreements, with Indians, 19, 62
  of Chouteaus, 8–20
  competition, in western Missouri, 36, 37, 42
  decline of, 34, 77–78, 160, 175
  described and analyzed, 16–20
  effects of Revolutionary War, 12
  European, 12
  extent of, for Francois, 25, 77–78
  factory system (U.S. government trading houses), 14, 33–34
  French ethos and protection of, 9, 10
  hazards of, 10, 32
  with Kansa, in Missouri, 19, 33, 34
  Maxent, Laclede and Co., 11, 12

with Mexico, 15
with Osage, in St. Louis, 11–13
prices on the frontier, 258g
Rocky Mountain rendezvous, 163, 171, 172
slump in (1821-1822), 25
supply-and-demand relationship, 15

Gauthier, Margaret. *See under* Bertholet
Gilliss, William (fur trader), 16, 37, 39, 41–44, 48, 61, 67, 68, 78, 80–81, 127, 154, 177, 240g
  financial negotiations, competition from, 93–96, 98–101, 104, 110–111, 113, 114, 116
  purchase of Metis land, 153–154
Giraud, Michel (post employee), 122
Glover, Colonel John (diarist), 49, 200, 240g–241g
Godin, Marie Therese Michelle. *See under* Menard
  first wife of Pierre (m. June, 1792), 5, 27
  mother of: Hippolyte, 241g; Marie Josephine, 241g; Marie Odile, 241g; Modeste Alzire, 241g; Pierre Jr., 241g; Therese Berenice, 5, 241g
Gonville
  family name, and "half-breed" tracts, 154
  Louis, son-in-law of White Plume (*q.v.*), 54, 87, 154
  Mary Josephine "Josette": daughter of Louis Gonville and (unnamed) Indian woman, 54, 154, 241g; wife of Joseph, 54, 168, 171, 241g
Gordon, William (Indian agent), 117
Graham, Richard (Indian agent), 27, 38, 44, 52, 61, 241g
Gratiot, Emily Ann. *See under* Chouteau
Gregoire, Adele. *See under* Chouteau
Grey
  Cecilia (*See under* Hunot)
  John (Ignace Hatchiorauquasha), 149, 184, 241g, 242g
  Mary, wife of John, 241g, 242g
Grinter
  Anna (Marshall), wife of Moses, 242g
  Moses (ferry operator), 242g

Guinotte
  Aimee: mother of Jules, Joseph Karl, Lydia, Emma, 226g, 242g; wife of Joseph, 226g, 242g
  Joseph, husband of Aimee, 226g, 242g
  Karl, 242g
  Mary Francis (Chouteau), wife of Karl, 242g

"half-breed" plots, 87, 154
"half-breed" settlement, **201**
Hancock, Julia. *See under* Clark
Hard Chief (Kansa chief), 34, 54, 82, 245g
Hatchiorauquasha, Ignace. *See* Grey, John
Hay, Aurora. *See under* Chouteau
health concerns. *See* illness and disease
Henrie, Guillaume (William), 176
Hill, James (steamboat master), 122
Hoblitzelle, Clarence (artist), **7, 20, 220**
holidays, New Year's Day, 26
Hopkins, Ashley (riverboat captain), 184, 186, 231g, 242g
Hopkins, Mary Brigitte, daughter of Francois and Berenice (*See under* Chouteau)
horses, care and necessity of, 88, 109–110, 112
Hudson Bay Company, 65
Hughes, Andrew S. (Indian agent), 14, 27, 131, 242g
Hunot/Uneau/Eanneau/Uno
  Cecilia (Grey), wife of Joseph, 184, 242g
  Joseph, 92, 242g
Hunter, James M., 169
Hunter & Simpson establishment, 169

Illinois Historical Survey, 2, 3
Illinois State Historical Library (ISHL), 2, 3
Illinois Territory, 11
illness, disease, accidents
  alcoholism, 102, 103, 105, 110, 113, 131, 131n13
  bilious fever, 121, 143
  chest trouble/heart disease (of Francois), 122, 144, 171, 173
  cholera, 88, 114, 185, 223g 231g; concern about, by Francois, 102, 104, 117–118
  and climate, 103, 143

illness, disease, accidents (*continued*)
  contagious "mouth disease," 104
  depression, 29, 31, 89
  eye problems, (of Francois), 117
  fever (malaria or typhoid?), 88, 119, 130, 133, 134, 136, 143
  frostbite, 55
  leg infection, 29, 51, 58
  liver/gallbladder problems, 119
  lung disease, 177
  malaria ("the fever"), 19–20, 88
  measles, 104
  personality disorders, 29, 35
  senility (senile dementia?), 86
  smallpox, 37, 85, 95, 118; vaccination program, 97–98
  train accident (P. M. Chouteau), 186
  tuberculosis, 88
  whooping cough, 99
  unspecified: (of Alzire), 175; (of Berenice), 122; (of Cyprien), 175; (of Francois), 89, 90, 102–104; (of Frederic), 177; (of Pierre Menard), 101
Independence, Missouri, 36–37, 48, 49–50, 87, 149
  Mormon immigration to, 155
Indian agencies, 219g
  Council Bluffs, cholera at, 117–118
  Fort Leavenworth, 239g
  Kansa Post, 14, 245g; closing of, 132
  Shawnee, 14, 22, 170
  structure of, under OIA, 14, 32–33
Indian agents. *See under* United States government
Indian Removal Act. *See under* United States government
Indians. *See also* Indian tribes and groups
  alcohol problems, 65, 102–105, 110, 113, 131, 131n13
  annuity payments (*See* annuities)
  Bureau/Office of Indian Affairs (OIA), 32–33, 254g
  business/credit arrangements with traders (*See* annuities)
  craftsmanship, 114, 166
  early French treaties, 10
  and fur trade, 9, 11, 12
  human rights abuse against, 31

Indian Removal Act (1830), 15
Osage country (Missouri), 8
  reception of the French, 10
  relationships with, 7, 8, 72, 82
  shoe manufacture, 115
  smallpox among, 95, 97
  smallpox vaccination program, 97–98
  socioeconomic change, 85
  trade licenses with (*See* licenses)
  Treaty of 1825, and tribal dissention, 34, 82
  westward migration, 17, 27, 34–35, 85
Indian Territory, 27, 33, 64, 85
  liquor sales prohibited, 113
  reservations established, 115
Indian tribes and groups, **45, 46**
  N.B.: those mentioned in letters are not indexed; nearly every letter mentions one or more tribes/groups
  Algonquin language group, 85
  Assiniboines, 85
  Comanche, 234g
  Confederated, chiefs, 64, 91, 156, 161, 256g
  Cree, 115, 235g
  Delaware, 19, 41, 44, **46,** 61, 92, 236g; reservation, 115
  Delaware-Loup, 61, 62, 62n28, 69, 97, 110; alcoholism, 103
  Flathead, 148
  Fox, 74 (*See* Sac and Fox)
  "Indians of the Marais des Cygne," 147
  Iowa, 10, 243g
  Iroquois, 148
  Kansa, 9, 19, 33, 63, 64, 97, 98, 244g; chiefs, 34, 41, 54, 82, 154, 245g; history and village of, 34; sociopolitical life, 34, 82–83
  Kaskaskia, 19, 64, 85, 93, 245g
  Kaw, 246g
  Kickapoo, 51, 61; Catholic mission, 148–149; financial dealings with, 113; treaty to establish reservation, 115, 247g–248g, 266g
  Kiowa-Apache, 85, 248g
  Kutenai, 148
  Loup (*See* Delaware-Loup)
  Mandan village, 6

Miami (so-called), 51, 85, 147, 254g
Osage, 9, 10, 44, 255g; chiefs, 267g; credit problems, 43; relations with Chouteaus, 8, 12, 72, 74; smallpox vaccination, 97–98
Otoe, 93, 171, 255g
Ottowa, 106, 255g
Padouca (Plains Apache), 10, 255g
Pawnee/Pani, 9–10, 53, 85, 256g
Pawnee Republicans, 97
Peoria, 19, 51, 61, 63, 64, 85, 93
Peoria Confederacy, 138, 256g
Piankeshaw, 19, 51, 61, 64, 93, 257g
Ponca, 256g, 258g
Potawatomi, 258g
Sac and Fox, 10, 24, 74, 97, 249g
Seminole, 262g; Second Seminole War (1835-1842), 169
Seneca, 85
Shawnee, 33, 40–41, **46,** 61, 64, 97, 263g; chiefs, 35, 54, 72, 146 (*See also under* individual names); credit risks, 43; emigration to Indian Territory, 27, 34–35; and Seminole war, 169; smallpox vaccination, 97
Shawnee village, 35, 263g
Sioux, 97
village of the Kansas (drawing), **108**
Wea (Piankeshaw), 19, 51, 85, 92, 93, 139, 266g; emigration to Indian Territory, 64, 113
Wyandot, 268g
Irving, Washington (writer), 124

Jackson
 Andrew (President), 87
 William (Chief Fish), 35, 54, 243g
Jackson County (Missouri), 14, 24, 50, 131
 1827 survey map, **198**
 first Chouteau child baptized on frontier, 112
 Mormon immigration, 155
Jarboe
 Joseph (merchant), 171
 Joseph, Joseph, and family, 243g
Jefferies, Thomas(? fur trader), 133, 134
Jefferson, Thomas (President), 6, 13
Jefferson Barracks, St. Louis, 31, 89, 247g
 court martials, 131

Jesuits, 243g, 260g
Johnson
 Mary Jane (Chick), wife of William, 152
 Thomas (missionary/schoolmaster), 106, 110, 111, 114, 116, 152, 243g
 William (missionary/schoolmaster), 106, 110, 111, 114, 116, 152, 243g
Johnson County, Kansas, 65
Jolliet, Louis (explorer), 9
Jones, Nancy, 105
Jumping Fish (Pashachahah), 115

Kane, Elias K., 212n12
Kansa Agency, 60, 200
Kansas, Chouteaus' name for western Missouri, 32
Kansas City
 Francois Chouteau, as founder of, 171–172
 Pierre Menard (Mack) Chouteau's activities in, 185–186
Kansas City, 1855, drawing by F. Buckeridge, **183**
Kansas City Post, 200, 202
Kansas Landing. *See* Town of Kansas
Kansas-Missouri border wars, 5
Kansas Outfit, 245g
Kansas River, 194, 259g
 mouth of, 200n3
Kansas Town Company, 92
Kaskaskia (Illinois Territory), wholesale store, 2, 5–7, 11, 27, 38, 143, 246g
 Menard and Valle store, 30
 Visitation Sisters convent, 128
"Kate Sweeny Bend," 186
Kawsmouth (West Bottoms) French community, 5, 148–149, 246g, 264g
Kearny, Col. Stephen W., 246g
keelboats. *See under* watercraft
Kelly, Price, 245g
Kennekuk (Kickapoo prophet), 115, 116
Kennerly
 George Hancock (military officer), husband of Alzire Menard, 36, 38, 42, 64, 247g, 331
 George Hancock (Jr.), son of George (Sr.) and Alzire, 89, 90, 187
 Harriet (*See under* Clark)

Kennerly (*continued*)
  Mme., mother-in-law of Alzire (Menard) Kennerly, 31–32
  Modeste Alzire Menard: daughter of Pierre and Marie Therese Menard; sister of Berenice, 5, 28, 31, 89, 132, 176, 247g; wife of George Hancock Kennerly, 32, 247g
Kiersereau, Pelagie. *See under* Chouteau
Kurz, Rudolph Friederich (artist), 16–17

Labaume, August (merchant), 155, 163, 165, 167–169, 248g
Labbadie
  Marie Pelagie (the younger) (*See under* Sarpy)
  Marie Pelagie Chouteau (wife of Sylvestre), 118
  Sophie (*See under* Chouteau, Sophie Labbadie)
  Sylvestre (husband of Marie Pelagie Chouteau), 118
Laclede
  Frederick (1865-1903), son of Frederic Donatien and Adele Chouteau, 248g
  Pierre de [Laclede Liguest]: cofounder of St. Louis, 8, 11, 248g; common-law husband of Marie Therese Bourgeois Chouteau (*q.v.*), 12, 248g; grandfather of Francois Gesseau Chouteau, 8; natural father of: Jean Pierre (Pierre Sr.) Chouteau, 12, 248g; Marie Louise Chouteau, 248g; Marie Pelagie Chouteau, 248g; Victoire Chouteau, 248g
La Croix, Charles de (priest), 8
La Liberte
  Eleonora, wife of Pierre La Liberte, 224g, 248g
  Pierre de, husband of Eleonora (Chalifoux), 105, 248g
La Liede (Shawnee smithy), 248g
Lamont, Daniel (fur trader), 64, 66, 248g
land acquisition, 68, 70, 71, 77–78, 134
  section, defined, 262g
Langham, Angus L., 24n7, 194

Langlois
  John Adrien, 136, 248g
  John Pierre, 136, 248g
La Salle, Robert de (explorer), 9
Latredo, John, 136
Latrobe, Charles Joseph, 124
Leavenworth, Col. Henry, 24, 42, 85
Le Coigne, Helen. *See* Decoigne, Helen
Lefevre, Francoise Nicolle
  stepmother of Angelique Menard, 32
  widow; third wife of Francois Saucier, 32, 248g
Lemme, J., 36, 37, 50, 248g
Le Roux, Joaquin Antoine, 133
Lessert
  Clement (interpreter), 64, 66, 98, 249g; gambling problem, 75
  Julia (Roy/Roi), wife of Clement Lessert, 66, 249g
letters
  as business records, 73
  challenges of translation and editing, 2–4, 133, 191–204
letters of Berenice Chouteau
  early correspondence, 23–46
  1827: Jan. 25, to *Cher papa* (Pierre Menard): mentioned, 176; anxiety about pregnancy and delivery, 28; April 18, to *Cher mama* (Angelique Menard): mentioned, 72, 128, 176; shopping, family strife, health of Angelique, 29; May 12, to *Cher oncle*, mentioned, 59, 176; May 19, to *Cher frere*, get well note, 31; Aug. 18, to *Cher mama* (Angelique Menard), mentioned, 143
  1831, Feb. 3, to *Ma cher souer* (Alzire Kennerly), deaths of brother and nephew; family illness; pregnancy; family, 89
  1840: May 9, *Cher papa*, family concerns, personal relationships; health concerns; lonesomeness; arrangements for slave Alexi, 175–176; Aug. 23, *Cher papa*, illnesses of son Frederic and brother Cyprien; arrangements for slave Alexi, 177; Dec. 29, *Cher papa*, grief over family

death; arrangements for Catherine Drips to attend convent, 178
1865, N.D.: FROM KANSAS CITY: *Edmond Menard,* mentioned, 185; *unknown recipient,* letters written in English thereafter, 185; FROM "LITTLE ROCK" HOME, STE. GENEVIEVE, *unknown recipient,* mentioned, 185
1871, N.D., FROM "LITTLE ROCK" HOME, *unknown recipient,* mentioned, 185
1871-1880, N.D., FROM KANSAS CITY, *Edmond Menard,* from various addresses in Kansas City, 187

letters of Francois Chouteau
1827, MAY 12, to *Cher oncle,* mentioned, 59, 176
1828: Nov. 5, to *Cher oncle,* business report, hope for good year, 36; DEC. 2, to *Cher oncle:* business report; new Shawnee post, 38, 40; mentioned, 173; DEC. 22, to *Cher oncle,* competition, proposal for new store, 43
1829: JAN. 12, to *Cher oncle,* complaints about Shawnee; praise for Kansa; proposal for new store, 48; FEB. 15, to *Cher oncle:* Shawnee and Kansa credit-debt; competitors; need for merchandise, 50; mentioned, 59; MAR. 3, to *Cher oncle,* business report; spring hunt; travel plans; family's health; merchandise, 52-53; MAR. 31, to *Cher oncle,* loss of *Beaver,* lives, cargo; discouragement; proposal for Independence store, 54-56, 153; MAY 26, to *Cher oncle,* death of mother; boat wreck, 57; AUG. 10, to *Cher frere,* settling of account, 60; AUG. 25, to *Cher oncle,* Indian annuities; merchandise, 67; SEPT. 24, to *Cher frere* (Cadet): annuities; supplies, personnel, 63-64; mentioned, 79, 81, 85; OCT. 15, to *Cher frere* (Cadet): barge arrival; claim against Vasquez, 69-70; mentioned, 61-62; Nov. 3, to *Cher oncle:* annuities; licenses; treaties; friends, 71-72; mentioned, 68, 177; Nov. 4, to *Cher frere,* annuities; licenses; treaties; friends, 73-74; DEC. 12, to *Cher frere,* annuities; credit-debt; recommendations, 74-75
1830: FEB. 15, to *Cher oncle,* hunting; annuities; business, 78-79; APRIL 22, to *Cher oncle,* good hunt; annuities; credit arrangements; family, 79-80; JUNE 6, to *Cher oncle:* annuities; dishonest agents; alcohol sold to Indians; health, 83-85; secondary usage as "receipt," 83-85; JULY 15, to *Cher oncle,* anger at Clark; unfair competition; dishonest agents; 86-87; SEPT. 18, to *Cher oncle,* family illness; the hunt; license; merchandise; horse, 88
1831: MAR. 20, to *Cher oncle,* sympathy; bad winter; business; family, 90-91; APRIL 16, to *Cher oncle,* birth of son, 92-93; JUNE 3, to *Cher oncle,* business, drought, family trip, shipping accident, 93-94; OCT. 27, *Cher frere,* salary negotiations, licenses, personnel, smallpox, 95-96, 134; Nov. 30, *Cher oncle,* personnel, salary negotiations, competition, family concerns, smallpox, slave purchase, 96-97
1832: JAN. 17, *Cher oncle,* optimism for business; competitors, new business, family illness; son in school; wagons, 98-99; FEB. 24, *Cher oncle,* missing letters; salary negotiations; personnel; competitors; land; family, 100-101, 134; AUG. 12, *Cher oncle,* safe boat trip; illness; family and friends' news, 102, 111; AUG. 30, *Cher oncle,* illness of Francois Menard; business matters, 87-88; SEPT. 7, *Cher oncle,* competition; business affairs; alcoholism; illness, 103-104
1833: FEB. 12, *Cher oncle,* business report; horses; evaluation of post potential; justification for action taken; effects

letters of Francois Chouteau
- **1833:** FEB. 12 (*continued*) of alcoholism on trade; Berenice's pregnancy, 109–110; FEB. 25, *Cher oncle,* birth of Benedict Pharamond; problems with Meyers' leaving his post, 111–112; APRIL 16, *Cher oncle,* financial business; Wea debt; annuities; need for merchandise; unfair competition;, 111–112, 139; MAY 20, *Cher oncle,* financial matters; personnel; Meyers and Frederick; shoes; Menard's education; cholera deaths, 114, 152–153; JUNE 17, *Cher oncle,* settlement of Gillis-Menard-Kickapoo matter; disappointment with Meyers; Indian preference for cash instead of merchandise; slave purchase; eye health, 116–117; AUG. 12, *Cher oncle,* business competition; alcoholism; cholera deaths; payment of personnel, 117–118; SEPT. 9, *Cher oncle,* Berenice's near death; sons' education and bad companions; business financial matters; cholera deaths, 117–118; SEPT. 22, *Cher oncle,* financial matters; family illness; sons' education; sympathy to Odile, 121; NOV. 25, *Cher oncle,* sons' education; Berenice's health; new post; employee; proposed new church, 122–123
- **1834:** JAN. 15, *Cher oncle,* sons' education; Berenice's gift to aunt; sympathy for Odile; treaty negotiations; business affairs; competition, 125–126; JULY 21, *Cher oncle,* family greetings; SS *Assiniboin,* 127–128; AUG. 4, *Cher oncle,* family greetings; grinding mill, 129; AUG. 16, *Cher oncle,* death of son Benedict; support of sons in school, 129–130; NOV. 25, *Cher oncle,* financial matters; Indian alcoholism; family health, 130–131; DEC. 4, *Cher frere,* concern for lost letters, 132
- **1835:** MAY 1, *Cher frere,* fur shipment via Shallcross; illness of personnel; financial arrangements, competitor, 133–134; MAY 5, *Cher oncle,* business disappointment; illness of personnel; poor postal service, 135–136; MAY 14, *Cher oncle,* complaints about Clark; annuities; competitors; poor postal service, 137–138; JUNE 21, *Cher oncle,* financial matters and annuities; postal service, 138–139; JULY 6, *Cher oncle,* financial matters and annuities; reclamation of W. Marshall; trade goods; family matters; cold weather. Addendum by Pierre Menard, 139–140; JULY 6, *Cher frere,* financial matters and annuities; trade goods; equipment needs; variable weather, 141; JULY 27, *Cher oncle,* financial matters and annuities; lost equipment; family illness; hot weather., 142; AUG. 30, *Cher oncle,* sons' expulsion from college; reflection on his own behavior; family illness; Berenice's pregnancy; business matters, 143–144; SEPT. 18, *Cher oncle,* birth of Mary Brigitte; family health; complaint about poor medical services; sons' education; annuities and credits, 145; SEPT. 25, *Cher frere,* note to accompany fur shipment, 146; OCT. 22, *Cher oncle,* sons' education; family health, 146–147; DEC. 16, *Cher oncle,* real estate transaction; family health; Gesseau's hatchet accident, 147–148
- **1836:** FEB. 5, *Cher oncle,* sons' education; defective guns; treaty; new stores in region, 151–152; APRIL 8, *Cher oncle,* scarce provisions; good shipping weather; optimism for coming year; land sale by Indians; family travel plans, 153; MAY 12, *Cher oncle,* Berenice's safe journey to St. Louis and Kaskaskia; impending Mormon crisis; niece's death; new

Index   295

competitors, 154–155; JUNE 6, *Cher oncle,* Berenice's safe return home; fur shipments; annuity negotiations; sons' education; Mormon crises subsided, 156; JULY 10, *Cher frere,* fur shipment; annuity payments, 157; JULY 18, *Cher oncle,* debt collection problems; fur and merchandise shipments; Mormon situation; deaths in Indian-settler conflict, 157; SEPT. 15, *Cher oncle,* annuities and debt collection report; business competition; impending Great Council at Fort Leavenworth, 159

1837: MAR. 24, *Cher oncle:* foiled land purchase; debt collection report; decline in hunting; Platte Purchase; slave purchase, 160–161; mentioned, 172; MAY 12, *Cher oncle,* slave purchase; mountain supply caravan; Decoigne land purchase; debt collections; gifts for children; family news, 162–163; JULY 14, *Cher oncle,* Decoigne land purchase; debt collections; Kansa prefer money to merchandise; recovery of fur packs; gifts for children, 164–165; OCT. 17, *Cher oncle:* son Menard; Maquaia Lorimier; Indians' choice of money instead of merchandise; Berenice's delayed trip because of children's illness, 166–167; mentioned, 173; Nov. 22, *Cher Gesseau,* Attachment to Oct. 17, 1837, letter re Decoigne land purchase payment, 167

1838: JAN. 28, *Cher oncle:* complaints about postal service; settlement of Decoigne matter; Bradshaw matter; Labaume matter; forthcoming hunting season; birth of second daughter, 168–169; mentioned, 50; FEB. ??, *Cher oncle,* mentioned, but missing from collection, 171; MAR. 3, Last letter to *Cher oncle,* Decoigne bill of sale and financial accounting; Bradshaw matter; Labaume matter; cold weather; forthcoming trip to St. Louis, 170–171

letters of others
   1822, JULY 19, Cadet Chouteau to Seres Chouteau, operation of Four Houses post and Randolph post, 203, 205–206
   1828, APRIL, Peter Menard to Pierre, concerning Peter's health (mentioned), 31
   1828, Pierre Menard, reply to Peter, concerning Peter's health (mentioned), 31
   1829, SEPT. 30, Pierre Menard to Francois, reply to Feb. 15, 1829, letter, 207–208
   1829, DEC. 24, Pierre Menard to John Ogle and to William Gilliss, unfair competition, 127n3
   1829, Peter Menard to Pierre, beaten by Indians, 31
   1830, FEB. 4, Pierre Menard to Francois Chouteau, reply to April 22, 1830 letter, 208–209
   1831, FEB. 22, Pierre Menard to Francois Chouteau, careful business practice, 209
   1833, FEB. 13, Pierre Menard to Francois Chouteau, draft of Feb. 20, 1833, letter, 210
   1833, FEB. 20, Pierre Menard to Francois Chouteau, replies to Francois' letters, 210–211
   1835, JUNE 24, Pierre Menard Chouteau to his grandfather Pierre Menard Sr., 214
   1836, JAN. 15, Gesseau Chouteau to grandfather Pierre Menard Sr., 215
   1836, AUG. 12, Pierre Menard to Francois Chouteau, unsettled debt between Marshall and Weas, 113, 212–213
   1838, Nov. 4, J. B. Sarpy to Pierre Menard Sr., 175
   1840, JULY 16, to Pierre Chouteau, violence on the frontier, 115n9
   1843, MAY 12 AND 24, Cyprien Menard, from Kawsmouth, to Pierre Menard, about flood, 179, 179nn74
Lewis, Merriweather, 13
Lewis and Clark Expedition, 13

licenses, for Indian fur trade, 249g. *See also* annuities
   of American Fur Co., 81–82, 120
   of Chouteaus, 9, 33, 44, 62, 80, 81, 96, 106, 185
   under French rule, 9, 33
   under Spanish rule, 12, 33
   under U.S. government, 14, 15, 15n22, 33–34, 44, 65, 82, 134
Liguest, Pierre de Laclede. *See* Laclede, Pierre de
liquor. *See under* Illnesses: alcoholism
Lisa, Manuel (fur trader), business relations with Chouteaus and Menards, 13, 171, 249g
Livingston, Martha (Mattie). *See under* Lykins
location: entrance to River, 132
Logan, Nancy, (wife of Frederick Chouteau?), 92, 174
Loisel, Regis (fur trader), 249g
Lorimier family, 98, 136
   described, 167–168, 249g
   Louis, husband of Marie Berthiaume, 167–168
   Maquaia, son of Lorimier and Indian named Francoise, 167–168
Louisiana Purchase, effect on fur trade, 13, 14
Louis XIV, king of France, 9
Loumus (servant of Berenice), 99, 100
Lulu, Joseph (slave), 55
Lutz, Joseph Anthony (priest), 40, 41, 172, 249g
Lykins
   Delilah (McCoy), first wife of Johnson, 249g–250g
   Johnston (physician; postmaster), 97, 112, 145, 249g–251g
   Martha/Mattie (Livingston, second wife of Johnson, 250g

M. Paku Shan, (Osage; wife of Noel Mongrain), 38
Magoffin, Susan (diarist), 71
Maiakita (deposed Osage chief), 267g
Maoumntameo. *See* Drips, Andrew
maps
   1827 Jackson County, **198**
   1878 survey of Missouri River, **204**
   Angus Langham's survey map, with "half-breed settlement" detail, **201**
   Curtis and Eley post, **22**
   homes of Chouteau family, **108**
   Missouri, **21, 22, 107**
Maquaia (French-Indian), 250g
Marais des Cygne River, 36, 250g
Marie (Osage woman), mother of James Chouteau, 8
Marquette, Jacques (explorer priest), 9
Marra, Dorothy Brandt, 2
Marshall
   Anna (*See under* Grinter)
   William (trader), 81, 93, 112, 113, 140-141, 242g, 250g
Maxent, Laclede and Co., fur traders, 11
Maximilian (prince), 250g
Maxwell
   Berenice, daughter of Hugh Herbert and Odile, 128
   Hugh Herbert (d. 1833), first husband of Marie Odile Chouteau, 121, 250g
   Lucien, son of Hugh Herbert and Marie Odile, 121, 250g
   Marie Odile Menard: sister of Berenice Menard Chouteau, 5, 32, 121, 126; wife of Hugh Herbert; mother of twelve children, 121, 250g
   Marie Therese a/k/a Lucretia (d. 1833), daughter of Hugh Herbert and Marie Odile, 126
Maxwell (Miranda) Land Grant, 121
Mayaweskata (Shawnee chief), 35
McCoy
   Delilah, daughter of Isaac (*See under* Lykins)
   Isaac (Baptist missionary), 35, 37, 92, 97, 250g, 263g; brother-in-law of Robert Polke, 185
   John Calvin (chronicler; postmaster), son of Isaac, 7, 24, 26, 30, 35, 49, 71, 78, 106, 112, 149, 152, 183, 251g; life of, and writing of Chouteau chronicle, 191–194; offers free lot to new Westport residents, 169
   Virginia (Chick), wife of John Calvin, 153
McDermott, John F., 135

Index

McGee, Milton (settler in Kansas City), 66
McKee, Henry (merchant), 132
McKenney, Thomas, 251g
McKenzie, Kenneth (fur trader), 66
McNair
    Alexander (first governor of Missouri), 41n55, 251g
    Dunning (Indian agent), 27, 41, 66; brother of Alexander, 251g
Menard
    Alzire (*See under* Kennerly)
    Amadee (Joseph Amadee), son of Pierre Sr. and Angelique (Saucier), 156, 251g
    Angelique (*See under* Saucier)
    Augustine (St. Gemme): mother of nine children, 252g; wife of Louis Cyprien Menard, 252g
    Caroline (Stillman), first wife of Pierre Jr. (Peter) Menard, 143, 252g
    Cyprien (Louis Cyprien): half-brother of Berenice Chouteau, 6, 103, 140, 177; illness of, 103, 177; later life of, 187; son of Pierre Sr. and Angelique (Saucier), 252g
    Edmond, son of Pierre Sr. and Angelique (Saucier), 176, 251g
    Eloise (Chenier), wife of Hippolyte (4) Menard, 252g
    Emily, half-sister of Berenice Chouteau, 6
    Emily (Briggs), second wife of Pierre Jr. (Peter) Menard, 252g
    Francoise Virginie, daughter of Hippolyte Menard; wife of Savinien St. Vrain; mother of Francois Pierre and Jean Theodule St. Vrain, 251g
    Francois Xavier (d. Jan. 8, 1831): death of, from lung ailment, 89–91, 103, 178; Son of Pierre Sr. and Angelique (Saucier), 251g
    Henri, half-brother of Berenice Chouteau, 6
    Hippolyte (1), (a/k/a Polite), brother of Pierre Sr.; uncle of Berenice Chouteau; husband of Rosalie Sequin (second wife); father of Hippolyte (4), 176, 251g
    Hippolyte (2), brother of Berenice Chouteau, 5, 251g
    Hippolyte (3), son of Jean Marie Menard; cousin of Berenice Chouteau; nephew of Hippolyte (the elder), 251g
    Hippolyte (4), son of Hippolyte (the elder) Menard; cousin of Berenice Chouteau, 176–177, 251g
    Jean Baptiste Edmond ("Edmond"), half-brother of Berenice Chouteau, 4, 6, 29, 30
    Jean Marie, brother of Pierre Sr., 251g
    Joseph Amadee, half-brother of Berenice Chouteau, 6, 103
    Louis Cyprien (*See* Menard, Cyprien)
    Marie Josephine, sister of Berenice Chouteau, 5
    Marie Odile (Menard), sister of Berenice Chouteau (*See* Maxwell, Marie Odile)
    Marie Therese Michelle (*See* Godin, Marie Therese Michelle)
    Matthieu Saucier, half-brother of Berenice Chouteau, 6, 103
    Michel B., son of Michael; nephew of Pierre Menard; cousin of Berenice; founder of Galveston, Texas, 148, 252g
    Pierre Jr. (Peter.; d. 1871): brother of Berenice Chouteau, 5, 29, 87, 104, 127–129; depression of, and concern for Indians' safety, 31; education, 124, 252g; fought in Black Hawk war, 128; husband of: Caroline Stillman (first wife), 143, 252g; Emily (second wife), 252g; Indian subagent, for Potawatomi, 31; son of Pierre Sr. and Marie Therese (Godin), 252g
    Pierre Sr.: biography, 252g–253g; business relationships: with Francois Gesseau Chouteau, 16, 51, 93, 95–96; letters from Francois (*See under* letters, of Francois Chouteau); with Lisa and Morrison, 13; death of, 179; education and early life, 13, 26–27; family, 253g; father of Berenice Chouteau, ix, 13, 29; illness, 101; Indian agent, 14, 27, 34–35; influence on Chouteau trade, 37;

Menard
- Pierre Sr. (*continued*)
  - lieutenant governor of Illinois Territory, 6, 14; *oncle* (father-in-law) of Francois Gesseau Chouteau, 2; personality and talents of, 26; social and spiritual responsibility, 98, 128; trip to Washington (D.C.), 6, 135; trip to Wisconsin, 36, 37
  - Sophie Angelique, half-sister of Berenice Chouteau, 6, 28, 29, 176, 177
  - Therese Berenice (*See* Chouteau, Berenice)
  - Therese Noemi, daughter of Hippolyte (Polite) Menard, 176
  - Xavier, 29, 87, 88 (*See* Menard, Francois Xavier)

Menard Family papers, Chicago Historical Society, 2
Menard farm, in Kaskaskia, 5–6
Menard & Valle stores, 253g
Mensing Island, 202
Metis (half-Indian, half-European), and Treaty of 1825, 154
Meyers/Myers/Mairs, William, unhappiness of, as Indian trader, 51–52, 92, 110–114, 116, 120–122, 253g
Miami County (Kans.), 51, 113
Michilimackinac, 13
migration westward, 4, 27, 34–35, 64, 77–78
military posts. *See also* trading posts
- Fort Carondelet, 238g
- Fort Cavagnial, 10, 11, 239g
- Fort Gibson, 239g
- Fort Leavenworth, 239g
- Fort Osage, 14, 33, 196, 239g

Miller, F. W. (Indian agent), 132
missionaries, 35–38, 123, 152, 234g, 236g, 263g. *See also* churches
Mississippi River
- exploration of (1682), 9
- keel boat travel, **14**

Missouri
- after Louisiana Purchase, 15
- ambush on Santa Fe Trail, subsequent unrest, 42
- French heritage of, 9, 11
- maps of, **21, 107**
- Vernon County, 8

Missouri Fur Company, 6, 171
Missouri Gazette, 62
Missouri Historical Society, 2
Missouri River
- exploration of, 9
- map of, **22**
- as *Pekitanoui* ("muddy waters"), 9

Missouri Saturday Evening News, reports death of Francois Chouteau, 172
Mongrain, Noel (interpreter), 36, 38, 53, 254g
Monroe, James (President), 15
Montardeau/Montardy/Montardine
- Calise, husband of Marianne (Valle), 49, 66–67, 254g
- Marianne (Valle), wife of Calise, 254g

Morgan (storekeeper), 254g
Morgan, Alexander G. (sutler; postmaster), 127, 157
Mormons. *See under* Churches
Morrison
- James, husband of Emily (Saucier), 58
- Jesse, husband of Eleanor (Saucier), 58
- William, business associate of Pierre Menard, 13

Mulkey
- Catherine Drips, wife of William, 178
- William, 178

music, Berenice's legendary piano and love of music, 128
muskrats, 135

Nancy (slave), 161
Native Americans. *See* Indians
New Madrid earthquake, 6
nicknames, use of, by French, 5
Notre Dame de Sion ("French Institute"), 2

Odin, John (priest), 147
O'Fallon (fur trader), 17
Ogle, John (fur trader), 36, 37, 43, 44, 51, 127, 254g
orthography, male *vs.* female, 3
Osage. *See under* Indians
Osage country (Vernon County), 8

Owens
"Mrs. Sam," 103
Samuel C. (merchant; Jackson County clerk), 69, 70, 155, 157, 169, 255g; death of, 71
William, 133, 134

Pal, Marie-Laure Dionne, 3
Paola, Kansas, 116
Papin
Joseph, husband of Mary Josephine "Josette" (Gonville), 171, 241g
Joseph, son of Marie Louise Chouteau Papin, 168
Mary Josephine (Josette) (*See under* Gonville)
Mary Louise Chouteau, sister to Pierre Chouteau, 168, 171
Papinsville, Missouri, 38
Parent, Emilie Forastin. *See under* Vasquez
Parks, Joseph, 255g–256g
relationship with Indians, 169–170
Pascal, Baptiste, 91–92, 135, 137, 167
Pashachahah (Jumping Fish), 115
patronage, and Indian trade licenses, 33–34, 53
Paul Wilhelm, Prince of Wuerttemberg, 196, 267g–268g
penmanship
of Berenice, 6, 216
of Francois Chouteau, 216
male *vs.* female, 3
Pensineau/Pinsonneau/Pensineaux
Laurent (Laurence), 120, 165, 166, 256g
Madame Rigauche, 6
Peoria
Baptiste (Confederated chief), 64, 91, 137, 138, 156, 161, 165, 256g
Illinois, 129
Perry
John (Shawnee chief), 35, 71, 72
William (Shawnee chief), 71, 72
Perryville, Missouri, site of St. Mary's of the Barrens (*q.v.*), 104–105
Philibert
Gabriel, 49
Joseph, 95, 256g–257g
Marie (*See under* Boone)

Piernas, Pedro (Spanish commander of St. Louis), 11
Pierre Menard Collection, Illinois Historical Survey, 2, 3
Pierre Menard Collection (PMC), Illinois State Historical Society, 2
Pilcher, Joshua (fur trader), 118
Platte Purchase (1836), 158, 160, 257g–258g
Platte River, 10
Point, Nicolas, S.J. (priest), 66, 148, 179, 233g, 258g
Plan de Westport (drawing), 179, 181, **182**
"Vue de la premiere hutte" (drawing), **108**
politics, of Menard family, 6
Polk, Mary. *See under* Chouteau
Polke, Robert, father of Mary Ann Polk Chouteau, 185
Pool[e]
G.W., 161, 258g
James, 258g
porcelain, dinnerware, 51
Porter, Clyde (chronicler), 173
postal service. *See* courier/postal service
posts. *See* trading posts
pot de bouillon (soup), 5
Prairie du Rocher (Illinois Territory), 11
Prudhomme
Gabriel, 92, 115, 149, 259g
Susan (Cree woman), wife of Gabriel, 114, 259g; a/k/a Margaret D. Durand, 212n11

Quick, John (Delaware chief), 92, 259g

Radford, Harriet Kennerly, 234g
railroad, convention in Kansas City, 185
Randolph Bluffs warehouse, 15, 23–26, 49, 68, 76, 196, 259g
Ravelette, Pierre (interpreter), 98
Renard, Mr. (St. Louis professional?), 29
Rigauche, Madame, 6
Riu, Francisco (Capt.), 11
River of Kansas. *See* Kansas River
map, 22
river travel
boating mishaps, 94–95
docking refused if cholera aboard, 118
ferry boats, 242g
fueling of boats, 56

river travel (*continued*)
   keelboats, 246g, 266g
   life expectancy of boats, 137
   steamboats, 103, 115, 122; accidents of 1836, 160
   uncertainty of, 54–56, 91, 111, 128, 134, 159
roads, 200
Robidoux, Joseph III (fur trader, founder of St. Joseph, Mo.), 7, 16, 74, 134, 259g
Rocky Mountain rendezvous, 163, 171–173
Rogers, Lewis (Shawnee chief), 146
Roi, Dr. (St. Louis physician), 29
Roux, Benedict (priest), 5, 24n5, 69, 105, 112, 132–133, 201, 233g, 260g
   departs to St. Louis, 145
   establishes "Chouteau's Church," 123
   opposed to dancing, 128
Roy (Roi)
   Joseph (river man), husband of Julia, 67
   Julia (*See under* Lessert)
   Louis, 49
   Mary Louise (Chalifoux), wife of Joseph Roy, 67
Ruland, John (Indian subagent), 129, 137, 260g
Russia, fur-trading partner, 17

Saint-Ange de Bellerive, Louis (St. Louis official), 11, 33
Saline County, Kansas, 10
Sanford
   Emilie, daughter of Cadet Chouteau, 144, 156
   John F.A. (Indian agent), husband of Emilie Chouteau; son-in-law of Cadet Chouteau, 144
Santa Fe (Louisiana Territory), 10
Santa Fe Trail, 15, 42
Sarpy
   Gregorie, 146, 261g; father of Jean Baptiste, 86, 261g; husband of Marie Pelagie Labbadie, 261g
   Jean Baptiste (J. B.) (trader), 17, 86, 94, 95, 174, 175, 261g
   Marie Pelagie (Labbadie): cousin of Francois, 86; daughter of Marie Pelagie (Chouteau) Labbadie; granddaughter of Pierre de Laclede, 261g; mother of Jean Baptiste, 86; wife of Gregorie, 86, 261g
Saucier
   Angelique (Menard): half-sister of Brigitte (Saucier) Chouteau, 27, 28; leg infection, 29, 51; mother of eight children, 261g; second wife of Pierre Menard (m. 1806), 5, 6, 27, 57–58; stepmother of Berenice Therese, 5, 6
   Angelique (Roi *dit* Lepensee) (d. 1787), wife of Francois, 32, 57; mother of Angelique (Saucier) Menard, 32
   Brigitte (1777-1829): daughter of Francois and Marguerite (Cadron) Saucier, 262; half-sister of Angelique (Saucier) Menard, 27; mother of: Charles B, Frederick, Cyprien, Francois Gesseau, Pharamond, three other sons, ix, 8, 58; second wife of Pierre Sr. (Jean Pierre), ix, 13, 57
   Francois: father-in-law of, Pierre Menard, Pierre Chouteau Sr., James Morrison, Jesse Morrison, 262g; father of: Angelique Menard, 13, 57; Brigitte Chouteau, 13, 57; Eleanor Morrison, 57; Emily Morrison, 57; eight additional sons, 57, 58
   Francoise Nicolle (*See* Lefevre, Francoise Nicolle)
Schermerhorn, John (minister), 124
schools. *See under* educational institutions
Seguin, Rosalie, second wife of Hippolyte Menard, 176
Shallcross, John (steamboat captain), 114–115, 134, 137, 262g
Shallford. *See* Chalifoux
Shane
   Anthony ("Mr. Chaine"), 35, 38–39, 48, 61, 78, 99, 105, 262g
   Charles, son of Anthony, 35, 79
   Lamatesche (Delaware Indian), wife of Anthony; mother of Charles, 263g
Shane and Wells, **22**, 35

Shawanock/Shouanock, son of William Anderson *(q.v.)*, 165, 263g
Shawnee, Kansas, 174
Shawnee village, 263g
shipping. *See* travel
Sibley, George (Fort Osage factory supt.), 9, 14
Siloqua, Dr. (physician), 102
Simpson family, 169
    James, 263g
    Richard "Duke," 169, 263g
Sister Betty Curtis White, 3
Six Mile Academy, Independence, 69
slaves, 19, 24, 56, 79, 116, 117, 144, 155
    Alexi, 175, 177
    Joseph Lulu, 55
    Nancy, 161
    U.S. Census of 1850, for Madame Chouteau, 184
social life
    of Kansa Nation, 34
social responsibility, of Menard/Chouteau family, 98
Society of Jesus. *See* Jesuits
Spain, and St. Louis (Louisiana Territory), 11
Spanish-Indian exploration, 10
St. Gemme, Augustine. *See under* Menard
St. Joseph, Missouri, 24, 134–135
St. Louis
    Chouteau residence, **7**
    co-founded by Chouteau ancestors, 8, 11
St. Louis Missouri Fur Company, founded (1808-1809), 13
St. Mary's, 261g
St. Vrain
    Francoise Virginie (*See under* Menard)
    Francois Pierre, son of Savinien and Francoise Virginie, 251g
    Jean Theodule, son of Savinien and Francoise Virginie, 251g
    Savinien, husband of Francoise Virginie (Menard), 251g
Ste. Genevieve, 261g
    The Asylum boarding school, 30
    wholesale store, 38
Ste. Philippe (Illinois Territory), 11
steamboats. *See under* boats/boating

Stewart, William Drummond
    international exploring trip, 187
    Rocky Mountain rendezvous, 172
Stillman, Caroline. *See under* Menard
Stokes, Montfort, 124
Sublette, Milton, and brothers, 166, 264g
Swinney, W. D. (boat owner and captain), 185

Tardiveau, Barthelemi (partner of Menard), 135
Tenskwatwa ("old prophet") (Shawnee chief), 72
Tesson, Baptiste, 168
Tesson family, 168
Timon, John (priest), 147
Todd, Joseph (settler), 158
Toler
    Ann (*See under* Chouteau)
    G. W., tenant of Chouteau Mansion, 184
Toniche (fur trader), 98, 99
Tooley, Elizabeth or Nancy, (wife of Frederick Chouteau?), 92, 174
Topeka, Kansas, "half-breed" plots, 87
Town of Kansas, 70, 115, 149, 264g, **264g**
Trading Post, Kansas (town), 122, 159–160
trading posts. *See also* fur trade; military posts
    of Andrew Woods, 25
    assignment of, to tribes, 74
    Berthold, Chouteau, and Pratte, 25, 62; sold to American Fur Company, 15
    Black Snake Post (St. Joseph), 7, 74
    Chouteau's Landing (Kansas Post), 104, 109, 120, 245g; dancing "balls" at, 128; decline of, 173–174; destroyed by flood, 1844, 179; disputed location of, 194–204
    Curtis and Eley, 25, 238g; (on map), **22**
    dual purpose, 106
    Fort Orleans, 10
    Four Houses (1819-1828), 9, 24, 24n7, 26, 81, 166, 240g, 245g
    Frederick's (*See* Kansa Post)
    French Fur Company (Berthold, Chouteau, and Pratte), sold to American Fur Company, 15

trading posts. (*continued*)
   Horseshoe Lake post, 40, 75, 81–82, 106, 245g
   Kansa Post, 120
   Kansas City Post, 202
   Kansas City warehouse (*See* River of Kansas Post)
   Kansas Post (*See* Chouteau's Landing)
   Kickapoo, 120, 124
   Randolph Bluffs warehouse, 15, 23–25, 196, 259g; destroyed by flood (1826), 25–26, 49, 68, 76
   River of Kansas Post (Kansas City warehouse), 25, 49, 134, 259g; destroyed by flood, 173
   Shane and Wells, **22,** 35
   Shawnee Post (a/k/a Cyprien's Post, Turner Site), 19, 25, 38–40, 104, 109, 112, 120, 173, 200, 263g
   St. Louis Missouri Fur Company, founded (1808-1809), 13
   Trading Post, Kansas, 265g
   as "warehouses," for Francois, 25
   Wea Post, 51, 116
travel, during 1800s in western Missouri, 15, 19, 24, 25, 32
   activity at Chouteau's Landing, 149
treaties (business agreements). *See also* credit arrangements
   defined, 19
treaties (political)
   1825 (with Kansa Nation), 34, 154
   1829 (Council Camp supplement), 92, 139
   1830 land preserved for Indian nations, Violation of, in 1835, 158
   1832 (*Castor* [Beaver] Hill), 115, 139
   1833 peace treaty, 126
   early French, 10
   Kickapoo reservation, 115, 116, 247g–248g, 266g
   of Paris, 11, 12
Tremble, Francis, 148
Troost, Benoist (physician), 146
Truteau, Jean Baptiste (educator), 8
Tucker, Maria, alleged wife of Cyprien Chouteau, 173
Turner, Kansas, nearby "half-breed" plots, 87, 154, **201**

Uneau. *See also* Hunot/Uneau/Eanneau/Uno
   Louis, 49, 92
United States government
   Bureau (BIA)/Office of Indian Affairs (OIA), est. 1824, 224g; smallpox vaccination investigation, 98; under War Department, 32–33
   Bureau/Office of Indian Affairs (OIA), est. 1824, under Dept. of the Interior, 87, 254g
   disputes with traders, 44, 166–167
   impact of, on fur trade, 13–16, 19, 32–34
   Indian agents and subagents (*See also* individual entries); John Campbell, 41; Liguest (Paul Liguest) Chouteau, ix, 34–35, 43, 81; Richard Cummins, 235g; John Dougherty, 237g; Andrew Drips, 238g; William Gordon, 117; Richard Graham, 241g; Andrew S. Hughes, 242g; Dunning McNair, 251g; Peter (Pierre Jr.) Menard Jr., 252g; Pierre Menard Sr., 253g; F. W. Miller, 132; John Ruland, 260g; John F.A. Sanford, 144; George Vashon, 266g; Antoine F., *dit* Baronet Vasquez, 245g
   Indian Removal Act (1830), 15, 34, 169, 243g
   Platte Purchase (1836), 158
   prohibits liquor sales to Indians, 65
   smallpox vaccination program, 97–98
   Treaty of 1825 (with Kansa Nation), 34, 40, 87
   War Department, 266g
University of Illinois, Urbana-Champaign, 3
University of Missouri at Kansas City, 2
Upper Missouri, 13

Vaill, William F. (missionary), 234g
Valencia (Missouri, Kans., or a street?), 106

Valle
- Felix, son of Jean Baptiste, 38, 86, 265g; house of, **253g**
- Jean Baptiste: husband of Jeanne Barbeau, **265g**; partner of Pierre Menard, 38, 53
- Jeanne Barbeau: mother of Felix, **265g**; wife of Jean Baptiste (J. B.), 86, 265g
- Marianne (*See under* Montardeau/ Montardine)

Valle, Felix, home of, **253g**
Valverde y Cossio, Antonio (governor of Mexico), 10
Van Bibber family
- Alfonzo/Alonzo B., 141, 265g
- intertwined with Boone family, 265g
- Jesse, 142
- Joseph, 142

Van Quickenborne
- Charles F., S.J. (priest), 148–149, 265g–266g

Vashon, George (Indian agent), 35, 51, 61, 63–65, 67, 69, 71, 73, 76, 78, 80, 86, 102, 266g
Vasquez
- Antoine F., *dit* Baronet (Indian agent; d. Aug. 1828), 41, 49, 54–55, 60, 68, 72, 74, 81, 245g, 266g; residence, 474
- Emilie Forastin Parent (Madame Baronet or Madame Vasquez): sale to American Fur Co., 91, 92, 103; wife of Baronet, 39, 55–56, 67, 68, 266g

Vasquez house, 68
Vernon County, Missouri, 8
Village of the Kansas (drawing), **108**
Villiers, Francois de (chevalier), 10
Vincentian fathers (religious order), 104–105
Virginia (friend? servant?), 29
Visitation Sisters convent, Kaskaskia, 128

Waldo, David (merchant; physician), 138, 145, 266g
Walker, Joel (mountain man), 99
Walls, Mr. (little Wells), 39, 52
Ware, Elizabeth, fourth wife of Frederick Chouteau, 174

warehouses. *See* trading posts
Wea Post, 51
Wells
- John B. (settler), 52, 158
- Mr. (trader), 52, 267g

West Bottoms. *See* Kawsmouth
Westport, drawing by Nicholas Point, **233g**
Westport, Missouri, 49–50, 112, 149, 152, 169, 174
Westport Border Times, 186
"Westport Landing," Missouri, 149
whiskey problems, 65–66
White
- Mathilda, second wife of Frederick Chouteau, 174
- Sister Betty Curtis, 2 , 3

White Hair (Osage chief[s]), 267g
White Plume (Kansa chief), 41, 54, 154, 267g. *See also* Gonville, Louis a/k/a Monconsia; Nampawarah, 87
- house of, near Topeka, , 87, **244g**

White River (Ozarks), 61
Widen (Wyden), Pierre (Raphael) Menard's assistant, 29, 30, 32, 72–73, 267g
Wilhite, P. G., later owner of Chouteau Mansion, 185
William Morrison Collection, Illinois State Historical Library, 2
Wilson, Moses Green, 162, 267g
Wind River, Wyoming, 186
women
- deference of, 4
- education, 6, 98, 226g
- hard life of, on frontier, 102, 111, 114, 116, 118–119
- independence of, 4
- "voting" by Indians, 166

Woods, Andrew (fur trader), 25, 195, 267g
Wuerttemberg, Prince Paul Wilhelm of, 196, 267g–268g

Yellowstone River, 94

Zabette, Frank. *See* Datchurut, Zabette

Contributors' Biographies

Dorothy Brandt Marra, native of Kansas City, received a B.A. from the College of St. Teresa (Avila College), Kansas City, and an M.A. from St. Louis University, St. Louis. She has written short stories, articles, and plays for magazines and newspapers, and two books: *The Story, Volume One of This Far by Faith*, a history of the Catholic people of western Missouri, and (co-author) *Ciao, Francesco*, a World War II airman's recollection. Marra is married, has four children, and lives in the area.

Marie-Laure Dionne Pal was born of French-speaking parents in New Brunswick, Canada. She attended Mount Carmel Academy, an English-speaking high school in St. John, New Brunswick, then earned a teaching degree from the University of New Brunswick. She has a B.A. from the University of the Philippines and an M.A. from the University of Missouri-Kansas City. Pal taught a complete schedule to French-speaking students in Canada, and French to English-speaking students in the United States. She is married, has three children, and is an area resident.

David Boutros is a native Kansas Citian who attended Raytown High School before going to Southwest Missouri State University and the University of Missouri-Kansas City to earned a B.A. and M.A. in history and an M.P.A. in non-profit administration. He has been Associate Director of the Western Historical Manuscript Collection-Kansas City since 1987, and active with a number of local historical organizations and projects. Besides occasionally teaching, he has authored articles on regional history and edited, *A Legacy of Design: A Historical Survey of the Kansas City Parks System*. David is married to librarian/historian Katherine Boutros and has two sons.

Sylvia D. Mooney, born in Kansas City, earned her B.F.A. in Illustration from Washington University in St. Louis, Missouri. She dedicated over thirteen years to historic trail preservation as Executive Director of the Cave Spring Association, retiring in 1988. During that period, Sylvia worked to nominate the Santa Fe Trail as a National Historic Trail. She returned to school, attending Longview Community College where she focused on life drawing and the plastic arts. In 1999, Sylvia earned her M.A. in Sculpture Studio from Central Missouri State University. She is presently teaching Basic Drawing and Art Fundamentals at Longview Community College. Sylvia is married, has five children, and thirteen grandchildren.